D1687137

REBEL MODERNISTS

Viennese Architecture
Since Otto Wagner

REBEL MODERNISTS

Viennese Architecture
Since Otto Wagner

Liane Lefaivre

Lund Humphries

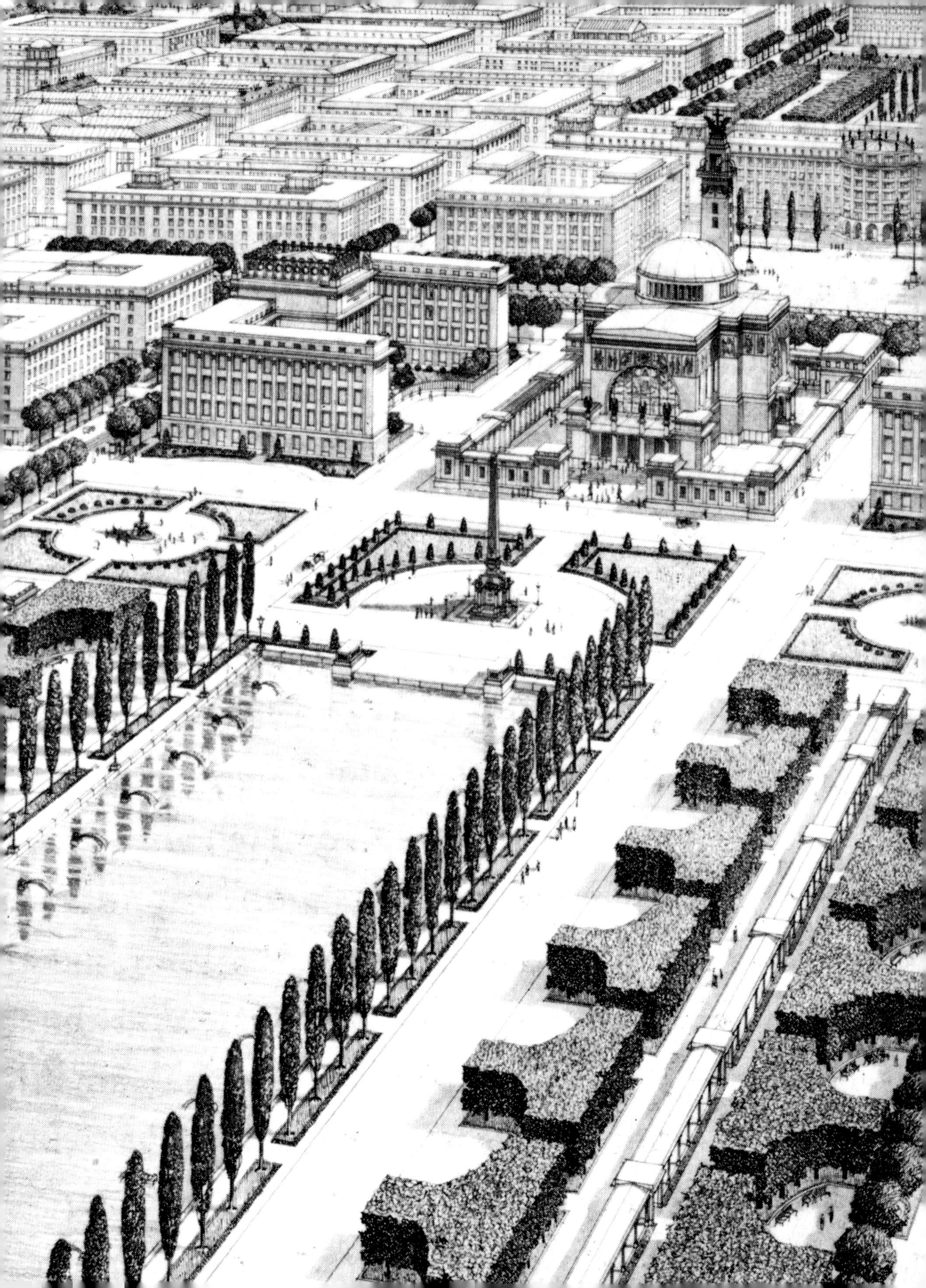

To the memory of my parents-in-law, Charichleia and Constantinos Tzonis, researchers at the Vivarium, founded by Hans Leo Przibram in the early 1930s

First published in 2017 by Lund Humphries

Lund Humphries
Office 3, Book House
261a City Road
London
EC1V 1JX

www.lundhumphries.com

Rebel Modernists: Viennese Architecture Since Otto Wagner
© Liane Lefaivre, 2017

ISBN: 978-1-84822-205-2

A Cataloguing-in-Publication record for this book is available from the British Library

All rights reserved. No part of this publication may be reproduced, stored in a retrieval system or transmitted in any form or by any means, electrical, mechanical or otherwise, without first seeking the permission of the copyright owners and publishers. Every effort has been made to seek permission to reproduce the images in this book. Any omissions are entirely unintentional, and details should be addressed to the publishers.

The author has asserted her right under the Copyright, Designs and Patent Act, 1988 to be identified as the Author of this Work.

Edited by Eleanor Rees
Designed by Adrian Hunt
Set in Posterama, Utopia and Neuzeit Grotesk
Printed in China

dɪːˈʌŋɡewʌndtə

Special thanks to the Universität für angewandte Kunst, Vienna, for its support.

Contents

	Prologue	8
1.	*Fin de Siècle* Vienna and the Culture Wars Modern and Anti-Modern	16
2.	Otto Wagner Rebel	32
3.	The Next Generation The Wagner School, Hoffmann and Loos	81
4.	After the Apocalypse The Social Housing of Red Vienna and Its Social Democratic Political Economy	104
5.	Between Two Wars: From Apocalypse to the Anschluss Other Modern Architectures 1919–1938	140
6.	Nazi Ostmark 1938–1945	180
7.	Reconstructing with a Memory Problem 1945–70	187
8.	The Kreisky Era From the late 1960s to the Present Day: Economic Prosperity and Culture Wars	210
9.	After the Shock Therapy Renewal	240
10.	Good Social Housing is Good for the Economy	260
	Conclusion	305
	Acknowledgements	308
	Notes	310
	Select Bibliography	326
	Image Credits	332
	Index	334

Prologue

It was a radiantly sunlit early June morning in 2003. I had arrived in Vienna three months earlier to take up my teaching position at the University of Applied Arts. I was on my way there, standing at the leafiest part of the Ringstrasse, at the corner of the Stubenring and the Weiskirchnerstrasse, looking toward the steeple of the Stephansdom in the distance. The mild westerly Alpine wind, the *Föhn*, was shaking up the abundantly planted, fragrant rose beds that lay in my immediate vicinity and rustling the deep dark green trees in the Stadtpark across the street, to my left.

I was getting used to being carried away by the history-laden aura that seemed to imbue everything in the city, not least its architecture. I had finished my *Mohnstriezel* (poppy-seed strudel) and *Melange* (cappuccino) at the outdoor terrace of the legendary Café Korb, in the center of the First District, near the Tuchlauben. The interior is extraordinarily plain, but Freud famously held some of his psychoanalytic meetings there for a time, and its downstairs bathroom, designed in 2002 by the Viennese architect Manfred Wolff-Plottegg, is an erotically charged biomorphic homage to Freudian dreamwork and a cult destination. Next to the toilet is the Art Lounge, also designed by him, but with the collaboration of three of Vienna's most internationally famous artists. Günter Brus painted the ceiling in a bold blue-and-white checkered pattern; Peter Kogler added to the ceiling with the same pattern he always uses obsessively, one that possibly represents colossal, vaguely menacing computer cables; and Peter Weibel papered the walls with ghostly pale images of a fully stacked library. Among the regulars was Nobel Prize-winning author Elfriede Jelinek, who gave public readings of her book there. Upstairs, the walls are crammed with black-and-white photographs of its larger-than-life, diva-like proprietor, Susanne Widl, an artist in her own right, with her many writer and artist friends. Once a year, on 'Poetry Day', she accepts poems in lieu of money as payment.

As I was leaving, I looked up from my table. A plaque on the adjacent apartment house indicated that Alban Berg had lived and worked there. Mozart had composed the *Entführung aus dem Serail* a few steps away, according to another inscription, one of the many plaques charting his nomadic peregrinations throughout the city.

In the ten minutes it took me to get from the Café Korb to the Stubenring, I came across at least 15 buildings of historical significance. First was the white gilded façade of Johann Lucas von Hildebrandt's eighteenth-century Baroque Peterskirche. With its taut series of undulating convex, concave, convex bays, it was a graceful tour de force which succeeded in compressing some grandeur into such a tight space, and a clear homage to that truly great masterpiece, Francesco Borromini's San Carlo alle Quattro Fontane in Rome. From there I gazed across the Graben at the diminutive black marble façade of Adolf Loos's Knize tailor shop and wondered if its sweeping ripples had been meant to harmonize with the Peterskirche. If I had deviated a couple of blocks in one direction, I would have seen his American Bar. If I had gone in another direction, I would have passed his Goldman & Salatsch tailor shop on the Michaelerplatz, standing insolently at one end of the domed nineteenth-century neo-Baroque Hofburg Palace. I would also have passed Hans Hollein's gleaming, bizarre, all-aluminum Retti candle shop. Instead, I turned to my left and saw his Schullin jewelry shop that looked like a gold vein in a rock. Then I walked past Otto Wagner's Anker building a few steps away. It stood out from its neo-Renaissance neighbors because it used shockingly naked glass and iron on its lower façade, the first building in Vienna to do so. From there I headed toward Vienna's great Gothic cathedral, the Stephansdom.

Proceeding down the Wollzeile, I passed the grand, time-worn, soot-covered grey stone frontage of an abandoned early nineteenth-century Biedermeier *palais*, and two apartment houses, one by each of the two most celebrated neo-classical architects of the mid-nineteenth century, Ludwig von Förster and Theophil von Hansen. Toward the end of the street was a small passageway, tucked into the façade, that led to the Jesuitenkirche, the finest example of Baroque splendor in Vienna, with its pink and cream and green faux-marble spiraling columns and its wondrous *trompe l'œil* ceiling by Andrea Pozzo. A little further down stood the old university building where Beethoven had premiered his Fifth Symphony under another frescoed ceiling. It was across the street from the apartment house where the inventor of the American shopping mall, Victor Gruen, had grown up. Perhaps the Wollzeile, the only really popular shopping street in the First District and certainly its most colorful, was his inspiration. The quirky display windows of Reimer's bonbon shop, with sculpted marzipan Cinderella-like brides and top-hatted grooms, mice, sunglassed bathing beauties, gartered legs or brown chocolate roses on multicolored cakes, and the bountiful, congested windows of Boehle's fine-foods shop, chock full of scalding hot yellow pepper sauce from Hungary, muscat grapes from Italy, prunes dipped in chocolate by his own hand, were exercises in creating irresistibly seductive popular shopping magnets.

From the corner where I now was, I faced the Café Prückel, a chandeliered masterpiece of kitsch 1950s rococo design by the one-time assistant of Josef Hoffmann, Oswald Haerdtl. To my right was the Museum für Angewandte Kunst (MAK), the Museum of Applied Arts. It was the second-oldest design museum in the world, and full of historic carpets, lace, glass. The director, Peter Noever, had had one room installed by the artist Donald Judd, devoted to the Baroque interior, and Jenny Holzer had installed the room devoted to Biedermeier porcelain and furniture. The artist Franz West had designed the sofas in the foyer. Just beyond the MAK was my university. The two were connected by Hermann Czech's airy MAK Café, with its delicately redesigned, sprightly Thonet chairs. Just beyond that, on the other side of the street, was Otto Wagner's Postsparkasse, a paean to aluminum, the then new high-tech amalgam, with its aluminum columns, aluminum sci-fi heaters, and two aluminum angels on the roof by the sculptor Othmar Schimkowitz.

At that very moment, the architectural historian Otto Kapfinger came by. He had been a member of Missing Link in the late 1960s, one of that period's most rebellious counter-culture architecture groups. He had also been one of the people responsible for saving the house Ludwig Wittgenstein had built for his sister from the wrecking ball, at about the same time. I told him how eager I was to visit the Wittgenstein house, which I had not yet had time to do. It was about a ten-minute walk from where we stood. 'But you have to see it at five in the morning,' he said. 'That's when the sun hits the breakfast room just so.'

'Have you?' I asked.

'Yes, of course,' he said matter-of-factly.

I spent the next 12 years being stunned time and again by the evocative power of the city and its architecture. I would have coffee along the narrow Göttweihergasse, just off the Neuer Mark where Mark Twain had lived from 1897 to 1899, because the outdoor terrace was flanked by the Erechtheion-inspired entrance to the apartment house that Theophil von Hansen had designed for Otto Wagner's mother, where Wagner had grown up. Salieri, Mozart's great nemesis, lived right across from it, at the corner of the lane and the Spiegelgasse. Zum Schwarzen Kameel served very good coffee, and had been frequented by Beethoven.

There was something somehow mythopeic about so much of Vienna's architecture that one came into contact with. My lawyer, Leopold Specht, had an office in the stately former headquarters of the Bodencreditanstalt, designed by Ludwig von Förster's son, Christian. This was the bank of the old imperial aristocracy that collapsed in 1931. The government obliged the Rothschild Creditanstalt to take on its debts, causing it to collapse in turn, setting off a chain reaction that damaged the world economy more than the Great Crash of 1929 had done. A building on the Landstrasse that I passed on my way to the university from the Rochusmarkt in the Third District was where Balzac stayed when visiting his mistress, Mme Hanska. Adolf Loos was a customer at the Storch pharmacy on the Tuchlauben, where I bought soap. At my very university, where I taught every day, Josef Hoffmann had been the director, Heinrich Tessenow and Koloman Moser had taught, and Gustav Klimt, Oskar Kokoschka and Margarete Schütte-Lihotzky had studied. More remarkably still, eventually I wound up living next to that same university building on the Wollzeile, the one in which Beethoven had premiered his Fifth Symphony. I even got to stay at the Wittgenstein House for four years, and was able to experience for myself Wittgenstein's ideal of *Klarheit*, in the form of the light that flooded the entire house in the early morning.

The future held more architectural revelations, of course. I was yet to see Wagner's Steinhof church and Hoffmann's Purkersdorf clinic, but I had seen Josef Maria Olbrich's Secession building, J. B. Fischer von Erlach's Imperial Library and his Karlskirche, and the church designed by the sculptor Fritz Wotruba. And these were only the tip of the iceberg.

'You get too carried away,' my friend Monica Wittgenstein, a niece of Ludwig Wittgenstein's whom I met for the first time in an elevator of the Hotel Wandl, would repeat many times. 'Vienna has a very dark side too. You just don't notice it at first. It's hidden behind the glittering façades, just as Vienna wants to it to be.'

This book has roots in that radiant morning at the corner of the Stubenring and the Weiskirchnerstrasse – and in that admonition.

The fact is, the dark side was in full view at that corner. I was facing Karl Lueger Square. Lueger, one of Adolf Hitler's heroes, had been so extreme in his anti-Semitism that the Emperor Franz Josef had put off granting him the title of Mayor of Vienna for two years after he was elected in 1897. Another person I met while staying at the Hotel Wandl was Maria Altmann, the niece of Adele Block Bauer, who had won a restitution case for five Klimt paintings stolen under the Nazi regime. My dentist's office gave on to the former court of the great historic synagogue in the Second District, designed by Förster, which was destroyed by fire on Kristallnacht, on 9 November 1938. The MAK museum used one of the fortress-like so-called *Flakturm* bunkers built by the Nazis.

Very soon, what came to impress me more positively about Vienna's architectural plethora was the extent of its public works, such as Otto Wagner's Danube Canal, with its bridges and sluices and water-management building, and his Stadtbahn stations. Then there were the city's more recent public places, such as the semi-pedestrian zone in the First District around the Graben, the Museumsquartier and the Mariahilferstrasse pedestrian area. More amazing still was the mass of now beloved social housing projects of the 1920s and those of the past 40 years, since 1970.

As I was to learn in the writing of this book, there is nothing banal about Vienna's architectural achievements. They have always been the result of a battle. This is true of the entire 120-year period beginning from the end of the nineteenth century, when Otto Wagner designed his Stadtbahn stations. Like Gustav Mahler, Arnold Schoenberg and Gustav Klimt, architects had to go into combat with the most conservative social order of Europe. Their history is a loaded one. The odds were stacked against them by the establishment. All had to take a rebellious stance to get things done.

Adolf Loos, Josef Hoffmann, Josef Frank and Josef Maria Olbrich; then Ludwig Wittgenstein, Victor Gruen and Friedrich Kiesler; then Richard Neutra, Rudolf Schindler, Bernard Rudofsky, Margarete Schütte-Lihotzky and so many others were all rebels. Vienna is a small city, but the list of representatives of its extraordinarily innovative architectural tradition over the past 120 years is long. It continues with the so-called Austrian Phenomenon of the late 1960s, including Hans Hollein, Coop Himmelb(l)au, Hermann Czech, Missing Link, Zünd-Up, Salz der Erde and Haus-Rucker-Co, followed by the late twentieth- and twenty-first-century generation, including Delugan Meissl, Jabornegg and Pállfy, Rüdiger Lainer, Elsa Prochazka, ARTEC's Bettina Götz and Richard Manahl, Geiswinkler and Geiswinkler, and PPAG's Anna Popelka and Georg Poduschka.

While it is not unusual for architectural historians to explore the interdependence of architecture with the broader cultural and even political world, this has not been done with regard to Vienna's architectural history since the *fin de siècle*. This book places architecture within the fraught and highly polarized culture wars, the *Kulturkampf*, that engulfed Vienna for most of the twentieth century. Of central importance here is the role of Jewish Vienna before the Anschluss, still systematically underplayed, but of overwhelming importance internationally in the flourishing of much that is modern in the arts and sciences today. Without being exhaustive, before the First World War the list of cultural figures connected with Vienna includes Karl Kraus, Hermann Broch, Stefan Zweig, Sigmund Freud, Gustav Mahler, Arnold Schoenberg, Eugen von Philippovich, Otto Bauer, Victor Adler, Otto Neurath, Gustav Klimt, Eugenie Schwarzwald, Berta Zuckerkandl and Mark Twain. After the Second World War, following the initial works of Ingeborg Bachmann and Paul Celan, the culture of protest was extreme, as exemplified by the Wiener Gruppe, the Actionist performance artists such as the angry Günter Brus, Otto Muehl, Hermann Nitsch and Valie Export, equally angry authors such as Thomas Bernhard and Elfriede Jelinek, and the great performance artist Helmut Qualtinger.

It is more unusual, though, to study the history of architecture in the context of political economy. But as the historian of Austria Charles Gulick pointed out, a unique feature of the history of Austria between the First and Second World Wars was an extreme polarization across political, economic and social fields.[1] This, as we shall see, is equally true about the period since the Second World War. As far as architecture is concerned, this would explain why the last 120 years have witnessed a striking spirit of anti-establishment modernist rebellion.

Throughout the twentieth century, Austria has epitomized how things can go terribly wrong. In the Gilded Age of the last years of the nineteenth century, under the inept last Habsburg emperor, Franz Josef, Austria's laissez-faire irresponsibility and incompetence made the imperial army into a laughing stock, stoked nationalist fervor in the various breakaway provinces, and turned Vienna into the city with the worst mass poverty in Europe. It then went on to plunge the country and the rest of Europe and North America into the killing machine of the First World War, what the Viennese satirist Karl Kraus called a 'laboratory for the end of the world,'[2] going from a country of 50 million to one of 5 million in the process. In 1938, continuing down the same path, the country welcomed Adolf Hitler and became a willing participant in the Third Reich's own even more efficient killing machine, serving its fraud-, plunder- and slave labor-based economy during the Second World War.

But the country has also been a case study in how to do things right and against great odds. Out of both world wars, socially and economically successful social-democratic governments arose, in the first case on the city wide scale of Vienna, and in the second, on the national scale of the country as a whole, creating remarkably robust modern capitalist political economies on which now rests one of the most harmonious countries in the world. Tellingly, Vienna consistently tops the official international rankings for 'livability'.[3] Another term for this is 'social justice'. In other words, social democracy has been good for architecture and vice versa.

The main focus of this book is how far architecture has been associated with what Vienna has done right since Otto Wagner broke with the backward world of the late Habsburg Empire and wrote his polemical manifesto, *Modern Architecture*. The modernization of architecture in Vienna was as multi-faceted as it was anywhere during this period. One of Vienna's particular features is the extent to which architects have been involved with design on an urban scale. But of all its dimensions, the most striking to this student of Austrian history is the tradition of social housing that emerged under the social-democratic government of Vienna after the First World War. Still robust today, it is probably the most distinctive contribution to world architecture that Vienna has made, and I have tried to build on the existing studies of it by Gulick, along with the works of Helmut Weihsmann and especially Eve Blau.[4]

Wittgenstein saw language as a game whose rules are not only affected by the forces of the real world but also capable of playing a role in shaping the *Lebensform*, the way of life. This book opens with *fin de siècle* Vienna, a period generally presented either as fatally angst-filled and backward-looking, or as a powerhouse of modernity. Here it is seen, instead, as a playing field where two polarized tendencies confront one another, an anti-modernist establishment on one hand and modernist rebellion on the other. This period laid the ground rules of the game that would play out over the next 120 years. To set Otto Wagner and the other modernist rebels in this embattled context makes their accomplishments all the more formidable.

1

Fin de Siècle Vienna and the Culture Wars
Modern and Anti-Modern

It is 1900. Twilight is spreading over the vast expanse of the Habsburg Empire. A sense of impending doom hangs in the air, from Bratislava to Tchernowitz, from Prague to Trieste, from Budapest to Sarajevo. Slowly but surely the old world is breaking apart. And to the sweet, vibrant, rapturous strains of a Johann Strauss waltz, Vienna is being swept, giddy and heedless, toward the abyss (fig.1).

This now clichéd image, of a frivolous society frolicking its way along an inexorably downward spiral into the harrowing vortex of the First World War, was first conjured up from the pen of one of Vienna's most renowned cultural critics, Hermann Broch. To him we owe the commonplace characterization of Vienna as made up of deluded 'sleepwalkers' caught in a 'gay apocalypse'.[1]

However pessimistic, this portrayal of late Habsburg Viennese society is benign compared to Karl Kraus's. From 1898 to 1936, he made a career out of writing incendiary articles fueled by a sense of moral outrage in the magazine he founded, *Die Fackel* ('The Torch').[2] Kraus coined the expression of the Austro-Hungarian Empire as a 'laboratory for the end of the world' in 1914, on the eve of the First World War,[3] and the metaphor re-emerged as the conceit of his still relatively unknown masterpiece, *The Last Days of Mankind*, written about the war as it was unfolding day by day, between 1915 and 1918. Set over a period of ten evenings, the 800-page drama is a cross between the theater of the absurd and the theater of cruelty, between farce and tragedy, between cabaret and documentary. It collages 200 often disconnected scenes that present the way in which the trenches were experienced as horror by the soldiers themselves and as entertainment by a well-heeled Viennese society more accustomed to the world of Franz Lehár's *Merry Widow* and similarly upbeat operettas. 'What's it like out there?' a jovial, light-hearted coffee-house denizen asks a friend back from the battlefield. 'Absolutely killing,' comes the answer, in one of the play's most celebrated quips. 'But it's a living.'[4] One scene requires 1200 horses to gallop out of the Danube in the wake of a flame-thrower,[5]

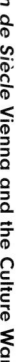

1   Emperor Franz Josef and the waltzers at the yearly Hofburg Ball. *The Court Ball*, Aquarelle by Wilhelm Gause, 1906. Vienna Museum

and another includes a dead forest that sings.⁶ In yet another, a sergeant chases after his troops brandishing a gun. 'Go and die for your country,' he orders, 'or I will blow your heads off.'⁷

There was no shortage of reasons for angst during the last years of the Habsburg Empire. Thomas Piketty and Anthony Atkinson point out that, in 1910, Vienna's 929 top earners had the highest incomes of any city in the world.⁸ Vast personal fortunes had been made in iron, steel, banking and real estate speculation, famously turning the city into a 'dream world for millionaires'.⁹ Christopher Clark notes that the years between 1877 and 1913 saw exceptional economic expansion.¹⁰

But during this period, which the Viennese refer to as the *Gründerzeit*, the 'era of entrepreneurs', and which Mark Twain more disapprovingly dubbed 'the Gilded Age', such great wealth was a thin veneer on a social order characterized by extreme inequality.¹¹ The early 1900s were also marked by runaway inflation. To protest against unsustainable rises in rents and food prices, on 17 September 1911, a crowd of 100,000 working-class urban poor staged an uprising known as the Hunger Revolt, the largest demonstration among many at the time, in which all the windows of the city hall were smashed.¹²

In 1894, Count Eugen von Philippovich, a political economist, social reformer and founding member of the Austrian Fabian Society, as well as Rector of the University of Vienna, wrote a book based on his investigation of the housing problem entitled *Wiener Wohnungsverhältnisse* ('Viennese Housing Conditions'). It became a bestseller. Philippovich described the misery of families crowded into dark, damp cellars and packed into tiny one-room apartments that had no running water, heating, or natural or artificial light, and compelled to use outdoor privies shared by 120 other people (fig.2). 'The dwelling is only a cover against the grimness of the weather, only a bedstead for the night which provides – in the narrow space, lacking air, cleanliness and quiet, into which people are pressed – rest only to a completely exhausted body.'¹³ By 1910 over 640,000 people had been homeless in Vienna,¹⁴ over 25 per cent of the entire population of the city.

Catherine Bauer, the American housing activist of the 1930s and 1940s, quoting Philippovich, noted that the empire had 'left a housing heritage that once more was the worst in Europe. In 1912, more than 50 per cent of the dwellings consisted of one room and a kitchen, with four people living there, with no sanitation and poor ventilation.'¹⁵ These apartments were not only 'small and ill-equipped'

2 Apartment of a family from Galicia, who had fled to Vienna with seven children, *c.*1918. Austrian National Library, Picture Archive

but 'expensive, absorbing one quarter of the average worker's salary. It was calculated that a Viennese worker paid more for one room and kitchen than did a Londoner for a living room, three bedrooms, kitchen and bath in relatively pleasant surroundings.'[16] Tuberculosis was known as the 'Vienna sickness'.[17] Of every 100 children an average of 24 died during their first year of life.[18] Slum landlords enjoyed a quasi-monopoly in the housing market. Most leases were for just one month and landlords could evict at short notice or increase rents. As a result of the high rents imposed by these landlords, almost 100,000 occupants were sub-tenants; another 75,000 were so-called *Bettgänger*, people who rented a bed left vacant during the working hours of the tenant.[19]

The inability to come to grips with extreme inequality was only one failing of the late Habsburg state apparatus, condemned, in the assessment of Viennese-trained economist Alexander Gerschenkron, as 'backward'.[20] The empire was the sick man of Europe.[21] It had failed to keep up with the fast pace of change that had engulfed most of the continent over the past 50 years.[22] The problems arising out of a failure to modernize were particularly acute at the turn of the twentieth century, the last years of the empire. Industrial capitalism had developed with much greater alacrity in England, France and Germany. The mindset of the imperial government was partly to blame. So out of touch with modern times was the Emperor Franz Josef that there were no toilets at the imperial palace at Schönbrunn before the newly wed German-born Empress Elizabeth introduced them. The emperor distrusted telephones, trains and especially automobiles.[23] The city of Vienna installed the Hofpavillon train station at Hietzing near his palace at Schönbrunn especially for him, designed by Otto Wagner, and he used it only once, on the day of its inauguration in 1899.[24]

Another example of this backwardness was the emperor's inability to recognize that it was an age of nationalism, when monocultural nation states were beginning to break away from multicultural empires. Austria was Europe's second-largest country after Russia. Yet its German speakers were a minority: they represented only 12 million citizens out of a total of 52 million. The empire included about 26 million Slavs, and 8.5 million Czechs and Slovaks. In addition, there were about as many Hungarians as Germans – 10 million, or almost 20 per cent.[25] Austria had become a morass of nationalist strife, with different nationalities rebelling against the emperor and at loggerheads with one another. Hungary had already managed to extract a special status within the empire with the so-called *Ausgleich* (Compromise) of 1867, which had established two states and two parliaments in what was now referred to as the Dual Monarchy of Austria-Hungary. By 1897 the Czechs were also demanding equal treatment. Mark Twain captured the comic side of the resulting parliamentary chaos in an article entitled 'Stirring Times', written from the visitors' gallery overlooking the chamber of the National Assembly. It described the inkpot-hurling, bench-overturning turmoil that erupted over the newly instituted requirement for German officials to learn Czech in the Czech-speaking provinces of Moravia and Bohemia.[26]

It was in the realm of economic policy that Gerschenkron saw the most glaring example of backwardness, putting the blame for the economic woes of the empire on the Gilded Age's *Gründerzeit* policies of parliamentary liberalism – closer in meaning to unfettered libertarianism than to what is often meant today by the term – in force since the aftermath of the March Revolution of 1848. The words of Count Eduard von Taaffe, one of the longest-serving prime ministers of the time, are telling. He depicted his own method of governing as *Fortwursteln*. This is usually translated as 'muddling through', although the literal meaning is more colorful, along the lines of 'going forth brandishing one's sausage'.[27] Victor Adler, the founder of the Social Democratic Party, was less euphemistic. Drawing from the earthy heaps of largely untranslatable Viennese slang, he described the imperial administration as a toxic mix: '*Absolutismus gemässigt durch Schlamperei*,' or, absolutism tempered with sleaze.[28]

There was one politician who did try to modernize Austrian capitalism by counteracting the laissez-faire politics of his predecessors, all noblemen like Taaffe who governed at the pleasure of the emperor.[29] This was Ernest von Körber, a commoner. He was prime minister from 1901 to 1904, after which he had a patrician 'von' attached to his name. He alone tried to transform the state bureaucracy into a responsively interventionist civil service for the sake of modernizing the industrial sector and to ensure a more equitable distribution of wealth, which he referred to as *Wohlstand* ('welfare' or 'prosperity').[30] Among the economically rational steps Körber took, he abolished press censorship and legalized unions, reversing one of the few measures imposed by Taaffe, who had banned the Social Democratic Party along with labor union meetings. Körber allowed the party to organize openly and thus to enter the government through elections. In this he was no doubt inspired by his internationally prominent Prussian counterpart, Minister President Count Otto von Bismarck, one of the founders of the welfare state, believing that the working class could be regarded as a reliable support for the economy.[31]

Körber's main strategy was to improve internal cohesion within the empire and redress the troubled state of its industrial sector by repairing its deficient communication system and modernizing the railroads and canals which linked the woefully inaccessible parts of the far-flung empire from Trieste to Prague. This meant changing the unfettered free-market mentality of the government and getting the state to support a deficit spending on public works.[32] The railroad construction was intended to reduce unemployment and to aid the ailing heavy industries. He went to work on rejuvenating the bureaucracy, instilling it with a novel sense of service.[33]

But, in his attempt to boost the economy, Körber made an unfortunate choice of Minister of Finance. He entrusted the prominent economist Eugen von Böhm-Bawerk with the task of developing the necessary economic policy reforms. As a result of Böhm-Bawerk's covert obstruction, however, Körber's plans miscarried, and his government was dissolved in barely four years under pressure from the conservative Archduke Franz Ferdinand.[34] From then on, the lack of political and social cohesion in the Habsburg Empire went unchecked and Körber's efforts resulted in what Gerschenkron deplored as the 'economic spurt that failed.'[35] According to Karl Polanyi, it was the failure to move beyond libertarian policies that brought on the First World War.[36]

Körber had better luck with his Minister of Culture, Wilhelm von Hartel, who held office between 1900 and 1905. He was a modernizer who actively supported the Secession (the avant-garde association of artists and designers formed by Gustav Klimt and Josef Hoffmann, among others) and took the side of Klimt in a dispute over the erotic frescoes he had painted in the medical faculty entrance. He also saw to it that Otto Wagner received imperial commissions for the Postsparkasse and the Steinhof church.[37]

Although Franz Josef saw himself primarily as a military leader, the imperial army too was in need of modernizing. Behind the emperor stood nearly six centuries of dynastic history crowned with military glory. True to his inherited values, he believed until the end of his days that the only truly noble activity worthy of a great monarch was warfare. According to Gerschenkron,

> . . . in the mind of Franz Josef things military and things economic were lodged in entirely separate compartments. His deep interest in the former was paralleled by his lack of interest, and understanding for, the latter. The old man knew how to insist vigorously on increasing the manpower of his army, but the relationship between the economic potential of the country and its military power appears to have lain outside his purview and concerns.[38]

Dreams of dynastic glory were unable to save the imperial army, which had been faltering since the very beginning of Franz Josef's reign. It was disastrously defeated by the French at Solferino in 1859 and went on to be gruesomely crushed at Königgrätz in 1867 by the technically and administratively superior Prussian army under Helmuth von Moltke and ultimately his superior, Bismarck. At Solferino, Austria lost the entirety of its Italian possessions except for Venice, which it was to lose to Napoleon III, who in turn ceded it to the post-Risorgimento kingdom of Italy under Vittorio Emanuele in 1866. After Königgrätz, Austria was excluded from power in Prussian-dominated Germany, at the cost of an unprecedented 31,000 Austrian soldiers' lives.

By the 1890s, the now notoriously inept army was also undermanned, with one soldier for every 132 civilians in Austria, compared to one per 98 in Russia and one per 65 in France. It also suffered from shortages of ammunition and artillery.[39] Finally, the dual monarchy's disorganized decision-making structure resulted in the eventual 'mad catastrophe' of defeat in the First World War. The lack of discipline in the army was such that in July 1914, while Austrian diplomats drafted hard-edged ultimatums which made the war unavoidable, Austria's generals were taking their summer vacation.[40]

Archduke Franz Ferdinand, the heir apparent from 1896 onward, was a just a brasher version of Franz Josef. The archduke was responsible for the appointment of the illustrious but incompetent General Franz Conrad von Hötzendorf as Chief of Staff of the Armed Forces.[41] From 1907 to 1915, the general was most famous for his affair with the married Gina von Reininghaus, to whom he wrote over 3000 love letters, some 60 pages long, but never mailed. This obsession not only eclipsed all matters political and military in his life, but meant that Gina's husband received lucrative military supply contracts.[42] Moreover, it was Conrad's counsel that prompted Franz Ferdinand to visit Bosnia-Herzegovina in 1914, which resulted in his own assassination and the igniting of the First World War.[43]

In addition to an imperial bureaucracy incapable of addressing the needs of a perilously unequal society, a fragmenting empire, an underproductive economy, and a tragicomically incompetent army command, there was one more cause for worry among the modernizers of *fin de siècle* Vienna. This was anti-Semitism. When, in the 1890s, the coalition between Austria's liberal political establishment and the crown collapsed, the liberals lost the election and scapegoats were needed. Franz Ferdinand declared that 'Jews, Free Masons, Socialists and Hungarians' were to blame.[44] Viennese anti-Semitism was resurfacing after an era of relatively peaceful coexistence during the *Gründerzeit*.[45] The first part of Hitler's *Mein Kampf* admiringly describes how Karl Lueger, elected as Vienna's mayor in 1897 on an anti-liberal platform, managed to mobilize the lower classes by playing on their economic fears, a strategy which he himself would later resort to. So overbearing was Lueger's anti-Semitism that the emperor delayed approving his election, blocking his assumption of duties for over two years.

Lueger was the opposite of Franz Josef. While the sleepwalking monarch was slowly edging the empire into world war, the supremely cunning and efficient mayor was not only running the city with exemplary vigor, but setting the stage for the Austro-fascist and Nazi movements which were eventually to lead to the Second World War and the Holocaust.[46] But the specter of the future was best embodied by another political figure of the time, the rabble-rouser Georg Ritter von Schönerer. Called '*Führer*' by his followers, he was a devotee of what he termed the 'German Reich', and coined the pseudo-medieval greeting *Heil*.[47] Schönerer was popular enough for members of his party to be elected to the Austrian parliament in the late 1890s. In 1896 Theodor Herzl published *A Jewish State: An Attempt at a Modern Solution of the Jewish Question*. Two years later, Mark Twain, living in Vienna, commented on the virulence of the anti-Semitic press in his article 'Concerning the Jews' in *Harper's Magazine*.[48]

Inimical as Vienna was to the modern, the city also became, to reverse Karl Kraus's dictum, the laboratory for much of what was to be modern in the century to come. At the very moment the Austro-Hungarian Empire found itself in the grip of a dying imperial political economy and culture, it suddenly emerged as the center of a liberating modernity, entering a feverish golden age of architecture, art, music, theater, science, the humanities and political thought. William Johnston's *The Austrian Mind* is the first, and remains the most systematic attempt, to draw an overall history of the modernists of the period from the 1890s to the late 1930s.[49] Friedrich Stadler termed the period a 'Late Enlightenment'.[50] This Viennese enlightenment extended beyond the cultural and scientific spheres, to politics and economics, shaping much that would define these fields.

The friction between modern and anti-modern gave rise to a highly polarized *Kulturkampf*, a culture war that was to become increasingly conflictual and politicized with time, evolving by the late 1920s into a battle between the social-democratic 'Red Vienna' and the fascist and Nazi 'Black Vienna' (fig.3).[51] One finds a disaffection with the city's conservative culture in many of the great literary and artistic works of the time. Arthur Schnitzler's plays pointed the finger at the abusive misogynist mentality of Vienna, in particular *Miss Else*, of 1924,

3 *'Ho-ruck, nach links!'* ('Heave-ho to the left!'). Poster by Victor T. Slama reflecting the polarization of Viennese politics between 'red' (*rot*) and 'black' (*schwarz*), 1932. Vienna Library, City Hall, Poster Collection

about a young woman driven to suicide by the sexually exploitative callousness of her upper-middle-class father and mother. Robert Musil's semi-autobiographical novel *Young Törless* caused a scandal with its open depiction of homosexuality, as did the painter Egon Schiele's polemical frankness on the subject of sexuality.

Karl Kraus (1874–1936) was the most strident protagonist in these culture wars. He was also the most popular. In 1899, the first issue of *Die Fackel* sold 30,000 copies in one week in Vienna.[52] Kraus's publications were complemented by his acclaimed public readings of his own works and those of others, which would regularly attract audiences of 2000 people.[53] Most prominent on his list of targets were the major newspaper of the time the *Neue Freie Presse*, Richard Wagner's purportedly racist operas and the miscarriage of justice in the case of Sacco and Vanzetti, two Italian anarchists executed in the US in 1927. He was at his most outraged at the political and cultural commentary on the 'opinion page' of the *Neue Freie Presse*, which in his view had become a perversion of the genre which Heinrich Heine had introduced into German culture and perfected in the 1840s. Kraus argued that these now merely masqueraded as legitimate journalism and were filled with nothing but warmongering, stock-market manipulation, smear campaigns and political machinations.[54] Among the works Kraus did champion were Jacques Offenbach's operas, for the way they mocked militarism and authoritarianism, and Frank Wedekind's play *Pandora's Box*, which would serve as the basis for Louise Brooks's famous performance in the film of the same title by the Viennese director Georg Wilhelm Pabst. He also supported pacifists and the Viennese social democrats immediately after the First World War.[55]

Adolf Loos (1870–1933), Kraus's very close friend, also inveighed against contemporary life and architecture, not in architecture journals, but in the livelier medium of newspapers, from the *Neue Freie Presse* to *Die Zeit*, *Die Wage* and *Wiener Rundschau*. He even attempted to start his own version of *Die Fackel*, publishing two issues of a magazine in 1903, outrageously titled *Das Andere. Ein Blatt zur Einführung abendländischer Kultur in Österreich* ('The Other: A Journal for the Introduction of Western Culture to Austria').[56] Though less popular than Kraus, he was nonetheless beloved. Ludwig Wittgenstein granted him a stipend on the death of Karl Wittgenstein, his father. Besides being saluted on his sixtieth birthday by architects such as Walter Gropius, Le Corbusier, Auguste Perret and Sigfried Giedion, the list of his well-wishers included Ezra Pound, Constantin Brancusi, Ilya Ehrenburg, Man Ray, Amédée Ozenfant, Tristan Tzara, Arnold Schoenberg, Stefan Zweig and, of course, Karl Kraus.

But these two writers were at least as widely despised as they were loved. Kraus had a full-time lawyer in charge of suing his detractors for defamation, and they managed to make a small fortune out of these court cases.[57] Attacks on Loos's Goldman & Salatsch tailor shop of 1909 on the Michaelerplatz have gone down in history. In his 1931 monograph on Loos, Heinrich Kulka wrote that 'the history of the Michaelerplatz building was the story of the painful birth of the modern style,' and implied that the architect was a martyr for the modernist cause: 'the man who bled for it, who was nearly tortured to death by a pack of philistines both outside and within the architectural profession, made it possible, through his heroic perseverance against the whole nation, to enable us to build as we build now.'[58] Because of all the negative press Gustav Mahler received for his compositions, Schoenberg called him a 'martyr.'[59] Wagnerites wrote off the music critic Eduard Hanslick as another 'Jew in Music.'[60] Oskar Kokoschka was as abhorred in the press as he was acclaimed.[61]

In fact, the Viennese anti-modernist and anti-Semitic reaction would eventually evolve into fanaticism, an early portent of the extermination lust that was to engross the German-speaking world under Adolf Hitler. In 1927 Adolf Loos would be taken to court on a politically motivated, trumped-up charge of paedophilia.[62] In 1925, the same year that his novel *Joyless Street* had been turned into a film by G. W. Pabst, starring Greta Garbo, Bruno Bettauer was murdered by a member of the Nazi Party. Anti-modernist fervor embraced scientists too. Paul Kammerer, the famed Jewish biologist, took his own life after being framed by an assistant in an incident involving a falsified experiment that ruined his scientific credibility.[63] The Catholic philosopher Moritz Schlick, head of the prestigious Vienna Circle, which was made up of Vienna's greatest minds in the sciences and human sciences, was assassinated in 1936 by a student who mistook him for a Jew.[64]

There is a systematic tendency to underrate Jewish Vienna's role in modernizing *fin de siècle* Vienna.[65] In fact, as Johnston remarks in *The Austrian Mind*, modernization was to an overwhelming extent made possible by the law that had emancipated Jews and brought them equal rights early in the reign of Franz Josef, in 1867, under the sway of his Foreign Minister, Klemens von Metternich, and Metternich's banker, Salomon Mayer von Rothschild. By 1910, Jews had disproportionate economic power.[66] Of the 929 highest-earning Austrians of that year, 60 per cent were Jewish, although Jews represented only 10 per cent of the overall population.[67] In 1860 Jews had been given the right to own property and, as Georg Gaugusch points out, by 1885, a third of the real estate owners of the Ringstrasse area were Jewish.[68] As for the luxurious Südbanhof Hotel in Semmering, the watering hole favored by the Viennese upper crust, after the Anschluss it was 'Aryanized' by the Nazis, which means it was considered to have been a Jewish building.

By the turn of the century, it was Jewish Vienna, as opposed to the traditionally dominant groups in Austria – the aristocracy, the church, the state bureaucracy and the army – that had become the powerhouse generating the modernization of the arts and sciences, something that was not true of Paris, London or Berlin. Viennese Jews provided almost all private patronage of modern art and architecture in the city. Karl Wittgenstein was the greatest among these, followed by Fritz Wärndorfer, who in 1903 was the sole patron of Josef Hoffmann's Wiener Werkstätte, Vienna's second great modern artistic institution after the Secession. Gustav Klimt's most celebrated portraits of women were all commissioned by Jewish families: the Wittgensteins, the Bloch-Bauers, the Zuckerkandls, the Beers, the Primavesis, the Riedlers, the Staudes.[69] The Lederer family sponsored Klimt's *Beethoven Frieze* at the Secession building. Vienna's most renowned dressmaker, Emilie Flöge, sold her loose-fitting 'reform dresses' as an emancipating alternative to the corseted garments of the time. Reform dresses appeared across Europe but gained particular popularity in Vienna once they became associated with the designs of Gustav Klimt, Koloman Moser and members of the Wiener Werkstätte for a mainly Jewish clientele.[70] And among the major collectors of modern art were three Jewish sisters, Serena Lederer, Jenny Steiner and Aranka Munk.[71]

As regards architecture, Ludwig von Förster and his son-in-law Theophil von Hansen, who designed the most remarkable apartment houses of the mid-nineteenth century, had Jewish patrons: the Pereiras, the Arnsteins, the Ephrussis, the Todescos and the Epsteins. So too did the great modern domestic architects, Otto Wagner, Josef Hoffmann, Adolf Loos and Josef Frank. Among their clients were the Wittgensteins, the Wärndorfers, the Primavesis, the Mautners, the Scheus, the Mollers, the Müllers, the Steiners, the Rufers, the Khuners and the Beers. The same is true of the commercial clients who commissioned buildings by these architects: Knize, Goldman & Salatsch, Mainz, Altmann, Lederer and Zuckerkandl.[72] The Belgian Stoclet family and Sonja Knips – a Frenchwoman, born Baroness Portier des Echelles, who wedded a wealthy industrialist – were rare non-Jewish art patrons of the time, who hired Josef Hoffmann to design their houses.[73]

Among Vienna's greatest architects were Richard Neutra, Josef Frank, Bernard Rudofsky, Victor Gruen, Friedrich Kiesler, Margarete Schütte-Lihotzky, Oskar Wlach, Oskar Strnad, Paul Engelmann and Ludwig Wittgenstein – all Jewish or of Jewish descent. The modernization of music was shaped by Gustav Mahler, Arnold Schoenberg, Alban Berg and Fritz Kreisler. Max Reinhardt founded the Salzburg Festival. Arthur Schnitzler's plays are still performed and adapted. Fritz Lang, Billy Wilder and Otto Preminger left their mark on German and Hollywood cinema.

The University of Vienna produced some of the most creative minds of the twentieth century up until 1938, when it was 'Aryanized' by the Nazis. Among Jewish Nobel Prize-winners were Max Perutz, Victor Hess, Wolfgang Pauli, Otto Loewi and Karl Landsteiner. In economics, Jews included Ludwig von Mises, Friedrich Hayek and Karl Polanyi, not to mention Alexander Gerschenkron. In the field of art history, many of the so-called Vienna School were Jews: Max Dvořák, Ernst Gombrich, Otto Pächt and Hans Tietze.[74] In the field of legal thinking, there was Hans Kelsen; in sociology Paul Lazarsfeld, Hans Zeisel and Marie Jahoda; in philosophy Karl Popper, Martin Buber and Ludwig Wittgenstein. In applied mathematics, the university was the birthplace of what came to be known as game theory, with students including John von Neumann and Fritz Morgenstern. In the sphere of medicine, Carl von Rokitansky, Emil Zuckerkandl and Sigmund Freud were Jews.[75]

Two of the most visionary scientific institutions of the period in Europe were founded by Jews. One was the Vivarium and the other was the Institute for Radium Research, both at the University of Vienna. The Vivarium was one of the first centers for experimental biology in history, founded in 1903 by the zoologist Hans Leo Przibram, the heir of a wealthy Jewish family. Przibram and his colleague and relative Leopold Portheim bought the building and turned it into a pioneering research institute, bringing together a multi-disciplinary team. It was among the first institutions in the world to synthesize the new subject of biology out of botanical, zoological, chemical and electrical engineering research.[76] The Institute for Radium Research, which opened in 1910, was notable among other things for its innovative modern architecture.[77] The lawyer Karl Kupelwieser,[78] who donated 500,000 crowns for its foundation, was not only patron of the institute but also its co-designer, along with the architect Eduard Frauenfeld. The new institute, which like the Vivarium brought together a range of disciplines, was conceived as one of a complex of three new structures, and was linked by bridges to the chemistry and physics buildings on either side of it. The French journal *Le radium*, the main forum of the international community of 'radioactivists', described the institute in 1924 as 'unique of its kind', with 'the most modern facilities in the world'.[79]

Viennese Jewish women were particularly active in the sciences. The Institute for Radium Research was 'a Mecca' for women working in radiochemistry and radiophysics, in the words of Peter Galison.[80] They included Mariette Blau, who was nominated twice for a Nobel Prize by Nobel laureate Erwin Schrödinger, and wrongly deprived of a Nobel that went to her colleague Cecil Powell in 1947.[81] Jewish women led the fight for women's education. Many had attended the private lyceum that Eugenie Schwarzwald had opened in 1901 to prepare Jewish and progressive non-Jewish middle-class girls for the day when the academy's gates would be open to them.[82] Jewish girls comprised almost half the students of Viennese public schools, over two thirds in progressive ones.[83] The actress Hedy Lamarr, who had only a high-school education, together with the American George Antheil – a self-proclaimed 'bad boy' avant-garde composer of industrial-aesthetic, electronic music – developed spread-spectrum and frequency-hopping technologies to defeat the jamming of Allied radio communications by the Nazis. Today these are used in wi-fi and Bluetooth devices.[84]

Jewish women were also active in the arts. They had dominated the field of art photography and portrait photography in Vienna since the famous Atelier Adele, run by Adele Perlmutter-Heilperin, opened in 1862. Dora Kallmus established her studio in 1907, with Trude Fleischmann and Edith Tudor-Hart belonging to the next generation.[85] Erika Giovanna Klien, Elisabeth Karlinsky and Maria Ullmann founded the Kinetismus movement in painting in the 1920s, a combination of cubism, futurism and constructivism.[86] Berta Zuckerkandl supported progressive modernizing circles through her renowned salon, where the guests included Mahler and Schoenberg, Schnitzler, Klimt, Kokoschka, Otto Wagner and Josef Hoffmann, along with her husband's colleague, the neuropsychiatrist Richard Krafft-Ebbing.[87]

The most important of the para-university associations was the Vienna Circle. Known initially as the Verein Ernst Mach, the Circle was founded by physicist Philipp Frank, mathematician Hans Hahn, Richard von Mises, the social-democratic brother of the free-market economist Ludwig von Mises, and the philosopher and sociologist Otto Neurath. It was made up of philosophers and scientists who were committed to a radical reform of philosophy, and who had a tremendous influence on Anglo-American philosophy through logical positivism. Peter Gallison claims that, to an astonishing degree, modern philosophy of science traces its heritage to the Vienna Circle.[88]

For the time being, then, in *fin de siècle* Vienna, the moderns were thriving. Without the benefit of hindsight, what the future held in store still appeared to be anyone's guess.

2

Otto Wagner
Rebel

This embattled, polarized Vienna was the Vienna of Otto Wagner (1841–1918). His own combative manifesto, *Modern Architecture*, first delivered as a lecture in 1895 and then published in 1896,[1] made him the first Viennese public intellectual to challenge the mediocrity and backwardness of the establishment. The lecture preceded by one year what is generally seen as the first skirmish in this battle, Karl Kraus's satirical article 'Die demolirte Literatur' ('The Demolished Literature'), which attacked all the major writers of Vienna, as well as Mark Twain's 'Stirring Times', published in 1896 and 1898 respectively.[2]

Otto Wagner's manifesto was a searing indictment of the entire architectural output that the Viennese establishment had invested in and treasured most dearly for the past 30 years: what has since come to be called historicism, but what he himself referred to as *Stil Architektur* ('style architecture'). He was brutal in his criticism. Catherine the Great's favorite lover, Grigory Potemkin, had allegedly erected cardboard towns along the Dnieper river in order to fool her into thinking that all was well in her empire. Wagner compared Vienna to these 'Potemkin villages', with its 'overdone apartment house façades' forming what he called a 'hodgepodge of styles, with everything copied, and given a patina'.[3] The result was 'sham architecture that seeks to cover nakedness with a lie'.[4] The 'deception

4 Otto Wagner wearing his *Légion d'honneur* medal. Portrait by Gottfried Kempf-Hartenkampf, pastels. Verwertungsgesellschaft Bildender Künstler, Vienna Museum

Otto Wagner

abounding in such designs', in his view, could not 'be sufficiently condemned'. He concluded that 'no epoch of art other than our own has exhibited such monstrosities; they present us with a rather sad picture of the artistic conditions of our time.'[5] In fact, Vienna's tendency toward pastiche gave 'an impression similar to that of someone attending a modern costume ball of the past century, even rented for the occasion from a masquerade shop'.[6] This was at odds with what a modern city should be. 'It should always be remembered that a great modern city cannot and should not have the appearance of ancient Rome or of Old Nuremberg,'[7] he declared. 'All we can do today' is 'simply look to the colossal mistakes of these architects with a pitying smile.'[8] When it came to Vienna's neo-Hellenistic parliament building, Wagner was especially vitriolic. Ornamenting the building in this way was as preposterous as riding around the city 'bare-legged in an antique triumphal chariot'. As for Vienna's pseudo-Gothic city hall, he saw it as the architectural equivalent of someone clowning around in 'a slit doublet.'[9]

Modern Architecture was a resounding success. Based on his inaugural lecture as professor at the Academy of Fine Art in Vienna, it won Otto Wagner the adulation of a younger generation who, like Josef Hoffmann, were only too happy to enlist as disciples of the 'Wagner School'; or like Adolf Loos, another ardent admirer, to claim some of Wagner's ideas, not to mention his fighting spirit, as their own. An instant bestseller, it went through three reprints, in 1898, 1902 and 1914. The book's incendiary stance went on to secure first place for Otto Wagner in Nikolaus Pevsner's now classic *Pioneers of the Modern Movement*, first published in 1936, followed by Louis Sullivan, Adolf Loos, Hendrik Petrus Berlage, Peter Behrens and Frank Lloyd Wright, among others.[10]

From Otto Wagner's point of view, whatever the merits of the plan of the Ringstrasse and the undeniable urban quality of the city as a whole, built on the ruins of the medieval fortifications which Franz Josef had ordered demolished in 1857, Vienna had become an architectural backwater by 1895. Like a reminder of its anachronistic attachment to an archaic *ancien régime*, historicism still characterized its architecture, unable to find a way out of what Wagner likened to a 'costume ball'.

It is common practice to group the architecture of Ludwig von Förster (1797–1863), and of his son-in-law and one-time partner Theophil von Hansen (1813–91), with that of the other architects

5 Ludwig von Förster and Theophil von Hansen, Pereira Mansion, 1848–9. From *Allgemeine Bauzeitung*, 1849, p. 228

of monumental historicist buildings on the Ringstrasse: Ferstel, Sicardsburg, van der Nüll, Baumann, Schmidt and Hasenauer. But there was a difference. Förster and Hansen's historicism displayed some distinctive features. One of Hansen's earliest domestic commissions, in 1849, was for the Sephardic Pereira family's villa in Woerden, northeast of Vienna, which was themed in a neo-Moorish style that is generally read as a coded affirmation of the 'Oriental' identity of the Jews (fig.5).[11] But the choice of Moorish precedents by a Sephardic family might also have been meant to recall medieval Spain, a symbol of cross-cultural harmony where Jews, Christians and Arabs had coexisted peacefully during the golden age of the Caliphate of Cordoba, between around 900 and 1149, before the Fall of Granada at the hands of the Catholic kings.

Certainly, the Alhambra was the inspiration for the Dohány Street Synagogue, built in Budapest by Förster in 1859, the first synagogue to be constructed in the Moorish style anywhere in the world. He used Owen Jones's *Plans, Elevations and Details of the Alhambra* (1835–45) as documentary evidence of the palace, a book which he might have been made aware of by the Ephrussi family. Gustav Epstein too had a copy.[12] This unifying aspect of the architecture would have been something the architects themselves identified with. Förster had married a Jew and their daughter married the Danish-born Hansen.

Hansen soon set up his own firm, producing some of the most prominent new buildings of the Ringstrasse: the Musikverein, the Stock

6 Theophil von Hansen's Musikverein concert hall with its neo-Renaissance façade surmounted by a neo-Greek pediment

Exchange and Parliament. These buildings did not draw from the more sober, stripped-down 'Attic' style of classical antiquity favored by his German and French predecessors – Schinkel, and Percier and Fontaine. Laden with polychromatic and glitteringly gilded ornamentation, they were the literal embodiment of the Gilded Age's version of Greek classicism, likewise obvious in the monumental public buildings that Hansen designed in Athens, such as the Academy and National Library.[13]

The distinctive formal style Hansen adopted in Vienna, which he himself dubbed 'Greek Renaissance' because it was informed by the incongruous combination of Greek classical and Italian Renaissance ornamentation,[14] appears to have struck a chord with the successful Jewish entrepreneurs of Vienna, eager to be identified with the highest forms of European culture along with financial power (fig.6). Between 1861 and 1873, the Todescos, Epsteins and Ephrussis all placed their orders with Hansen for profit-making *Zinspalais* (rent-earning apartment houses). By favoring, these, as it were, non-denominational Mediterranean styles, both Moorish and 'Greek Renaissance', these clients were avoiding the northern, essentially Catholic styles of other Ringstrasse architects – neo-Gothic and neo-Baroque. The Ephrussi Palais went so far as to feature the crowning of Esther as Queen of Persia and the judgement of Haman, the deceitful enemy of the Jews, as the theme of the frescoed ceiling of its ballroom, along with more usual scenes from Greek mythology.[15]

The Viennese public itself, accustomed to the more restrained, traditional, Biedermeier-era architecture of the early nineteenth century, had not initially approved of the new, highly wrought, monumental historicism. The very first building on the Ring, the Wiener Hofoper (Vienna Court Opera) by August Sicard von Sicardsburg and Eduard van der Nüll, was badly received. Bringing together elements of French and Italian Renaissance, it was ridiculed for its '*Stil mischmasch*' ('mishmash style') and criticized for lacking the grandeur of Theophil Hansen's Heinrichshof, the apartment house that had been constructed across the street for the building tycoon Heinrich Drasche in 1861–3. The opera house was even referred to as the 'Königgrätz of architecture', a reference to that disastrous defeat of the Habsburg Empire by Prussia in 1866. Faced with this negative reception, one of the architects, van der Nüll, already sickly, committed suicide. Sicardsburg died of a heart attack six months later.[16]

Historicism's initial lack of popular appeal did nothing to stem its rapid spread. The first monumental project of Franz Josef's reign was the colossal military barracks, the Arsenal. It comprised 31 separate units, built between 1849 and 1856 by a team made up of Sicardsburg and van der Nüll, along with Carl Rösner and Antonius Pius de Riegel, and Hansen and Förster. Its purpose was not to keep the external enemies of the country at bay, but to secure the power of the new emperor, Franz Josef, in the event of other upheavals, such as the March Revolution of 1848, which had pitted the revolutionaries against Franz Josef's predecessor, Emperor Ferdinand.

The Viennese Arsenal bears a resemblance to the colossal Arsenale of Venice, begun in the twelfth century. This symbolic reference would have served as an assertion of imperial might, as Franz Josef derived much of his prestige from his control of the great Italian port and its hinterland.[17] The Viennese complex incorporates features of its Venetian precedent without being a literal copy of it. Like the Venetian Arsenale, the Viennese one is finished in naked brickwork, unprecedentedly brutalist for a monumental building in *fin de siècle* Vienna. And like the Venetian complex, built over a period of centuries, the Viennese Arsenal is a cluster of distinct and divergent units.

A northern neo-Gothic style was chosen for Heinrich von Ferstel's design of the Votivkirche, built between 1856 and 1879 –

the first architectural pearl on the Ringstrasse – and for Friedrich von Schmidt's City Hall, built between 1872 and 1883. A pleasant, but unremarkable, neo-Renaissance style was selected for Ferstel's Kunstgewerbeschule (today the University of Applied Arts) of 1884 and for Ludwig Baumann's Kunstgewerbemuseum (today the Museum of Applied Arts) of 1871. The neo-Baroque Burgtheater of 1888 and the Kunsthistorisches Museum (Museum of Fine Art) and Naturhistorisches Museum (Natural History Museum) of 1872–91 were all designed by the German Gottfried Semper, working with the Viennese-trained Karl Freiherr von Hasenauer. These historicist buildings were remarkably conservative when compared with the art nouveau wrought-iron masterpieces which were then being constructed in Paris, Barcelona and Brussels. In fact, Semper and Hasenauer's Kunsthistorisches and Naturhistorisches museums were heaped with scorn in the foreign press and, by the early 1890s, when they opened to the public, their anachronistic style was looked down upon in France.[18]

The major train stations of Vienna were built in unexceptional historicist styles which pale in comparison with those of Budapest. Viennese historicism also spread to the grand hotels of Semmering, the Alpine watering hole of the Viennese well-to-do, especially the grand Hotel Panhans and the Tyrolean-themed Südbahn Hotel, the latter reminiscent of Ludwig of Bavaria's fairytale castles of the 1880s in southern Germany. The new glazed-fronted department stores – the Herzmansky of 1898 by Maximilian Katscher and the Gerngross of 1902–4 by Ferdinand Fellner and Hermann Helmer – also fail to impress beside Paris's Le Printemps, Bazar de l'Hôtel de Ville and La Samaritaine.

The reverse side of Viennese historicism was technological backwardness. The acoustics of Semper and Hasenauer's Burgtheater were so poor that the director Max Reinhardt complained he had to rely on his imagination because he could not follow the dialogue on stage.[19] One of the reasons for the poor reception of Sicardsburg and van der Nüll's opera house was that they were not up to the structural problems entailed.[20] The commission for the main exhibition hall for the World's Fair of 1873, held in Vienna, was awarded to Karl Freiherr von Hasenauer. But since the Viennese-trained Hasenauer lacked the expertise to construct a building on such a scale, he had to employ a foreign engineer, the Scotsman John Scott Russell. Scott Russell's part of the building used 4000 tons of iron and rose to 84 meters. If Austria had intended to present itself as an industrial world power alongside England and France, it failed. After paying a fortune for this modern metal structure, rather than making a feature of it as London had done with Joseph Paxton's cast-iron and glass Crystal Palace in 1851, Hasenauer covered it with a neo-Renaissance pastiche, ornate and heavy-handed, inspired by the Pantheon in Rome. To set this building in perspective, in 1873 Henri Labrouste had just recently finished his light iron structure for the Bibliothèque Nationale in Paris – and it won the first architectural prize at the Vienna World's Fair. Commissioned to commemorate Franz Josef's Golden Jubilee in 1897, even the Ferris Wheel at the Prater, which was to be designed by an Englishman, expressed in its iron structure the reality of the new industrial materials.[21]

One exception to this lack of homegrown expertise was provided by the engineer and entrepreneur Carl von Ghega, born in Venice to an Albanian family. His Semmering Railway, built between 1848 and 1854, a project that had been judged impossible because of the steepness of the gradients, comprised 14 tunnels, 16 viaducts and 100 stone and 11 iron bridges. It was considered a masterpiece and is now a Unesco World Heritage site.

In 1895, the year Otto Wagner wrote *Modern Architecture*, a theme park called Venedig in Wien, or Venice in Vienna, was built in the city. This no-holds-barred expression of Viennese historicism gave physical form to the dream of recapturing a bygone past – one in which Venice, which had won its independence in 1866, was still part of the Austro-Hungarian Empire. Conceived by the theater director Gabor Steiner and designed by the architect Oskar Marmorek in the former Imperial Gardens in the Prater in the Second District, it was an exact replica of the original Venice, spread across 50,000 square meters, including a system of canals, with replicas of the Palazzos Priuli, Cammello, Dario and Sernagiotto, along with the Abbazia San Gregorio and Ca' d'Oro; there was even a Campo dei Mori that offered a view of a perfect replica of the Piazza San Marco. According to the guide book, 25 real gondolas had been brought from Venice to ply the 8000 meters of canal. Venice in Vienna contained souvenir shops, travel agencies, restaurants, cafés, champagne bars, taverns, *Biergarten*, music halls, theaters and a post office. This stage setting was where Johann Strauss, the 'king of the waltz', chose to live.[22]

Viennese *fin de siècle* apartment interiors could be just as schmaltzy. Their leader of fashion was the painter Hans Makart

(1840–84), Gustav Klimt's former master, against whom he was to rebel in founding the Viennese Secession. Makart epitomized the historicist zeitgeist of the Ringstrasse, delving into a hodge-podge of bygone styles. The interior of his studio was the perfect match for the historicist stage setting provided by the Ringstrasse architects. Dubbed from the early 1870s the 'painter-prince' of the Ringstrasse, dressed up as Rubens, he made a killing by painting poorly executed canvases representing the daughters and wives of patrician Vienna as ersatz Valkyries, Cleopatras and seventeenth-century Habsburg nobility.[23] At Makart's death from syphilis in 1884, his studio, full of his signature palm fronds and peacock feathers, which had been the cherished model for many nouveau riche living rooms of the day, contained no fewer than 1083 'antiques'. Cosima Wagner, the wife of Makart's friend Richard Wagner, treasured its memory as a 'wonder of decorative beauty'.[24] One reason for Cosima's admiration might have been that among Makart's sources of inspiration was Richard Wagner himself, who had decorated his sumptuous villa, not far from Schönbrunn, with ankle-deep rugs and heavy draperies while working on *Die Meistersinger von Nürnberg* in 1863–4.[25]

There was someone whose aversion to the modern world outdid even that of these historicists. This was the architect and town planner Camillo Sitte (1843–1903). Born just two years after Otto Wagner, he was Wagner's sworn enemy. Sitte was not just nostalgic for the past; dressed in medieval garb and donning a faux-Gothic velvet beret, he sought to recreate it. The architectural historian Sigfried Giedion dismissed him as 'a kind of troubadour, ineffectually pitting his medieval songs against the din of modern industry,' and believed that he had 'lost contact with his period'.[26]

In Sitte's defense, he was immensely learned. After training as an architect with Ferstel at the Technische Hochschule from 1863 to 1868, he pursued art-historical and archeological studies under Rudolf Eitelberger, working on the documentary history of art along with his friend, the great art historian Albert Ilg, author of the first scholarly work on the Renaissance, *Hypnerotomachia Poliphili*.[27] He also investigated the physiology of vision and of space perception. After this he travelled to Germany and Italy to focus on Renaissance art.

The conservative Sitte was the polar opposite of the modernist Otto Wagner. He was, like Makart, a worshipper of Richard Wagner, whom he considered to be the supreme hero of German art, and whose

Meistersinger von Nürnberg showed, in Sitte's view, the *Volk* 'fully developed'. He went so far as to assert that 'to make the Wagnerian Siegfried is to make the future, the new German man'. He even named his first son Siegfried. During one of his trips to Bayreuth in the early 1880s, he met his idol and seems to have been commissioned to design stage sets for *Parsifal*.[28] He also wrote a rhapsodic article, 'Richard Wagner und die deutsche Kunst', in *Jahresbericht des Wiener Akademischen Wagner-Vereins* in 1875 and an article on *Lohengrin* in 1877.[29] Sitte's most Wagnerian project was for a so-called 'Holländer Turm', an immense tower on an empty beach, its many floors devoted to a presentation of Germanic creativity.[30]

As for the Ringstrasse, Sitte simply found it too modern – that is to say, too cosmopolitan. He fancied himself waging battle against the forces that repressed *Alt-Wien*, the *völkisch* Vienna that was dominated by the church, the old nobility and the traditional tradesmen.[31] Sitte's own manifesto, *City Planning According to Artistic Principles*, of 1889, was at least as popular as Otto Wagner's book when it was published six years later. It immediately went through two editions in 1889 and a third in 1901. The remarkable success of Sitte's book can be explained at least in part by its undisputed quality, the way in which he substantiated each point in modern art-historical fashion by a clear visual image drawn from the plan of an existing European city. The book has gone down in history as a defense of urban conservation and of the traditional, humane city, in particular in the wake of the disastrous 'urban renewal' projects of post-Second World War planning in the US.[32]

What is usually overlooked by his many twentieth-century admirers, however, is that Sitte was categorically opposed to any modernization in cities and believed that straight streets were symptomatic of 'a very new and modern ailment'. His reason was that one 'naturally feels cozy in small, old plazas, and only in our memory do they loom gigantic, because in our imagination the magnitude of the artistic effect takes the place of actual size. On our modern gigantic plazas, with their yawning emptiness and oppressive ennui, the inhabitants of snug old towns suffer attacks of this fashionable agoraphobia.'[33] Discussing squares in Padua, Syracuse, Padua, Palermo and Verona, he wrote: 'It is generally realized from personal experience that these irregularities do not have an unpleasant effect at all, but on the contrary, they enhance naturalness, they stimulate our interest and,

Fig. 30. Padua: Piazza degli Eremitani

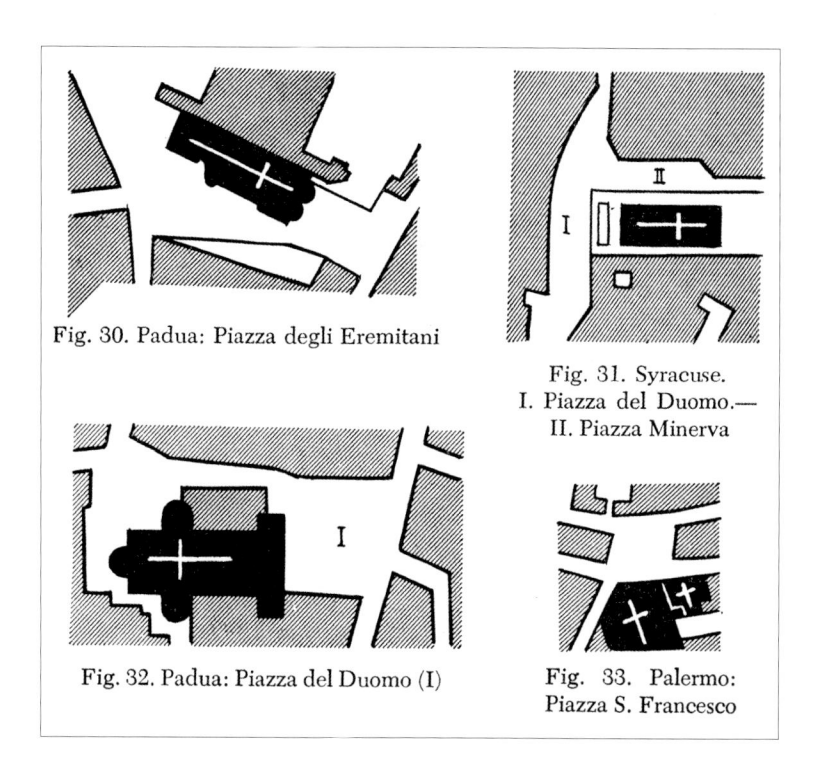

Fig. 31. Syracuse.
I. Piazza del Duomo.—
II. Piazza Minerva

Fig. 32. Padua: Piazza del Duomo (I)

Fig. 33. Palermo: Piazza S. Francesco

7 Church-centered urban design principle by Camillo Sitte, *City Planning According to Artistic Principles*, 1889

above all, they augment the picturesque quality of the tableau.'[34] The unmentioned feature shared by all these squares is that they were located in Catholic cities, centered on a church (fig.7).

An alternative to Sitte's conception of public space was set out by Otto Wagner. Two years before the publication of his manifesto of 1895, he had won the competition for the position of artistic advisor for the Stadtbahn, the city's new rail system. The colossal project included three different lines extending over a distance of 40 kilometers. The first was the Gürtel (Girdle), located on the so-called Linien Wall, which was a fortification line like the Ringstrasse but further out. It was meant to link outlying areas to the center of Vienna. The other two rail lines ran along the Wien river and the Danube canal. Wagner was also in charge of a massive reinforcement of the embankments of the waterways. The most complex part of the commission was the weir at the Nussdorf Dam.[35] The overall project required the coordination of viaducts, bridges, tunnels, and more than 40 railway stations between 1894 and 1910.

Otto Wagner's Stadtbahn substituted a new architectural language for the old. It turned a public transport infrastructure project into an aesthetically exciting, sensual, egalitarian public space which was meant to bring together working-class people with the more affluent population. The colors were white and what has since become a typically Viennese shade of green, possibly borrowed from the oxidized copper roof of the Karlskirche, which the contemporary art critic Ludwig Hevesi named 'Secession green', referring to the Secession building, where it was also used.[36] The two most famous buildings, co-designed by Wagner and Josef Maria Olbrich, the architect of the Secession building, are the two former station entrances on the Karlsplatz (fig.8). Their walls were white marble slabs suspended by a visible cast-iron structure painted in Secession green, with shining, gilded sunflower-themed ornamentation. The Hofpavilion near the palace at Schönbrunn was decorated in mahogany, with frescoed panels, a specially designed chandelier and wall-to-wall carpeting.

Otto Wagner's stations are all masterpieces of detailing. Their white outer walls are rendered in an aggregate containing powdered marble, giving them a literal aura. The Jugendstil rosettes and garlands in green-painted wrought iron that decorate the entrances to the Kettenbrückegasse and Rossauerlände are especially beautiful.

The roofs of all the platforms are supported on delicately proportioned, slender wrought-iron classical columns. Even the lamps were designed by Wagner. The Nussdorf Dam, the Kaiserhof Dam near the Schottenring, the bridges across the Zeile and the Währingerstrasse, and the Ferdinandbrücke were all faced with bright white-and-gold glazed tiles.[37]

8 Otto Wagner, urban design using two modern Stadtbahn stations to frame the entrance to the square in front of the historic eighteenth-century Karlskirche by Johann Bernhard Fischer von Erlach. Postcard, author's collection

The sheer excitement created by this new kind of modern public place was captured by the very young Richard Neutra. He writes that his decision to become an architect was the result, at eight years old, of 'a ride in the new, much talked about subway, the stations of which were designed by Otto Wagner'. For the young boy, Otto Wagner was 'Hercules, Achilles, Buffalo Bill, all rolled into one: he stood for all the heroes and pathfinders . . . Here was a missionary and one who was breaking with a worn-out past.'[38]

Wagner landed the Stadtbahn commission just in time. In 1897, after Franz Ferdinand's designation as heir apparent and Karl Lueger's appointment as Mayor of Vienna, he fell victim to a conservative backlash. Contrary to standard practice following such a prestigious and successful public commission, he was never to receive any other commissions from the municipality, except to make a chair for Lueger's birthday in 1904 in opulent rosewood incrusted with mother of pearl.

Thus the first casualty of Otto Wagner's declaration of war against the establishment was his own career. His treacherous embrace of modernity would never be forgiven, and his practice was about to plummet because of it. He was now seen by the Viennese establishment as an 'evil revolutionary'.[39] One anonymous critic accused him of being 'a worshiper of an affected brutal, Gallic architectural materialism'.[40] His only two large projects following his manifesto, the Postsparkasse and the Steinhof church, were given to him by Lueger's enemy, the emperor, under the aegis of the Minister for Culture, Hartel.[41] This only encouraged criticism. The church, in particular, drew comments with strong overtones of racial prejudice. When the building opened in October 1907, some critics claimed that instead of a house of God, it resembled a 'tomb of an Indian maharaja'. One anonymous pamphleteer attacked him as a traitor and corruptor of youth, who socialized with Jews and freemasons. Others attacked the church as an example of 'Assyrian Babylonian idiot style' and '*l'art juif*'.[42]

Otto Wagner's manifesto was not only an assault on the Ringstrasse architects. It was also a rejection of everything he himself had stood for up until that time. He had spent the first 30 years of his professional career as the consummate insider. He had been brought up in one of Theophil von Hansen's first Viennese *palais*, built in 1848, in the very heart of the patrician First District, on the Göttweihergasse, between Seilergasse and Spiegelgasse, on the site of Antonio Salieri's apartment and, later, Franz Schubert's. Adolf Loos perceptively noticed the striking influence of this building on Otto Wagner's subsequent oeuvre.[43] While a student at the Academy of Fine Art, Wagner had not only studied in the studio of the two Opera architects, van der Nüll and Sicardsburg, he had also been their teaching assistant. He even worked with Makart on the pompous design for the processions for the emperor's silver wedding anniversary in 1879. When he set out on his own career, the building boom around Vienna's Ringstrasse was just starting and his mother ensured that his first job upon graduating in 1862 was at the great Ringstrasse office of Theophil von Hansen and Ludwig von Förster. Hansen and Wagner swiftly became the two favorite architects of industrialist and banker Gustav Ritter von Epstein, who entrusted them with the creation of his Palais Epstein, Hansen providing the design and Wagner supervising the construction. Otto Wagner opened his own office as early as 1864, and soon became a highly successful architect in the mold of his Ringstrasse predecessors, collaborating with Hansen and Förster. Epstein retained him to build a summer residence at Baden (1867), his second independent commission. And it was to Epstein's intervention that Wagner owed his third commission: the construction of a synagogue in Budapest (1872).[44]

At that time another architect had the German-speaking architectural establishment under his sway. This was Gottfried Semper (1803–79), once a revolutionary anti-monarchist who had fought on the barricades of 1848 alongside Bakunin, who was now currying favor from the absolutist Emperor Franz Josef in Vienna. Wagner's fantasy monumental complex, *Artibus*, of 1880, has long been recognized as a close copy of Semper's design for the Kaisersforum of 1869, intended to exalt Franz Josef.[45] It even bore Semper's own motto, *Artis sola domina necessitas* ('Necessity is the only mistress of art'), as a show of allegiance.

Otto Wagner laid his career on the line in 1895 by writing his manifesto and joining the ranks of the anti-establishment, firebrand Secessionists. He was 55 years of age, and the Secession was a club of 'angry young men'; Wagner was Josef Hoffmann's senior by 30 years, Olbrich's by 26 and Klimt's by 21. When one looks outside Vienna at other major modern architects of the period, Otto Wagner was 26 years older than Hector Guimard, 20 years older than Victor Horta, 15 years older than Louis Sullivan, and 11 years older than Antoni Gaudí. The fact is that he was swept up in the liberating, progressivist spirit that was engulfing the cultural, scientific and political life at the time not only of Vienna, but also Paris, London, Berlin and Chicago.

In Wagner's case, the precipitating factor was the Secession, started by Gustav Klimt, who, like Wagner with his once revered role model, Semper, now turned against his own master, Hans Makart. The Secession stood against everything the Semperian and Makartian historicists worshiped. Instead of embracing the universals of the past, it sought out the right architecture for the times. 'To each epoch its own art' was its motto. Like the art nouveau movement in Paris and Brussels and Modernismo in Barcelona, Viennese Jugendstil threw off what had by then become a conservative, backward architectural movement and looked to nature and its naked forms for inspiration.

If Otto Wagner made the leap, it was with the certainty of a relatively soft landing. He relied on the cushioning effect of his business success during the great building boom of the Ringstrasse, which had coincided with the start of his career. Although he received 16 major commissions throughout his life, he built, as a developer, an additional 15 apartment houses and villas on his own account. The fact that he had been not only an architect but also a highly successful entrepreneur for 25 years, living in the buildings he had financed and designed until he sold them to fund the next venture, stood him in good stead. He was able to build a second villa for himself in Hietzing in spite of the dip in his earning power. It also mitigated the financial risk involved in morphing from old boy to counter-culture firebrand. In this respect he differed from his fellow rebel, Louis Sullivan. Sullivan wound up destitute in the wake of the Chicago Columbian Exhibition of 1893 that turned the tide of public taste away from his kind of modernism, towards a conservative and pompous Beaux-Arts historicism, which Lewis Mumford later decried.[46]

One aspect of Wagner's non-conformist streak was his refusal to participate in the generalized anti-Semitism for which Vienna was known. Throughout his career, he included synagogues among the specialisms listed on his calling card.[47] This was in keeping with his first important career choice, to work for the firm of Förster and Hansen. As we have seen, one of the distinguishing features of their practice was that, unlike the major Ringstrasse architects who were followers of Semper, they worked for Jewish clients, designing great palaces for the Ephrussi, Epstein, Arnstein and Todesco families. Wagner's design for the Rumbach Street Synagogue in Budapest of 1872 is a case in point. His neo-Moorish façade followed Förster's example for the Sephardic Leopoldstadt Temple in Vienna in suggesting the Alhambra (fig.9).[48]

Otto Wagner became a fighter who ceaselessly campaigned to open up Austria's architectural language to the modern world of the industrial revolution. In *Modern Architecture* he turned his back on the anti-modern, anti-machine-age architectural and urban ideas that typified the country. A keen Francophile, he held up the example of modern-day France, where industrialization had been adopted by architects to great success. Rejecting the faux-grand, historicist 'Pompier' style, the French, Wagner wrote, 'have shown the first signs of this new style with the realism of the Eiffel Tower and *plein air* genre painting. Architecture, too, must reflect its time.' He roundly condemned the Italian-inspired Grand Tour, classic capstone of the traditional Viennese architectural education, on the grounds that Italy's architecture said too little to modern men. Let the architecture novitiate visit Paris instead, 'the metropolis' and 'those places where modern luxury resides'.[49] When he commissioned his own portrait at the height of his career, he made sure it featured his French award, the medal of the *Légion d'honneur* (fig.4).

Pompier style was the dominant cultural expression all over Europe and America in the late nineteenth century, in the wake of the rapid pace

9 Otto Wagner, section of the Rumbach Synagogue. From *Einige Skizzen*, 1889, vol. 1

of economic growth and the then-unprecedented rise of the nouveaux riches of the international Gilded Age. But, whereas in Paris, London, Barcelona and Chicago, there were ingenious alternatives, in Vienna there had been none. Before Otto Wagner, there were no attempts to advance architecture in such a way as to adapt to the new realities. Vienna had no Paxton, Viollet-le-Duc, Baltard, Garnier, Labrouste, Eiffel, Guimard, Horta, Gaudì or Sullivan. There was no Crystal Palace, no Gare Saint-Lazare, no Printemps, no Les Halles, no Opéra Garnier and no Carson Pirie Scott Department Store.

Otto Wagner broke with Gottfried Semper over the use of iron in architecture. Semper had declared in his *Der Stil in den technischen und tektonishen Künsten* (1861–63) that monumental architecture could never be based on naked iron structures,[50] although he did use the material when necessary on the inside of buildings, where it would not show.[51] Amazingly, this was a decade after Victor Baltard had designed Les Halles in Paris (1851–7). Yet Semper was to spend the rest of his life arguing for the use of costly, inefficient traditional stone façades.

It was one of Semper's precepts that architectural dressing did not have to reflect a building's interior. It could instead express faithfulness to tradition in the face of a disrupting industrial revolution. This was an excuse to conserve the traditional vocabulary of stone on the outside of a building while adapting to new, modern functions on the inside. This idea, put forth in his *Der Stil*, however modern it may have been when it was published, was no longer modern by the 1890s. In a major attempt to turn German architecture away from Semper's influence, the German architect and diplomat Hermann Muthesius (1861–1927) was assigned as technical attaché to London to report on English architecture, which was deemed more modern. The result was his *Die Englische Baukunst der Gegenwart* ('English Architecture Today') of 1900. By then, Semper's authority was regarded as a straitjacket on creativity, particularly in relation to the new realities of iron, which fascinated Wagner, along with Louis Sullivan and his modern followers internationally.

Although Wagner went to great lengths to declare his admiration for Semper in *Modern Architecture* – he would do the same for Karl Lueger in his *Grossstadt* (1911) – the book seems to be a series of stabs in Semper's back.[52] He cited Semper's motto, *Artis sola domina necessitas*, which even Wagner had adopted in 1880, only to note that Semper himself was now deviating from it.[53] With regard to *Der Stil*, he accused its author of having 'lacked the courage to complete his theories'.[54]

He then went on to condemn the Semperian method of construction that consisted in chiseling large blocks of stone and stacking them in place, with 'great expenditure of time and money'.[55]

Even Otto Wagner's earliest works reveal a subtle anti-Semperian streak, including his own early apartment house of 1877–8 near the Schottentor. The flat, geometric black-and-white pattern on the first floor of its façade, a two-dimensional, abstract version of Renaissance stone masonry with a diamond-shaped projection, ran contrary to Semper's precept that only stone was acceptable for a building's exterior. His Rumbach Street Synagogue of 1872 used slender cast-iron columns as the sole elegant supports for the dome in the interior, as Henri Labrouste had done in the Bibliothèque Nationale in Paris, among others. Wagner's design for the interior of the Österreichische Länderbank (1882–4) in Vienna, one of the city's first bank buildings, was also the first Viennese example of an atrium covered with a large cast-iron and glass skylight, prefiguring his future embracing of steel and glass in his ceiling of the main hall of the Postsparkasse (1904).

Two more overt examples of opposition to Semper's dictates were Wagner's Neumann Department Store (now demolished) on the Kärntnerstrasse (1895) and his Anker building (1895) for the Anker insurance company on the Graben. These two buildings were the only two comprising iron and glass in the heart of Vienna's exclusive shopping area in the First District. In the Anker building, the cast iron and glass extended up the first two floors of the façade, and a cast-iron and glass attic structure housing a photographer's studio adorned its top storey instead of a masonry roof (fig.10). Each one of the buildings that Wagner designed after publishing *Modern Architecture* in 1896 can be seen as a negation of his former historicist self and an attempt to rethink architectural solutions along the lines of what he believed was a modern alternative. His design work for the Vienna Stadtbahn was his first major riposte to Semper's ideas concerning the use of iron.

The irony is that Wagner was applying something akin to the conservative and notoriously convoluted concept of architectural *Bekleidung* (dressing, cladding) which Semper had put forth in his *Der Stil*,[56] but taking it to its logical conclusion – as Semper himself had not. In Semper's view, textile art and ceramics were the first fields in which the desire to beautify could be seen to take an important place alongside functionality. This could be interpreted to mean either that cladding should be structural, or that a wall construction

FOTOGRAFIE
NEW-YORK
S. BRAUN
M. GOLDSCHMIDT & COMP. JUWELIERE
CHOCOLADE
A. KAINRATH
C.M. FRANK
WINDERLE

only exists to enable textiles or carpets to be fixed onto it – two different ideas that Semper kept confusing. What Wagner did in both the whimsical, brightly colored and glazed Majolica House and in the apartment next door to it, the Köstlergasse House (1898–9) on the Linke Wienzeile, was to replace the dark and heavy garments of Semper's overdressed neo-Renaissance and neo-Baroque buildings with more modern, lighter and certainly more sensual material, similar to the billowing, liberating Viennese 'reform dress' (fig.11). *Modern Architecture* does, after all, contain a panegyric to women's clothes, which Wagner claimed to prefer to men's.[57] Actually, his friend Gustav Klimt was in the habit of dressing in this way (fig.12).

Like Klimt, Wagner was caught up in a wave of luxuriant sensuality. Both these buildings – one clad with a floral motif executed in majolica tiles produced by Wienerberger Keramik, designed with the help of his former student Alois Ludwig, and the other embellished with gilded jewel-like moldings designed by Koloman Moser, as if to reveal the creamy texture of the façade underneath – stood as a shocking iconographic rupture with Semperian tenets. First, both façades are purely surface ornament applied onto the building's real, hidden structure. And second, as in the case of the forerunners noted above, the Neumann department store and the Anker building, the first two floors of these buildings were a blatant, almost exhibitionist display of naked iron and glass, as decried by Semper.

When Wagner's repressed rebelliousness finally burst forth in his Majolica House and Köstlergasse House, it was a cry from the heart. This, at least, is how his long-time collaborator, the Secession sculptor Othmar Schimkowitz, appears to have understood it. Schimkowitz

10 (opposite) Otto Wagner, Anker building. From *Einige Skizzen*, 1906, vol. 3

11 (top) The Majolica House and the Köstlergasse House, revealing the cast-iron and plate-glass ground floor. From *Einige Skizzen*, 1906, vol. 3

12 (bottom) Moritz Nähr's photographs of Gustav Klimt and Emilie Flöge wearing billowing 'Reform' dresses in the garden of Klimt's studio, 1905/6

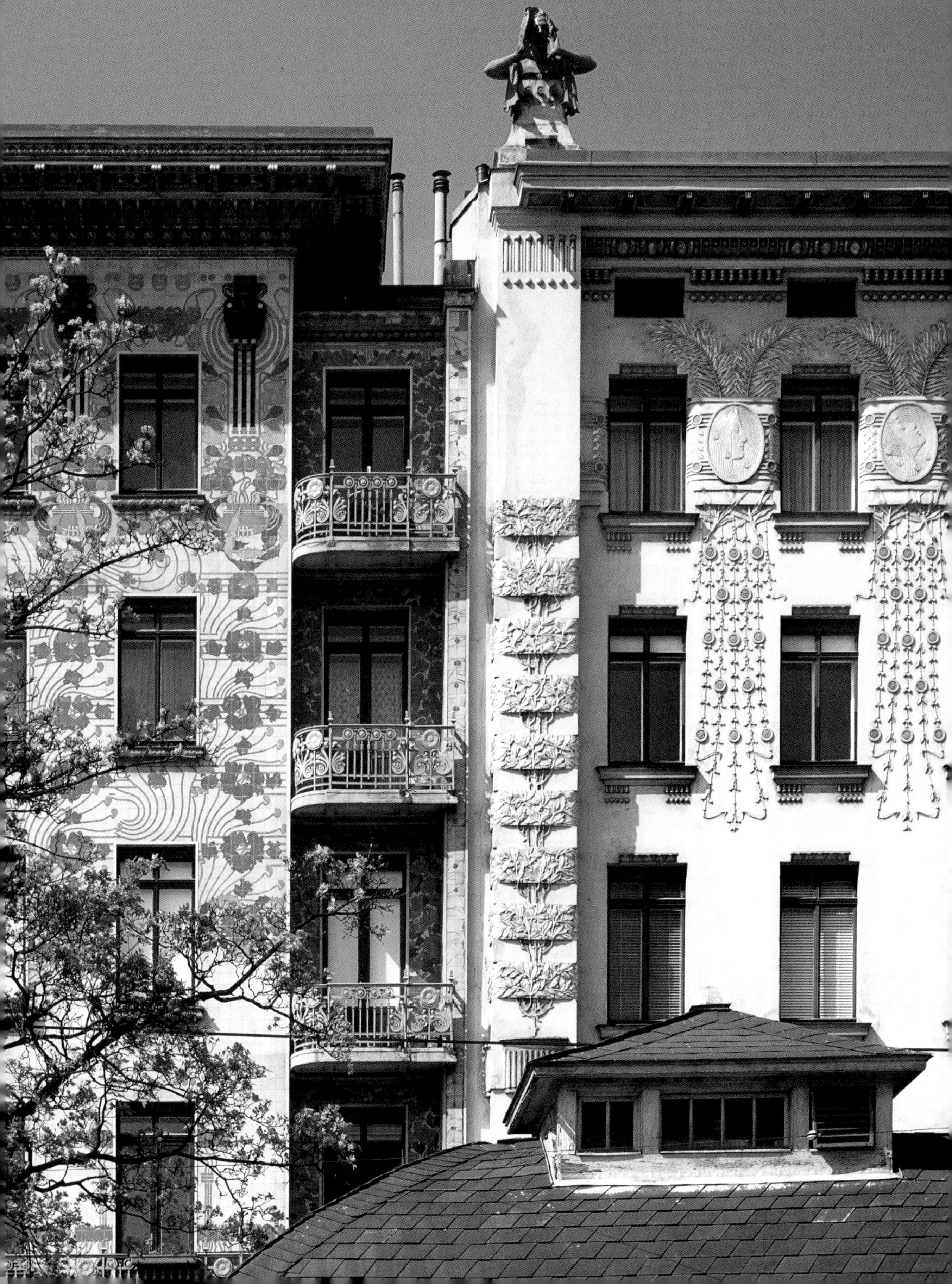

captured the buildings' spirit in the form of the two identical busts of a young woman on the top of Köstlergasse House, shouting through cupped hands. It was the call of the modern (color plate 1).

The dressing of the Majolica House is the product of an exuberant creative energy. This is where Otto Wagner became a master of ornamentation. A swirl of magenta poppies fans out over the entire façade amid a waving pattern of plump turquoise poppy buds, all on delicately undulating tendrils, intertwined with prickly sea-blue and emerald-green thistles regularly interspersed with small, intricate leafy vignettes. At the highest part of the façade, from the jaws of ten sculpted lion's heads in a row, glazed in teal blue, hang large botanically themed vignettes made up of flowering sprigs and loose wreaths of thistles twisted around giant lyres. The most brightly colored element of all is the underside of the cornice and of its soffit. It features three rows of moldings: a pattern of aligned magenta rosettes, followed by more thistles, now in pairs extending upward and then gently bending toward one another in a slender arc, and then a row of distended, glistening, strange turquoise pomegranates that open up along a slit to reveal a glimpse of their seeds (color plates 2–4). The tiled walls of the balconies are decorated a pattern of lush nasturtium leaves (fig.13). The Köstlergasse façade next door, with its palm fronds, laurel branches wound around pillars, giant medallions and tumbling cascades of coins, all dazzlingly gilded against the creamy skin of the façade, is no less imaginative (color plate 5).

Perhaps inspired by Klimt's erotic female nudes that seem to be floating in space, in 1899 Wagner furnished his own apartment with a transparent bath for his wife, made out of plate glass mounted in nickel (fig.14). Adolf Loos lavished praise on it in an article,[58] and appears to have grafted it into his own design for a house for Josephine Baker that included a transparent glass pool, in which he dreamed of seeing its occupant bathe naked (as we shall see in Chapter 5).

Once Otto Wagner swerved off the beaten path, there was no holding back his innovative impulses. In his design for the avant-garde modernist journal *Die Zeit*'s telegraphic dispatch office of 1902, on the corner of Annagasse and Kärntnerstrasse in the heart of Vienna's historicist First District, he covered the entire façade in metal (fig.15). It was unheard of. Its only elements were iron, nickel-plated iron, glass and, last but not least, the newly discovered, still expensive and bauxite-rich, Austrian-processed aluminum. The shock effect must have been

13 (opposite)   Balconies with nasturtium pattern between the Majolica and Köstlergasse Houses

14 (below)   Plate glass and nickel bathtub in Otto Wagner's apartment adjoining the two apartment houses on the Linke Wienzeile, on Kostlergasse 3. Photograph, 1898–9. Bildnachweis, Austrian National Library

like that of Hans Hollein's all-aluminum Retti candle shop or Frank Gehry's all-titanium museum in Bilbao when they were first seen.

With his Postsparkasse (1904–6), Wagner shed the last remnants of his previous Secession-inspired tendency and adopted a purely industrial aesthetic. Here he sheathed the relatively low-cost structural brick and reinforced-concrete framework with thin, mass-produced, factory-polished panels of granite, anchored in place with iron bolts whose heads were encased in aluminum caps, underlining the fact that there was no stone masonry in the building (figs 17 and 18). On the contrary, it was just veneer – another anti-Semperian affront. The inspiration for these caps in the industrial vernacular of the late nineteenth century is clear. No one was more familiar with the language of cast-iron structures than Wagner, thanks to his involvement with the Stadtbahn. His drawing of the monumental gate to his Ferdinandbrücke of 1905, published in his *Einige Skizzen* ('Some Drawings') of 1906, depicts panels anchored in place with iron bolts whose heads are encased in caps, which one finds in all the similar structures in Paris at the time (fig.19). They are identical in shape to the caps dotting the cast-iron beams of the bridge structure below. In the Postsparkasse aluminum was used demonstratively in the columns outside and in the heaters inside (fig.20). The two winged figures on the roof of the building, again by Schimkowitz, overlooking its entrance are also aluminum and clearly visible, their wings secured to the building with the same bolts (fig.16). Wagner was to include this detail derived from the new industrial vernacular in all his architecture from then on, in a continual challenge to the traditional Semperian abhorrence of metal.

Wagner's Leopoldskirche am Steinhof (1904–7) is part of one of the most enlightened architectural complexes of the turn of the century. It was part of a sanatorium for the treatment of about 1000 poor and destitute people, along with affluent mentally ill patients. It was

15 (opposite) Otto Wagner, entrance to the dispatch office of the journal *Die Zeit*. Reconstruction by Adolf Krischanitz and Otto Kapfinger, 1985. Vienna Museum

16 (below) Othmar Schimkowitz, 'high-tech' all-aluminum angel with wings fastened to the top of Otto Wagner's Postsparkasse with alumium-capped bolts

ÖSTERR. POSTSPARKASSE

17 (opposite)   Otto Wagner, Postsparkasse, Vienna

18 (left)   Otto Wagner, Postsparkasse, Vienna. From *Einige Skizzen*, 1906, vol. 3

19 (right, top)   Otto Wagner, project for the rebuilding of the Ferdinandbrücke in Vienna, showing the standard use of capped studs on the bare cast-iron base of the structure and Wagner's use of them as pure ornamentation on the marble panels above. From *Einige Skizzen*, 1897, vol. 2

20 (right, bottom)   Otto Wagner, Postsparkasse, aluminum ventilation shafts

commissioned by the Minister of Culture, Wilhelm von Hartel, to celebrate the emperor's Golden Jubilee. The Steinhof complex was revolutionary from a medical viewpoint. Corresponding to the new belief – inspired by French psychiatrists like Charcot who were having a great influence on Sigmund Freud among others at the time – that mental problems were illnesses that could be cured, it replaced the cruelty of the seventeenth-century Narrenturm ('Fool's Tower'), intended to punish the insane. Otto Wagner had already mapped out the center in his general plan for Vienna of 1892–3 on a 33-hectare site just outside the city's border, planted with fruit trees, designed by the garden architect Johann Müller. The surrounding colony was conceived along the lines of a therapeutic village, with no fewer than 60 villa-like pavilions designed by Carlo von Boog, in what was referred to as the White City. They included an indoor swimming pool, heliotherapy terraces, conservatories, a skating rink, tennis courts, bowling alleys, winter gardens, a dance hall, farm buildings, pigsties and nurseries.[59] The only building not designed by von Boog was Otto Wagner's church.

Wagner's church could not have been less Semperian (color plate 6). Its luminous spaciousness was achieved thanks to its cream-colored majolica ceramic tiles jointed in a sparkling brass-colored metal framework inside. Outside, the glinting dome achieved its own radiance by a reversal of the pattern inside. Here the tiles were of gilded brass, inserted into a framework of green-colored metal. In the abundant gilding of the building's cupola and of its winged figures, Wagner was no doubt directly inspired by Olbrich's Secession building and indirectly by the golden domes of the shrines in Jaipur, Isfahan and Jerusalem among others, which were becoming known thanks to the Orientalism that was sweeping Vienna in the wake of Josef Strzygowski's immensely popular *The Orient or Rome: Contributions to the History of Late Antique and Early Christian Art* of 1901. The critic who assailed the building as resembling the 'tomb of an Indian maharaja' was correct.

Indeed, for all his conservatism, Franz Josef approved of this most modern project, perhaps as the father of the suicidal Crown Prince Rudolf. He even declared in a letter to his mistress, Katharina Schratt, in 1902 that it would almost be a pleasure to be imprisoned there, praising in particular Wagner's church.[60] Commissioned for 800 celebrants, the church was by far Otto Wagner's most extravagantly funded building. As with the Postsparkasse, the structure is sheathed with thin sheets of Carrara marble, set in a mortar bed and seemingly anchored to the wall with metal bolts, now capped not with aluminum (as in the Postsparkasse) but with copper heads. All the exposed metal of the building is copper and the tiles on the roof were originally gilded. The all-white interior contained exquisite mosaics and stained glass by Koloman Moser on the two side walls, as well as inlaid on the surface of the dome covering the main hall of the church. Schimkowitz again provided the personification of the protective, welcoming spirit of the building in the form of four towering, stately but resplendently gilded winged figures on the façade.[61]

The final years of Otto Wagner's architectural career saw him transform once again, this time with the two almost totally unadorned Neustiftgasse apartment houses in Vienna (1909–12, fig.21) and the Lupus Sanatorium (1910–13). He was perhaps influenced by his student Josef Hoffmann's drastically naked Purkersdorf, finished in 1904, a building

21   Otto Wagner, apartment house on the Neustiftgasse. From *Einige Skizzen*, 1922, vol. 4

22 Aerial view of the plan for the 22 District of Vienna. From Otto Wagner, *Die Grossstadt*, 1911

which was arguably more radical in its rejection of ornament than Adolf Loos's more celebrated Goldman & Salatsch's tailor shop (1909–10).[62]

Wagner's ultimate feat of self-reinvention was in the form of a book that came late in his career, just as the ideas of the proto-social-democratic Progressive Era were spreading internationally, in favor of tighter planning regulations after the period of Gilded Age laissez-faire. This was *Grossstadt* ('Big City') of 1911, written three years before his death. It was based on a lecture given at the prompting of Professor Alfred Hamlin of the engineering department of Columbia University, where Wagner had been invited to participate in a conference on municipal art.[63] With it, Otto Wagner made an important contribution to the field of modern urban planning. His ideas stand out from the more reductive, one-dimensional approaches of other major architects who wrote about cities during this period, as exemplified by Tony Garnier's *Cité Industrielle* of 1904–17, Le Corbusier's *Ville Radieuse* of 1924, Ludwig Hilberseimer's *Grossstadt* of 1927 and Cornelis van Eesteren's *Functionele Stad* of 1928.[64]

Otto Wagner did not favor the new automobile-based urban transportation, unlike the later Le Corbusier, Hilberseimer or van Eesteren. He preferred the equally novel public transport:

> Rapid transit must be provided in such a manner that there will be constant circulation through the different zones of

> the city, in a constant movement to and fro through the radial streets, so that any desired point can be reached with a single change of cars. Elevators should provide the means of connection between elevated, subway and street car lines.[65]

This was no doubt a result of his personal hands-on experience in urban infrastructure planning through his commission for the Vienna Stadtbahn network.[66] Moreover, Wagner opposed laissez-faire policies, just as the reformer Ernest von Körber had at the federal level. Both were for government-regulated planning. Wagner praised the principle of the City Expansion Fund (*Stadtsweiterungsfond*), which had harnessed through levies on the sale of public property the financial basis for public works, contributing to defraying the cost of streets, parks and public edifices, complaining only that it did not go far enough compared to similar funds in Paris and Berlin.[67] He brought a staunchly anti-free-market stance to bear against what he called the 'vampire' of real estate speculation the very year the suburban population rose up during the hunger protest of 1911. In order to guarantee what he called a 'democratic' city, he wrote that this kind of speculation, 'which now makes the autonomy of the city almost an illusion, may be reduced to a minimum'.

> It will not do to leave the expansion of a city to blind chance and artistic incompetence . . . or to abandon the development to miserable land speculators. The resulting injury to the inhabitants and government is, from a politico-economical point of view, nothing short of colossal. It will continue to grow greater, for the onward march of time will make it ever more irreparable.[68]

He endorsed 'systematic planning' instead.

Wagner sought feasible ways to enhance the common good through a socially and economically sustainable municipal political economy. His vision of a 'metropolis without end' was not a call for sprawl. He proposed strict regulation in the form of public acquisition of land and that the urban fringe and its subsequent release into the private building market should only be permitted with strict controls governing the terms of its use and built form. 'The profit for the municipality would be largely increased in this manner,' he argued:

some years later, when the city had expanded, the result would be an increase in the price of property which would 'create a profit amounting to hundreds of millions'.[69] With this return on investment, the city could afford 'things which are scarcely thought of now, but which cannot be omitted from the plan of the future metropolis', such as 'People's clubs and dwelling houses, municipal sanatoriums, city warehouses, promenades, fountains, observatories, museums, theaters, waterside pavilions'.[70] This would be in line with what is 'imperiously demanded by a progressive culture'. Wagner also called for the creation of new public places at transport infrastructure hubs, an example of which is illustrated in a contemporary postcard showing the original layout, now destroyed, of his two Stadtbahn stations which served as a gate to the square in front of the Karlskirche.

The provision of massive perimeter-block housing units was predominant in his plans for the new Vienna (fig.22). In contrast to the other great architects who wrote about the city at the turn of the century, Otto Wagner believed that housing could enhance the common good by fostering a sense of community. Concerned with the social quality of everyday life of the city dweller, he favored the rented apartment, which he maintained was the only proper urban dwelling form. He made the point that the

> . . . longed-for detached house in the still more longed-for garden city can never satisfy the popular need, since as a result of the pressure of economy in living expenses, of the increase and decrease in the size of families, of change of occupation and position in life, there must be constant shifting and change in the desires of the masses. The needs which arise from such changing conditions can be satisfied only by rented apartment dwellings, and never by individual houses.

In direct opposition to Camillo Sitte, Wagner added:

> To hark back to tradition, to make 'expression' or picturesqueness the controlling consideration in designing homes for the man of today is absurd in the light of modern experience. The number

of city dwellers who today prefer to vanish in the mass as mere numbers on apartment doors is considerably greater than those who care to hear the daily 'good morning, how are you' from their gossipy neighbors in single houses.[71]

Having read Philippovich's report on the housing condition of the poor, Wagner believed, in particular, in the need for social housing. 'Our democratic existence, in which the masses feel the pressure of the necessity for economy in their methods of living, and call for homes once sanitary and cheap,' could be enhanced through the supply of 'multi-storey houses'.[72] Interestingly, he was also a proponent of allowing residential and office buildings in the city's center to rise to seven or eight storeys, and indeed to become skyscrapers.

His capacity as a proponent of housing, anti-sprawl and pro-density policies make Wagner a forerunner of the housing policies of the so-called Gemeindebau phase of Red Vienna (as we shall see in Chapter 3) and of today's Vienna with its own policies favoring social housing, public transportation and public places. For him 'the new and undeveloped quarters' were to be the site of systematic 'regulations on a large scale'.[73]

Otto Wagner's many feats of reinvention in the face of great odds guaranteed him an enthusiastic following among the younger generation. The energy he poured into his modernist mission against the background of Viennese conservatism makes the reason for his appeal apparent. He ignited the spirit of modernity that was spread all over the Austro-Hungarian Empire by his students. Jože Plečnik in Vienna and his native Slovenia, Viktor Kovačić in Zagreb and Jan Kotěra in Prague became founders of their countries' iconoclastic modernist movements. But it is in Vienna that the influence of Wagner's modernization of architectural language, what he referred to as 'art', and most particularly his vision of the role of the architect as a socially engaged intellectual and as a public servant – working for the welfare of all, including 'the masses', on the scale of the entire city, shaping its public life through progressive policies – has been greatest, extending up to the present day.

Color plates

1 Othmar Schimkowitz, embodying the call of the modern

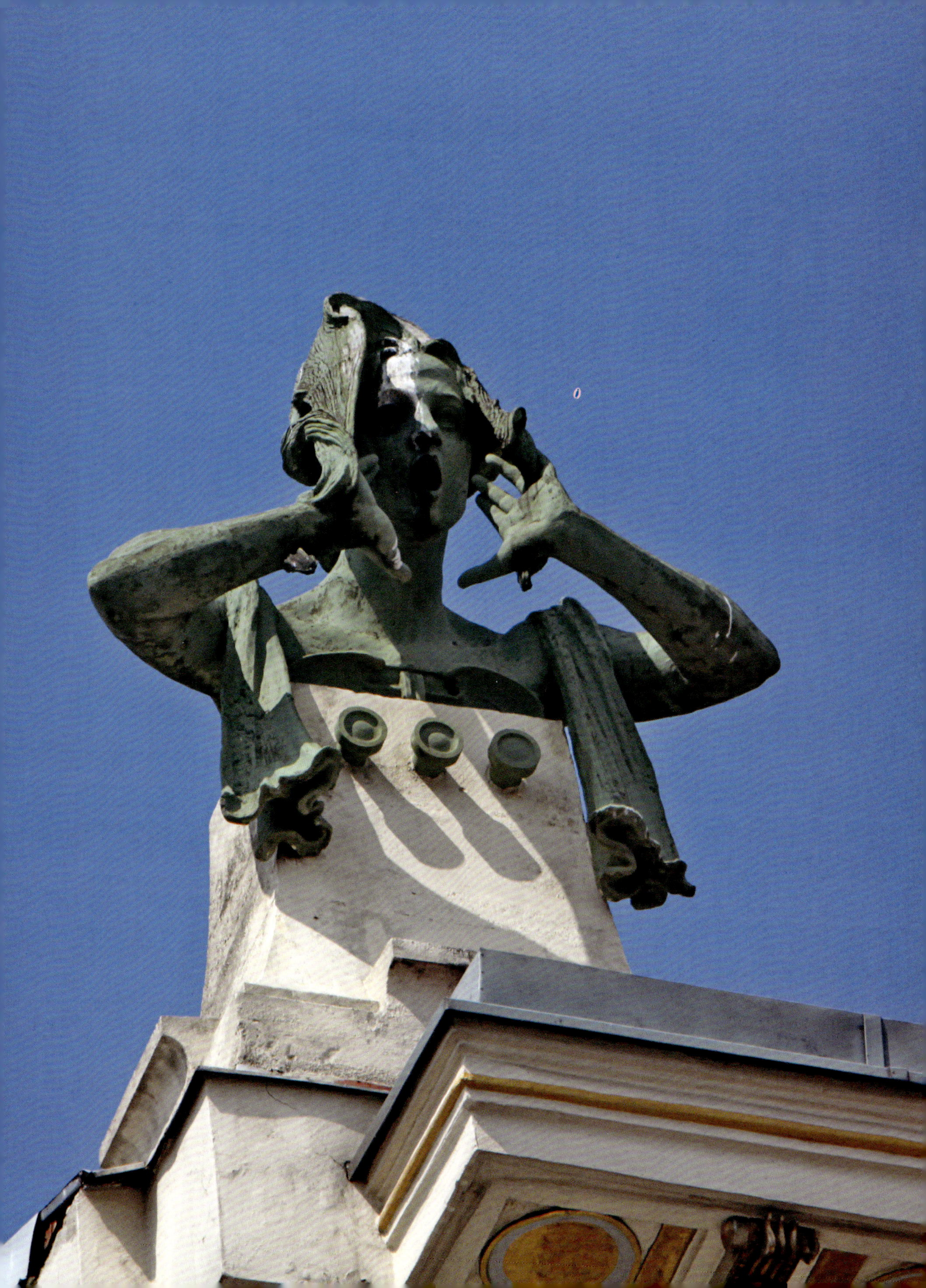

2 (top)   Majolica House, detail

3 (bottom)   Majolica House, floral pattern

4 (opposite, top)   Majolica House, detail of the soffit

5 (opposite, bottom)   Köstlergasse House, medallion

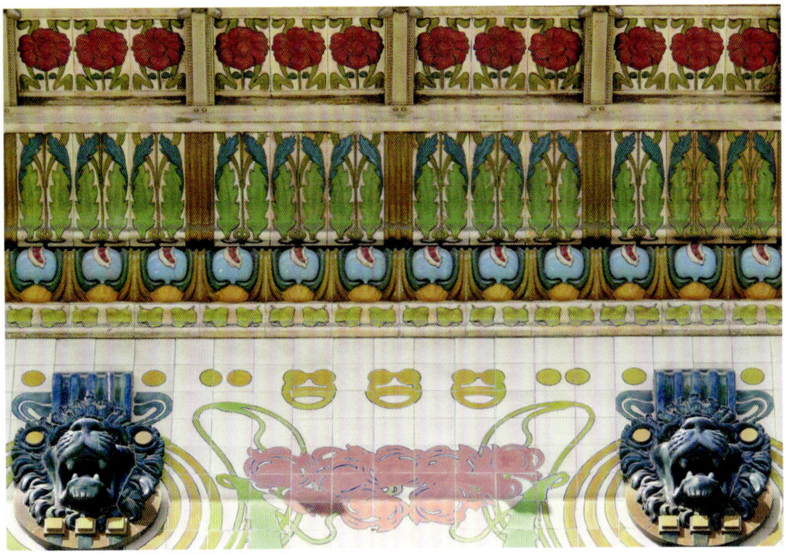

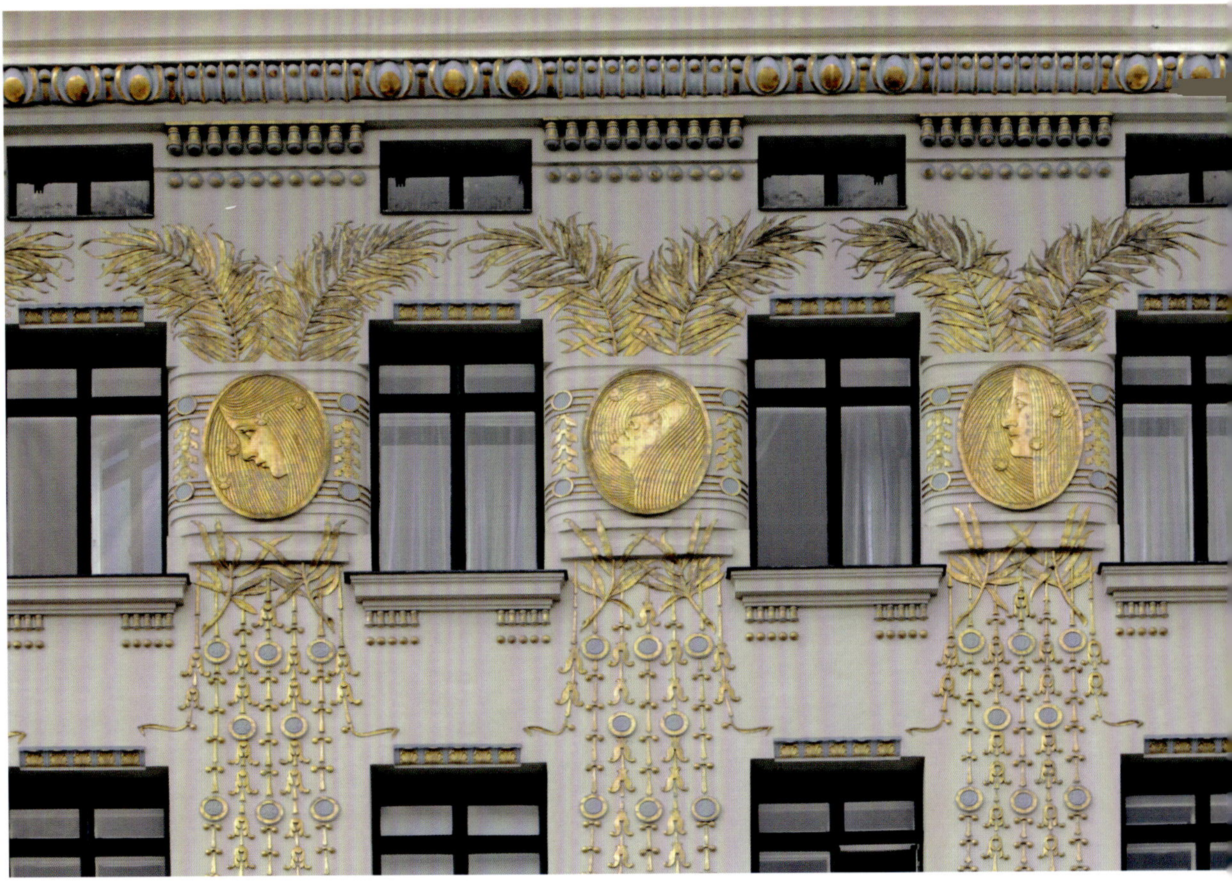

6 Otto Wagner, church at Steinhof

7 (top)   Josef Maria Olbrich's stark Secession building, 1897

8 (bottom)   Frieze over the entrance of the Secession building sculpted by Othmar Schimkowitz. Contrasting radically with the stark white walls, it is highly wrought, each mask representing a different art, fraught with serpentine lines and gilded leaves, similar to the sculpted ones forming the dome above

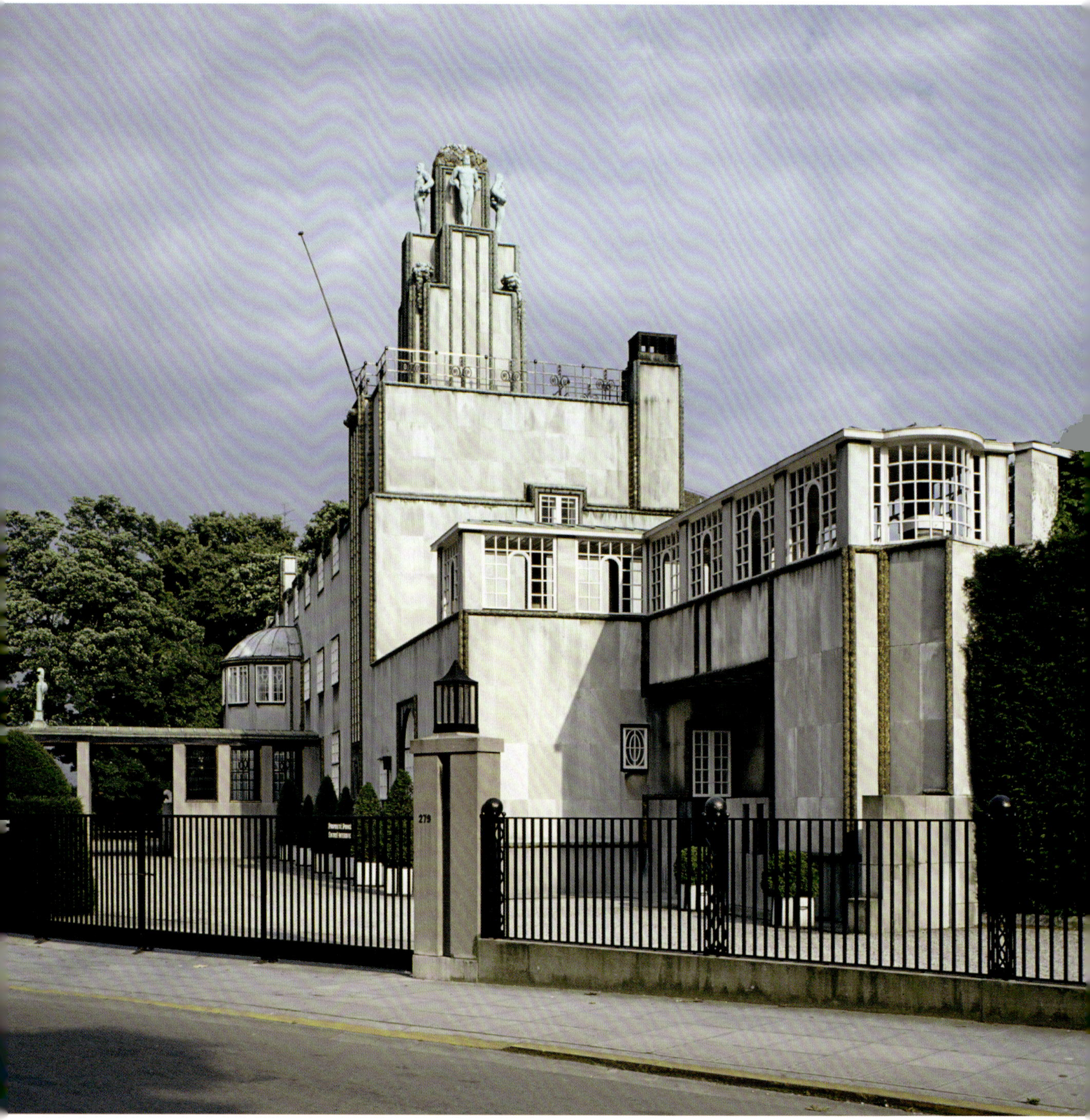
279

9 (opposite) Josef Hoffmann, Palais Stoclet, façade

10 (top) Josef Hoffmann, interior of the Primavesi country house. Drawing, *Das Interieur* 39 (1914)

11 (bottom) Josef Hoffmann, Cabaret Fledermaus, 1907. Over 7000 pieces of tile were designed by Bertold Loeffler and Michael Powolny for the bar room. Wiener Werkstätte, postcard no. 74, 1907. Museum of Applied Arts (MAK), Vienna, KI 13748-4

12 (below)   Adolf Loos, interior of the luxuriously panelled American Bar revealing the infinity effect created by the mirrors on the upper walls

13 (opposite)   Adolf Loos, Goldman & Salatsch shop, reflective interior

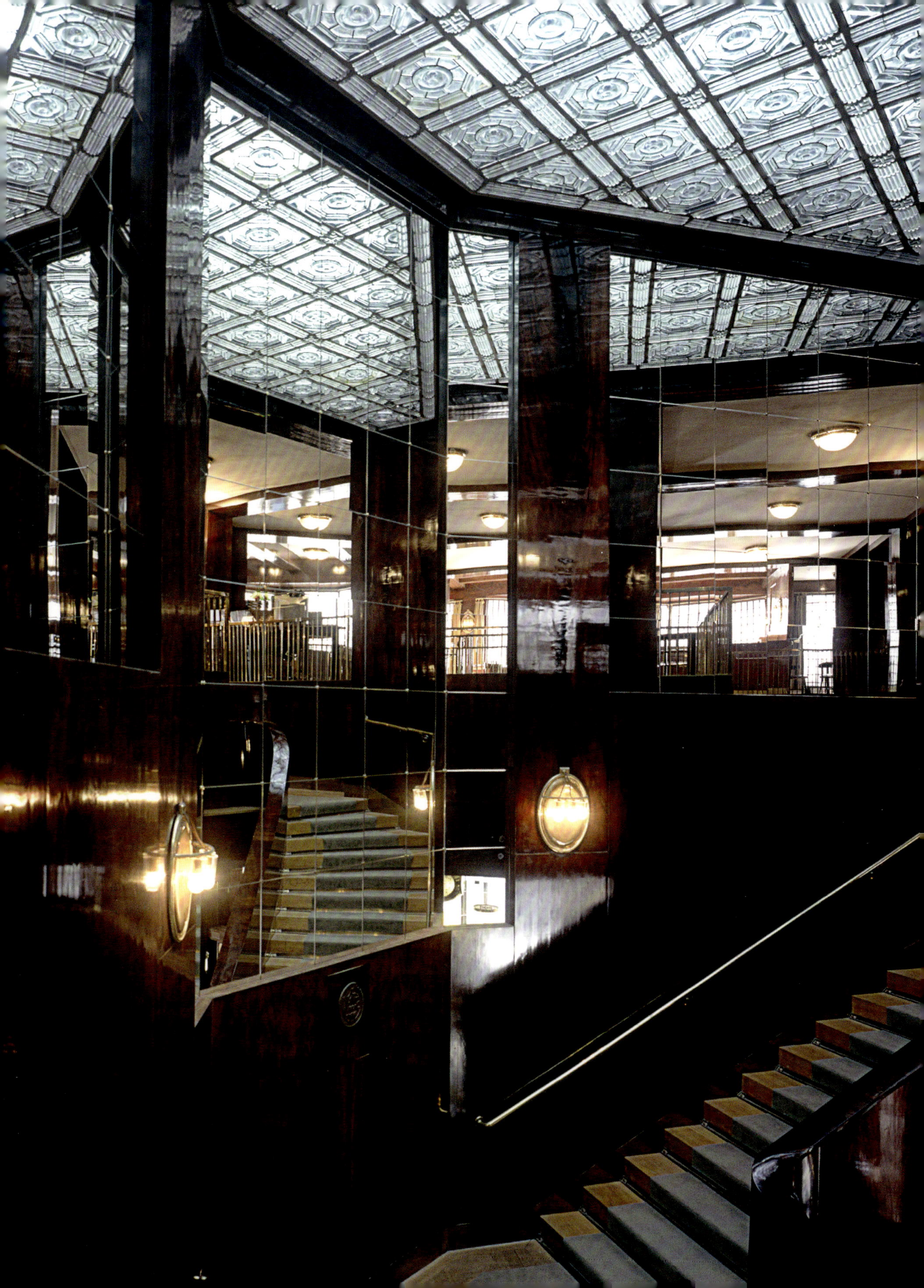

14 The Karl Marx Hof, designed by Karl Ehn, 1927–30

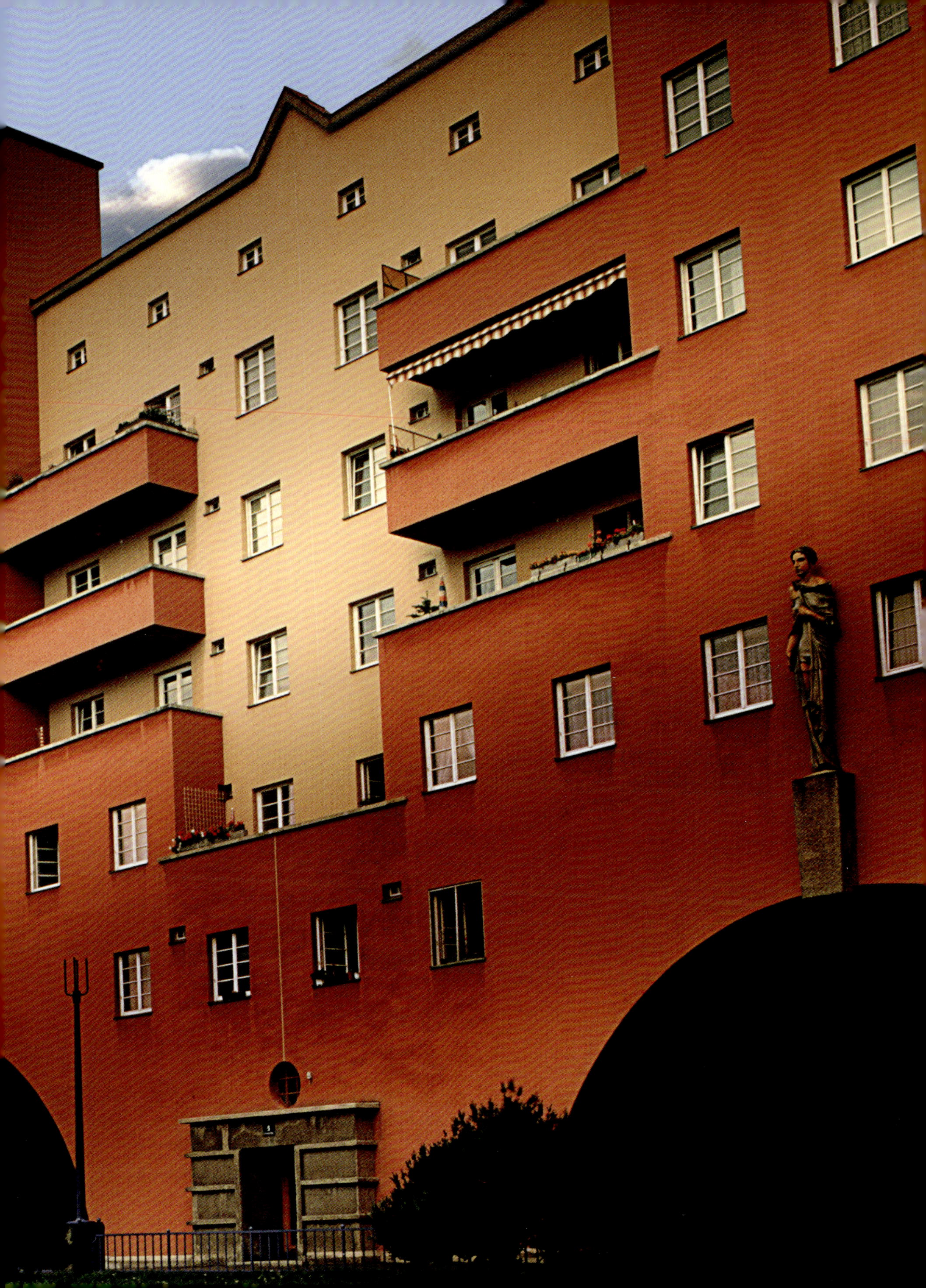

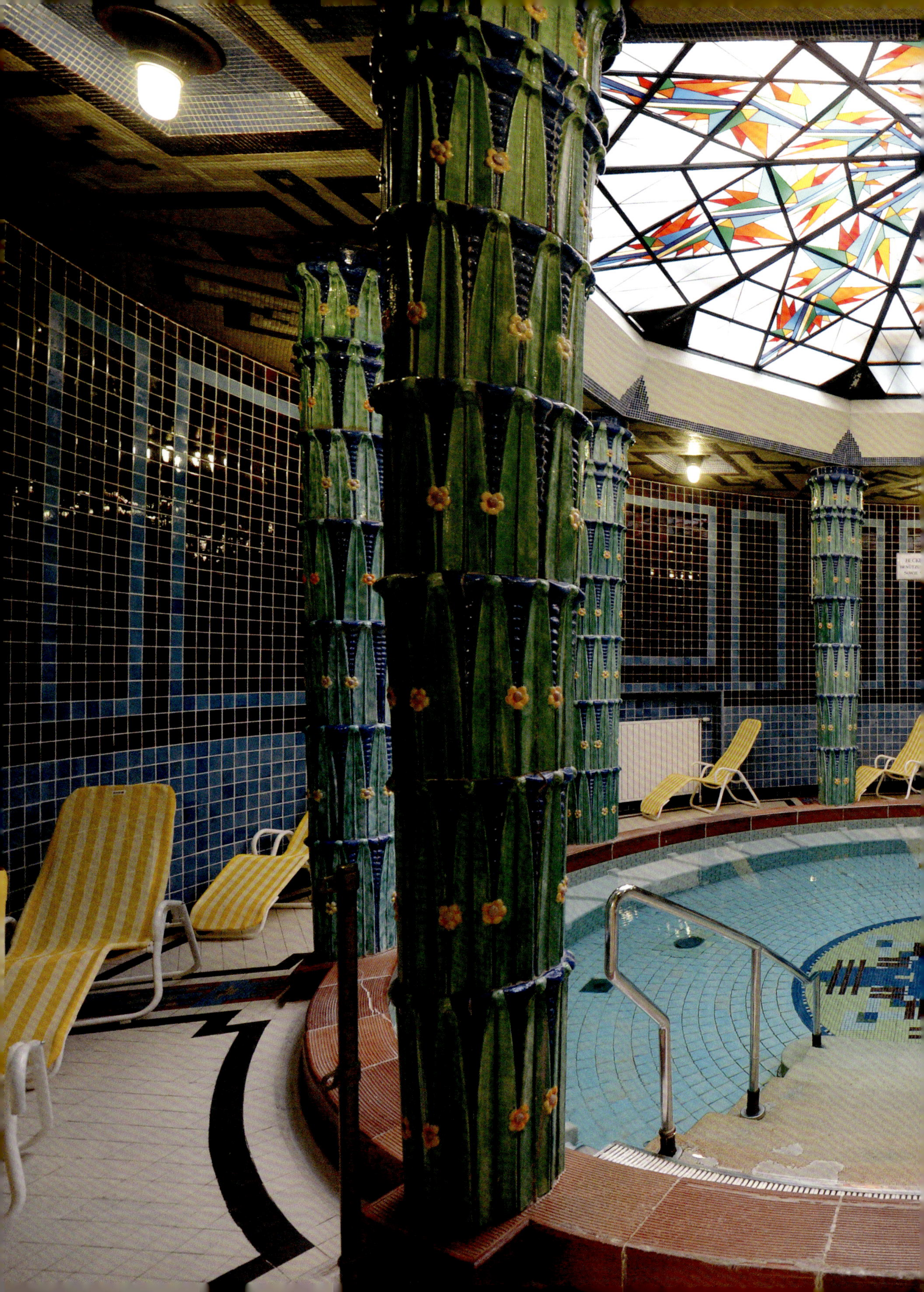

15 Amalienbad, art deco majolica details around one of the pools

16 (top)   Adolf Loos, Moller House, entrance

17 (bottom)   Adolf Loos, Moller House, elevated nook overlooking the reception area with adjacent staircase leading to the upstairs bedrooms

18 (opposite, top)   Adolf Loos, Müller House, reception area and stepped-back wall containing the steps of an actual staircase leading to the reading-room nook above

19 (opposite, bottom)   Adolf Loos, Müller House, study nook off the landing of the staircase

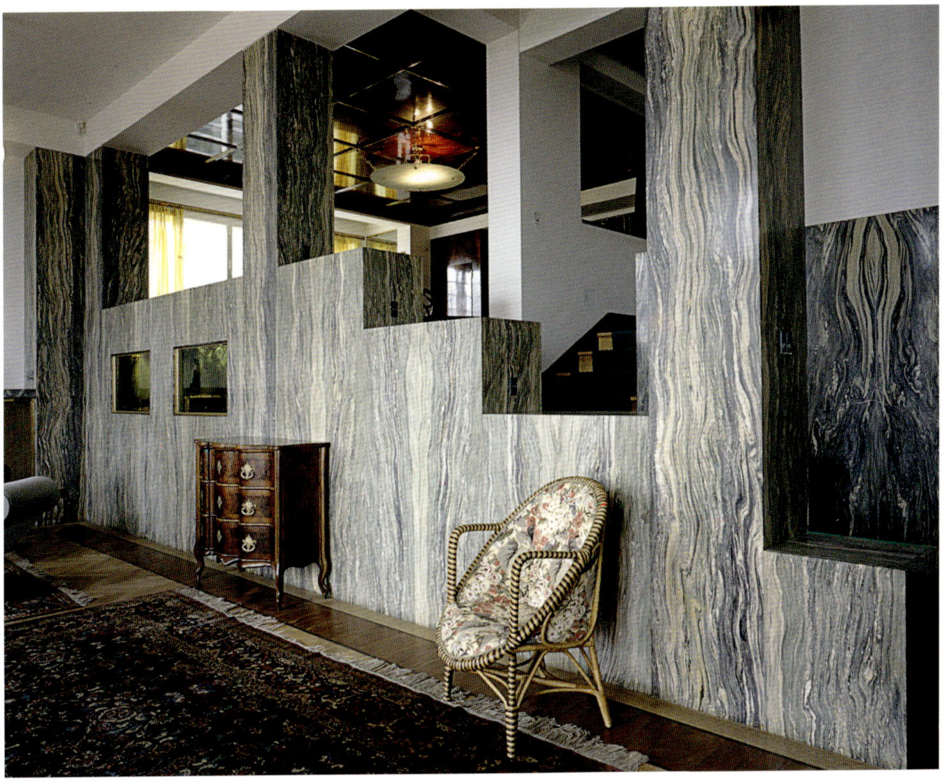

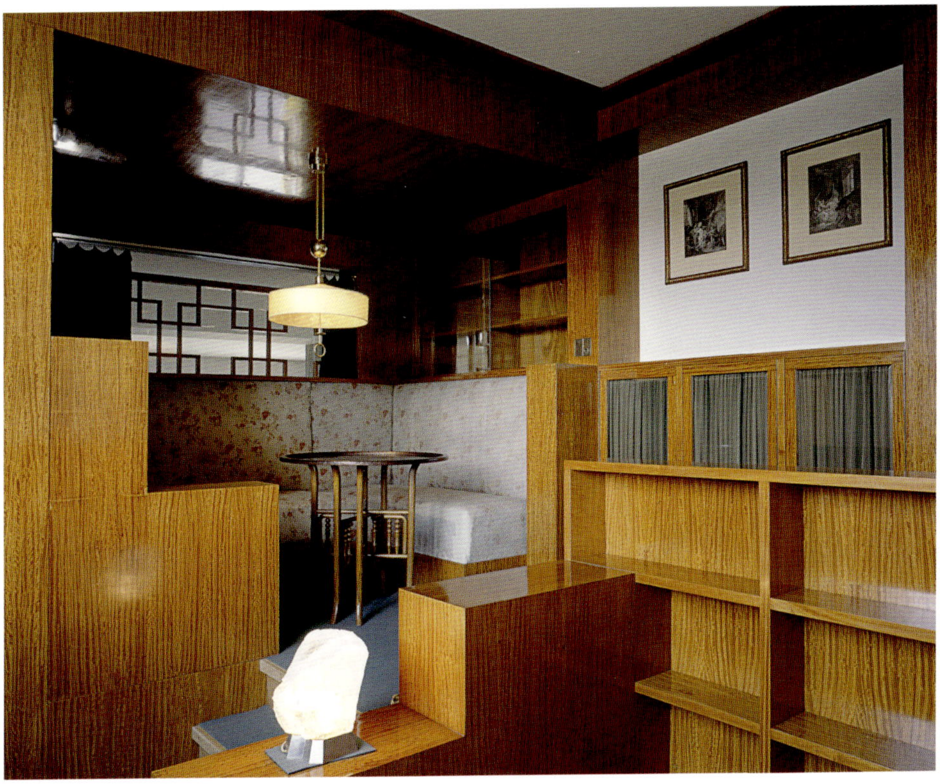

20 (top)   Josef Frank, project for the United Nations Headquarters, New York, 1947. In the tradition of Otto Wagner's Majolica House, it is clad in a something like a dress

21 (bottom)   Josef Frank, project for slum clearance in New York, 1942. It is in pastel colors, germane to the ones he had used in his master plan for the Wiener Werkbund of 1932

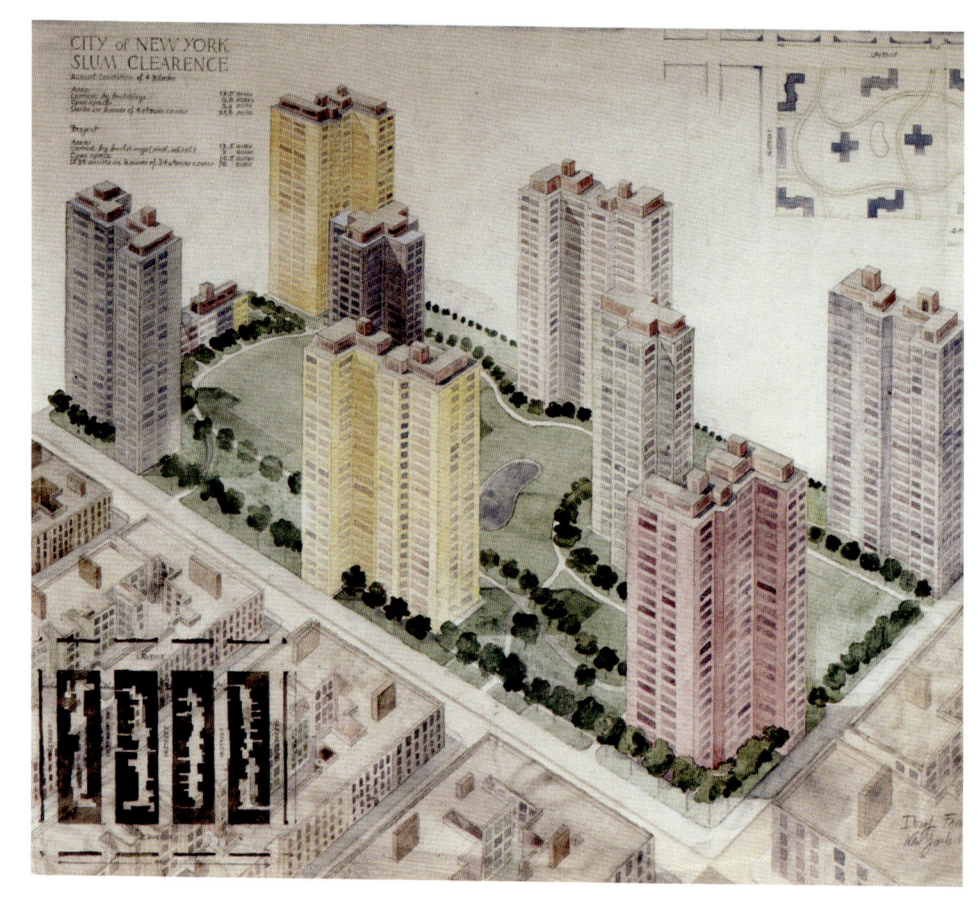

3

The Next Generation
The Wagner School, Hoffmann and Loos

Two buildings illustrate the polarization between modern and anti-modern in turn-of-the-century Vienna. They face each other across the Stubenring in the First District. One is Otto Wagner's Postsparkasse of 1904–6, the first modern institutionalized deposit and savings bank in Vienna for private individuals. Postal savings banks had already been instituted in Great Britain in 1861 thanks to William Gladstone, then Chancellor of the Exchequer, who saw them as a cheap way to finance the public debt, and they served much the same function for the imperial administration. In Vienna, in addition, thanks to an invention of the Viennese bank's founder, Georg Coch, every owner of a postal check account was enabled to transfer money nationwide and to receive credits as well, representing a major democratization of the banking sector.[1] Otto Wagner's architecture expressed the spirit of this enlightened, modern institution.

The other of these buildings, across a small square, is the bombastic, faux-Baroque Ministry of War, built between 1909 and 1913 by Ludwig Baumann, one of the last disciples of Gottfried Semper (fig.23). Its most remarkable feature is the series of 42 lintels that adorn the *piano nobile* windows along the façade and two wings. Each one of the lintels bears the cast-concrete head of a soldier in the specific battle gear of one of the multi-ethnic battalions of the Imperial Army. Some of the heads are barking orders, some look perplexed, most seem aghast, and at least one appears to be dead (fig.24). The overwhelming impression they convey is of things gone awry. Indeed, barely one year after the building's completion, hundreds of thousands of soldiers were marched off to die in a war administered from this building.

But there was no going back for a new generation who had studied with Wagner at the Academy of Fine Art and who came to be known

23 (top)   Façade on the Stubenring of Ludwig Baumann's Ministry of War, 1908–10

24 (bottom)   Two of the soldiers on the lintels above the windows on the main floor of the Ministry of War

25 Otto Schönthal, Villa Vojcsik. Vividly colored turquoise majolica detail, 1902

as the Wagner School. Each architect, in his own way, exploited a vein opened up by Wagner's angry manifesto, *Modern Architecture*, and his daring designs. His signature use of brightly colored lead-glazed majolica, for example, showed up in the whimsical, vaguely tumescent details of Otto Schönthal's Villa Vojcsik of 1902 (fig.25) and his fondness for floral pattern in Jože Plečnik's whirls imprinted on the concrete façade of his Langer House of 1901. Max Fabiani's headquarters for the furniture manufacturers Portois & Fix of 1900 also reflected the lessons of Wagner in its imaginative use of majolica tiles. More a follower than a student of Otto Wagner, Fabiani had graduated from the Polytechnic Institute in 1892, but from 1894 to 1898 he was a key figure in Wagner's practice, collaborating with him and running his office. Most fittingly for a furniture company, the pattern he applied to the Portois & Fix building's façade resembled an embroidered upholstery fabric, with red-brown granite cladding at the lower levels and a shimmering abstract composition of light and dark green tiles covering the upper surface. The windows were framed in bright red and copper punctuated with small decorative dots.[2]

The winged figures seen in Wagner's Postsparkasse and Steinhof are referenced in Oskar Laske's mosaic angels at the Apotheke zum Weissen Engel of 1907 (fig.26) and in Plečnik's Zacherlhaus office building of 1905, clad in grey granite tiles, unornamented except for some sculpted caryatids high on the top floor and a sculpture of the Archangel Michael a little lower down.

Of course, as is often the case, the most famous of Wagner's bona fide students was the one who broke the mold. This was Rudolf Schindler, who became a follower of Frank Lloyd Wright, whose work had been introduced to him by Otto Wagner himself. Another architect of this generation who was sui generis, and had nothing to do with Otto Wagner, was the flamboyant, and eventually phenomenally successful, Josef Urban, most famous perhaps as the architect of the Ziegfeld Follies in New York.

Three architects of this generation stand out among the others who practiced in Vienna, however. The first is Josef Maria Olbrich (1867–1908). Although he had worked for Wagner from 1894 to 1898, he owed nothing to his master. If anything, the reverse was true. In 1897, Olbrich received the commission, funded mainly by Karl Wittgenstein, for the Secession building, whose purpose was to provide a venue for the rebellious artists who had seceded from the annual salon of the

26 Detail of the mosaic ornamental façade of Oskar Laske's Apotheke zum Weissen Engel, Vienna, 1901–2

ultra-conservative Künstlerhaus. Just as iconoclastic as anything Otto Wagner designed, its use of ornamentation and space was radically new, in accordance with the Secessionist art of the time (color plate 7).[3]

The building was a synthesis of two extremes, on one hand unbridled excess and, on the other, asceticism. It was no doubt influenced by a work of the Orientalist Viennese art historian Josef Strzygowski, *The Orient or Rome: Contributions to the History of Late Antique and Early Christian Art* of 1901. Strzygowski had argued, drawing on his expertise in early Renaissance, Egyptian, Coptic and Byzantine art, that stylistic innovation in late antiquity had been the product of a cross-fertilization of Oriental and Semitic influences with early Christian art. The Secession artists assembled details from these various sources and came up with a jarring mix of ascetic restraint and pagan gorgeousness consistent with what they saw as a burgeoning *Ver Sacrum*, or Sacred Spring, the emblematic phrase fixed onto the façade. The embodiment of Athenian classicism had been the owl associated with the goddess Athena. Here the pre-classical spirit is embodied by the 12 young owls on friezes usually attributed to Koloman Moser (fig.27).

27 Secession building, detail: one of the four panels depicting stylized owls, symbols of the virginal Athena, the only ornament of the pristine white side exterior walls. Designed by Koloman Moser

The incorporation of the serpentine line has been a hallmark of excess since the sixteenth-century Mannerists. Accordingly, for the planters on either side of the entrance, Robert Oerley designed a marine-inspired tentacular pattern typical of the pre-classical Minoan art that had just been discovered by Sir Arthur Evans at Knossos. Othmar Schimkowitz designed the three female masks representing art, architecture and sculpture, with serpents twisting about them, as well as the gilt foliate architrave above the entrance and the gilded dome made up of 3000 leaves and 700 berries (color plate 8). Gustav Klimt designed the celebrated luxuriant *Beethoven Frieze* of 1902. Painted directly onto the walls of one of the exhibition rooms in the basement, it is seething with gilded coiled elements.

In the other vein, Olbrich found inspiration in the early fifth-century temple of Segesta in Sicily. Even by its own Doric standards, the temple, which was adorned only with triglyphs and whose columns were not fluted, was exceptionally minimalist compared with the more mature Athenian classical style. Olbrich wrote that it was so 'white and gleaming, holy and chaste' that it sent 'a shudder through me as I stood alone before it.'[4] Hence the Secession's large expanse of naked white wall, sparsely ornamented.

More importantly from the architectural point of view, because the temple of Segesta had been left unfinished, it had no empty inner walled chamber at its center, that is, no 'cella'. Following its example, Olbrich's interior was an open, airy universal space, with no permanent partitions. Because the roof of the great exhibition hall was supported by only six columns, its gallery space could be rearranged at will, to fit the objects being exhibited. This was unprecedented in gallery design. In omitting internal walls, Olbrich pioneered the use of movable partitions in a completely flexible space, preceding by 80 years Cedric Price's design for the Fun Palace in London and Richard Rogers and Renzo Piano's Pompidou Center. As one critic observed, the exhibition space had to be mutable, for that was the nature of modern life, 'of the hurrying, scurrying, flickering life, whose manifold mirror image we seek in art in order to pause for a moment of inward contemplation and dialogue with our own soul.'[5]

Josef Maria Olbrich died too soon, aged 41, to fully realize his potential. But the two other great designers of his generation were able to do so. These were Josef Hoffmann and Adolf Loos. Both were innovators who benefited from the spark of modernization that energized Vienna during the empire's short but heady economic boom from the mid-1890s to 1914.[6] In particular, they reaped the fruits of a transformation in Jewish-Austrian patronage at this time, although the new patrons were not as wealthy as those of the *Gründerzeit*. Of course, the tycoon Karl Wittgenstein, who had made his fortune in the iron industry, was enormously rich but he did not invest in real estate at the same scale. He did, however, fund the construction of the Secession building. Robert and Otto Primavesi, Zuckerkandl and Wärndorfer, Goldman & Salatsch – once more, all Jews. Their commissions were not for *palais*, but for more modest private houses, shops and clinics.

Hoffmann and Loos, who were bitter opponents to the end, ignited one of the most contentious and heated debates of the time. This was the debate about the status of ornament in architecture. The conflict itself has long roots. It flared up several times over five centuries in European culture. The first of its most radical formulations was the invective of the ascetic Cistercian Bernard of Clairvaux against the lavish indulgence in precious gems, gold and pearls by the Capetian kings and Eleanor of Aquitaine in their church of St Denis in Paris, under the direction of Abbot Suger. Criticism raged throughout the eighteenth century in the polemical writings of Algarotti, Cordemoy, the Abbé Laugier and Francesco Lòdoli, along with other 'rigoristi', against the excessive ornamentation of what has come to be called the Baroque and the rococo.[7] Of special relevance here, the restrained Viennese Biedermeier style that marked the beginning of the nineteenth century in all fields of design was the direct outcome of the 'rigorist' stance against superfluous ornamentation. In the present case, Hoffmann was for ornament, and Loos was almost histrionically against it. At least, this is how they have gone down in history.[8] Of the two positions, it is certainly the rejection of ornament, erroneously identified with Loos, that became more dominant in architecture in the next 150 years, down to the present. The attempt to modernize historicist ornamentation shared the fate of the artisans and craftsmen who survived the industrial revolution for long enough to shape it. It was a losing battle. Hoffmann, Sullivan, Gaudí and the followers of art nouveau were the last of a dying breed.

Traveling the 160 kilometers from the idyllic Baroque hillside town of Brtnice (Pirnitz) in the province of Moravia, to which he would return throughout his life and whose interior decoration, like that of his future apartment in Vienna (fig.28), was a constant source of inspiration to him,[9] the affable, extraordinarily gifted Josef Hoffmann (1870–1956) arrived in Vienna at the right time and place to study under Wagner and took full advantage of his good fortune. As one of the founding members of the polemically modern Secession, along with his friends Olbrich, Klimt and Moser, he never deviated from the path toward the modernization of architectural ornament that the master had blazed. As a result, Hoffmann was to become one of the most sought-after architects and designers – of interiors, furniture, porcelain, metalwork, textiles and glass – in Vienna before the First World War.

Less closely linked with the Secession, Hoffmann's work is inseparable from the Wiener Werkstätte (Vienna Workshop) – the workshop modeled on the Arts and Crafts movement begun in England by John Ruskin and William Morris – which he founded with the artist Koloman Moser in 1903 and which gave him the means to turn every project into a *Gesamtkunstwerk*, that is, a 'total work of art' in which architecture, art, interiors and design were conceived as one. In other words, he opened up each of these fields to the idea of crossing over, with each incorporating concepts from the others (figs 29 and 30).

The movement could be two-way, as in the extraordinarily fruitful and creative twenty-year-long exchange of design ideas between Hoffmann and Klimt which has come to light only recently.[10] If his surprisingly brief autobiography of 1948 is anything to go by, Hoffmann considered the main achievement of his life to have been the creation of the Wiener Werkstätte. Its description takes up 15 of the autobiography's 19 pages.[11]

The Wiener Werkstätte brought together architects, designers, and artists. By 1905, it employed 100 craftsmen. As Hoffmann recounts, it was founded with the support of the Jewish industrialist Fritz Wärndorfer, who had married into the textile industrialist family of Marienthal, the Mautners. The Wiener Werkstätte was, in Hoffmann's mind, the logical next step after the Secession: it was a way of marketing and mass-producing its products. In 1913, Hoffmann combined the Werkstätte with his teaching activities, institutionalizing the private workshop by making it an official part of the curriculum of the Kunstgewerbeschule (Arts and Crafts School), of which he had just become director. In turn, the works produced by this combination were exhibited at the affiliate museum next door, today the MAK (Museum of Applied Arts).

Hoffmann was also a supreme networker. In addition to being a co-founder of the Secession and founder of the Wiener Werkstätte, he also was part of both the Austrian Werkbund and the German Werkbund. The Austrian Werkbund, founded in 1912, was modeled on the German

28 (opposite, left)   The enfilade succession of rooms in Josef Hoffmann's own apartment, in which he experimented with design patterns, just as he did in his parental home in Brtnice, Moravia. Muzeum Josefa Hoffmanna, Brtnice

29 (opposite, right)   Josef Hoffmann, summer dress, 1911. Example of the *Gesamtkunstwerk* transfer of the same aesthetic shared by all areas of design. Wiener-Werkstatte-Archiv-Fotoband 'Mode', Museum of Applied Arts (MAK), Vienna

30 (above)   Josef Hoffmann, decanter and various glasses

one, founded in 1907, whose aim was to bring together modern architects and designers with modern industrialists. Among the figures attached to them were major architects of the day, including Hoffmann, Hermann Muthesius, Peter Behrens, Ludwig Mies van der Rohe, Lilli Reuch, Josef Frank and Dagobert Peche. Hoffmann was a tireless impresario for all things Viennese. He used his connections to promote the Wiener Werkstätte by organizing the extravagant, 54-room *Kunstschau* exhibition of June 1908 with Gustav Klimt and other artists who had just broken away from the Secession. The exhibition broke with the pure aestheticism of the Secession, blurring the boundary between art and design and turning its high ideals into marketable goods.[12] The exhibition featured Klimt's opulent, sybaritic, sexually charged *The Kiss*, counterbalanced by the work of the fiercely anti-aesthetic young expressionist Oskar Kokoschka. Hoffmann was also an exceptional teacher and proved himself a devoted promoter of young, original, non-conformist talent in his capacities as the director of the Kunstgewerbeschule, where he was appointed professor at the age of 29.[13] Carrying on the legacy of Otto Wagner, he backed youth and creativity, even if it did not always align with the direction of his own work. For example, he selected Friedrich Kiesler to go to Paris to represent Austria at the World's Fair after the First World War. He also opened up the school to women, uniquely for the time. As a result, Vienna gained Margarete Schütte-Lihotzky, Vally Wieselthier, Felice Rix, Erika Giovanna Klien, Elisabeth Karlinsky, Maria Ullmann and many other designers.

In his own eyes, Josef Hoffmann was a modernizer, more precisely a modernizer of ornamentation. To him, this meant he was not only liberated from the monopoly of historicism but free to pick and choose among the stylistic trends of the day. Given these conditions, he chose to be an eclectic. Every one of his important buildings signals a new stylistic departure. His oeuvre became chameleonic, mimicking one after the other the major stylistic schools of his time: that of Otto Wagner, Charles Rennie Mackintosh, Klimtian Jugendstil, Cubism, expressionism, neo-classicism, Neues Bauen and even Moravian regionalism.[14] The same chameleonic spirit also infused his designs for objects, from crystal glassware to metalwork, jewelry and textiles. What Hoffmann lacked in originality he made up for amply in design agility and exquisite detailing.[15] His sets of glasses designed for the Lobmeyr crystal shop are cases in point.

His commissions for members of the Wittgenstein family typify this eclecticism. His first job, a remodeling in 1899 of a small farmhouse in Lower Austria, Bergerhöhe, for Paul Wittgenstein, was inspired by the Arts and Crafts style. For Paul's father, Karl, he outfitted a hunting lodge in 1907 with golden faucets. In 1905, for Hermann, Paul Wittgenstein's son, he delivered a sparse interior design for a Viennese apartment using only black and white. Margaret, Karl's daughter, had an apartment in Vienna similarly furnished according to designs by Hoffmann and Moser. Paul Wittgenstein's Vienna apartment was decorated in striking neo-classical and Biedermeier style. A final project, the most highly decorated, lavish and expensive object ever produced by the Wiener Werkstätte, was purchased in 1908 at the *Wiener Kunstschau* (Vienna Art Show) by Karl Wittgenstein for his *palais* on the Alleegasse in Vienna. It is a solid silver vitrine decorated with enamel and moonstones, designed by Hoffmann and Carl Otto Czeschka, for which Wittgenstein paid 25,000 crowns.[16]

Again the Arts and Crafts movement in England served as the source of inspiration for Hoffmann's designs for more modest clients, the artists' colony of Hohe Warte in Vienna's leafy, suburban Nineteenth District, where he built houses for Koloman Moser, Carl Moll, Helene Hochstetter (fig.31) and Sonja Knips, among others.[17] Around the same time, between 1904 and 1906, Hoffmann pursued a

31 Josef Hoffmann, house for Helene Hochstetter, Steinfeldgasse 7, 1906–7. Drawing, *Der Architekt* XIV (1908)

32 (above)　Josef Hoffmann, drawing of the Purkersdorf Sanitorium (1904–6). Museum of Applied Arts (MAK), Vienna

33 (opposite, top)　Josef Hoffmann, Palais Stoclet, drawing of the kitchen. Museum of Applied Arts (MAK), Vienna

34 (opposite, bottom)　Joseph Hoffmann, Palais Stoclet, dining room. Marburg Photoarchiv

restrained minimalism in creating the Purkersdorf Sanatorium in the Vienna Woods for Victor Zuckerkandl, who purchased the plot for it in 1903 (fig.32). This was the way in which the industrialist Zuckerkandl – the brother of two of Vienna's most famous doctors, Emil the anatomist and Otto the urologist – channeled his own concern for health. The sanatorium was one of the first important commissions given to the Wiener Werkstätte, and represents Hoffmann's earliest *Gesamtkunstwerk*, unifying a building and its furnishings. Hoffmann's famous *Sitzmaschine*, the 'machine for sitting', was originally designed for it. The aim of the sanatorium was to treat neurosis and hysteria through mineral baths, therapeutic massage, physiotherapy, music recitals, and through the soothing, uncomplicated pristineness of the architecture. The clientele was much the same as the well-heeled guest list of the salon of Emil Zuckerkandl's wife, Berta. It included Arthur Schnitzler, Gustav Mahler, Arnold Schoenberg, Hugo von Hofmannstahl and Koloman Moser.[18]

Hoffmann's design persona then underwent another metamorphosis with the extravagant, sybaritic display of wealth which was the Palais Stoclet, constructed in Brussels for the Belgian banker, financier and industrialist Adolf Stoclet (figs 33, 34 and color plate 9). It is generally considered to be the masterpiece of Hoffmann and the Werkstätte. Stoclet had met Hoffmann in Vienna, where his family sent him as a representative of their railway business. It took no less than five years, 1906 to 1911, for Hoffmann and the Werkstätte to complete the house. Among the objects they produced was a statue of Pallas Athena (who also stood on a column at the entrance of the Parliament building in Vienna), placed over the front gate of the house, along with not one but four Herculean figures who survey the four corners of the universe. The materials were outlandish. The building is faced in white Norwegian

marble with a gold leaf trim. The walls of the main entrance are clad in Paonazzo marble and the floor inlaid with African padauk and teak woods in a double square grid pattern, which was then covered by a carpet designed by Hoffmann himself. The music room is clad in marble from Portovenere, outlined in gilded bronze, with bronze moldings defining its corners and upper edges. The parents' room is dressed in rosewood, the 36-square-meter bathroom completely clad in marble and the children's room incrusted with mosaics. Most extraordinary of all is the dining room, lined with white-veined Paonazzo marble from Portovenere and Macassar ebony. The Werkstätte designed everything, from the gardens to the furniture, light fixtures, cutlery, upholstery, toilet articles, dinnerware, and chandeliers hung with glass pearls. In this *Gesamtkunstwerk* environment, one cannot help thinking that Gustav Klimt's gilded mosaic compositions, 'Expectation' and 'Fulfillment', including the famous 'Tree of Life', were meant to set off Madame Stoclet's new dresses by the Werkstätte designer Eduard Josef Wimmer-Wisgrill, with which he demanded she replace her famed Paul Poiret collection (fig.35).[19]

Hoffmann's Villa Skywa-Primavesi (1913–15) was created for his fellow Moravian Otto Primavesi, an industrialist who had commissioned a portrait of his wife from Gustav Klimt. This marks yet another stylistic departure. It reflects the architect's turn toward classicism, especially in the two decorated tympana which are set before the raised hip roof, highlighted by pilasters. More noteworthy is the country house he designed for the Primavesis in 1914 in Winkelsdorf, Moravia, a rare example of regionalism conceived by Josef Hoffmann. As his biographer Eduard F. Sekler points out, Moravian popular tradition served as his source of inspiration both in the interior and on the exterior.[20] Only materials and architectural forms of the area were used. This does not mean that the ornamentation in any way aimed at authenticity. The folk motifs, on the contrary, were given a highly geometric stylized interpretation by Hoffmann. Based on local tradition, the building had a projecting hip roof made out of straw. The interior decoration was influenced by the serrated lozenge motif found in north Moravian folk art. This design theme is to be found throughout colored, painted decorations of carved wood, painted furniture and wall panels, and hand-printed textiles from the Wiener Werkstätte (color plate 10).

Hoffmann's association with the Wiener Werkstätte also took more modest but no less remarkable forms. Cabaret Fledermaus was commissioned by the Werkstätte's sole patron, Fritz Wärndorfer, in 1907. Marble lines the walls but the foyer and auditorium are covered with plain black-and-white checkered floor tiles. The café is furnished with relatively inexpensive bentwood tables and chairs designed by Hoffmann, which are in turn decorated with a butterfly textile designed by Dagobert Peche. Besides Hoffmann, the designers involved in the *Gesamtkunstwerk* were Klimt, Kokoschka, Czeschka, Wimmer-Wisgrill and Anton Kling. They collaborated on postcards, furniture, stage design and posters. One of the remarkable features was the 7000-piece majolica mosaic that covered the walls, the bar and the entrance (color plate 11).[21]

35 Avant-garde pantsuit in silk for women designed by Eduard Josef Wimmer-Wisgrill with textile pattern by Dagobert Peche, both of the Wiener Werkstätte, 1920. These predate by almost 20 years Coco Chanel's campaign for pants for women in 1937. Museum of Applied Arts (MAK), Vienna

The architect most often seen in opposition to Hoffmann, Adolf Loos, was born in the same year, 1870, in the small bustling industrial town of Brno in Moravia, near Brtnice. Loos's father, a master stonemason, died when Adolf was nine, which devastated him. His relations with his mother were strained and he changed boarding schools four times because he had trouble fitting in. Loos was a contrarian and an *enfant terrible*. Having failed to gain entry to the School of Fine Art, where Hoffmann was a student, he studied architecture at the Polytechnic in Dresden, in northern Germany, for three years. From there, in 1893, he left for the United States, where he spent three years and became enamored of Anglo-Saxon culture, particularly the modernist dynamism of Louis Sullivan, and the English gentleman's modern style of clothing – simple, but masterfully cut and using fine material.[22]

When he reached Vienna in 1897, Adolf Loos was hankering for a fight, as usual. It was a good time and place to be an angry young man. The Secession was being founded, and the group of writers known as Jung Wien (Young Vienna) were debating in cafes. Like Otto Wagner, whom he idolized, and his close friend Karl Kraus, he used his pen as his weapon of choice and began a series of sensationalistic satirical articles. In fact, in his first years in Vienna, between 1897 and 1903, Loos was more of an architectural writer than an architect. To his credit, he was the first architect to break the mold, with the exception of the Viennese architect J. B. Fischer von Erlach, who in the early eighteenth century had commented on areas of design and culture. Even though Loos's writing slowed after 1904, when his career as an architect took off, beginning with his commission for the Villa Karma in Switzerland, he continued to write. In fact, his most forceful statement of the period came in the form of *Das Andere* ('The Other'), the magazine he launched in 1903, which bore the subtitle: 'A Journal for the Introduction of Western Culture to Austria'. Only two issues were published. Like Kraus, he was beloved as much as reviled.

The person Adolf Loos judged most worthy of contempt was Josef Hoffmann, who was, in his view, guilty of the worst possible offense, that is of being an eclectic, of reducing ornament to a mere grab-bag of knick-knacks. In fact, Loos's best-remembered article, '*Ornament und Verbrechen*' ('Ornament and Crime'), was an incensed review of the famous *Kunstschau* art fair organized by Hoffmann in 1908. Loos first delivered the text as a lecture that year and published it in French in *Cahiers d'aujourd'hui* in 1910. About the interiors exhibited at the fair that were based on Hoffmann's principles he wrote: 'When I visit such an apartment, I pity the poor people who spend their lives there. Is this then the backdrop that these people have created for the small pleasures and great tragedies of this existence?!!! This?? . . . Alas, you wear these apartments like a Pierrot costume from a fancy-dress shop.'[23] Loos not only abhorred the aesthetics of Josef Hoffmann and the Wiener Werkstätte, he also condemned historicism, going so far as to parrot Wagner's simile of the Potemkin villages to describe it. There may have been an additional gut reaction in Loos's animosity. Although Hoffmann worked with Jews and Social Democrats, he was to become a supporter of the fascists after 1932 and designed the Austrian Pavilion at the Venice Biennale for the Dollfuss regime. Loos also slammed the functionalist machine aesthetic of the Werkbund and of its chief theoretician, Hermann Muthesius.[24]

It is because of his writings that Loos has gone down in history as the first twentieth-century architect to banish ornament. Gropius described him as a 'seer' and declared that 'when everything still lay in the slumber of eclecticism, he predicted, from the loneliest of positions, the future developments.'[25] Just how much the Imperial era held his belligerent courage against him is attested by the fact that 'Spoken into the Void', his far-reaching and still valid essay written between 1897 and 1900 for the *Neue Freie Presse*, did not find a publisher in either Austria or Germany until after the war. Le Corbusier wrote that, 'in the middle of our architectural problems in 1913, Loos suddenly appeared with a splendid article, "Ornament and Crime"'.

> We found ourselves at the closing of our sentimental period: We had found the connection to nature again and had completely conquered the new technologies (iron and concrete, new machines, new materials). All that meant a crucial break with the past, which had been tended artificially by the academies, and a longing preparation for the future. Loos swept beneath our feet with a Homeric cleansing – strict, philosophical and lyrical. In this way Loos influenced our architectural fate.[26]

Sigfried Giedion thought of him thus:

> He cleaned up architecture. He helped many, primarily the most important ones today, because he showed them 'that's

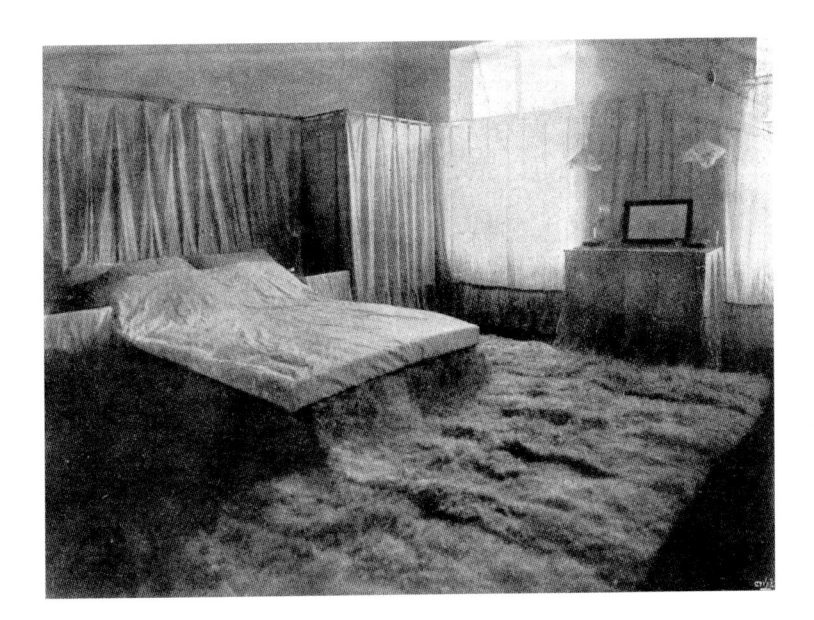

the way.' A pathfinder. His work is not continuous. But he has moments. In these moments he saw more boldly, cogently, and further than any who began with him. There is not one architect today that does not carry a piece of Loos in him.[27]

These commentators may be correct when it comes to Loos's writings. But there is a glaring inconsistency between his writings and his own architecture, in particular his interiors, as many readers have noticed. The most extreme of these readers, the English architectural critic Reyner Banham, famous for his love of 'gizmos' and ornaments, dismissed Loos's writings as '*Schlagobers-Philosophie* [whipped cream philosophy] that whisks up into an exciting dish on the café table, and then collapses as you look at it, like a cooling soufflé. It is not a reasoned argument,' he continues, 'but a succession of fast-spieling double-takes and non-sequiturs holding together a precarious rally of clouds of witness – café Freudianism, café-anthropology, café criminology.'[28] Indeed, what is one to make of the white angora rug that extended from the floor up to the bed in Loos's wife Lina's bedroom of 1903 (fig.36)? If this is not a Loosian crime, what is?

Loos waited until his last article to add a proviso to his statement that ornament was a crime, explaining that he meant not ornament in general but 'superfluous' ornament. This clarification appears in the foreword he wrote shortly before his death to a collection of his essays called *Trotzdem* ('Despite Everything'), in 1931. 'After a thirty-three-year struggle, I have emerged victorious: I have liberated humanity from superfluous ornamentation.'[29]

In this light, Loos appears as what he truly was, a modern reformer of ornamentation, no less than Josef Hoffmann, whom he reviled.

36 Photograph from Adolf Loos, 'My Wife's Bedroom', in Peter Altenberg (ed.), *Kunst und Alles Andere* (Vienna, 1903). White cambric curtains run all the way around the room. The angora carpet rises up along the base of the bed. Museum of Applied Arts (MAK), Vienna

If the one had an eclectic approach, the other had a rigorist one. Loos was not abandoning ornament but reducing it to what he saw as its most essential expression, that is the cladding of the wall and the craftsmanship in treating it. In his mind he was, as he avowed, in the tradition of the rigorist German architect Karl Friedrich Schinkel, who had reacted against the excesses of the overwrought rococo.[30] In fact he was returning to the nineteenth-century Viennese Biedermeier tradition, that drew from eighteenth-century rigorist strictures. He reduced ornamentation to the epidermal cladding of the design object, whether it was wood or stone. Loos simply took this concept of the ornament, which had been applied to furniture and household objects, and applied it to the interior walls of the building.

Without this proviso, there is an irreconcilable contradiction between what Loos says and what he does. For example, Loos wrote in 'Ornament and Crime':

> The Papuan covers his skin with tattoos, his boat, his oars, in short everything he can lay his hands on. He is no criminal. The modern person who tattoos himself is either a criminal or a degenerate. There are prisons in which eighty per cent of the inmates have tattoos. People with tattoos not in prison are either latent criminals or degenerate aristocrats.[31]

This statement stands in contradiction to his lavish use of richly veined marble, precious wood wainscoting, beveled mirrors and polished brass as the very kind of architectural tattoo he so roundly condemned, applied to the 'skin' of the walls of his domestic buildings. His Villa Karma (1903–6) in Montreux, Switzerland, is one example. His design consisted in the addition of a top floor to an existing three-story villa. He wrapped the villa in a structure 3.5 meters wide on all four sides. Walls were in red Skyros marble in the entrance, with a black-and-white checkerboard marble pattern on the floor. The hall was paneled in dark oak; the floor in the dining room was, again, black-and-white marble with walls in white marble. The smoking room was covered with wallpaper and built-in oak furniture. The library had an oak floor and bookshelves in black marble with mahogany wood surfaces. The bathroom on the first floor had two marble tubs. Although it was built before the publication of 'Ornament and Crime', it set a pattern in Loos's designs that was unbroken.

In the same vein, his famous diminutive American Bar (1908) just off the Kärntnerstrasse was equally lavishly decorated, with its black-and-white checkerboard marble floor, mahogany wainscoting on the walls divided into three equal bays, and pilasters in dark green marble. Ceiling beams are in dark green marble from Tinos, with rectangular coffers made of darker-veined marble (*rosso antico*), and the gaps are inlaid with brass. The exterior consists of four Skyros red-and-white marble pillars and brass door frames with glass panels. The most notable feature may well be the addition of large wall mirrors above head level, which gave an infinity effect to amplify its cramped space (color plate 12).

The shop Loos designed for his tailors, Goldman & Salatsch (1909–12), is a five-story structure on which an unadorned white stucco façade is surmounted on a monumental entrance, consisting of a frame resting on four Doric columns, all in a precious green Cipollino marble from Greece (fig.37). These columns were merely decorative, the load-bearing function being taken up by the hidden steel structure around the frame. In other words, being purely ornamental, the columns are effectively a 'crime'. The other load-bearing elements, inside the building, were located around the staircase, giving Loos the chance to accommodate a flexible layout of living and office space which came to be called the *Raumplan*.[32] To make the customer feel at home, he included a den-like suite with armchairs and a Persian rug and an open fireplace on the first floor. But it was more than just 'homey'. The entire interior space was what Walter Benjamin would go on to call 'phantasmagoric' in his *Arcades Project* (1927). It was a feat of marketing, somewhat in the spirit of the genius which the heroine, Denise, deploys in her design of fantasy worlds of consumerism in Emile Zola's *Au Bonheur des Dames* ('The Ladies' Paradise', 1883). Loos stripped his shop of outmoded Zola-esque frills in favour of what he saw as a modern male consumer's kind of ornament. He created a looking-glass paradise of cunningly arranged polished surfaces – stained oak paneling, brass fittings and omnipresent beveled mirrors of crystalline glass (color plate 13) – where the masculine shopper could everywhere see his own reflection surrounded tantalizingly by shoes, pants, ties and suits tailored to the new modern style worn in London. This was meant to be a man's dream world, calculated to allow the consumer to feel filthy rich, terribly elegant and consummately modern.

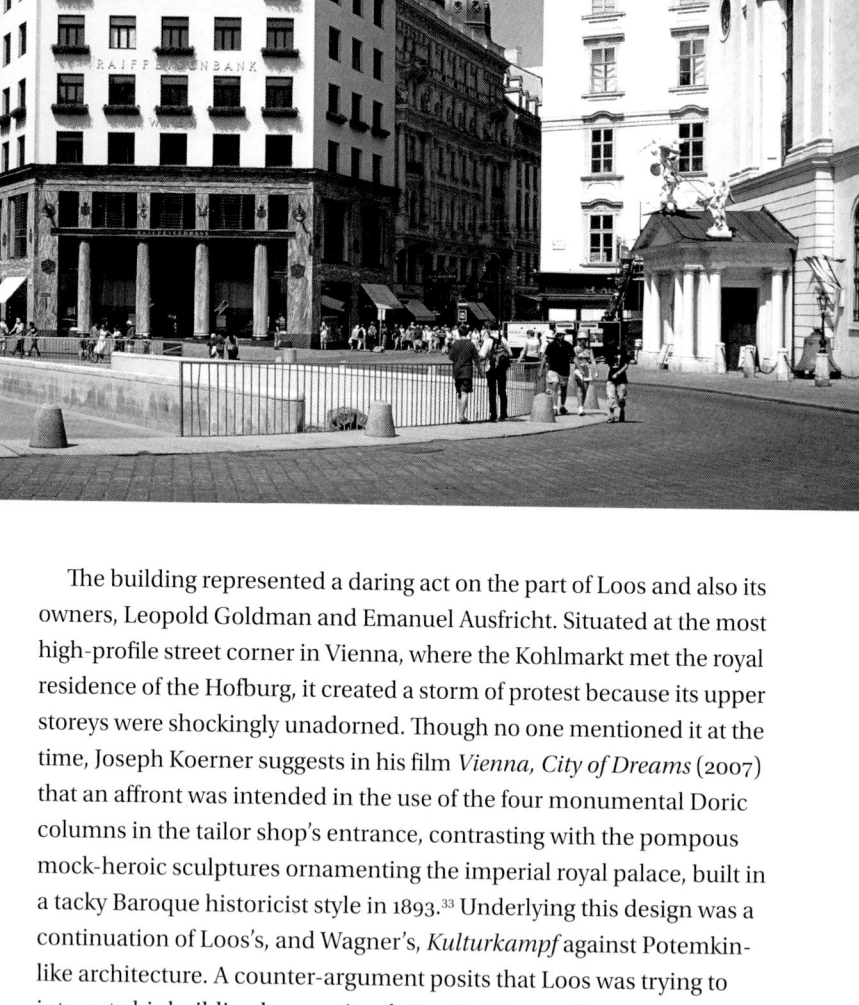

The building represented a daring act on the part of Loos and also its owners, Leopold Goldman and Emanuel Ausfricht. Situated at the most high-profile street corner in Vienna, where the Kohlmarkt met the royal residence of the Hofburg, it created a storm of protest because its upper storeys were shockingly unadorned. Though no one mentioned it at the time, Joseph Koerner suggests in his film *Vienna, City of Dreams* (2007) that an affront was intended in the use of the four monumental Doric columns in the tailor shop's entrance, contrasting with the pompous mock-heroic sculptures ornamenting the imperial royal palace, built in a tacky Baroque historicist style in 1893.[33] Underlying this design was a continuation of Loos's, and Wagner's, *Kulturkampf* against Potemkin-like architecture. A counter-argument posits that Loos was trying to integrate his building harmoniously into its historical context by taking its cue from the undistinguished, nondescript neo-classical façade of the church of St Michael across the way, built in the late eighteenth century under Josef II. This would be surprising, as there is no trace in Loos's writings about a desire for integration into the historical fabric of Vienna. What is certain is that this was Jewish Vienna at its most confident, however misplaced this confidence might be. Leopold Goldman was to die on an overcrowded cattle train before reaching the concentration camp he had been sent to by the Nazis, 27 years after the controversial shop's opening.[34]

Although the building has gone down in the annals of architectural history as the one that foretold the banishment of ornament in twentieth-century avant-garde architecture, it was far less radical than Josef Hoffmann's Purkersdorf clinic in the Vienna Woods from four years earlier. But Hoffmann's building was far from the city center, and he had little interest in polemics. And so the clinic never made it onto the radar screen in the way Loos's building did.

Loos's much smaller Knize tailor shop (1913), on the Graben shopping street in the city center, is a more coherent expression of his rigorist approach to ornament. Whereas Goldman & Salatsch was a temple to shopping, this was a small shrine whose seductive, exquisite, richly gleaming cherry-wood interior customers reached through a gently curved, enfolding entrance of charcoal-grey Swedish granite, past display windows made of expensive curved glass in cherry-wood frames, the whole surmounted by the glistening Knize emblem in gold-plated brass (figs 38 and 39).

37 (opposite)   Adolf Loos, Goldman & Salatsch shop, façade

38 (below, left)   Adolf Loos, Knize shop, reflective façade

39 (below, right)   Adolf Loos, Knize shop, polished interior

40 (above)   Adolf Loos, Duschnitz House (1915–16), the typically ostentatiously decorated interior of a building that appears sober from the outside

41 (opposite)   Adolf Loos, Scheu House

Among Loos's projects for private houses following the Villa Karma were the Steiner House (1910), Goldman House (1910–11), Stössl House (1911–12), Horner House (1912–13) and the Mandl House (1916–17). All flouted his dictum of ornament as crime. Taking the Duschnitz House (1915–16) in particular, designed for an industrialist and art dealer, it is, again, every bit as lavish as Hoffmann's Palais Stoclet, with its profuse use of white and grey-violet Pavonazzetto marble and limestone walls, wood ceilings and fireplace copied from a French Renaissance palace (fig.40). Loos's problem was not how to create an ornamentless architecture, it was how to express luxury in a way that conformed with the dominant 'tastefulness' of the time. As he wrote in an unpublished paper: 'The house should be closed on the outside, and wealth should only be displayed in the interior.' Indeed, what characterizes all the interiors behind these stern façades is that they were made of the most luxurious marbles and woods, nearly equaling those of the Palais Stoclet in terms of conspicuous consumption. In addition, Loos lectured to his Jewish clients that these façades were the architectural equivalent of the modern, assimilated – or in Loos's word 'emancipated' – Jewish taste in clothing, 'a dinner jacket as opposed to the caftan of the Middle European Orthodox Jew'.[35] Outwardly, the houses gave the impression of restraint. Internally, they could be every bit as ostentatious as a silk kaftan.

Loos's Scheu House (1912–13) comes closest of all to his idea of absence of ornamentation (fig.41). It was designed for two lifelong friends, his lawyer Gustav Scheu and his wife, Helene Scheu-Riesz. They were Jewish intellectuals, followers of Ebenezer Howard's Garden City movement and ardent social reformers. The house does not match the excesses of the Duschnitz villa, although its walls were still covered with oak wainscoting. It was Loos's first house with stepped terraces, one per floor, the result of a request from Mrs Scheu-Riesz. Both in these and in its relative decorum, it was a harbinger of what was to follow, after the First World War.

For the time being, the immediate future in Vienna was bleak: 1914 would arrive and war would be unleashed on Europe. All these architects would see their careers suspended. But four years later, by the end of the war, much of the old world would be swept away. Historicism would be a thing of the past. New modern architectural styles – shaped by Otto Wagner and these other modernist rebels and more adapted to the hard realities of a very different world – were to triumph.

4

After the Apocalypse
The Social Housing of Red Vienna and Its Social Democratic Political Economy

Karl Kraus was right. Austria did become a laboratory for the end of the world. The Habsburg heir apparent, Archduke Franz Ferdinand, in full military regalia, strutted his way into the ill-advised state visit to Sarajevo that provoked not only his own assassination, but the collapse of the Habsburg monarchy and the Austro-Hungarian Empire. Although the causes of the conflict that lasted between 1914 and 1918 are more complex,[1] it was this senseless act of bravura on the part of the imperial government that set off the First World War, pulling Europe and North America down into a senseless bloodbath. Sixteen million people died on blood-soaked battlefields and 20 million were physically maimed.[2]

John Maynard Keynes, in his international bestseller *Economic Consequences of Peace* (1919), deplored nonetheless the revanchist, scorched-earth policies of the victors, Woodrow Wilson, David Lloyd George and Georges Clemenceau, toward the defeated Germany. He likened the Treaty of Versailles to a 'Carthaginian Peace' – a reference to the Roman annihilation of the Phoenician city of Carthage – whose only purpose was to eradicate the enemy population, simply to punish rather than to create a framework for stability and a balance of power, the way the Congress of Vienna had in 1815 under Metternich, inspired in turn by the Treaty of Westphalia of 1648. Keynes correctly predicted that the untenable terms of the peace treaties which they had meted out would have disastrous long-term consequences, leading to a new world war.[3]

'*Ce qui reste*' – the leftovers – was how the French president Georges Clemenceau, whose ferociousness earned him the nickname Le Tigre, described Austria after the Treaty of Saint-Germain-en-Laye had dismembered the old empire. The new republic fared even worse than Germany under the Treaty of Versailles. Before the war the Habsburg Empire had been the largest in Europe, surpassed only by Russia. It had extended to present-day Hungary, Croatia, Bosnia, Ukraine and the Czech and Slovak Republics. These were the industrial and resource-rich regions of the empire. It had been an extremely rich country. Now Austria was left with nothing but Vienna and the most backward, rural, Alpine provinces. A population of 53 million fell to 5 million, with many living in poverty. It was an unmitigated catastrophe except for one thing. The monarchy succeeded at self-destructing, clearing the way for democracy.

42 The children's wading pool at the Fuchsenfeld Hof. Of all the Viennese Gemeindebau output, it especially impressed the American housing specialist Catherine Bauer, who published it in her *Modern Housing* (1934)

The great history of the period is the 1600-page publication by Charles Gulick and (not fully acknowledged as co-author) the Viennese-trained economist Alexander Gerschenkron. They established how the dissolution of the Habsburg monarchy in 1918 had left Austria utterly bereft. As they pointed out, industrial activity came to a standstill, resulting in massive unemployment.[4]

Yet despite the ravages of war, Austria, now freed of the imperial political and economic straitjacket, emerged almost immediately as an innovative economic force in redefining modern capitalism. In other words, it reversed typical Austrian 'backwardness' by reinforcing the role of the state, at least in regard to the municipality of Vienna. On 4 May 1919 the first municipal election in Vienna in accordance with the universal, equal, direct and secret right to vote for both women and men brought the Social Democratic Party to power with a landslide victory. With Jakob Reumann as mayor, it was the first major city in history to have a social-democratic government.

But the country was split into two strongly opposed entities. Throughout the 1920s antagonism grew between the federal government, composed of conservative, libertarian, proto-fascist Christian Socials and Pan-Germans and dominated by the Austrian School of Economics, which revered free-market capitalism,[5] and the social-democratic municipal government of what eventually came to be called 'Red Vienna'. The city contained one third of the country's population.[6] A right-wing paramilitary group, the Heimwehr, was formed in various provinces with financing from Austrian industrialists and Italian fascists. In response, in 1923 the Social Democratic Workers' Party created the Republikanische Schutzbund, a workers' force intended to protect Austria's young democracy. At its peak in 1928 the Schutzbund had 80,000 members, armed with light weapons, principally in Vienna, but also in Upper and Lower Austria and Styria.[7]

The first major confrontation occurred in July 1927, when the Palace of Justice was burned following angry popular demonstrations. The crowds were protesting against the acquittal of three men from the right-wing militia for the murder of a social democrat war veteran and his eight-year-old nephew during a peaceful demonstration. The police killed 89 and wounded 1600 in the turmoil.[8] This marked what Gulick called the 'turning point' in the increasingly ruthless measures of 'Black Vienna' (the fascist element) to gain total control, funded by Mussolini, by the biggest business concern of the country, the Alpine

Iron and Steel Company of Linz, and by the major landowner and figure of the old nobility, Prince Stahremberg, *inter alia*, paving the way for the Nazi takeover in 1938.[9]

The antagonism finally came to a head during a parliamentary crisis in which Engelbert Dollfuss was appointed chancellor on 20 May 1932. In early 1933, he led a military putsch and assumed dictatorial powers. On 12 February 1934 he sent the security forces to attack social democrats. A two-week-long civil war broke out, in which the social democrats were defeated after many battles. Fighting around the country resulted in hundreds dead and more than a thousand wounded. The Social Democratic Workers' Party and its militia, the Schutzbund, were banned, and nine of the uprising's leaders were executed. On 1 May 1934, the new constitution, replacing that of the First Republic, was instituted, as was Austro-fascism. The replacement of Red Vienna with Black Vienna signaled the demise of democracy in Austria for the next 11 years.

Faced with an antagonistic federal government from the start, the municipal government placed its major emphasis on social housing.[10] The political rationale was clear: providing government-supported housing on a grand scale guaranteed votes for the social democrats. The Karl Marx Hof, for example, which housed approximately 5000, was built in the patrician Nineteenth District of Vienna to help assure victory for the social democrats at the ballot box there. Robert Danneberg, a leading figure in the municipal government of Red Vienna, published his *Kampf gegen die Wohnungsnot! Ein Vorschlag zur Lösung der Aufrechterhaltung des Mieterschutzes* ('Battle against Housing Need! A Proposition to Maintain Rent Control') with this in mind.[11] But there was also a proto-Keynesian economic rationale to the program, as we shall see.

Although the city's infrastructure was in exceptionally good shape thanks to the rail and riverine transportation network designed by Otto Wagner, the municipal policies of the Christian Socials under Karl Lueger had done little to benefit the urban working class, which in 1910 comprised 56 per cent of the population of Greater Vienna. As Eve Blau points out 'in 1892 a law had exempted owners from real estate taxes for 30 years, whatever the reason, it 'triggered a decade of widespread speculation by slum landlords'. Investors built tenements that 'exploited' the building prescriptions to build on every centimeter allowed by law.[12]

Vienna's housing problem went back a long way. One of the first housing projects for workers was initiated by the heir apparent to the imperial throne, Prince Rudolf, but it was ineffectual. The Rudolfshof in Vienna's Ninth District was designed by Theophil von Hansen, who, as his own charitable contribution, supervised the construction for free in 1870–71.[13] The emperor sold the land to the housing society for half its designated price and donated 3000 guilders to the project, while the construction magnate Heinrich Drasche contributed 10,000. The building, designed in accordance with the perimeter-block model that Hansen used in his high-end Zinspalais, contained only 42 units and was reserved for relatively well-off imperial civil servants displaced by the rapidly increasing costs of renting in the newly built First District.[14]

Another attempt to institute social housing came in the wake of Eugen von Philippovich's book on the wretched housing conditions of the poor in Vienna. Such was the public outcry that four years after its publication, in 1898, in honour of his Imperial Golden Jubilee, Franz Josef sponsored a public housing competition, which resulted in the so-called Lobmeyrhof in the Sixteenth District. The 26 blocks of family dwellings, finished in 1903, housed 1700 people in 392 apartments. The blocks were five stories high and enclosed large courtyards. All the dwellings were provided with their own toilet, although half of these were outside the apartment itself. The major innovation was the access to light and air. Multi-functionality was a feature: facilities included steam-powered laundries, showers and baths, a public library, lecture hall, plots for vegetable gardens, play areas for children and even a house doctor.[15] But the project failed because of the resulting prohibitive cost of the apartments. Most of the tenants were not members of the poor working class, but skilled blue-collar or white-collar workers.[16]

By 1910 over 640,000 people were homeless in Vienna,[17] over 25 per cent of the entire population. In 1913, with the situation no better, a bill intended to ameliorate the condition of the poor was coming up for a vote. The parliament had to decide whether to back an enormous state bond issue that would finance decent housing or else to finance fractious tribes in Albania, in a bid to establish an ally client state that would be a thorn in the side of nationalist Serbia, which was threatening to break away from Austria-Hungary. This strained the empire's finances, but the emperor preferred the costly military intervention, which only pushed Austria-hating Serbia to the brink. Sixteen months later, Franz Ferdinand was to die from a Serb nationalist's bullet, igniting the First World War.[18]

During the war, as a result of long-term neglect, according to the housing census the number of the smallest dwellings (one room and kitchen) represented 73 per cent of the 554,525 living quarters in Vienna. In the working-class districts, 90 per cent of the housing stock fitted this description. There were also thousands of homeless people who lived in makeshift shacks, under bridges, on boats and in caves under railway embankments. In addition, hungry, homeless Viennese otherwise unconnected to the land began to plant vegetable gardens on the Wald and Wiesengürtel, and on military parade grounds and in inner-city parks. Soon slums began to spread on the periphery of Vienna.[19] The inhabitants started to cultivate the soil around the cities and the industrial areas to grow vegetables and breed small livestock illegally, in what were referred to as *wilde Wohnen*, 'wild settlements'. Thus Vienna became gradually encircled by perhaps as many as 150,000 allotments.[20] The housing shortage pressed further. The users of the allotments started to build cabins in their gardens.

After the war, the appalling housing problem was compounded by a massive influx of veterans, the great majority of whom were maimed and disabled in the wake of the war. The poverty was such that famine struck parts of the population.[21] On 17 April 1919, when a horse died in the street, the crowd threw itself upon the animal's carcass and sliced it into bits which they carried home.[22] The 'wild' allotments had become slums. A measure of the destitution of Vienna's slum-dwelling population is that, when they were finally given social housing, its residents had to be taught how to furnish their apartments and adhere to hygienic standards. This was the work that the larger-than-life Otto Neurath would take on, as we shall see in the following pages.

The hardship prompted three pioneering psycho-sociologists, Paul Lazarsfeld, Marie Jahoda and Hans Zeisel, to write their classic *Die Arbeitslosen von Marienthal* ('The Unemployed of Marienthal') in 1927, commissioned by the Social Democratic Party and largely funded by the Rockefeller Foundation. It warned that support for the social-democratic alternative among the working class was, counter-intuitively, waning in the face of continuing job losses and poverty.[23] Vienna's urban poor also became the subject of the arts for the first time in Vienna, which had not had a Victor Hugo or a Charles Dickens to describe their plight in the nineteenth century. Georg Wilhelm Pabst directed the film *The Joyless Street* in 1925, written by Hugo Bettauer and featuring Greta Garbo, about the bankruptcy of countless households due to the hyperinflation of the early 1920s in Austria and Germany, both countries crushed under the weight of war reparations impossible to meet. The photographer Edith Tudor-Hart captured the plight of the pauperized population, including one maimed former soldier reduced to selling yo-yos in the street.

In response to the near-total economic collapse, the social-democratic government of Vienna developed, funded and managed in quick succession two different, but equally prototypical, Keynesian-style planning policies for the common good in the field of social housing. Both were forerunners of the welfare-state social housing models that were adopted in Austria and most other European countries after the Second World War. The first was based on the idea of Siedlungen, 'settlement housing units'. It was heavily influenced by the approach taken by the German Weimar Republic (1919–33) to social housing, that is, an association-based communitarian system on the model of Ebenezer Howard's garden cities, with government funding and planning. This housing took the form of single, semi-detached or terraced family houses with their own garden plots on the outskirts of the city. Its adherents, most notably Otto Neurath, developed a complex logistic system to make it workable economically. This model, which was a combination of bottom-up and top-down policies, was pursued by the administration of Jakob Reumann from 1919 to 1923.

The second yielded the so-called Gemeindebau ('Municipal Building') program. In stark opposition to the first sort of housing, these massive apartment blocks were to a certain degree homegrown, drawing on the precedent of the typical bourgeois Viennese Ringstrasse apartment block and partly inspired by Amsterdam's perimeter housing blocks as embodied by Michiel de Klerk's Het Schip, De Dageraad and the Spaarndammerplantsoen, all built during the First World War. Moreover, it was all top-down. The Gemeindebau program developed its own unique combination of perimeter-block configuration, colossal in scale, inserted within the existing urban fabric. Just as original was its concept of multi-functional planning, with the inclusion of cultural, sporting, hygienic and educational facilities that broke away from the one-dimensional dormitory concept of housing. The unusually high quality of social amenities

5.1 Graph comparing number of housing units provided in *Gemeindebauten* and *Siedlungen* between 1919 and 1926. [*Der Aufbau*, nos. 8/9 (1926): 129].

was enhanced by another truly innovative interpretation of the garden city idea. Instead of the housing units being placed in nature, nature was placed inside the social housing units in the form of internal green areas that often took up 80 per cent of the lots. This phase also had its own managerial and financial modus operandi, without which it would have been impossible. It was carried out under the administration of Mayor Karl Seitz from 1923 to 1934.

As a result of both housing programs, within 14 years the city of Vienna completed 348 Gemeindebau council housing estates with 61,175 apartments, and 42 Siedlung settlement groups with 5257

43 Otto Neurath, table indicating the number of housing units built between 1919 and 1926. Above, the number of perimeter housing blocks (Gemeindebauen); below, the number of individual row houses (Siedlungshäuser). *Der Aufbau*, nos 8–9 (1926), p. 129

terraced houses and 2,155 commercial premises; 190 architects had worked on their design (fig.43). By 1934 one tenth of the inhabitants of Vienna lived in publicly financed social housing.

The first Siedlung housing policy arose as a response to the grassroots, back-to-the-earth movement of settlers' organizations that wrote petitions and organized demonstrations with up to 100,000 participants. The resulting housing consisted of small-scale single units, semi-detached or in terraces of family houses with a small garden which was used for growing food.

The lawyer Gustav Scheu was appointed in May 1919 by Mayor Jakob Reumann as advisor on housing matters. Scheu, like all of the main supporters of the settlement movement, was a follower of Ebenezer Howard, favoring the development of suburban tracts of land funded by voluntary associations of like-minded communitarian settlers in outlying areas.[24] This went hand with hand with a commitment to a common ownership of the land, exclusion of individually owned property, and a community based on cooperative rather than competitive principles.[25] He would also have been influenced by another movement: the Weimar Republic's Siedlung settlements. Under his direction, a total of 3,209 housing units were provided in Vienna with municipal help, and of these 673 were cooperative Siedlungen. Among the movement's most devoted and prolific propagandists was the art historian, journalist and writer Max Ermers. One of the projects he most enthusiastically supported was the Siedlung Rosenhügel ('Rose Hill'), one of 'the largest and most politically active cooperative associations',[26] whose future residents made their own bricks (*Pax Ziegel* or Peace Bricks) out of cinder, sand and cement pressed into hollow blocks.[27] The communal center was in Ermers's words 'the heart and the brain of a settlement, simultaneously a town hall and a home for recreation, a club, a theater, a concert hall, a people's university'.[28]

The German Siedlung movement involved many remarkable figures, all linked in a tightly knit network. The Siedlungsamt (municipal settlement office) was headed by Hans Kampffmeyer, a founding member of the German Garden City Society who had been campaigning for garden city settlements in Vienna since 1908 and who founded the journal *Der Siedler* ('The Settler') with Otto Neurath in 1920, publishing advice on all aspects of life for the future occupants of the garden cities. Several newly created housing associations joined the socialist government in promoting Siedlungen between 1919 and 1934 (only 11 per cent of Vienna's housing was in this form). The concept of the house-with-a-garden that characterized this phase was influenced by Leberecht Migge, a German socialist regionalist landscape architect, influenced by the anti-state, pro-self-sufficiency ideas of the Russian anarchist Peter Kropotkin. Migge was best known for the incorporation of gardening principles into the Siedlung designs of Martin Wagner, Ernst May and Bruno Taut, among others, during the Weimar Republic. The resulting settlements were like pre-industrial villages with an emphasis on cultivation and subsistence gardening.

Hugo Mayer, who favored a neo-Biedermeier style, was the most active designer of the early garden villages built along these lines. He designed the first of the Siedlungen, Siedlung Schmelz (1919), filling 25 per cent of its plot of land with rows of two- and three-storey multi-family houses, and Siedlung Rosenhügel (1921) in the Twelfth District for railway workers. Adolf Loos too was associated with this phase of Red Vienna's housing policy. Like so many Viennese intellectuals, he joined the ranks of committed social democrats. Loos had designed Scheu's house in 1912 and was a close friend of his as well as a garden city enthusiast. Scheu's first decision after taking office was to appoint Loos as his assistant. The architectural direction of the Siedlungsamt was entrusted to him as its chief architect from May 1921 till June 1924 when Scheu resigned. He set up a zoning plan approved in July 1921.[29]

Given Loos's propensity for luxurious furnishings, it is remarkable how he became a functionalist, concerned with economy, structural efficiency and the well-being of the inhabitants, as well as a pioneer of ecological sustainability. One of his most urgent tasks was to establish design and construction guidelines. Much of the early settlement housing was judged to be unsightly and unsafe. The houses had been built without regard for the existing building codes and with substandard materials. 'To become settlers, we have to learn how to live as settlers . . . We must start with the garden . . . It should be 200 square meters at the most.' Of primary importance, Loos determined, were waste collection facilities and workplaces. The toilet was to be located in the garden where its contents could be turned into fertilizer. Loos's recommended that sites be oriented east–west so that gardens could receive sun all day. Bedrooms and the principal work spaces of the house all faced south.[30]

Loos's ecological ideas were influenced by Leberecht Migge. The Siedlungen he designed, like the German counterparts Migge had created, emphasized real kitchen gardens, which were to provide food and make each family self-sufficient.[31] Leopold Bauer, an architect who had studied with Otto Wagner and published a proposal in 1919 entitled 'Healthy Living and Joyful Work: Problems of our Time', also advocated 'ecologically correct' row housing for Vienna interspersed with green spaces.[32]

Loos designed between 40 and 50 houses in several settlements during his association with the Siedlungsamt between 1921 and 1924, including Hirschstetten, Friedenstadt and Am Heuberg in the area surrounding Vienna. Interestingly, they display the two signature features of houses he is most famous for, the Rufer House, the Tristan Tzara House, the house for Josephine Baker and the Moller and Müller houses. These are the *Raumplan* and the ascetic, cuboid, white stucco façade. The houses of Am Heuberg had flat roofs, which make them the forerunner of the better-known Weissenhof Siedlung of 1927, organized by the German Werkbund in Stuttgart, usually considered to be one of the foremost precedents of the International Style.[33]

Margarete Schütte-Lihotzky (1897–2000), Loos's closest associate at the time, was another of the major cultural figures attached to the Siedlung movement. She met Loos in 1920 and by early 1921 was working with him on the Friedensstadt Siedlung. When it closed down for financial reasons, she then worked with Ernst Egli on the Eden Siedlung.

History has shortchanged Schütte-Lihotzky. She was one of the first Austrian women to get an architecture degree from the Kunstgewerbeschule, headed by Josef Hoffmann, the only institution that granted diplomas to women. There she attended masterclasses between 1915 and 1919 with three architects linked to the Siedlung projects, Josef Hoffmann, Heinrich Tessenow and Oskar Strnad.[34]

Her most celebrated contribution was the design of the Frankfurter Küche, the Frankfurt Kitchen, of 1926 (fig.44). By using modular parts, she could cost-effectively mass-produce her kitchen-in-a-box for the 15,000 new social housing flats built by the design team of Ernst May at the height of the Weimar Republic. Her references for the kitchen were far removed from those of the conventional female sphere of interior decoration, instead grounded in the kind of scientific thinking that characterized the work of many other Viennese women at the time. With its repositionable gas range, industrial-style oven, metal sink and chopping board combination, integrated removable garbage drawer and fitted glass cabinets – prefiguring Buckminster Fuller's clip-on Dymaxion units – her kitchen was conceived as an assembly-line work station where all implements were ergonomically designed for maximum efficiency, following the time-and-motion studies of Frederick Winslow Taylor. Below one counter were 18 drawer-like containers for sugar, flour and other dried foodstuffs, each with a handle and a spout that served to pour out its contents as needed. A dish-drying rack hung over the sink and an ironing board tucked next to the window could be dropped down (fig.44).[35]

Schütte-Lihotzky's career was as well rounded as that of any of her male colleagues. At a time when it was inconceivable for a woman to have her own architectural practice, her projects included a home for invalid soldiers in 1918, a Culture Palace in 1918 for promoting peace, and housing for war veterans in France in 1920. On joining the office of Otto Neurath's Österreichischen Verband für Siedlungs-

44 Margarete Schütte-Lihotzky, Frankfurt Kitchen, 1927

45 One of Heinrich Tessenow's many exquisite drawings expressing the arcadian *völkisch* German idea of the *Dorf* (village), Bautechnische Zeitschrift, 18 January 1904

und Kleingartenwesen (Austrian Association of Settlers and Small Gardeners), she was the only woman to be accepted by her peers to collaborate as an equal participant in the Winarsky Hof with Behrens, Hoffman, Strnad and Wlach, and the Otto Haas Hof with Dirnhuber and Schuster.[36] Once she arrived in Frankfurt, she designed Siedlung Praunheim. She was, in other words, way ahead of other women architects of her generation, with the exception of Liane Zimbler, five years her junior, who had also graduated from the same school. Zimbler built a successful commercial practice although her designs were mainstream.[37]

In 1937, the political situation having deteriorated, Schütte-Lihotzky left Frankfurt for Moscow and enlisted in Ernst May's design team for the new industrial city of Magnitogorsk. She then moved to London and Paris with her husband, Wilhelm Schütte, but, finding no work, they traveled to Istanbul at the behest of fellow Austrian architect Clemens Holzmeister, who found himself in Turkey at the time of the Anschluss and remained there for the duration of the war.

Among other notable collaborators with Adolf Loos and Schütte-Lihotzky was her former professor at the Kunstgewerbeschule, Heinrich Tessenow, who put her in contact with the Weimar Republic avant-garde. He had been part of the Deutsche Werkbund, a friend and collaborator with Ernst May, Peter Behrens, Erich Mendelsohn and Ludwig Mies van der Rohe, a professor at the Technical University in

Berlin and a disciple of the Garden City movement. Tessenow designed houses for the Kolonie Rannersdorf for the officials of the city-owned Schwechat beer company, based on simple, cottage-like designs with pitched roofs and picturesque courtyards harking back to an idyllic pre-industrial German peasant vernacular. His drawings capture better than any words or photographs the bucolic romanticism that infused the Siedlung movement and its back-to-the-land dream (fig.45).

But it was the brilliant polymath and socialist political activist Otto Neurath (1882–1945) who was the managerial mastermind in this first phase of Red Vienna's social housing program. His intellectual roots lay in political science. He had worked on his doctorate thesis under the German socialist sociologist Ferdinand Tönnies, who was renowned for his attempt to revive traditional forms of community (*Gemeinschaft*), such as guilds, that were being threatened in the new, industrial-age society (*Gesellschaft*).

During the turbulent period of the social-democratic Bavarian Soviet Republic, otherwise known as the 'Bavarian Revolution of Love,'[38] Neurath ran the central economic planning office between 1918 and 1919 alongside the economist Luigi Brentano, who served as the People's Commissar for Trade. Upon his return to Vienna, Neurath filled several positions in the administration of the Siedlungen, remaining true to the concept of what he called 'total socialism' (*Vollsozialisierung*) based on all-inclusive community participation, which he developed from the work of his mentor, Tönnies. Brought into the municipal government of Red Vienna as a planner, he came up with a novel combination of, on the one hand, guild-socialist Fabianism and the Garden City Movement and, on the other, the nascent field of operations research and systems theory, a field of Neurath's own making on the basis of his experience in wartime planning.

Neurath's concept of planning strove to be an extreme combination of centralization and self-help, in other words of both top-down and bottom-up processes. He set up structures for managing the flow of people, materials, money and information with regard to the Siedlungen. In 1921, now that he was in the municipal government, he founded the Siedlungs-, Wohnungs- und Baugilde (Settlement, Housing and Construction Guild), with 400,000 members, who were already well trained through their experience in workers' unions. This organization dealt with building and maintenance for the different associations, facilitating centralized purchasing of materials and furniture and providing technical assistance on design, construction and farming matters. By 1923 Neurath had also set up a Workers' Bank and a Siedlungsmuseum for housing and city planning in Vienna. In 1925 he renamed the latter the Gesellschafts- und Wirtschaftsmuseum (Museum of Society and Economy) and founded its own association, of which the Vienna city administration, the trade unions, the Chamber of Labour and the Workers' Bank became members. The museum was provided with exhibition rooms at the city administration buildings, the most prominent being the People's Hall at the Vienna City Hall. To make the museum accessible for the unschooled, Neurath worked on graphic design and visual education with the illustrator Gerd Arntz and with Marie Reidemeister. Finally, he created what he called Isotype, a symbolic way of representing quantitative information via easily interpretable icons.[39]

Also in 1921 Neurath created the Österreichischer Verband für Siedlungs- und Kleingartenwesen, the ÖVSK, a fusion of 230 cooperative associations with a total of 50,000 members. The organization provided public lectures for the settlers. Adolf Loos lectured on 'The Settlement House'; Hans Kampffmeyer on the history of the Garden City Movement; Max Ermers gave courses on cultural and social aspects of settlement development; Margarete Schütte-Lihotzky taught domestic furniture and interior design, and Josef Frank gave a course on home construction. As for Neurath, he dealt with the economics of settlement development.[40]

Out of the ÖVSK emerged GESIBA (an acronym for Public Utility Settlement and Building Material Corporation) as a non-profit enterprise, partly owned by the municipality and partly by ÖVSK. The settler movement had received funding from the Quakers, probably through Scheu's wife, Helene Scheu-Riesz, an author and Quaker herself. But in 1921 the mayor, Reumann, created GESIBA for the purchase and development of land, the supply of building materials and professional assistance and the city established its own Siedlungsamt, later to become an important housing developer.[41]

By 1924, Neurath's political fortunes were waning, as was the popularity of his extreme views about systems of governance. Through the ÖVSK, however, he managed to receive municipal funding to prepare a comprehensive development plan for consideration by the city building department. Four architects were commissioned: Adolf Loos, Josef Frank, Josef Hoffmann and Peter Behrens, who had just taken over Wagner's job at the academy. The purpose was to designate certain areas as allotment and settlement zones as well as to create a plan for the future of Vienna. Neurath, working with Franz Schuster, proposed a greater cultural, economic and aesthetic unit than the city's previous regulatory plan, which had only looked at street planning and transportation infrastructure, along with land division. Neurath, instead, favored returning to Otto Wagner's 1911 work, *Die Grossstadt*. In keeping with Wagner's ideas, in his *Städtebau und Proletariat* Neurath emphasized the importance of social and cultural infrastructures such as parks, playgrounds, schools, churches, traffic routes, markets, municipal buildings, department stores, morgues, theaters, museums, libraries, barracks and asylums, all connected with the technical infrastructure of the city. He also envisaged the improvement of working-class areas, leaving the historic city as a business district. Interestingly, at this time he turned also to the idea of the Gemeindebau.[42] In 1925, however, Neurath turned his attention to the realization of a Settlers and Urban Planning Museum instead, after the ÖVSK suspended him over infighting.

Although this phase of the social housing policy of Red Vienna, dominated by Neurath, has been described by Peter Marcuse as 'probably the most widespread example of physical self-help in housing in the twentieth century in an industrialized nation,'[43] the garden city model proved to be unviable. The Siedlung experiment was halted after barely four years. Because of their wide dispersal, the settlements incurred greater expenses for schools, transport infrastructure, water and electricity supply. Superblocks, on the other hand, thanks to their density, could make more economical use of existing facilities. Moreover, by 1923 the postwar food shortages were over, so the allotments had lost part of their purpose. Finally, public opinion was not in favor. Throughout the 1920s, a debate raged in parliament, the city council, and the architectural and general press between back-to-the-land reformers and those who favored urban density. The latter offered social and cultural advantages, it was argued. The city was a stimulant to body and intellect, the locus of creative energy and the ethnological and social progress that were shaping the modern world. And, finally, Vienna – unlike Frankfurt or Berlin, where the Siedlung movement had spread out – could not expand because it had little hinterland, bordered as it was by the province of Burgenland to the north. It was much more practical to

Internationale Ausstellung Wien

Werkbund Siedlung

5. Juni - 7. August 1932

9-20 Uhr Eintritt S 1.-

70 eingerichtete Häuser

densify than to spread out, a solution that turns out to have been ecologically sound, as luck would have it.[44]

Before disappearing altogether, however, the Siedlung movement breathed a 'last gasp'.[45] In order to muster support for the ÖVSK, an International Urban Development Conference was organized by Otto Neurath in 1926 with the help of Josef Frank, featuring Ebenezer Howard's International Federation for Housing and Town Planning, along with the big guns of the movement from Germany, Ernst May, Bruno Taut, Heinrich Tessenow and Martin Wagner, among others.[46] One thousand people came, the greatest attendance for an international Garden City movement to date, with Raymond Unwin participating along with a French delegation.[47]

There was also the Vienna Werkbund Siedlung, a commercial enterprise initiated by Josef Frank, another vocal and militant defender of the Siedlungen, and funded by GESIBA, which was persuaded to act, for this once, as a developer whose aim was to sell houses on the open market rather than as a source of municipal funding for social housing. Frank had participated in the Weissenhof Siedlung exhibition in Stuttgart in 1927, organized by Mies van der Rohe and subsidized by the municipality, and intended to create a counter-project to it. He succeeded in his goal. Whereas the other architects had stressed the new machine aesthetics, he filled his building with multicolored pillows, which earned the house the moniker 'Frank's Bordello'.[48] His complex adopted a color scheme proposed by the artist Laszlo Gabor, which called for randomly painting the houses in a variety of bright pastel hues – yellow, blue, green, pink and off-white – in order to look different from the pristine all-white Weissenhof Siedlungen.[49] The only architect Frank chose from the Weissenhof was Hugo Haring, who had been the most idiosyncratic. Other architects Frank invited were Gerrit Rietveld, André Lurçat, Oswald Haerdtl, Walter Loos, Richard Neutra, Margarete Schütte-Lihotzky, Ernest Vetter, Adolf Loos, Josef Hoffmann, Oskar Strnad, Oskar Wlach and Clemens Holzmeister.[50]

The Vienna Werkbund Siedlung exhibition was no more a success than the Siedlung housing program had been (figs 46 and 47). The architects who had worked on the Stuttgart Weissenhof exhibition were not invited, thus excluding the majority of the international avant-garde. The opening had to be postponed from 1930 to 1932 for organizational and financial reasons. Unfortunately it followed the worldwide economic depression, triggered by the collapse of the

46 (opposite) Austrian Werkbund, International Exhibition of the Werkbund Siedlung, 1932. The image emphasizes the stylistic ideals of the project, in line with Neues Bauen aesthetics rather than with the art deco-inspired style of the Gemeindebauen. Offset. University of Applied Arts, Vienna, Collection and Archive Inv. Nr. 2547/P

Viennese bank, the Creditanstalt, in 1931. The 70 houses were too expensive and only some could be sold, the remaining units managed by the city of Vienna until today.[51]

In 1922 the second experimental phase of the housing policy began under the newly elected mayor, Karl Seitz, who favored large complexes. Rather than providing the poverty-stricken population of Vienna with provisional shelter and the means to supply its own food, the municipality chose the task of providing permanent living space, social services and employment. Hence the solution of colossal, multi-storey social housing apartment houses, or council housing blocks, inserted into the existing urban fabric.

Several features of these Gemeindebau projects made them more attractive than the Siedlungen. First, whereas the Siedlungen were scattered in outlying areas without public transport links to the city center, the Gemeindebauen were either built within the urban fabric in an interstitial way or located along lines of public transportation, that is, along Otto Wagner's Südgürtel train line, which, with its concentration of workers' housing estates, became known as the 'Ringstrasse of the Proletariat' (fig.48). Second, whereas the

Siedlungen, and for that matter all the housing projects of the time in Europe, were conceived as individualist and mainly dormitory units, the Gemeindebauen were multi-functional, with an emphasis on community-enhancing shared amenities. Some were so large and so multi-functional that they became self-sufficient. They were cities within the city, thanks to the number of services and amenities such large units could support. Their communal facilities typically included washhouses for bathing and laundry, kindergartens, mothers' advice centers, youth centers, libraries, post offices, walk-in health centers, dental clinics, pharmacies and a multitude of shops. Third, they were as arcadian in concept as the Siedlungen. The difference was that instead of locating housing units in nature, the Gemeindebau turned the idea of the garden city upside down. It brought nature into the urban fabric, and turned each complex into a big garden city of its own. And fourth, because of their economies of scale, they were more cost-effective and serviceable.[52]

The most influential architect of the housing program was Otto Wagner's student and one-time collaborator, as well as Adolf Loos's schoolmate in Brno, Hubert Gessner (1871–1943). Through his friendship with Victor Adler, the co-founder along with Otto Bauer of the Austrian Social Democratic Party,[53] he received many commissions associated with the party, including the Vorwärts-Gebäude (1909) on the Weinzeile, which served as a headquarters for the party and of its newspaper, the *Arbeiter Zeitung*. But he is most noteworthy as

47 (opposite)   Josef Frank's idea of how Siedlungen ought to be furnished. This is the interior of the housing units he contributed to the Wiener Werkbund of 1932. National Library of Austria, Bildarchiv

48 (below)   'Ringstrasse of the Proleteriat', *Die Unzufriedene*, 30 August 1930, no. 35, Year 8, Vienna

the architect who set the format for all the subsequent Gemeindebau housing projects. The most important aspect of his initial project, which was carried over to all the following buildings, was the idea of the huge perimeter block.

Gessner's Gemeindebau format has been seen as adapting the monumental perimeter housing units that appeared in Otto Wagner's *Grossstadt*. In fact, the concept goes further back.[54] One finds it in the aristocratic palace or *Hof*, and in the Ringstrasse *Zinspalais* (profit-making apartment houses), in the Arkadenhof of the working-class Viennese and in Hansen's housing project for civil servants, Rudolfshof of 1872.[55] This was followed by the imperial Jubilee housing project of 1898 by Bach and Simony, the Lobmeyrhof, with its 392 apartments in which 1700 people were living by 1905.[56] In contrast to private nineteenth-century buildings, and incidentally also to de Klerk's perimeter housing blocks in Zuid Amsterdam, these courtyards were publicly accessible, thanks to the porosity of the walls, as paths led off the sidewalks through multiple openings into the internal communal spaces.

Whatever the case, Gessner's Metzleinstaler housing project (1923–5) was to become the prototype for all further council housing. Like the Jubilee housing project, each apartment now had a toilet and water supply facilities, as well as a small anteroom. Typical for council housing was the Wohnküche, a living room with kitchenette which allowed heating with a coal stove and later a gas stove; to reduce costs, private bathrooms and central heating were not provided.[57]

Gessner's most high-profile project was the Reumann Hof (fig.49), which he originally planned as 'Vienna's first skyscraper' but for cost reasons had to reduce to eight storeys; characterized by an imposing central courtyard, this estate forms the core of a vast housing area with almost 2500 apartments along the former Linienwall (the outer defense line of the city). Gessner went on to design three more of the most celebrated of the Gemeindebauen: the Lassalle Hof of 1924, Karl Seitz Hof of 1926–32 and Robert Zangerl Hof of 1927–8.

Contrasting sharply with the Siedlung developments, Gessner's new Gemeindebau was a perimeter block with a planted courtyard at the center, like the traditional Viennese *Hof*. The courtyards occupied up to 60 per cent of the land on which the housing complexes were located. This meant that, unlike the Siedlungen, this council housing used nature as a shared social space. Furthermore, the scale of the natural environment each resident now had access to was immense.

The Karl Marx Hof, the most famous of the Gemeindebauen because of its outstanding formal qualities, stretched over 1.5 kilometers, with 1382 apartments housing over 5000 people. Designed by Karl Ehn, it has gone down in history as the symbol of Red Vienna's social-democratic architectural movement. This is because it is the most formally striking of all the municipal social housing buildings, inspired perhaps by de Klerk's Het Schip of 1919. De Klerk's architecture, indeed, is the first among the early housing projects of this period to embrace a sweeping megalithic horizontality by letting the estate stretch out for its entire length uninterruptedly rather than breaking it down into an aggregate of smaller units (color plate 14).[58]

The Karl Marx Hof was one of a series of mega-projects with remarkable landscaped courtyards. Sandleiten in Ottakring, with 1587 apartments, was the largest of all. It was designed by a group of some

49 Hubert Gessner, Reumann Hof (1924–6). With 392 units and 19 shops, typical of the upscale amenities of the massive Gemeindebauen, it was one of the first to be located along Otto Wagner's Stadtbahn on the Gürtel, dubbed the 'Ringstrasse' of the working class

50 The George Washington Hof, one of the five idyllically landscaped courtyards

of Otto Wagner's best students, Emil Hoppe, Otto Schönthal, Franz Matuschek, Franz Krauss, Josef Tölk along with non-Wagner students Siegfried Theiss and Hans Jaksch. The complex was made up of a great variety of individual buildings linked by wandering footpaths which led through a bucolic natural setting that had once been a vineyard. The George Washington Hof by Robert Oerley and Karl Krist (1927), with 1084 apartments, is particularly noteworthy for its picturesque landscaping thanks to its five spacious courtyards, interconnected through meandering paths, each named after the particular trees planted there, birch, oak, lilac, acacia and elm (fig.50). The Rabenhof, with 1112 units, by Heinrich Schmid and Hermann Aichinger (1925–8), was again appreciated because of its landscaping and also for its exquisitely crafted patterned brickwork incorporated into an art deco aesthetic. The same architects' Fuchsenfeld Hof (1925) was famed for its photogenic children's wading pool (fig.42).

The size of the individual apartments conformed to the international standards of the time. Although the floor space was small, their scale was no different from, among others, Le Corbusier's, the Bauhaus's and the Congrès International d'Architecture Moderne's (CIAM) definition of *Existenzminimum*. There was no stigma attached to small apartments in the 1930s. In fact they became cult destinations: Agatha Christie, for example, chose to live in the similarly proportioned Isokon Flats in Hampstead in London, designed by the Canadian architect Wells Coates, as did Walter Gropius, Henry Moore and the Soviet spy Kim Philby. The Isokon bar drew regulars, including Barbara Hepworth and Ben Nicholson, who met there and later married.[59] Moreover, the small scale of Vienna's Gemeindebau apartments was more than counterbalanced by the access to fresh air and green space, with the unique added benefit of having a semi-enclosed community gathering space, as well as their transport links. As Helmut Gruber has pointed out, because of the overall large scale of the housing blocks, the projects could sustain health and education programs, and parades, festivals and sporting events designed to create a 'new' working class.[60]

Most of the Gemeindebau architects, such as Hubert Gessner, had been part of the Wagner School and their formal aesthetics, often incorporating majolica art deco elements, were decorative and strangely mediocre when compared to the quality of art deco internationally. But alongside this tendency was another. A group of architects, including Adolf Loos, Oskar Strnad, Margarete Schütte-Lihotsky and especially Josef Frank, found the Wagner School buildings to be anachronistic. Loos was part of this minority who preferred the minimalist aesthetics of the German so-called Neues Bauen ('New Building'), adopted by most members of the Bauhaus when designing social housing in Germany. One of the Viennese housing projects designed in the Bauhausian spirit, but never built, was possibly based on Loos's Scheu House. Like the latter, the Terrassenhaus Project of 1923 was designed by him along with Behrens and Strnad. Loos was also involved in another complex, at least in its very early design phase. This is the massive block made up of the Winarsky Hof and the Otto Haas Hof in 1924. Through the lobbying of Josef Frank, the city agreed to commission a Gemeindebau that would be built according to the Neues Bauen aesthetic tenets of Bauhaus architects such as Mies, Gropius, May and Martin Wagner, rather than those of what Frank derogatorily referred to as the *Volkswohnungspalast* ('People's Housing Palace'), espoused by architects of the kind we have just seen, whose work was perceived by the Neues Bauen adherents to be anachronistic.⁶¹ The Winarsky Hof and the Otto Haas Hof were massive perimeter blocks sectioned into nine different parts, each one designed by a different architect. Besides Loos, the team included Behrens, Frank, Hoffmann, Strnad, Schütte-Lihotzky, Franz Schuster, Karl Dirnhuber and Josef Wlach. Surprisingly, neither the Winarsky nor the Otto Haas Hof were eventually designed according to the rigorous Neues Bauen aesthetics. They adopted pitched roofs rather than modernist flat ones, probably for construction-related reasons.⁶²

Rudolf Perco's Friedrich Engels Platz Hof (1930–33; fig.51), the second biggest Gemeindebau after Sandleiten, with 1467 apartments, was, with its stark white cuboid aesthetics, a more successful, purer and more inventive application of the Bauhaus style than the Otto Haas Hof. It transposed the Bauhaus formal language, which had by then been applied to small-scale projects such as the houses in the Weissenhof Siedlung of 1927, Mies's Tugendhat House of 1929 and the Wittgenstein House (1927–9), to a composition on an extraordinarily large scale – and with what enviable elegance. Ernst Lichtblau's Paul Speiser Hof (1929), with its columns of projecting, slickly glazed balconies, was another fine example of the Bauhaus influences present in Viennese architecture at this time.

The municipal housing programs were part of a broad political and cultural agenda, the scope of which was unique. Indeed, one of the features that set Red Vienna's housing programs apart from those of other cities – Paris, Berlin and London most notably – is the sense of civic duty which led major cultural and scientific figures to contribute to the common good. The Social Democratic Party's two founders, Victor Adler and Otto Bauer, who abandoned prestigious professional life to serve the municipality, set the tone. Among the politically committed, socially engaged social democrats who participated in Vienna's Gemeindebau program was Sigmund Freud, from 1922 onward.⁶³ In order to help guarantee the well-being of Vienna's working-class population, he operated a clinic called the Ambulatorium, where people of all ages and social classes were treated at no cost. The clinic's innovations were a reflection of Freud's commitment to free treatment and his view of the importance of psychoanalysis in social reform. Many of the clinicians at the Ambulatorium were feminist activists, including Karen Horney, Helene Deutsch, Edith Jacobson, Hermine von Hug-Hellmuth and

Theresa Benedek.⁶⁴ Then there was Karl Kraus. He gave readings to working-class audiences on Offenbach, Gogol, Ibsen, Strindberg, Wedekind, Brecht and Rosa Luxemburg, in venues such as the Musikverein and the Konzerthaus. The earnings from these readings were often given to radical social causes.⁶⁵ Both Kraus and Arnold Schoenberg contributed to the text of Adolf Loos's 1920 public lecture 'Guidelines for an Arts Office', which was intended to bridge the gulf between the people and artists.⁶⁶ Max Ermers, now head of the urban planning section of the art history department of the University of Vienna, became the first official advisor for settlement housing in 1920. Although not involved in the housing program, other major intellectuals also collaborated with the social democratic administration. The novelist Robert Musil, originally trained as an engineer, was appointed to advise on the reform of the army. The great philosopher Ernst Mach bequeathed a major part of his estate to the *Arbeiter Zeitung*, the fascinatingly multi-faceted official newspaper

51 Rudolf Perco, Friedrich Engels Platz Hof, with its Neues Bauen aesthetics, including a communal kitchen

of the Social Democrats.[67] Although Ludwig Wittgenstein was not a social democrat but a Tolstoyan populist, he produced a spelling dictionary for the public school system in 1926, one of only two books he published during his lifetime, along with his *Tractatus Logico-Philosophicus* of 1921.

As for the three main administrative figures of the Gemeindebau program, they abandoned distinguished and lucrative careers to become civil servants in Red Vienna. Hugo Breitner left his position as the vice-president of one of Vienna's biggest banks, and Robert Danneberg his law practice. Julius Tandler had been associated with the Institute for Radium Research, where he had been a student of the anatomist Emil Zuckerkandl, the brother of Viktor Zuckerkandl who founded the Purkersdorf Clinic designed by Josef Hoffmann. Tandler had been one of the pioneers in using radium against cancer. He became the main force behind the social programs attached to the housing blocks.[68]

The coming together of so many motivated modernists had an impact on the quality of life inside the housing projects. Among its multi-functional aspects, the Gemeindebau program was remarkably female-friendly, for example. Politicians stressed that the 'liberation of housewives' could be promoted by transferring household functions to the communal facilities.[69] Inspired by women's rights campaigners such as Auguste Fickert, Adelheid Popp and Anna Boschek, Otto Bauer had argued in favor of apartment houses in his *Der Weg zum Sozialismus* of 1919 largely on feminist grounds, because they freed women from individual household chores. While women were working, the one-kitchen house's kindergarten looked after the children. There would be food from the central kitchen when the women got home and the house's washing service would take care of the laundry. The kindergartens turned the Gemeindebau into a *Kinderparadies* ('children's paradise'). There were often children's baths and milk halls. Catherine Bauer was so struck with the children's wading pool at the Fuchsenfeld Hof that she included a photograph of it in her *Modern Housing* (1934). Thanks to the education reformer Otto Glöckel, schools once dominated by the Catholic Church became non-denominational, and women were allowed free access to universities in 1919.

The Gemeindebau program also promoted a unique level of musical life. The Austrian Social Democratic Arts office pressed for participation in amateur orchestras. A Workers' Symphony Orchestra was created. The party's gains in the 1927 Viennese municipal elections were due in large part to its cultural programs. The concert commemorating the tenth anniversary of the republic placed the span of Western music at the service of the proletariat. The program opened with Bach, his 'St Anne' Prelude and Fugue in E flat, orchestrated by Schoenberg, followed by Brahms. Its highlight, however, was Mahler, who was, albeit mistakenly, taken to be a socialist hero.[70] The work chosen was his First Symphony, which progressed from nature (the bird calls at the opening) to the urban to the archetypical heroic finale. The path from nature to the city was thematically prepared by Schoenberg's folk song arrangements, 'Naturbetrachtung' ('Contemplation of Nature'), and 'Auf den Strassen zu singen' ('Singing in the Street'). The following season, the same songs preceded Mahler's Sixth Symphony, with its inverted relationship between nature and urban modernity. In 1928, the Social Democratic Party's Sozialistische Kulturbund (Socialist Cultural Association) announced a competition for a less romantic symphony, suitable for proletarian listeners and amateur performers. The jury included Paul Hindemith.[71] Music was highly politicized at the time. Theodor Adorno, for example, was about to begin advising composers on how to Nazify music.[72]

The Gemeindebau community had its own weekly cultural magazine, *Der Kuckuck* ('The Cuckoo'), which covered current economic and social affairs both locally and internationally. In addition to articles on faraway places such as China, Palestine, Africa and the USA, it carried the latest women's fashions, articles on architecture and engineering, skiing and mountain climbing, and a series of detective stories that took place in remarkable social housing estates. Victor Gruen wrote on how to furnish an apartment. There was even an article on Greta Garbo and one on Charlie Chaplin.[73]

Finally, the Gemeindebau program promoted the idea of healthy bodies for the poor through athletics, sports and, somewhat surprisingly, dancing (fig.52). The *Arbeiter Olympiaden*, the Workers' Olympic Games, was organized in 1927. The most famous Viennese working-class spa, the spectacular art deco mosaic-embellished Amalienbad in the Tenth District, designed by Otto Nadel and Karl Schmalhofer and produced by the Brüder Schwadron ceramics firm, was completed in 1926, with a sauna, a wading pool and a swimming pool, which remains to this day one of the largest in Europe (color

52 Outdoor athletics and leisure activities, including dancing, in the Ottakringer Bad, the municipal recreation area in the working-class neighbourhood of Ottakring, 1930. With kind permission of Stadt Wien, MA44

plate 15). At 33 meters long, it was intended to serve 1300 people, under a glass roof which could be opened to the sky. Although much of the building was destroyed during the Second World War, it is considered a unique work of art because of its intricate ornamental mosaics.

The Gemeindebau program was a financial success. The construction of 348 colossal Gemeindebauen between 1922 and 1934, when the economy was depressed, turned publicly financed housing into a profitable economic engine.[74] In December 1929, following the great depression that wiped out many of the world's stock markets, *Der Kuckuck* ran a cover article referring to Hugo Breitner, one of the program's main movers: 'A Million Cities without Breitner – Bankrupt' (fig.53). It claimed that in the wake of the crash, Chicago, Philadelphia, Budapest, Warsaw and Berlin were bankrupt, but Vienna was in the black.[75] *Der Kuckuck* was correct: Vienna's coffers were full in 1933, in spite of the crash.[76] The incoming fascist chancellor Dollfuss knew this, and on 22 July 1933 he wrote to Mussolini that what he had in mind was to 'take a big chunk out of' the funds of 'Red Vienna' which the 'Marxists' had at their disposal. In order to do so, the Council of Ministers voted to impose a tax of 36 million schillings on the city of Vienna, backdated to the beginning of the year.[77]

The success of the Gemeindebau program poses the following question. How is it that such massive public spending, which Catherine Bauer estimated at $60 million between 1924 and 1928,⁷⁸ enabled the country to do so well economically in the midst of the postwar collapse? Why is it that the Jubilee housing project, as we have seen, was a financial disaster in 1898, even though it was sponsored by the emperor at a time when the economy was relatively vigorous?⁷⁹ It would seem that the imperial project, to which Franz Josef contributed a mere 3000 florins in addition to the industrialist Drasche's 10,000, was not sufficiently well funded. This was the result of a pre-capitalist, paternalistic philanthropy model versus a modern social-democratic capitalist one.

The answer lies partly in the municipal political economy devised and managed by Robert Danneberg and Hugo Breitner. Danneberg, a lawyer, as president of the Regional Assembly of Vienna, is generally

53 *Der Kuckuck*, 1 December 1929, p. 4, announcing that Vienna was still in the black because of Breitner and his tax-supported massive spending on social housing following the stock market crash, unlike Chicago, Philadelphia, Berlin and Warsaw

credited with having thoroughly modernized the administration of public works by reorganizing the city's municipal and provincial structure and setting up the network of interlocking institutions that constituted Red Vienna's housing program, known as the Stadtbauamt (City Building Office), a division of the Public Works department.

Another reason for the success of the social housing program lay in economies of scale. While architects were free to design the buildings as they wished, the city enforced strict regulations on the size of apartments, the amount of infrastructure and the use of standardized building parts. The building program of 1923 provided just two types of apartment. The smaller one, at 35 square meters, had one room, a kitchen, an anteroom and a toilet, while the larger apartment, at 45 square meters, also included a small bedroom. From 1925, these basic types were gradually enlarged up to 57 square meters and most were equipped with balconies.[80]

Doors, windows, door knobs, banisters, fittings, hand basins, gas stoves, even garden benches were all standardized, subject to tender and ordered in great volume, often to cover the building program for a whole year, as Eve Blau points out. Large contracts over a number of years ensured stability and cheapness of production. Purchasing in bulk directly from producers, the municipality eliminated middlemen and was able to control the quality of materials. Construction techniques were selected which required little expertise and were labour-intensive, thereby providing jobs for unskilled workers. The extensive millwork, joinery and other carpentry work involved in the buildings, as well as the specially commissioned sculpture, painted decoration, and ornamental stucco, metalwork and ceramic tile work with which the buildings were embellished, employed thousands of additional skilled craftsmen.[81]

The Stadtbauamt's Architecture Bureau was charged with drawing up the guidelines for ground coverage, layout and general disposition. Besides vetting and supervising the design of the buildings, the bureau was also in charge of commissioning craftsmen and artists for their decoration, and it oversaw repairs once the buildings were constructed. The 13 remaining sections of the Stadtbauamt were responsible for installing gas, electricity, water and sewage lines; providing bathing and laundry facilities, childcare and healthcare services; planting trees and gardens, laying out parks and equipping them with outdoor furniture, playgrounds and paddling pools; and constructing and maintaining streets and access roads, as again, Blau points out.[82]

Hugo Breitner (1873–1946) was the chief inventor of Red Vienna's proto-Keynesian political economy of social housing,[83] and Robert Danneberg (1885–1942) its chief pamphleteer and defender.[84] Breitner was uniquely qualified. Before becoming the city councilor responsible for finance in 1920, he had been one of the four directors of the Länderbank (incidentally designed by Otto Wagner, in 1882–4), one of Austria's biggest banks. The novel financial model he created for the municipal housing program was the result of his expertise in devising leveraging schemes, something which he combined with a municipal proto-welfare state concept. In addition, the Länderbank by 1898 had become the bank of choice for Karl Lueger's public works borrowing, under two of Vienna's richest bankers, Samuel Hahn and Ludwig Lohnstein, allowing anyone in its employ to become familiar with municipal finance.[85] Breitner's experience was in the bank's private equity section, which turned failing industrial companies around and made them profitable.[86] This he was to use in order to turn the amenity-rich, community-enhancing Gemeindebau program into a wealth-generating investment.

The Rent Control Act of 1922 destroyed private building speculation and Breitner chose to implement his municipal program by taking advantage of this at the federal level. A tenant now paid half the rent which had previously been asked for a given apartment in August 1914. Because of the depreciation of the Austrian krone through hyperinflation from 1921 to 1923, this meant that rents were reduced to practically nothing.[87] In 1923 Breitner introduced a luxury tax (fig.54), a new concept after the First World War, to finance elementary and secondary education, medical care and housing. According to Helmut Gruber, 'By shifting the forms of taxes from indirect to direct, from necessities to luxuries, and by introducing a graduated scale that favored wage earners, the socialists created a source of revenue for public projects truly unique at the time.'[88] Before Breitner, the tax burden in Vienna had weighed more heavily on working people. Breitner succeeded in shifting city taxes on to the relatively well-to-do and the rich. Beer in particular was one of the main sources of revenue. Other luxury goods now taxed included servants, horses, cars and theater tickets. Now at least 60 per cent of this revenue came from luxury property and business. Vienna was on its way to becoming a more equal society.[89] Breitner's policy of funding the building program out of taxation, rather than the usual mortgage loans, meant that he

54 Victor T. Slama, poster caricaturing the champagne-drinking sugar daddy horrified at the idea of paying Breitner's luxury tax. Vienna Library, City Hall, Poster Collection

avoided financing through mortgages with high interest rates which would have increased rents.[90]

Breitner's policy also included a new kind of property tax. He taxed square meters of space that the owners had not rented out. This meant he could tax high-end 'cottages' in the suburbs and luxurious palaces in the center of the city. According to this innovative scheme a simple worker's apartment was taxed annually at an average of 2 per cent of its pre-war rent, luxury apartments up to 37 per cent. In other words, 0.5 per cent of the most expensive housing now brought in 45 per cent of the overall tax on rent. This strong progressive move distinguished the financing of Austria's public housing from that of all other European countries. By 1927, the 'Breitner taxes' accounted for about 36 per cent of all tax revenues, or 20 per cent of the total revenues, of the province of Vienna.[91] As Breitner himself wrote, this was in sharp contrast to 1913, where every crown of rent, whether paid on palace or hovel, was taxed at exactly the same rate. A worker living in a cheap apartment in 1926 paid for the entire year in house-construction tax only 60 per cent of what he had paid for rent taxes in a single month in 1913.[92]

The next innovative aspect of Breitner's scheme was what he did with the tax revenues. Part went into purchasing private land and making it public. Breitner exploited federal tax regulations in order to depress land values. The housing construction tax was based on the market value of property; because it added to the cost of ownership, it caused property prices to drop. Between 1922 and 1928 Breitner had steadily accumulated land holdings for the city of Vienna at a fraction of pre-war real estate prices. In 1918 the municipality had owned 17 per cent of the total urban land. By 1924, Breitner had doubled the city's real estate holdings to 35 per cent, and by 1929, it owned approximately one quarter of Greater Vienna.[93]

The potential benefits are obvious. As Catherine Bauer noted, 'low rents allowed for low wages to act in turn as a boost for Austrian industry. The Rent Control Act was therefore supported by businesses and tenants, but opposed by landowners.'[94] The building policy of the city also encouraged employment through labor-intensive building, and the houses created by the city represented genuine capital formation, despite the fact that it abstained from charging rent which included more than maintenance and running costs. Breitner put into practice the notion that borrowing to pay for public works should be considered investment, not expenditure, and that public works would soon pay for themselves through taxation revenue from those newly re-employed. It proved a useful alternative to the approach being widely used in an attempt to pull nations out of depression – printing money. Breitner could not print money as he was working for a city, not the federal government, and because he refused to borrow at high interest rates.[95] This meant there was no inflation.

Red Vienna's Gemeindebau program came to an abrupt end in February 1934, strangled by Black Vienna. Afraid of losing the next federal election to the Austrian Social Democrats, the Austro-fascist Dollfuss outlawed the social-democratic Schutzbund and then the Social Democratic Party itself. A civil war broke out as a result, which lasted two weeks. Among the fiercest fighting occurred when, under Dollfuss's orders, the paramilitary Heimwehr besieged the emblematic Karl Marx Hof in February. The social-democrat mayor, Karl Seitz, was stripped of his title and replaced by an Austro-fascist. By May, Dollfuss assumed full dictatorial powers, only to be murdered by members of the Nazi party a couple of months later and replaced with Kurt Schuschnigg. Schuschnigg's own Austro-fascist regime was to last barely four years until the Anschluss in 1938, when Hitler made Austria part of Nazi Germany.

Robert Danneberg would be arrested and tortured by the Gestapo and then murdered in Auschwitz. Julius Tandler would die in exile in the Soviet Union. Hugo Breitner was able to escape to the US, thanks to the progressive department store tycoon Edgar Kaufmann, the client of Frank Lloyd Wright's Fallingwater (1936–8), and his son, Edgar Kaufmann Jr., who had studied sculpture in Vienna at the Kunstgewerbeschule. Indeed, the Kaufmanns put up Breitner and his family on their way to California. Among other Viennese social democrats who were recipients of Edgar Kauffman's generosity, incidentally, was Otto Neurath, to whom he sent monthly instalments of $400 to support him in exile in the Netherlands after 1938.[96] Kaufmann Sr also gave a prize to the 26-year-old Catherine Bauer in 1931 for an article she wrote on art and industry that preceded her classic *Modern Housing*.[97] But Breitner did not fare well in the US. His considerable property had been seized by the Nazis and 'Aryanised'. He ended up teaching some courses at Claremont College in Los Angeles, but as he knew no English, his contract was not renewed, and his final job was as a freelance accountant. He died of a heart attack at the age of 72 in 1947.[98]

Red Vienna's social housing program has had its share of critics. The main one was Friedrich Hayek, who argued in his *Road to Serfdom* (1944) that Viennese social-democrat tax policy had been the cause of ruin, blaming it for the economic collapse of Austria and the resulting rise of fascism, and predicting that any Keynesian policy would ultimately have the same consequence.[99] However, Gulick observed that, contrary to Hayek's view, Red Vienna 'worked like an exemplary social savings and insurance institution'. They further pointed out:

> Whether and to what extent there were instances in which city taxes actually hampered capital formation or increased consumption of capital is not certain, albeit it was probably one of the factors which induced entrepreneurs to embark upon rationalization schemes . . . it contributed toward enhancing the productivity of Austrian industry and toward improving its competitive position, particularly against German industry. Nor can it be overlooked that Breitner's method of reducing taxes on condition that businessmen employ the resultant savings as capital investments in their undertaking amounted to compulsory formation of private capital under pressure.[100]

In fact, what Breitner had already worked out as a banker and implemented in real life as a municipal policy maker, John Maynard Keynes was only starting to mull over in 1924 in his: 'Does employment need a Drastic Remedy?' He argued that 'the ultimate cure of unemployment' was that '100 million pounds be spent on public housing, better roads and improvements to the electricity grid. Let us experiment with boldness on such lines, even though some of the schemes may turn out to be failures, which is very likely.'[101]

By the time Keynes had made the case for public spending on welfare programs such as housing, Breitner had already spent the best part of a decade putting the hypothesis of this new political economy to the test in the real world. Moreover he had been successful. As in the Keynesian policies of the Roosevelt administration and the European post-Second World War welfare state, Hugo Breitner was using government expenditure on infrastructure as an attempt to spend Vienna's way out of an economic crisis. His policy was a precocious municipal New Deal in this respect. His thinking corroborates what some economists claim, that not taxing the rich is disastrous for the economy as a whole. Their analysis shows that top marginal tax rates could rise to levels near those of the Eisenhower administration – 91 per cent – and not hurt growth.[102] (In addition, after the First World War, it was commonly felt that anyone with a lot of money must have come by it as ill-gotten gains, either from weapons profiteering or as a slum landlord.)

In fact, there is evidence that the real cause of the economic crisis which Hayek blamed for the rise of fascism was the federal government's monetarist policy, informed by the Austrian School of Economics with its doctrine of laissez-faire non-intervention. The austerity policy of Christian Social prime minister Ignaz Seipl did not stimulate the economy, and his government failed to initiate a program that would boost industrial production.[103] The country's biggest steel mill, in Linz, would have to wait for the state interventionist policies of the Nazi government of Austria to become productive once again. A further problem was the unproductive way in which tax revenues were used by the fascist government.

The crucial factor was the bankruptcy of the imperial Bodenbank and subsequently of the private sector Rothschild Creditanstalt Bank in 1931, after the state forced it to bail out the Bodenbank. What ensued was a credit crisis which shook the entire industrialized world. The Austrian National Bank, and ultimately the Austrian state, were in turn forced to come to the rescue of the Creditanstalt, in what became the largest bank failure in history, pulling down the Austrian economy and the world economy with it. This points to federal policy as being responsible for the ensuing political crisis that brought on Dollfuss's military coup of 1933, and ultimately opened up the 'road to serfdom' that was Hitler's takeover of Austria.

5

Between Two Wars: From Apocalypse to the Anschluss
Other Modern Architectures 1919–1938

Not all of Vienna's creative energy went into social housing projects. The pathos of war was visible everywhere in the form of maimed men begging in the streets and the slaughter of loved ones was still fresh in people's minds. Viennese intellectuals entered a Europe-wide moral crisis, a rebellion against the past and the entire set of traditional values. This rebellion yielded great iconoclastic works by Oskar Kokoschka, Arnold Schoenberg, Alban Berg, Joseph Roth and Robert Musil, not to mention Karl Kraus's *Last Days of Mankind*. All were damning indictments of the pre-war militarism of the Habsburg Empire.

Buildings designed for a new social entity for Vienna, a struggling postwar middle class, mostly Jewish professionals, were an important part of the multi-faceted post-First World War modernization of Austria. This aspect of architectural modernity was part of the tradition initiated by Otto Wagner's polemic *Modern Architecture* that sought to develop new formal languages suited to the new realities of the day.

By far the most radical of the attempts to create a postwar architectural language is the house Ludwig Wittgenstein (1889–1951) designed for his sister Margaret Stonborough between 1927 and 1929 in Vienna's Third District (fig.55). This is not surprising. Wittgenstein

55 Margherita Spilutini's photograph of Wittgenstein House, façade

himself is recognized as the most radical philosopher of language of the twentieth century for the way he revolutionized Western philosophy's conceptions of the subject. Architectural historians tend to look at the building divorced from Wittgenstein's philosophy, and philosophers tend to consider it as inconsequential in the evolution of his philosophical thinking. But the design of the house must be seen as a turning point in the shaping of his new philosophy. For the two years it took to construct the unique house, Wittgenstein the architect was inseparable from Wittgenstein the philosopher.

This was not an ordinary house. Margaret, like all her siblings except Ludwig, who relinquished his own inheritance, had one of the biggest inherited fortunes of Europe at the time the house was being conceived.[1] Her father, Karl Wittgenstein (1847–1913), had been an exceptionally shrewd and ruthless self-made iron and steel tycoon of the Gilded Age before resigning from his business ties in 1899. He was still the thirty-seventh richest person in Austria in 1910 and had been known as the Andrew Carnegie of Europe.[2] An indication of this wealth is that in 1938, the family had 40,000 pounds of gold. We know this because it was the amount that the Nazi government demanded from the Wittgensteins in order to buy a retroactive Christian identity for their grandfather, the price they paid for two sisters to be permitted to remain in Austria free from the threat of deportation.[3]

But in building this house Margaret was renewing her elite social standing by partaking in the latest intellectual and scientific trends of the day. In spite of her vast wealth, she abandoned the grand *piano nobile* of the patrician Baroque Palais Schönborn-Batthyány, designed by Johann Bernhard Fischer von Erlach at the end of the seventeenth century in the center of Vienna, to move into the spartan and decidedly cramped quarters of the house designed by her brother.[4] Her bedroom and library measured no more than 70 square meters. Nevertheless, no private client had deeper pockets than she in 1920s Vienna. As far as her new house was concerned, 'time and money were never allowed to matter', as another Wittgenstein sister, Hermine, wrote in her diary. 'Gretl' gave a totally free rein to her little brother 'Lukie'.[5]

Margaret was following in her father's footsteps to some degree. Karl Wittgenstein had been a major architectural patron. He had been the only private funder of the construction of the Secession building. He not only bought the land, but also paid for the building and for the running of the exhibitions. He had his daughter's portrait painted by Gustav Klimt, one of the Secession's firebrand founders. He also hired Josef Hoffmann to design her conjugal apartment in Berlin and the family vacation house in the picturesque village of Hochreit, in Lower Austria.[6]

By the time Margaret was having her house built, in the mid-1920s, she had, naturally, moved beyond the 1890s cult of the Secession. In fact, she so disliked Klimt's portrait that she may have redone her lips with her own paint brush and, in any event, never exhibited it in her house.[7] In the tradition of other Jewish *Salonieren*,[8] she opened her living room to intellectuals, but she limited her invitations to one group: those logical positivist members of the Vienna Circle who held her brother in awe. Her one purpose was to integrate him within this supportive group of colleagues in Vienna.[9]

Why did Ludwig Wittgenstein accept an architectural commission in 1927? He had no architectural training. His only previous design experience involved building a rudimentary summer shack overlooking a fjord in Skjolden, Norway, in 1913, the year his father died. More significantly, not only was he architecturally illiterate, but upon the publication of his *Tractatus Logico-Philosophicus* he had become one of the most famous logicians of his generation and was seen as the intellectual heir of the then towering figure of Bertrand Russell. Ludwig Wittgenstein's treatise was seen as the next step following Russell and Alfred North Whitehead's monumental *Principia Mathematica* (1910–13).[10] He was feted by most of the Vienna Circle. Rudolf Carnap, a leader of the circle, described him in 1926 as the thinker who had given him the greatest inspiration. Wittgenstein was also admired by two Austro-Hungarian geniuses who were to found the applied mathematics department at Princeton, Felix Morgenstern and John von Neumann. Another of Wittgenstein's genius admirers, John Maynard Keynes, captured this adulation at Cambridge, joking that 'God arrived on the 5.15' when Wittgenstein came in by train in the fall of 1929 – once he had competed Margaret's house.[11]

In order to get a sense of what might have made Wittgenstein abandon his own field for architecture, one must understand that in the year his *Tractatus* was published, 1921, he underwent a crisis. Although he was celebrated internationally, his personal life had been rocked by tragic events. He had been on active duty for the full duration of an apocalyptic war before being taken prisoner. He shared in the trauma of the whole of Europe, eager to rid itself of the remnants of a culture which had created the conditions for the most horrendous war in history, and begin anew.

And an angst haunted the family. Karl Wittgenstein was not a nurturing, supportive father. He could not abide any signs of weakness among his sons. His three daughters escaped his scourge, as did the seventh child in line, the resilient Paul, slightly older than Ludwig, who became a famous pianist and continued to play professionally to great acclaim, even after he lost one of his hands in the war.[12] But the three older brothers committed suicide over a period of five years. One symptom of Ludwig's own self-punishing tendency was that in 1921 he relinquished his share of the inheritance which he had received in 1913, upon the death of his father, and distributed it among his sisters. Another was that for the next six years, up until 1927, he abandoned an assuredly glorious academic career at Cambridge and went into a self-imposed exile. He enrolled at a primary-school teachers' college, then set off for small villages in the backwaters of nearby Lower Austria –

Trattenbach, Puchberg, Otterthal and Kirchberg am Wechsel – to teach the children of the illiterate local farm communities in a program initiated by the social-democrat educational reformer Otto Glöckel.

Given the high suicide rate among the Wittgenstein brothers, by 1927 Margaret was seriously concerned about Ludwig's mental health and made it her duty to include him in her project to build a radically modern house, in order to draw him back to Vienna. She had first hired the architect Paul Engelmann to design the house. He had been a close friend of Ludwig's since before the war and, along with Richard Neutra and Rudolph Schindler, among others, had studied under Adolf Loos. Her ruse worked. Ludwig threw himself into the task, even signing the plans alongside his friend. Eventually he came to dominate the entire project, enlisting another of Loos's private pupils, Jacques Groag, to act as his foreman.[13] Engelmann's subsequent commissions for domestic architecture in Israel were very different. He adopted the Loosian *Raumplan* ('space mapping'),[14] of which there is no trace in the Wittgenstein House.

The house Ludwig Wittgenstein designed with Engelmann was in the international architectural vanguard. By 1929, however, when the house was completed, there was nothing unique about a stark, unornamented, white stucco cuboid exterior that used the new lightweight but strong ferro-concrete construction technology. The house belonged to a movement that had already swept across Europe. By 1927, this movement in fact had reached a climax with the Weissenhof Siedlung Exhibition, organized by Mies van der Rohe, featuring houses designed by Walter Gropius, Ernst May, Le Corbusier, Mart Stam and Hannes Meyer, among others. All of them, except for Josef Frank's, as we have seen, were logical conclusions of Loos's 1908 dictum that ornament was a crime.

Ludwig Wittgenstein would have had an insider's knowledge of these projects through Paul Engelmann. In addition, he had already known Loos for about ten years. Upon receiving his share of his inheritance in 1913, Ludwig had made a gift of a small part of his fortune to deserving Austrian artists, one of whom had been Adolf Loos (among the others were Oskar Kokoschka, Else Lasker-Schüler and Rainer Maria Rilke). It was through Loos that he had originally met Engelmann.[15] Ludwig Wittgenstein maintained an ongoing relationship with Loos until after the war, though he reported to Engelmann that he found him 'infected with the most virulent bogus intellectualism'.[16]

The interior of the Wittgenstein House, like the exterior, was conceived as a tabula rasa. The floors were covered with large black plates made of an aggregate of iron and stone. In the entrance hall a bare 200-watt light bulb hung directly from the ceiling on an exposed electric cable and the walls were left in coarse, unpainted concrete. On the landing between the ground and first floors, exposed I-beams made up the support for the glazed winter garden, while four more I-beams placed at the edges of the staircase at the entrance of the house were also left exposed. At the top of the columns, there was a bizarre indentation, a stripping away of the concrete, disclosing, in lieu of a decorative capital, the dimensions of the iron beam at its reinforced ferro-concrete core (fig.56).

Its industrial aesthetic set the house apart from all other Viennese domestic architecture of the time, particularly that of Loos, who, as we have seen, had tended to indulge in richly detailed and often cosy interiors. It also set it apart from the gleamingly luxurious house Mies van der Rohe was building in nearby Brno for the Tugendhat family, with extravagantly costly stone and wood. However, Richard Neutra had incorporated Model T headlights in the staircase of his Lovell

56 Margherita Spilutini's photograph of the foyer of Wittgenstein House, the bare lightbulb and the columns recessed where a capital is usually placed

57 (left)   Wittgenstein House, window with handle

58 (right) Wittgenstein House, elevator

House by 1929. The Wittgenstein House pales next to Pierre Chareau's Maison de Verre in Paris, built at the same time (1928–31), with its even more emphatic machine aesthetic, translated into rubberized flooring, perforated sheet-metal walls and heavy industrial light fixtures.

More impressive, and in a certain sense extravagant, were the bespoke mechanical details of the house. Wittgenstein had trained at one of the leading engineering schools in Europe, at the University of Manchester, where he became one of the early inventors of the jet propeller.[17] The house is a showcase of his obvious mastery of engineering. He designed all the technical features, including small details like the iron window frames, metallic doors, door handles, double windows, window frames, door and window hinges, and even the door locks (fig.57). His love of locksmithing continued: in a film that was made of his life in Cambridge, the only person interviewed who was not a philosopher or an academic was the local locksmith, Andrew Mackay, who claimed that Wittgenstein would drop by and discuss locks with him.[18] He designed the elevator that went from the ground floor to the second floor, the dumb waiter that led from the upper kitchen on the ground floor to the lower one in the basement (figs 58 and 59), and the radiant heating system under the aggregate iron and stone floor that turned the whole house into a very effective heater. And, finally, he designed one-centimeter-thick iron 'curtains' that could effortlessly be pulled up to the ground floor from the basement by a pole inserted at the top, thanks to a system of pulleys (fig.60). All the doors between the different rooms on the ground floor were also iron. Clearly, Wittgenstein was concerned with making a lasting contribution to architecture.

But, again, with the exception of the iron curtains, the mechanics of the Wittgenstein House had at least near equivalents. One was

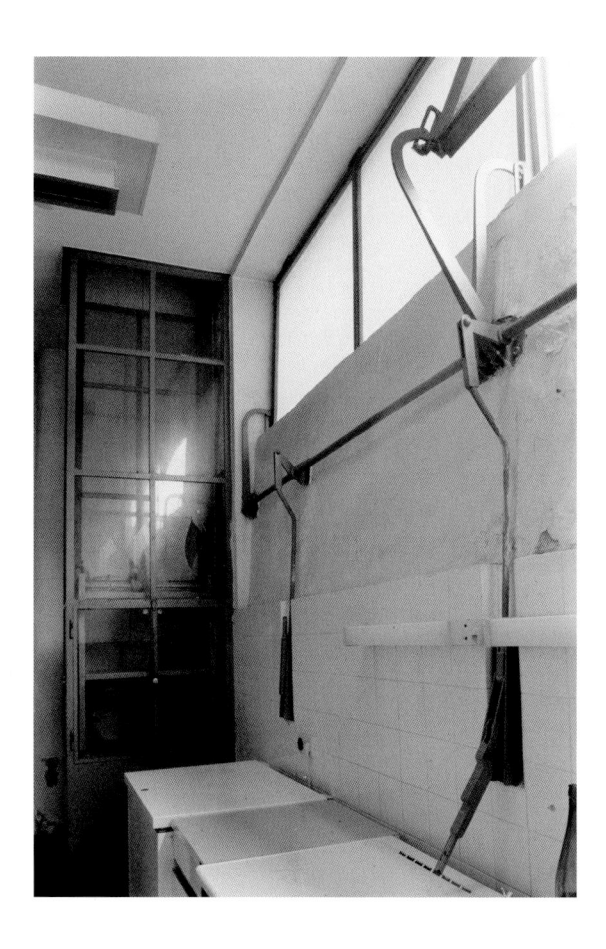

Leendert Cornelis van der Vlugt's Van de Leeuw House in Rotterdam. In Neutra's words, this was 'one of the most modern houses I have ever dreamed of', with its 'English sheet rubber to cover the floors and winding metal stairways to microphonic conversations at the entrance, exhausts for cigarette smoke as soon as it leaves your mouth, complicated dashboards of switches for our guest beds to activate all kinds of illumination, move the window drapes, electronically turn on and off the hot and cold water in the bathroom'.[19] Chareau's Maison de Verre displayed mechanical fixtures such as wheels for opening the ventilators, pivoting shelves concealed in the wall between the small sitting room and the pantry hallway, a curved metal closet door with an inner wooden door fitted for storing shoes, and a semicircular dressing table of glass and tubular steel attached by a hinge to a column, allowing it to pivot on a conical roller. Even in Mies's luxuriously clad Tugendhat House in Brno (1928–30), the two large windows opposite the onyx wall and the dining area could be retracted via electric motors all the way to the floor.

What makes the Wittgenstein House arguably unique, and not just noteworthy, is the role it played in its creator's self-reinvention as a philosopher of language. Between his *Tractatus Logico-Philosophicus*

59 (left)   Wittgenstein House, dumb waiter

60 (right)   Wittgenstein House, succession of windows in the reception area on the ground floor. Originally mirrors were placed between them. These windows were blocked with bespoke 'iron curtains'

in 1921 and his *Philosophical Investigations* (published in 1953), his thinking underwent a radical transformation. In the first book, Wittgenstein was firmly within the tradition of Russell and Whitehead and the logical positivism of Carnap and other members of the Vienna Circle, all of whose works followed on from the great Gottlob Frege's *Foundations of Arithmetic*. Like the other notable Fregeans, Wittgenstein thought it made sense to try to construct a logical system from simple axioms that would guarantee a valid outcome. Moreover, he believed that all valid conclusions could be built out of these basic axioms, and, in turn, that the sciences would be unified by these shared starting points. He clung to the idea that language, made up of these truths, was a mirror of the world, one that could be purified or rationalized.

By the time of his *Philosophical Investigations*, these assumptions were overturned. For Wittgenstein, it no longer made sense to try and purify language in order to make it into a more perfect mirror of reality. Language, in fact, did not mirror reality. It had an instrumental rather than a reflective function. It acted, rather, as a 'language game' or a 'toolbox' in directing actions upon reality.

The house Wittgenstein designed appears to have been pivotal in this transformation, but not in the way it is usually understood. One of Wittgenstein's biographers has equated it with the *Tractatus*:[20] according to this interpretation both the book and the house express a predilection for rigorous rationality.[21] In other words, the house was an example of the 'purification' that Wittgenstein had upheld as his aim in the *Tractatus*.

The idea of a building representing a purification or rationalization of architectural language might have been germane to the architecture of Wittgenstein's architect contemporaries, such as Mies, Gropius, Le Corbusier or Rietveld. Rudolf Carnap was invited by Gropius in November 1929 to present his *Logical Construction of the World* in order to reveal the link between logical positivism and Bauhaus architecture. Carnap used the metaphor of the house to describe how a representation of the world could be corrected, perfected, made complete. The idea was that all knowledge should be codified by a single standard language of science, and above all that there should be a project of rational reconstruction, in which ordinary-language concepts were gradually to be replaced by more precise equivalents.[22]

But it is unlikely that the purification of architectural language was the ultimate aim of Wittgenstein in the design of his house. He was not interested in perfection. The house was more of an attempt to create a tabula rasa on which to design a new world, one which eschewed a single hierarchical order, imposed top-down, and one whose logic was not unitary but distributed. What is certain is that the book he wrote in 1929 while building it, *Philosophical Remarks*, generally thought of as a forerunner of his more mature *Philosophical Investigations*, had nothing to do with Fregean views. On the contrary: they were anti-Fregean.

Wittgenstein's anti-Fregean turn predates by just four or five years the revolutionary works on incompleteness in 1931 by the two greatest logicians of the twentieth century, Kurt Gödel and Alfred Tarski, both students at the University of Vienna. They are famous for overturning the Fregean system that had underpinned work by Russell, Carnap, the logical positivists of the Vienna School and the young Wittgenstein.

Although Wittgenstein lacked the mathematical and logical training of Gödel and Tarski, he already sensed the Fregean theory was flawed, that it could not take some inconsistencies into account. Indeed, his book ends on a note of extreme skepticism regarding Frege: '*Wovon man nicht sprechen kann, darüber muss man schweigen*' ('What cannot be talked about must be left unspoken').[23] This would seem to imply that Wittgenstein sensed that the explanatory power of Frege's theoretical construct was fundamentally flawed. By the same token, this meant that he felt – correctly – that the value of his own work, in spite of his present fame, would eventually be cast in doubt. It would not be unreasonable to assume that this was an important factor in the punishment Wittgenstein inflicted upon himself for six years.

In *Philosophical Investigations* Wittgenstein used the house as a metaphor, just as Carnap had done at the Bauhaus lecture. But, rather than searching for a clarification of the Fregean concept of language, he threw away the concept altogether and drew up a new one, on a totally clean slate.

It was in the process of building the house that Wittgenstein grasped his important realizations. The first page of the *Investigations* reveals that his insights about the nature of language came from the use of it by builders. No wonder that for the rest of his days he carried around a cherished notebook in which he had glued photographs of the house. Building the house changed his life.

We have seen what architecture meant for Wittgenstein's radical new philosophy of language. But this philosophy also informed the architectural language of the house. It would explain the building's

61 Wittgenstein House. The door heights differ from room to room, as do the patterns of the iron and stone aggregate floor plates

most original feature, namely that there does not seem to be one unifying compositional logic uniting its different rooms. It lacks, in other words, what he may have seen as a Fregean idea of overall completeness. Each room, each floor, is a self-contained unit.

One of the most legendary stories about the building of the house is that Wittgenstein returned to the site one day after an absence and, upon surveying the construction work, made the builders change the height of one ceiling by three centimeters.[24] Unfortunately, the current owners of the house have repaired the walls and ceilings, and therefore it is no longer possible to get an exact idea of the original proportions of the rooms. But there are two oddities in the house that can only be the result of extreme meticulousness. One is the height of the doors. They differ, even when they are contiguous (figs 61 and 62). The door to the room I stayed in was a different height from that leading to the immediately adjacent bathroom, and from that of the the bedroom next to mine. Each door, in Wittgenstein's terminology, might be leading to a space structured on the basis of its own, individual 'language game'. Each, in other words, might have had its own autonomous proportional system, dictating its proportions in their minutest detail. The second oddity is the pattern of the floor slabs on the ground floor. It is not continuous. Each room – the bedroom, the study, the music room, the foyer, the dining room – has a pattern of its own.

This does not mean there is no relation between these different units. The house is a construction which is built from the ground up, from the different parts. It is an order made up of sub-orders. Although incomplete and imperfect, there is a higher standing order that accommodates sub-orders. Alan Turing, Wittgenstein's student, might have described it as the design of a distributed algorithm capable of recreating concurrent systems. When, in 1929, Wittgenstein was granted a doctorate at Cambridge on the basis of his book, he wrote in his diary that he hoped his examiners 'would never understand it'; in other words he hoped they would never realize how dated it was soon to become.

62 Wittgenstein House, entrance seen from the foyer, photographed by Margherita Spilutini. The doors on either side differ in height

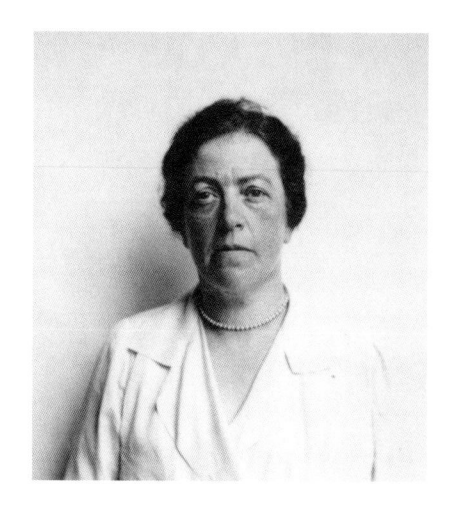

63 (left)   Margaret Wittgenstein. Photograph by Ludwig Wittgenstein and Moritz Nähr. Wittgenstein Archive, Cambridge

64 (middle)   Hermine Wittgenstein. Photograph by Ludwig Wittgenstein and Moritz Nähr. Wittgenstein Archive, Cambridge

65 (right)   Helene Wittgenstein. Photograph by Ludwig Wittgenstein and Moritz Nähr. Wittgenstein Archive, Cambridge

By now, Wittgenstein had solved what had become a profound existential problem, one he had been wrestling with during his six-year exile from academia. All he now needed was the free and stimulating intellectual world of Cambridge to start working on his revolutionary *Philosophical Investigations*, which was finally published by his disciples in 1953, two years after his death.

By involving him in the design of her house, Margaret gave her adored brother a second life. The notebook he took back with him to Cambridge contains, besides images of the house, four photographs taken by him shortly before the construction began:[25] head shots of each of his three sisters and himself. To these is added a fifth, a single composite face fusing that of Wittgenstein with those of his sisters, resulting from the overlay of all four negatives (figs 63–7). This composite was developed by Moritz Nähr, one of Vienna's best photographers and a close friend of the Wittgenstein family. This may be the origin of yet another concept he worked out in the *Philosophical Investigations*, that of 'family resemblances'.[26] This could mean a couple of things. It could indicate that he had transgender impulses and saw himself as a woman. It may also reveal that he identified with his caring, life-affirming sisters rather than with his tortured brothers. The fact is he was now acting according to his sisters' 'rules of the game' and as part of their *Lebensform*, that is, life itself.

With Adolf Loos's houses of this period, we leave the exalted sphere of Ludwig and Margaret Wittgenstein and enter a less radical world, although equally innovative and anti-conformist. From 1920 to 1924, while Loos was working on the Siedlung program as a militant social democrat, he was also receiving commissions for what were to become the most celebrated private houses of his career. The first of these was his Rufer House, for Joseph and Marie Rufer, sugar importers and members of Arnold Schoenberg's avant-garde circle. The next was for Tristan Tzara, the founder of the Dada movement in Paris. This was followed by his Moller Haus in Vienna and his Müller House in Prague. The house he designed for Josephine Baker, which was never built, also belongs to this series.

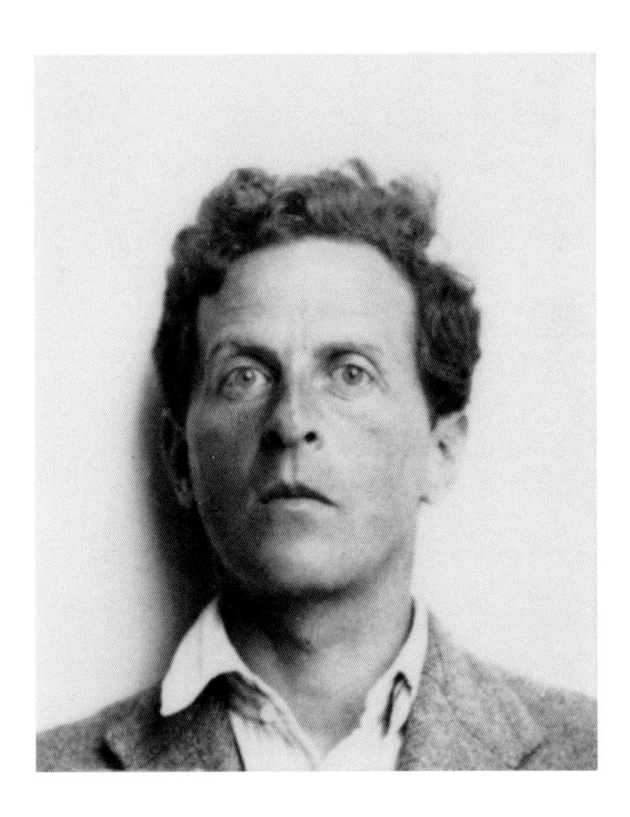

What characterizes these houses is that they constituted architectural split personalities. The impenetrable exterior served as a mask for an opulent interior, as opposed to the modernist houses by Le Corbusier, van der Vlugt or Neutra, not to mention Ludwig Wittgenstein, who all employed modestly priced materials. What also makes them unique is that they are the clearest examples of what Loos's student Heinrich Kulka called the *Raumplan* ('space mapping'), an intricate network of interlocking spaces of vastly contrasting proportions, all connected by a discontinuous network of stairs of different lengths.[27] Before 1916, the floors in a Loos house had been uninterruptedly even, as in the Steiner House of 1910, the Stössl House of 1911, the Horner House of 1912, the Scheu House of 1912 and the Duschnitz House of 1915. However, in the Mandl House of 1916 and the Strasser House of 1918–19 Loos devised a split level at the entrance, a cloakroom surmounted by a sitting room.[28]

The Rufer House of 1922 is the first to display in a fully fledged way this new design principle of Loos's. Here it is no longer just a case of stacking two rooms, but of creating this entirely new spatial concept. Four drawings Loos made of the almost perfectly cubic house, measuring 10 by 10 by 12 meters and with deceptively simple, all-white

66 (left) Ludwig Wittgenstein. Photograph by Ludwig Wittgenstein and Moritz Nähr. Wittgenstein Archive, Cambridge

67 (right) Composite photograph by Ludwig Wittgenstein and Moritz Nähr. Wittgenstein Archive, Cambridge

68 (above)   Adolf Loos, Rufer House

69 (opposite)   Adolf Loos, Rufer House

and stucco façades, reveal a new, complicated distribution of floor and ceiling heights within, requiring a multitude of staircases of varying lengths and rotating patterns (figs 68 and 69). The strickingly irregular placing of the windows relates to the different internal units of the house, where its pinwheel plan opens out into spatial complexity: low-ceilinged, intimate, private, small, nook-like spaces connected by staircases to much grander and more airy two-storey reception areas. 'My architecture is not conceived by drawings,' he would state in retrospect, 'but by spaces. I do not draw plans, facades or sections . . . For me, the ground floor, first floor does not exist . . . There are only interconnected continual spaces, rooms, halls, terraces . . . Each space needs a different height . . . These spaces are connected so that ascent and descent are not unnoticeable.'[29]

Next came the house Loos designed for the Jewish Romanian founder of the Dada movement, Tristan Tzara (1896–1963), a Communist, future Spanish Republican anti-fascist combatant, then member of the French Resistance. Tzara was a prolific writer, an essayist, playwright, literary critic, composer, gallerist, film director and art collector. The two had met in Zurich, perhaps through their common friend Oskar Kokoschka, who had written a puppet play that had been staged by Tzara in that city in 1917.

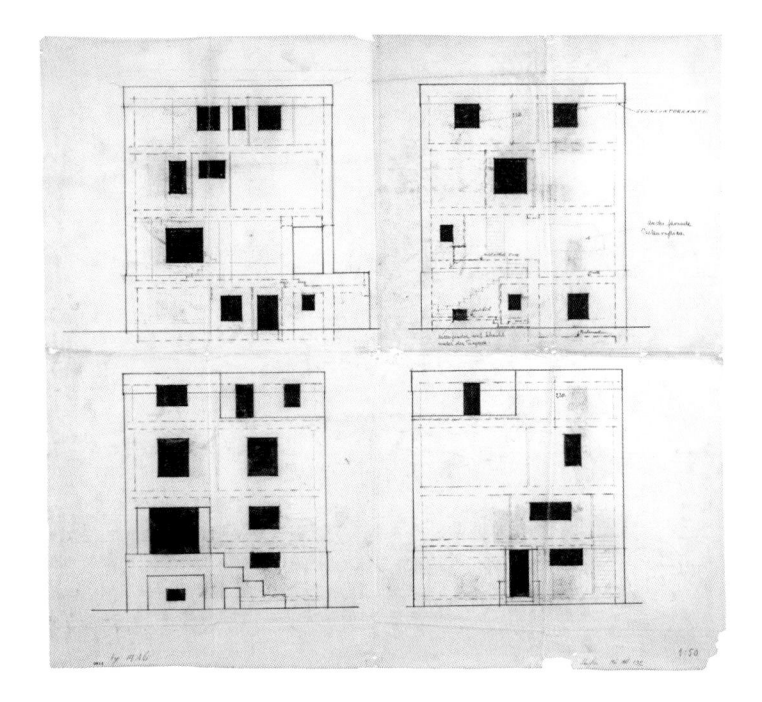

By 1925, Tzara could afford any architect. The dowry of his new wife, the Surrealist poet Greta Knudson, brought him a small fortune. He was in close contact with an astonishing number of the myriad artists and musicians who came together in *entre-deux-guerres* Paris. His circle included André Breton, Francis Picabia, Paul Eluard, Louis Aragon, Giorgio de Chirico, Man Ray, Marcel Duchamp, Max Ernst, Hans Arp, Igor Stravinsky, Kurt Schwitters, Eric Satie, Ezra Pound, Theo van Doesburg, Ossip Zadkine, Sonya Delaunay, El Lissitzky, Serge Diaghilev, René Char, Nancy Cunard, Pablo Neruda, Ilya Ehrenburg, Elsa Triolet, Pablo Picasso, Michel Leiris, Raymond Queneau and Claude Levi-Strauss, not to mention Le Corbusier, whom he had helped to organize the opening event at the Esprit Nouveau Pavilion in 1925, a paean to industrial aesthetics. So why did he choose Adolf Loos?

One can only guess, but perhaps Tzara was attracted by the *Raumplan* and the novel discontinuities it created, disrupting familiar sequences of spaces with its way of nesting them one inside the other. Perhaps he saw in it a device that he could appropriate in the service of his own playfully subversive, iconoclastic artistic vision. In 1924, the year the house was commissioned, Tzara had presented his *A Handkerchief of Clouds: A Tragedy in Fifteen Acts*, which had been performed by the Ballets Russes and whose libretto was illustrated by Juan Gris. Based on a rewriting of Shakespeare's *Hamlet*, it disrupted the continuity of the original play in the same way the *Raumplan* did with space. It fragmented and disconnected its parts and reassembled them following a dream-like labyrinthine logic. The result in both cases was a complex structure, marked by disruptions and fragmentation, in which disparate pieces which had been dislocated from the whole were incongruously 'nested' together.

There is, of course, a functional dimension to the layout of the house. The bottom two floors are occupied by a rental unit, while the upper three, of which only two were actually built, was home to Tzara and his wife. This division is clearly expressed on the façade, which is divided horizontally in two. On the inside, one staircase leads from the ground floor and connects only with the rental unit, while another circumvents the rental unit and leads up two flights to the apartment above. Basically, it is in the apartment of the Tzaras that an element of Dada 'aesthetics of discontinuity' exists thanks to the almost absurd fragmentation of spaces created by the proliferation of stairs, excessive even by Loos's standards.[30]

The stairs may have provided an additional interest for Tzara, who was, at the time, moving from Dadaism to Surrealism, possibly because of his wife's influence. *A Handkerchief* is generally considered his transition work.[31] Freud was of major importance for the Surrealists. Among the subjects they picked up on was what Freud had written about the sexual symbolism of mounting staircases, ladders and flights of stairs in his *Sex in Dreams* of 1921.[32] One memorable Surrealist photograph by Man Ray shows Tzara pensively sitting on a ledge at the top of a ladder facing a gigantic photograph of a seductive, bare-breasted woman (fig.70). From this perspective, two sequences of stairs in the Tzara House in particular invite a Freudian reading. One is the extremely narrow, five-storey spiraling flight in the so-called

70 (opposite)   Man Ray, *Portrait of Tristan Tzara*, 1921. Gelatin print

71 (above)   Adolf Loos, Tristan Tzara House façade

72 Adolf Loos, Tristan Tzara House entrance hall

servants' stairwell, to the left of the house, a typical Freudian reference to the vagina. The other is the superfluous two flights of stairs intended to lead from a study to the couple's bedroom (which was never built), a his-and-hers way of reaching the bedroom.

Finally there is the façade. If Loos's façades are masks, the façade of the Tzara House, with its two eye-like apertures, has something of the look of an African mask (fig.71). The smooth upper surface rests on a lower one that is rougher. At a time when much of Parisian avant-garde art was coming under the influence of African art, Tzara had one of the best collections of African masks and sculpture in the world and they were housed in the apartment. In fact, upon entering the house one was immediately faced with two identical African masks, on either side of the door leading to the staircase to the Tzaras' own apartment (fig.72).

It would appear from his next project that some of Tzara's Dadaism and Surrealism rubbed off on Loos. Two years later, in 1927, he designed a house for the 21-year-old Josephine Baker in Paris, where she had just begun to perform her own uninhibited, absurdist Dada version of burlesque. It is not certain whether Loos ever actually met Baker and doubtful whether the house was even buildable in the first place. In any event it was never realized. Like all Loos's houses, it was designed to have a severe, almost puritanical façade, in black-and-white striped marble cladding which belied the complexity of the interior (fig.73). The spaces of the three-storey interior are laid out with the usual Loosian profusion of stairs, but what is most astonishing is the transparent glass and steel swimming pool at its epicenter. It is

73 Adolf Loos, model of Josephine Baker's house

strikingly similar to the glass bath Otto Wagner had installed in his own apartment on the Köstlergasse in 1898, with which Loos had been so smitten.[33] Directly accessible from Baker's bedroom on the second floor, the glass pool was meant to be a vessel in which the immersed body of the bathing beauty would be visible from above the surface and from a sideways corridor that ran around it. In Loos's wishful thinking, she was even visible from outside the building, through a series of windows on the outer walls of the corridor. This is not a case of simple voyeurism. From the Freudian perspective typical of the Surrealists, the orgasmic symbolism of the figure swimming in a dreamlike aquatic receptacle is clear.

The Tzara House also left a mark on Loos's next private house. It has a face-like façade in which one can discern eye-like, nose-like and mouth-like openings. Loos's obsessive playful repetition with different-sized rooms connected by stairs is also present. The Moller House of 1927–8, constructed for a textile manufacturer and his wife in Vienna (fig.74). Here one finds Loos's by now signature lavish use of precious woods as wainscoting or as wall cladding. In addition, as in the Tzara House, access to the living room is by a narrow, claustrophobic flight of stairs which one encounters upon entering the front door, with a sharp twist toward the top. From the living room in the Moller House one accesses either the dining room (fig.75), via a short staircase, or a smaller inglenook-like alcove. Up another flight of stairs, from the inglenook, one reaches a library. Yet another flight leads to the bedrooms above (color plates 16 and 17).

The Müller House in Prague, Loos's last great masterpiece before he died three years later, was larger than the Moller House (fig.76). It was commissioned by the civil engineer and building contractor Frantisek Müller, partner in the building firm Kapsa & Müller, and was completed in 1930. It is Loos's most structurally complex project,

74 (left)   Adolf Loos, Moller House

75 (right)   Adolf Loos, Moller House, elevated dining room seen from the more expansive reception area

mainly because the client's company was a pioneer in the use of reinforced concrete, and he wished to turn the house into a showcase for his professional expertise as well as conspicuous consumption. Besides being his grandest and most opulent house, with the main living room completely clad in Cipollino marble and the dining room in Okoumé wood and entered through a travertine door frame, the Müller House, with its array of diminutive nooks and crannies and double-height halls, all linked by stairs, is also the most grandiose expression of his *Raumplan* concept (color plates 18 and 19). Access to the living room is once again by a narrow twisting staircase. From this very large room, not only must all the other rooms of the house – the music room, the reading room, the library, the salon, the dining room, the bedrooms – without exception be climbed up to by means of stairs, but there is at the back of the room a hypertrophic version of a flight of stairs in the form of a stepped wall (in turn concealing a normal flight of stairs).

The Wittgenstein House and these Loos houses were exceptional buildings for exceptional families in exceptional circumstances. At the same time, demand also sprang up for everyday houses for everyday people in everyday worlds, ones that were medium-priced, more down-to-earth and with a feel of hominess. This demand for quality, modern middle-class domesticity was met by the architectural firm of Strnad (pronounced 'Stranad'), Wlach and Frank (all of whom were also social democrats engaged, like Loos, in Vienna's Gemeindebau program). Founded in 1916, it specialized in interiors and single family homes. In order to complement their architectural practice, Wlach and Frank launched a medium-priced home furnishings shop that sold furniture, carpets and textiles, called Haus & Garten, in 1925. Pieces could be purchased individually or as ensembles or could be custom-ordered. The partnership was successful until anti-Semitism and the Anschluss forced Frank and Wlach into exile, respectively to Sweden in 1933 and to New York in 1938.

Oskar Wlach (1881–1963) was in charge of managing the office and Oskar Strnad (1879–1935) was the chief designer. Strnad was a friend of the conductor Bruno Walter and the director of the Volkstheater, Alfred Bernau, for whom he had designed a *Rundtheater* ('round theater') in 1918. As a friend of the celebrated actor and director Max Reinhardt, he also worked on a *Simultheater* ('simultaneous theater'), a three-part stage with a circular auditorium, in 1923 with Margarete Schütte-Lihotzky. His involvement in the theater explains why his houses too seem theatrical, as Christopher Long has noted.[34] For example, the great staircase in his Haus Wassermann (1914) in the Nineteenth District had various stage-like landings.[35]

76 Adolf Loos, Müller House

Of the three, Josef Frank (1885–1967) was the most ambitious and successful. He also belonged to what was becoming the Viennese tradition of combative architects. Like Loos, he was a friend of Otto Neurath and had worked for the ÖVSK. He also helped Neurath build his Wirtschafts- und Gesellschaftsmuseum.[36] He was an internationally recognized cultural figure with passionately held, unconventional views, on which he wrote abundantly and around which actively organized his fellow architects.

Frank took on both Josef Hoffmann and Adolf Loos for what he believed to be the dictatorial way in which they imposed their ideas on their clients. Central to his concerns, however, as it was for Hoffmann and Loos, was the status of ornament in architecture. Frank advocated an attitude of deference on the part of the architect to what he called the individual *Wohnkultur,* or lifestyle, of the client. In a 1912 essay on Frank's 1910 apartment design for his sister, Hedwig Tedesco, Wlach wrote that it was one 'in which a Persian rug, an English table, a Chinese lamp, and a Swedish blanket, etc., would form a resonant harmony which remains mutable and lives along with the life of its owners'.[37]

In his many writings, Frank would go on polemically defending his own approach versus what he saw as the overbearingly purist, regimenting approach of architect over client. The concept that perhaps best sums up his lifelong design principle appears in a late article, dated 1958 and titled 'Accidentism', in which he warmly accepts the purely emotional combination of often mismatched possessions owned by his clients.[38]

Accidentism would explain Josef Frank's manner of designing not only the architectural ornament but the order of the building, for example in the asymmetric façade of the Summer House for Hugo Bunzl (1913–14), with its seemingly arbitrarily placed windows and doors. It is also apparent in the house he designed for the Weissenhof Estate exhibition, whose multicolored pillows and divans so riled the Bauhaus architects. Frank's best-known house, for Julius and Margarete Beer (1930), is a perfect illustration of accidentism both inside and out. By the time the house was finished, there was nothing innovative about arranging rooms in a series of different sizes linked through staircases. It had become a Loos hallmark. As for the idea of the house as a pathway, presented by Frank in a mid-1930s article, 'Path and Place', this again was no longer new.[39] Le Corbusier had developed it earlier and much more daringly in the Villa Laroche

(1923–5) as the *promenade architecturale*. What was unique was the element of unpredictability and disconcerting disorder in the overall plan. The anti-CIAM, anti-Bauhaus accidentist strain of Frank's work became more extreme over time.

Josef Frank flourished in the United States. Some of his most whimsically anti-Bauhaus designs were conceived there, although never carried out, between 1940 and 1946. This was when he created his most distinctive towers for the City of New York Slum Insurance Company Housing Project, as well as a design for the UN Building. Both projects are the only ones of their kind, painted in the pastel colors and quirky decorative patterns he loved (color plates 20, 21).

For all his activity as a writer and architect, Frank is more celebrated for his textile and carpet designs, which are perhaps the ultimate statement of his anti-rationalist approach to ornament. Indeed, once he arrived in Sweden, he was fortunate to find the ideal patron for his prodigious creative energies. This was the unusually supportive textile and household goods firm of Svenskt Ten. The exuberant flora- and fauna-themed patterns, bold colors and asymmetric styles probably come closer to any of his architectural work in expressing his aesthetic vision (fig. 77).[40]

Ernst Plischke (1903–92) stands out among Viennese architects because of his commitment to a cold, functional, Bauhaus-like modernism, a result no doubt of the influence of the German architect Peter Behrens (1848–1940), who had taken over the chair of architecture at the Academy of Fine Art. His Viennese output included the much admired Employment Center in Vienna-Liesing (1930–31) and the Gamerith House on Lake Attersee (1933–4). He continued in this style in New Zealand, building a series of social housing projects around Wellington and Auckland during his stay between 1939 and 1947.[41]

Sheer elegance was the sole aim of the Hochhaus ('Tall House') of 1931–2 by Siegfried Theiss (1882–1963) and Hans Jaksch (1879–

77 (left)   Josef Frank, drawing for a hand-knotted carpet, *c*.1940. Watercolor, gouache and pencil on paper. Svenskt Tenn Archive, Stockholm

78 (right)   Josef Frank, ensconced among his accidentist textile designs in Stockholm, *c*.1950. Svenskt Tenn Archive, Stockholm

1970) in its use of the new spare, unornamented, international architectural style. This was the first high-rise in Vienna (fig. 79). Like the Gemeindebauen, it was public sector, although funded by Dollfuss's fascist federal government, which provided 60 per cent of the construction costs, probably in an attempt to act as a foil to the 234 Gemeindebauen for the working class built by Red Vienna's social democrats.[42] It was a 16-storey building containing 225 stylish apartments, 105 of which were for single young urban professionals. Like Loos's Goldman & Salatsch haberdashery just down the street, the Hochhaus was built in Vienna's historic center, in the vicinity of the imperial residence of 1893, the Hofburg, and of a great many of the patrician eighteenth-century Baroque *palais*. But, unlike the Loos building, its intention was to fit right in. The foyer, visible through a glazed entrance, was elegantly clad in finely veined white marble. After the first eight storeys, whose top aligned with that of the surrounding buildings, it was discreetly stepped backwards in a series of receding floors invisible from the street, diminishing in area until they reached the top level with its dramatic two-storey, glass-enclosed restaurant. The building was multi-functional. Residents could order gourmet food to be delivered, use various large terraces for gymnastics, and dine and dance at the panoramic rooftop restaurant.[43] The top of the building allowed for extraordinary views, notably from the elegant

79 (below, left)   Theiss and Jaksch's high-rise Hochhaus emerging from the low-rise Vienna of the 1930s

80 (below, right)   Hochhaus, dramatic spiral staircase leading to the restaurant/dance hall upstairs, with a view on to the rest of the city

81 (opposite)   A fashion magazine shot taken from the roof of the Hochhaus in the mid-1930s. Vienna Municipal Library

semicircular steel stairwells, mullioned in glass and thin steel, in the interior courts (figs 80 and 81).

Among the residents of the much sought-after building was the dapper stage actor Paul Henreid.[44] To his escape following the fascist putsch of 1934 he owes the best role of his career: Victor Laszlo, the debonair resistance hero on the run in *Casablanca* (1942). Four other major characters of the film had also been members of the thriving Viennese cabaret and experimental theater scene: the director Michael Curtiz (born Mihály Kertész); the score's composer, Max Steiner; Peter Lorre, who played Ugarte, the sleazy underworld figure; and Szöke Szakáll, who played Carl, the lovable head waiter.

The commercial sector, although relatively sluggish in the 1930s, was a source of income for at least one notable architectural office. Victor Gruen (born Viktor Grünbaum, 1903–80), a member of the younger generation, managed to make a small fortune in Vienna by using his keen business acumen to set up a profitable practice in store design. The offspring of a prominent Jewish lawyer's family in the First District, he had been such an active social democrat since high school that he was chosen to write Loos's obituary in the *Arbeiter Zeitung* in 1933. Although he had had to leave architecture school early to support his mother and siblings when his father died immediately after the First World War, he opened his own practice in 1932, just two years before the Social Democrats' housing program was forcefully shut down by the Austro-fascist government in 1934. Otherwise, he would have thrown himself into social housing. An article he wrote in 1931 in *Der Kuckuck* details his ideas of functional modern furniture design for the typically small apartments of the program as 'the foundation for a new culture that is authentic rather than fake'.[45] He also practiced interior design. Among the small remodeling commissions he received in 1934 was one for the design of an apartment of Otto Bauer, the head of the Social Democratic Party.

Having been brought up on the Wollzeile, one of the liveliest of the First District's shopping streets, Gruen, like Loos, was remarkably successful at shop design. Ultimately he was also more innovative and a more successful businessman. His first design was the Parfumerie at the exclusive Bristol Hotel. Like Loos, he used the device of a reflective surface on the rear wall with an additional band of mirror across the ceiling to give the tiny store, only 2.5 meters wide, a feeling of spaciousness. But instead of expensive wood and marble, he used shiny white lacquer. His lighting effects were part of his general tendency to replace the snobbish Loosian element with more egalitarian bling. This came naturally to Gruen. When he was not designing, he was pursuing his love of acting in the Jewish socialdemocratic Politische Kabarett (Political Cabaret), which he founded in 1926 on the Riemergasse, next door to his family's apartment. At the Singer shop, and at Deutsch's tailor shop, he created an even more recessed arcade than the one Loos had included in his Knize shopfront. The entrances were flanked by display windows that were fully glazed and where goods were dramatically spotlit, like actors on the stage (fig. 82). His work earned him early international recognition, and he was published in *Architecture d'aujourd'hui* and *Architecture Review* in 1938. His growing success unfortunately coincided with the Anschluss and Gruen had to flee for his life to New York through Switzerland, famously carrying nothing but his passport, having been forewarned by a stagehand, Felix Slavik, who went on to become Mayor of Vienna in the early 1970s.[6]

Gruen was as active when he got to New York as he had been in Vienna (fig. 83). He pursued his love of cabaret performance and joined the troupe known as the Refugee Artists Group. In his role as an architect, he started out in 1939 by designing Lederer de Paris, a shopfront on a prime location in Manhattan, for Hermann Lederer, the owner of a luxury leather goods store in Vienna and the sponsor of Gustav Klimt's *Beethoven Frieze* at the Secession building. His second design was on Fifth Avenue, for the Viennese confectioners Emil Altman and Ernest Kühne, also Jewish refugees from Vienna, whose shop on the Graben, designed by Josef Hoffman, still stands today. Eventually Gruen moved to California, where he conceived what he is most famous for, namely the first shopping mall in history. He initially envisioned shopping centers as a communal space that brought people together. Developers found his ideas interesting, but he had a hard time securing finance. One of his first major projects, Northland Center in Detroit, incorporated many elements of his original vision, including public gardens, a bank, a post office, auditoriums, artworks and fountains.

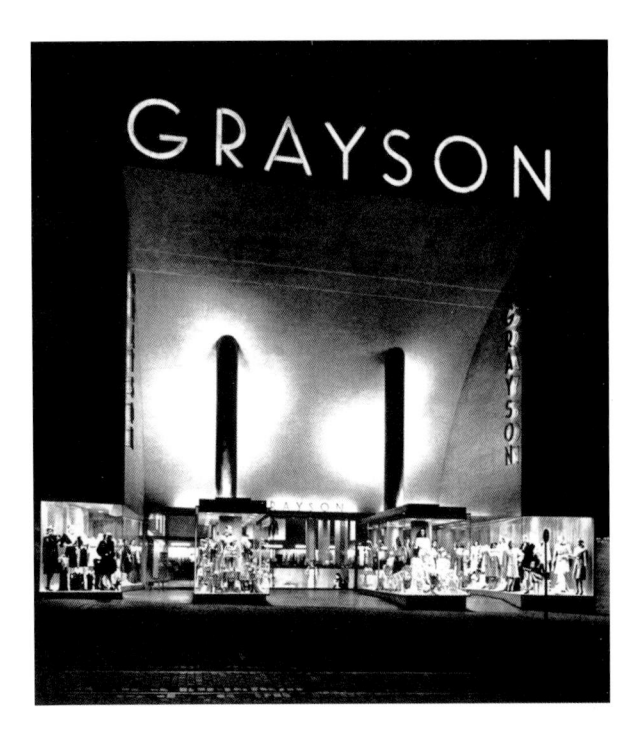

It was with a commission from the owners of Dayton Department Stores for the Southdale Center in Edina, Minnesota, that Gruen made history, albeit unwittingly. He had conceived the Southdale Center as bringing vitality and social interaction to the suburbs, with houses, apartments, schools and offices surrounding the mall. It was not to be. His clients threw out all the extra amenities, which would have made the center a little more like Gruen's Wollzeile in nature, and opted for a mono-functional shopping area. Beyond its collection of shops, Southdale Center did provide a light-filled interior, however, which he called the 'Garden Court of Perpetual Spring' – a large open space with a goldfish pond and aviary, sculptures and a sidewalk café – and more than 75,000 people attended the grand opening. But its influence ultimately contributed to suburban sprawl and urban decline as shopping malls displaced downtown retail stores. What Gruen had not anticipated was that, far from bringing the cosmopolitan energy of the urban plaza to the suburbs, his innovation – and the many copycats it inspired – encouraged the very kind of sprawl he sought to mitigate. His critics were legion. Even Frank Lloyd Wright later weighed in; he said Gruen 'should have left downtown downtown'. Eventually, Gruen would turn against his own work. In his own words, he now wanted to liberate American cities from 'the terror of the

82 (left)   Victor Gruen, Deutsch Men's Shop, Vienna. *Architecture d'Aujoud'hui*, April 1938, p. 18

83 (right)   Victor Gruen, Grayson Department Store, New York. *Architectural Forum*, September 1941, p. 196

FACADE OF THE PROPOSED MAX REINHARDT THEATRE IN NEW YORK CITY

automobile'. He envisioned 'livable' and 'lovable' spaces that would get people out of their cars and interacting with each other.[47] He started writing books in this vein, but it was when he returned to Vienna in 1968, and spent his last years there, that he was able to mend his ways and help save the city from plans to construct a freeway through the First District and turn it into a multi-functional pedestrian zone only partly devoted to shopping, as we will see in Chapter 7.[48]

Gruen was not an exception. A significant proportion of this phenomenally gifted generation of Viennese architects flowered far from the fertile ground which brought it forth. For many of them, mostly Jewish but not all, there was no choice but to emigrate. The reasons were financial or racial, but mostly the latter.

One beneficiary of the Austrian-Jewish brain drain was the United States.[49] Cape Canaveral owes its engineering to the Technische Hochschule-educated engineer Anton Tedesko,[50] and the Ziegfeld

Follies owes much of its spectacular stage design to Josef Urban. Urban, a graduate of Otto Wagner's class at the Academy of Fine Arts, was an exceptionally prolific architect, stage and graphic designer. It might be said that he was to architecture, design and scenography what Florenz Ziegfeld was to musicals: larger than life, and lavishly over the top. Upon immigrating to the US in 1911, he almost immediately found fame and fortune, first as designer and stage director for the short-lived but influential Boston Opera Company, with 51 productions for the Metropolitan Opera of New York between 1917 and his death on 10 July 1933. His stage designs included *Apple Blossoms*, a 1919 musical in which Fred and Adele Astaire, also of Viennese extraction through their father, made their debuts. But his biggest break was in 1914, when Ziegfeld commissioned him for the design of the Ziegfeld Follies Theater, along with all of its stage designs. He also designed the never-built Reinhardt Theater in 1928 for his compatriot and fellow émigré, Max Reinhardt, and went on to create the classic art deco New School for Social Research in New York in 1930, along with much of boom-town Miami Beach, including the palatial Mar-a-Lago, now owned by Donald Trump (figs 84–86).[51]

Friedrich (Frederick) Kiesler (1890–1965) was another classic American success story. His designs had been somewhat sui generis in Vienna, where he had copied the work of the Suprematists and De Stijl, notably in his 'electro-mechanical' stage. In 1925, Josef Hoffmann,

84 (opposite)   Josef Urban, design for the Max Reinhardt Theater, New York, 1928. Watercolor on paper. Josef Urban Collection, Rare Book and Manuscript Library, Columbia University

85 (above, left)   Josef Urban, shop for the Kaufmann Department Store. Josef Urban Collection, Rare Book and Manuscript Library, Columbia University

86 (above, right)   Josef Urban, New School, façade. Josef Urban Collection, Rare Book and Manuscript Library, Columbia University

who was the director of the Austrian section of the International World Fair in *entre-deux-guerres* Paris, had given Kiesler the task of installing the Austrian theater exhibition at the Exposition Internationale des Arts Décoratifs et Industriels Modernes. Like Loos, Kiesler was in his element. As the area for his exhibition in the Grand Palais was far greater than his original plan had allowed for, he used the leftover space to build his Raumstadt, a suspended 50-meter-high structure made of intersecting wooden beams (fig. 87), in keeping with the Russian Pavilion by Konstantin Melnikov and Le Corbusier's Pavilion de l'Esprit Nouveau. It was accompanied by a manifesto entitled *La Contre-architecture* co-signed by the disciple of cubism, the art historian Maurice Raynal.[52] It was a sensation. Helped by the American expatriate Sylvia Beach, who had just founded her bookstore, Shakespeare and Company, and published James Joyce's *Ulysses*, Kiesler then decamped for New York.

New York provided Kiesler with the stimulating environment in which he could keep evolving the extraordinary ideas he had been nurturing in Vienna. Among the masterpieces he produced there is the 1929 interior of the Film Guild Cinema in Greenwich Village, featuring a screen in the form of an eye whose iris could contract and expand, as he explained, in relation to the geometry of the projected film (fig. 88). He also developed plans for a 'projectoscope', offering projections on multiple surfaces, which were not realized at the time, but which were a precursor of Charles and Ray Eames's multiple projections for the US pavilion in Moscow in 1958.[53] Kiesler also developed 'co-reality' – an 'exchange of interacting forces' – and 'correalism', the 'science of the laws of interrelationships' which express 'the dynamics of continual interaction between man and his natural and technological environments . . .'[54] He made sure that his most high-profile designs were recorded by some of the greatest photographers of the time, something no other architect had done. For Peggy Guggenheim's legendary Art of This Century gallery, he designed a new kind of correalist setting for surrealist art, not only the rounded walls and projecting arms on which the paintings were thrust forward, away from the walls, but also its furniture, the Correalist Rocker and the Correalist Instrument. Guggenheim was photographed by Berenice Abbott on the Rocker (fig. 89).[55] Kiesler also asked Irving Penn to photograph him and his Endless House (fig. 90). Still, he would have to

87 (opposite)   Frederick Kiesler, Raumstadt, *The Endless City*

88 (above)   Frederick Kiesler's Film Guild Cinema, 1928, meant for avant-garde cinema. The eye, which opened to reveal the screen, turned the entire theater into a surreal metaphorical camera obscura, to make the experience of the film more immersive, unlike showings in the ornate movie palaces of the day

89 (above)   Friedrich Kiesler photographed by Berenice Abbott, sitting in the gallery he designed for Peggy Guggenheim's Art of This Century gallery, on a chair he also designed, called the Correalist Instrument

90 (opposite)   Irving Penn, *Frederick Kiesler with his Endless House Model*

wait until 1965, the year of his death at 75, for one of his architectural masterpieces, the Shrine of the Book, constructed in Jerusalem in partnership with Armand Bartos, to be memorialized.

One could say that Urban and Kiesler were working in architectural idioms that were international. Surprisingly, perhaps as a way of overcompensating for the trauma of being uprooted, the majority of Viennese architects who went into exile at this time transformed themselves into regionalists in their adoptive countries. This is true of Josef Urban's late works in Florida. The architecture of other Viennese émigrés was very different. The regionalist architecture and writings of most Viennese émigrés were shaped by Adolf von Hildebrandt's concept of space. Hildebrandt had written the bestselling *Das Problem der Form in der Bildenden Kunst*,[56] which argued for a conception of sculpture not just as an isolated object but as one that shaped the space around it. Theodor Fischer translated into architecture and urban design the notions that Hildebrandt had developed for sculpture. How architecture related to the *Raum*, the space which framed it – that is, nature itself – became of utmost importance for him. 'The strength of building lies not in contrasting with nature,' he wrote, 'but in fusing with it in the highest sense.' Fischer advocated the incorporation of 'regional reference in the new architecture' through a new design process that would follow what he called the laws of 'associative connections'.[57] Hildebrandt's concept of *Raum* influenced the turn away from the folksy *Heimat*-style Tyrolean regionalism of the day, in particular by the architect Franz Baumann, who gave his buildings curvilinear forms inspired by the outlines of the surrounding Alps rather than by the vernacular architecture. The masterful ski-lift stations of the Nordkettenbahn (1927–8), in three pieces, were totally free of any vernacular reference and perfectly embedded into the contours of the Alpine topography. They incorporated new technology into a harmonious composition with the landscape.[58] This idea, which first saw the light of day in the Alps, now found its way into the work of the immigrants wherever they settled – Turkey, Japan, China, Palestine, New Zealand, Brazil and the US.

The young Turkish Republic under the modernizing Kemal Atatürk took every measure to become a haven for Austrians forced to emigrate by the Nazis.[59] Among the architects who found a refuge there was Clemens Holzmeister (1886–1983),[60] who happened to be in Ankara as Hitler's troops entered Austria in 1938. He had been professionally involved with Turkey since 1926, working for Atatürk, who had been the first president of the republic since 1923 and who was bent on attracting Europe's best and brightest in all fields. Because Holzmeister had been a supporter of the fascist government of Engelbert Dollfuss and Kurt Schuschnigg, after the Anschluss he was officially expelled from his post at the architecture section of the Academy of Fine Art by the Nazi administrators in Vienna.

Atatürk hired Holzmeister to design the government buildings of his new capital, Ankara, to help fulfill his dreams of a modern Turkey as the equal of any European country. The official architecture that had emerged in the last years of the Sultanate during the failed reform efforts of the Young Turks was in the elegant Ottoman revivalist style. It was characterized by ornate tile decoration, wide roof overhangs, scalloped broken arches, and domes carried on sculpted pendentives. Much of the capital, Istanbul, had been built in this style. When Atatürk assumed power, he moved the capital from what was perceived as the symbol of a decadent, corrupt and genocidal regime of pashas to the new location of Ankara, symbolically in the middle of the country, in the Anatolian plain. In addition, he officially rejected neo-Ottoman revivalism in favor of modern Bauhaus-inspired reinforced-concrete architecture. It became known in Turkey as the 'cubic' style.

While the main representative of the neo-regionalist 'cubic' style is generally recognized to be Sedad Hakki Eldem (1908–88),[61] it first appeared in the buildings Holzmeister designed for Ankara. While in the service of Atatürk, he designed 11 government buildings in the city, including the Grand National Assembly (1938), the Ministries of Agriculture (1934), War (1931) and the Interior (1932), the seat of the Turkish General Staff (1930) and Atatürk's private palace. From 1940 to 1945 he was Director of the Architecture Section at Istanbul Technical University. He stayed on after the war until 1954, when he retired and returned to Austria, assuming his former position at the Academy of Fine Art in Vienna until 1957.

Holzmeister is remarkable not only for the sheer quantity of buildings he designed, but equally for the central role that one particular building played in shaping the subsequent course of regionalist Turkish architecture. This is the Ministry of Defense (1929). Here the reinforced-concrete construction remained, but it was combined with elements from traditional vernacular Anatolian architecture: in particular, the practice of breaking up the façades of buildings with projecting masses in the 'cubic' manner. Some of Holzmeister's earlier buildings in Austria make use of this signature stylistic quirk, dividing the flat surfaces of buildings into a series of cubic projections whose purpose was to create a play of light and shadow. In Ankara this tendency lost its purely abstract dimension and became associated as a precedent with the Anatolian House, with its characteristic three-sided balconies. Thereafter a generally massive and monumental appearance, use of projections, large eaves and windows in traditional proportions became typical of his buildings.

Although he was a Tyrolean and built in that area, strangely, Holzmeister did not become an Alpine regionalist until he returned from Turkey after the war. Unlikely as it may seem, he appears to have imported his regionalist sensibility from Anatolia to the Tyrol. It is one of the ironies of this early phase of globalized practice that the façades of his most celebrated Tyrolean regionalist hotels, the Drei Zinnen and the Hotel Post, recall the 'cubic' form of Atatürkesque regionalism.[62]

Holzmeister was not a writer. Ernst Egli (1893–1974), who was his assistant in Turkey, on the other hand, not only wrote about Turkish regionalism, he never abandoned it. Egli's biographer argues plausibly that he was the one, in fact, who suggested the model of the Anatolian House to Holzmeister. Moreover, Sedad Hakki Eldem had been Egli's assistant at the university.[63]

Egli's writings on regionalism are a clear echo of the writings of Fischer and Hildebrandt. In 1930 he published in the Turkish journal *Türk Yurdu* an article entitled '*Mimari Muhit*' ('Architectural Environment'). He explained the title as follows: 'What I mean by the word "environment" is everything around the building, what is near, but also what is far. Light, air, sun, wind, topography, water, plants, climate, night and day . . . One can compare the environment to the embrace of a mother.' He went on to say that 'the uniqueness, superiority and movement of a person are more a product of their environment than of their race or nation.'[64]

Palestine of the 1930s became another homeland for Viennese architects, who also became regionalist once they settled in their new country.[65] Moshe Gerstel (1886–1961), who had studied at the Technical University of Vienna, arrived in Palestine in 1935 and became one of the chiefs of the Hadar District on the lower flank of Mount Carmel overlooking the sea in Haifa. His major commission was for the non-regionalist Talpiot Market. What singles him out, however, is the great number of vernacular-inspired residences he designed for wealthy Arabs outside of Hadar, which incorporated many elements from the local vernacular. Paul Engelmann, Wittgenstein's collaborator on the Wittgenstein House, was not explicit in the Mediterranean character of his architecture, but Leopold Krakauer (1890–1954), who left Vienna in 1924, was. He rejected the historicist Orientalizing style of Alexander Baerwald (1877–1930), with whom he first worked upon arriving in Haifa, in favor of something closer to the architecture of the Tyrolean Baumann. His masterful charcoal and pastel renditions of the landscapes reveal a deep fascination with the mountainous terrain of the Judean Hills,[66] something which is obvious in the way his Hotel Teltsch in Haifa (1934–5) fits into its landscape (figs 91 and 92). It is another trace of the influence of Hildebrandtian neo-regionalist sensitivity to space, in other words to the surrounding topography, a concept transposed from the Alps and adapted in this instance to Mount Carmel.[67]

China is another country where regionalism was influenced by Hildebrandt and Fischer's concern for the harmonious relationship between buildings and their surroundings. This was thanks to one Chinese student who studied in Vienna, Feng Jizhong (1915–2009), one of the major influences on the Pritzker Prize-winning architect Wang Shu, who was his student. Feng was enrolled at the Technical University of Vienna between 1939 and 1945, and then returned to China, where he became a professor and then chairman of the architecture department at Tongji University in Shanghai. Because of his run-in with the regime, his oeuvre was limited to a classic book on Chinese gardens and the design of an exquisite, poetic tea house called Helou Xuan ('Not a Simple Pavilion'), which was built in 1981 in the Square Pagoda Garden in Songjiang near Shanghai. Both are highly esteemed for the way they returned to tradition during the period when it was banned in Maoist China. In fact, Wang Shu organized an exhibition of it in 2010 at the Art Academy in Hangzhou with reconstructions in model form. The tea house was conceived, according to Feng, as a composition in which the basic element was space, something for which there was no precedent in Chinese architecture, but which echoes Hildebrandt's concept. The classical Tang Dynasty garden in which the tea house is located contains not only a famed square pagoda but other archeological remains of the Song and Tang dynasties. Markedly irregular in plan, the tea house is meant to be a place of contemplation, with the gaze of the onlooker being directed in three different ways, each one pointing toward an important view, one of which is the celebrated artificial pond dating from the founding of the garden.[68]

Even Japanese regionalism had a small Viennese component. In 1933, the Viennese designer Felice Rix (1893–1967) and her German-trained architect husband, Isaburo Ueno (1892–1972), two Josef Hoffmann protégés, invited the exiled German architect Bruno Taut (1880–1938) to visit Katsura Palace. Arata Isozaki believes this was a turning point in the redefinition of 'Japan-ness' in architecture, away from the 'big roof' style, which consisted in placing a pastiche traditional Japanese roof on top of a Western building, and toward a more profound identification with traditional spatial compositional elements and the minimalism embodied by the Katsura Palace.[69]

The two newly arrived graduates 'believed that modernism in architecture might replace the elevational eclecticism of the *teikan* style, if only they could isolate the key compositional elements common to traditional Japanese architecture and modern design. They needed, however, an authoritative spokesperson. Taut intuitively understood his role and played it to the hilt.'[70]

As far as American regionalism is concerned, Max Moses Heller (1919–2011) is an unlikely case of a non-architect having a major impact on both architecture and urban design. Born in Vienna, he escaped the Anschluss with the help of Mary Mills, a native of Greenville, South Carolina. He had encountered her, a young woman traveling in Europe, only once by chance in an outdoor café in Vienna. Following Hitler's entry into Vienna, he wrote to her out of sheer desperation requesting support for his application for residency in the US. Her father accepted and, after landing a job making shirts in a factory, Heller eventually made his way up to become mayor of the town. Under his leadership, the whole place was revitalized, based on preservation of historical buildings and landscaping of the picturesque river banks running through the heart of the town, balanced with sensitive new construction. He hired the landscape architect Laurence Halprin to convert the almost derelict Main Street into a lush, tree-lined, revitalized town center.[71]

But by far the most prominent regionalist expatriates to the US were Rudolph Schindler, Richard Neutra and Bernard Rudofsky. Although Schindler and Neutra had been disciples of Adolf Loos, both became devotees of Frank Lloyd Wright after seeing the spectacular Wasmuth Portfolio edition of 1911 featuring Wright's designs. Following Wright, both architects made 'site' – the way their buildings fitted into the surrounding landscape – a key factor in their designs, in a spirit similar to that of Fischer and Hildebrandt. Schindler and Neutra not only practiced regionalism, they preached it, as did Rudofsky.

91 (left) Leopold Krakauer, Hotel Teltsch, Haifa, 1940

92 (right) Leopold Krakauer, *Judean Hills*, 1930. Drawing, charcoal on colored paper, private collection

Rudolph Schindler (1887–1953), who arrived in the US in December 1920 at the age of 33, was a self-conscious regionalist from the start. As his biographer Judith Scheine recounts, he was immediately attracted to the work of Irving Gill (1870–1936) and to the adobe architecture in Taos. He then worked for Wright, at the time when Wright was famously excluded from the International Style exhibition because of his regionalism.[72] Schindler repeatedly complained that MoMA in New York focused on Europeans and failed to include regionalists like himself, Gregory Ain and Harwell Hamilton Harris.[73] And indeed, Hans Hollein recounts that when he tried to convince MoMA to devote an exhibition to Schindler, it was categorically turned down.[74] But Schindler called his own work 'Space Architecture', influenced perhaps by Hildebrandt and Fischer. It focused on the way interior space flowed and melded with the surrounding space. 'In my own house in 1921,' Schindler wrote in 1952, just before he died, 'I introduced features which seem to be necessary for life in California: an open-plan flat on the ground; living patios; glass walls; translucent walls; wide sliding doors; clerestory windows; shed roofs with wide shading overhangs. These features have now been generally accepted and form the basis of the contemporary California House.' He went on to criticize his master, Wright, for introducing 'modernized versions of Aztec details' which were a 'superficial attempt, completely false historically, climatically and functionally, and died at birth'.[75]

Neutra too was a Hildebrandtian regionalist from the moment he arrived in the US. Whereas Schindler had come straight from Vienna, Neutra had seen more of the world and its modern architecture before alighting in Wright's office. He had worked with Erich Mendelsohn in England and Israel, and, more importantly, he had travelled to the Netherlands and seen the architecture of van der Vlugt. He was soon off to Cuba, Brazil, Mexico, Guam and India, not to mention Switzerland. This was symptomatic of the difference between Schindler and Neutra. Neutra thought bigger. Whereas Schindler remained focused on mostly domestic architecture in Los Angeles, Neutra's regionalism took in the city as well as the building. The mere title of his book *Mysteries and Realities of Site* (1951) reveals the same concerns for the harmonious flow of space between a building and its surroundings, but the surrounding space was larger, stretching out in the case of the Desert House of 1946, commissioned by the Kaufmann family, to the foothills around Palm Springs. In addition, Neutra was an early advocate of what was to become the ecological movement, as again is obvious in the title of his *Survival through Design* of 1969.[76]

As for Bernard Rudofsky (1905–88), he was a convinced regionalist all his life. His love of Mediterranean island architecture took him from Vienna, where he had studied at the Technical University, to Procida and Capri in southern Italy and to Santorini in Greece, where he painted architecture in its relationship with the mountainous landscape. Just before the outbreak of the Second World War, he left Italy for Brazil, where his love of the vernacular led to the design of three houses, one of which won a design first prize at MoMA, and later to a long association with the museum that eventually resulted in the bestselling book about regionalist architecture based on his exhibition of the same title, his celebrated *Architecture without Architects* of 1964.[77]

Not all exiled Austrians were so fortunate. Herbert Eichholzer (1903–43) had trained as an architect in his home town of Graz and worked with Le Corbusier and Pierre Jeanneret in 1929. In 1932 he had joined the anti-fascist Schutzbund. He left Austria on the day of the Anschluss and went to work unpaid for Atelier Albert Laprade in Paris, where he built hotels and housing for the French Alps. In November 1938 he heeded the call of Clemens Holzmeister, who was eager to protect his fellow countrymen, and departed for Ankara, as did Margarete Schütte-Lihotzky. As a collaborator of Holzmeister, Eichholzer worked on projects in Ankara, including the Turkish Parliament and ministry buildings, but at the end of April 1940 he left the safe haven of Turkey and returned to Graz where, as a member of the underground, he joined the government administration. Both Schütte-Lihotzky and Eichholzer were captured in 1941 and imprisoned. In 1943 Eichholzer was executed.[78] Schütte-Lihotzky survived.[79]

This brings us to the next period in Austria's architectural history, the period of Nazi occupation, from 1938 to 1945.

6

Nazi Ostmark
1938–1945

Hitler's *Mein Kampf* (1925) opens with the demand for the restoration of Austria to Germany. 'German Austria must return to the great German Motherland, and not because of any economic considerations. No, and again no: even if such a union were unimportant from an economic point of view; yes, even if it were harmful, it must nevertheless take place. One blood demands one Reich.'[1]

This union was opposed by the Austrian fascist government, but once Chancellor Dollfuss had been assassinated by a Nazi, the coast was clear. The Anschluss took place on 12 March 1938, when Hitler declared what was now Ostmark to be part of the Third Reich. After the unopposed entry of the German army, 200,000 people gathered on Vienna's Heldenplatz to cheer Hitler as a 'liberator'. Barely two weeks later, on 10 April, a plebiscite showed that 99.73 per cent of the voting population welcomed the new status quo.[2]

Vienna descended into an orgy of violence and looting against Jews by Austrian Nazi sympathizers. 'Hell was unleashed,' wrote the playwright Carl Zuckmayer, describing the day before the Anschluss. 'The city turned into a scene from a Hieronymus Bosch nightmare.' It was, he went on, worse than anything he had ever experienced. Jeering onlookers surrounded Austrian Jews as they were forced to scrub the sidewalks on their hands and knees, doused with pails of excrement.³ In no other city of the Reich did crowds of ordinary people eagerly join in.⁴

Among many buildings that were 'Aryanized' as an instrument of anti-Semitic terror was the Rothschild family home in the Fourth District of Vienna. The house was requisitioned by Austrian Adolf Eichmann (1906–62)⁵ to serve as the headquarters for his new Central Office for Jewish Emigration. By October 1938, he was boasting that 350 applications were being dealt with daily. In less than two years, Austria's Jewish population dropped from 192,000 to 57,000 as Jews were intimidated in this building and robbed of their property in exchange for being allowed to leave the country.⁶ The Ephrussi Palais was also taken over by the Gestapo in 1938. The Alpine castle-themed Südbahnhotel in Semmering had become so identified with its Jewish clientele, such as Peter Altenberg, Sigmund Freud, Arthur Schnitzler and Arnold Schoenberg, that it was Aryanized as well.

The importance of Vienna dwindled in Nazi Ostmark. It was in Klagenfurt, the capital of the province of Carinthia, that the seven new Gauleiters, or regional governors, were sworn in by the Deputy Führer of the Third Reich, Rudolf Hess (1894–1987).⁷ One figure who played a critical role was the Austrian Odilo Globocnik, whom Hitler had appointed Gauleiter of Vienna in 1938. Lasting only a few months until he was sacked for corruption, Globocnik's career was resuscitated when he went on to become police commander in Lublin in eastern Poland and the organizer of the extermination camps of Belzec, Sobibor and Treblinka, reporting directly to Heinrich Himmler.⁸ Under Globocnik, 15 synagogues were destroyed in the Kristallnacht pogrom of November 1938. The only one to be saved was the City Temple on the Seitenstettengasse, designed by Joseph Kornhäusel in 1826, because it was so well integrated into the urban fabric of the district.⁹

Upon Globocnik's departure in 1940, the German officer Baldur Benedikt von Schirach (1907–74) was appointed Gauleiter of Vienna, a post in which he remained until the end of the war. During his tenure 65,000 Jews were deported to Poland, a measure which he called a 'contribution to European culture'.¹⁰

Not only did architectural commissions keep coming, they were, for many architects, irresistibly megalomaniac. Several architects who had been major contributors to Red Vienna's housing program – no less than Karl Ehn, the architect of the Karl Marx Hof, and Rudolf Perco, the architect of the Friedrich Engels Hof, along with Siegfried Theiss and Hans Jaksch, who had contributed to Sandleiten – sought out and received work.[11] It was under von Schirach that Vienna's *Flaktürme*, or flak towers, were commissioned, to be built by slave labor between 1942 and 1944. They were designed by the German architect Friedrich Tamms (1904–80), who had studied with Albert Speer at the Technical University of Berlin. The towers – two each in Arenberg Park, the Augarten and Esterhazy Park – formed a triangle with the Stefansdom at the center. Each pair consisted of a 'G-Tower', which housed guns, and an 'L-Tower' crowned with searchlights for detecting targets. The latter towers were also equipped with radar installations and rangefinders. The guns were able to fire 8000 rounds per minute, with a range of up to 14 kilometers in a full 360-degree field of fire.

These massive reinforced-concrete buildings each had room for up to 30,000 civilians and could function simultaneously as bunkers, shelters, hospitals, military headquarters, industrial units, barracks, and even for the storage of art treasures from museums. The walls of the bunkers were up to 3.5 meters thick, meaning they could withstand hits from the majority of Allied bombs. In the early days of the war and indeed into 1942, flak towers were responsible for more than half of all Allied aircraft losses, and they forced Allied bombers to fly far above the altitudes that allowed for high accuracy, thus allowing Germany to hold out far longer than it might have otherwise. Toward the end of the war, however, as materials became scarce, specialized soldiers were transferred to fight in Russia and elsewhere, and skilled radar operators were moved to the Western Front, their effectiveness was curtailed and they increasingly failed to protect Vienna from Allied bombing raids.[12]

Hitler was also interested in the planning of Vienna. In 1940 Vienna's overall plan was, after several different proposals were considered, given to Hanns Dustmann, who had been in the employ of Albert Speer and who was Baldur von Schirach's most trusted architect.[13] Under him, the emphasis was on an urban renewal of the Second District, also known as Leopoldstadt. This was the Jewish neighborhood of Vienna, and home to the city's biggest synagogue, on Tempelstrasse. Hugo Hasslinger, a professor at the University of Vienna, wrote at that time that it was a 'traditionally loathed part of the city with noxious streets, most of which were occupied by rootless foreign people'.[14] The plan was to raze 70 per cent of the residential area of the district, along with a part of the more upscale Jewish neighborhood, and to replace it with a monumental *Allee* exalting the Third Reich with a triumphal arch at one end and a colossal domed hall at the other, designed by an obscure Berlin architect by the name of Pöcher and meant to hold 130,000 people. The project was a slightly miniaturized version of Albert's Speer's plan for the Gauforum of Vienna's age-old enemy, Berlin, which also entailed the razing of Jewish neighborhoods.[15]

Dustmann's Vienna plan came to naught. Hitler decided he would not 'give Vienna a pfennig, and the Reich won't give it anything either.'[16] In addition, the war put an increasingly heavy strain on the national budget.[17]

Linz, on the other hand, was a high priority. Neither of Vienna's architects, Dustmann or Pöcher, was held in high regard, and the architect who in 1941 was finally put in charge of the city's planning was Hermann Giesler (1898–1987), one of Hitler's two favorite architects, the other being Albert Speer, who himself had been commissioned with the plan in the beginning.[18] As Hitler's biographer Brigitte Hamann writes, one of the last photographs of the dictator depicts him shortly before his suicide in the bunker of his Chancellery.[19] While the Red Army advanced into the ruins of Berlin outside, he was pondering on Giesler's most recent model of Linz, its gigantic buildings illuminated by spotlights which could be adapted to show Linz in the morning, at midday, at sunset and at night. Hitler sat in front of the model 'whenever he had the opportunity during those weeks', Giesler reported.[20]

Hitler appointed Linz 'the Führer's sister city' and called it the 'most beautiful city on the Danube', a jab at Vienna, declaring that 'Linz owes everything it has and is as yet to obtain to the Reich. Therefore this city must become the carrier of the idea of the Reich. Every building in Linz should have the inscription "Gift from the German Reich".'[21] In fact, he had planned to spend his retirement on an Alpine peak, the Freinberg, above the old part of town, in a building modeled on an upper Austrian farm. 'I climbed these rocks when I was young. On this hilltop over the Danube, I daydreamed. This is where I want to live when I'm old.'[22] Josef Goebbels, the Minister of Propaganda for the Reich, shared this view. On visiting Linz he declared that it was made of 'genuine German men. No Viennese scoundrels.'[23]

Giesler's plan for the left bank of the Danube, in the old town of Linz, was monumental. It called for a party and administration center with a gigantic assembly area for 100,000 people and grounds for celebrations accommodating 30,000, an exposition area with a Bismarck monument, and a technical university. In addition, a 'district center' was to be built around a national commemorative site for Hitler's parents' tomb. Its steeple was to be higher than Vienna's Stefansdom and visible from far away. The bells would ring out with a motif from Austrian composer Anton Bruckner's *Romantic Symphony*, a homage to Richard Wagner's operas based on love stories, *Lohengrin* and *Siegfried*.[24]

On the right side of the river, a boulevard wider than the Ringstrasse in Vienna was to be laid, along with a hotel for 2000 guests with a direct connection to the new expanded train station. The most modern hospitals and schools, among them an Adolf Hitler School, a district school and a Reich Motor Flying Club for the Luftwaffe, would also be established. Other projects included a model settlement for workers and artists, two homes for SS and SA invalids, new streets and an access road to the Autobahn.[25]

The planned cultural center was to have metropolitan proportions, in particular the Linz Art Museum, plundered from Jewish private collections.[26] In his last will, made the day before his death, Hitler wrote: 'I collected paintings over the years, never for private purposes, but always exclusively for enlarging a gallery in my home town Linz on the Danube. It would be my most fervent wish for this legacy to be realized.'[27]

Hitler's plans for a future postwar Linz were partly fulfilled, as opposed to those for Vienna. Among the projects that were built was the so-called Nibelungen Bridge, named by Hitler himself after the Wagnerian opera, and two new buildings flanking it. Massive housing projects were also undertaken from 1939 to 1945, as Linz's population went from 112,000 to 195,000. They comprised 1200 new apartments, 50 semi-detached houses and 420 individual houses in 1939 alone. Speer himself designed temporary housing for workers in 1940. By 1944, 10,873 housing units had been built, accommodating 82,999 people. Unlike the multi-functional housing of Red Vienna, these projects, designed by Herbert Rimpl (1902–78), were planned as dormitory communities with no communal facilities. The housing was located to the south of the town, in Keferfeld, Spallerhof and Bindermichl.

The sudden massive demand for manpower triggered by the renewal of industry prompted an influx of immigrants, mainly from Italy. Workers were needed in the south of Linz, where there was a cluster of steel mills which had been owned by Alpine

Montangesellschaft AG (once chaired by Karl Wittgenstein). Hermann Göring, minister in charge of the Reich's Four-Year Plan, absorbed these in May 1938, just two months after the Anschluss, into the German state-owned conglomerate which he called Reichswerke Hermann Göring.[28] In so doing, he replaced the laissez-faire political economy of the federal government under Dollfuss with massive state support, effectively turning production around. This interventionist, Keynes-like policy was generalized to the country's industrial production under Nazi rule.[29] The demands of war required increasingly larger quantities of steel, concrete and manpower.[30] In Linz, with an infusion of 60 million marks, a modern industrial complex was constructed along with a nitrogen plant, a chemical works and other large-scale enterprises manufacturing aluminum, artificial fibers and armaments.[31]

Linz had one final advantage for the Nazis in addition to its military-industrial facilities. In the hills just 20 kilometers away, near the small villages of Mauthausen and Gusen, was a granite quarry, the Wiener Graben, owned by the City of Vienna.[32] The stone it produced had previously been used to pave the streets of Vienna, but the Nazi authorities envisioned a complete reconstruction of major German towns, in accordance with the plans of Speer, among others, for which large quantities of granite were needed. Speer wanted stone buildings because, in contrast to those made of brick and plaster, they would have '*Ruinenwert*' ('ruin value') in what he foresaw as a Reich with a thousand-year future.[33] Speer's theory was an extension of Gottfried Semper's dictum. As we have seen, Semper had believed that only stone was suitable for lasting cultural monuments.

Unlike the industrial mills, work in the quarry was supplied by slave labor – one of the pillars of the Nazi political economy, along with plunder. By August 1938, Heinrich Himmler, the director of the SS, ordered the construction of a concentration camp to house these prisoners.[34] Mauthausen-Gusen Concentration Camp was built in the immediate vicinity of the quarry under the management of Austrian Gauleiter August Eigruber, who had trained in geodesy and mine engineering at the Austrian Federal Teaching Institute for Iron and Steel.[35] Inmates spent their days carrying 45-kilo stones on their backs up the 186 steps of the quarry.

As the war progressed and the fear grew that industrial facilities would be bombed, German planners decided to move production underground. Again slave laborers from the concentration camp were used, this time to dig out the space for a hidden arms factory. By the end of the war, the prisoners had tunnelled 29,400 square meters beneath the sandstone hills surrounding the camp at Mauthausen and roughly 50,000 square meters beneath the nearby village of Sankt Georgen. Here the Messerschmitt Company built a rocket assembly plant. But the most remarkable was Bergkristall, an underground factory that produced the Messerschmitt Me 262, the world's first operational jet-powered fighter. It was built in six months by 6600 slave laborers. The work was directed, ultimately, by Albert Speer, who was by then the Reich's Minister of Armaments.[36] This was the second-largest plane factory in Germany after the one at Mittelbau-Dora concentration camp, a sub-camp of Buchenwald in Germany, which was also underground. In 1945, the Germans were able to assemble 1250 planes a month.

Recently, a network of underground tunnels and bunkers that may have been used by the Nazis to develop an atomic bomb was discovered in Austria by Andreas Sulzer, an Austrian filmmaker. Its location was determined using intelligence reports and radiation tests, which revealed higher than normal levels of radioactivity. Covering up to 75 acres, the site is believed to have been connected to the Bergkristall factory.[37]

By the summer of 1940, Mauthausen-Gusen had become one of the largest concentration camps in German-controlled Europe. The camp and its sub-camps were designated 'Grade III', for the extermination through labor of 'Incorrigible Political Enemies of the Reich'. In January 1945 there were roughly 85,000 inmates. The full death toll remains unknown because the Nazis burned many of the archives, but sources place it between 122,766 and 320,000 for the entire complex.[38] More than 14,000 – 13 per cent – of the inmates were Jewish; the rest were Germany's political and ideological enemies: Spanish anti-Frankists, Greek partisans and Poles, among others.

7

Reconstructing with a Memory Problem 1945–1970

At the end of the war American bombers were unrelenting over Vienna, as they had been in the rest of the Third Reich. For 20 days in April 1945, before Austria finally surrendered, Vienna was pounded by 52 air raids. Over 11,000 people were killed. On the day Russian troops entered the city, 13 April, 21,317 buildings had been totally or partly destroyed in the bombing and 86,875 apartments rendered unusable.[1] Twenty-eight per cent of the housing stock were demolished, more than had been built by Red Vienna.[2] Twenty eight per cent of the city's buildings suffered some damage and four per cent were totally destroyed. Over 800,000 cubic meters of rubble had to be cleared. The damage touched all parts of the city. The greatest destruction was concentrated in industrial sections such as the district between the Danube canal and the river Danube itself. But even the cathedral was not spared: it was bombed by American planes on the last day of the war, 12 March 1945, along with the Albertina museum, the Burgtheater, the Staatsoper and, across the street, Theophil von Hansen's Heinrichshof.

As part of the former Third Reich, Austria was now an occupied, war-torn country. Each of the four Allied powers – France, Britain, Russia and the United States – claimed part of the country. The Americans occupied the area around Salzburg, the Russians the east of the country. Vienna itself was partitioned into four occupation zones, although it was never divided as severely as Berlin. In 1955, thanks to a

93 Arbeitsgruppe 4, Seelsorgzentrum in Ennsleiten in Styria, 1961

thaw in the Cold War brought on by Nikita Khrushchev's rise to power in the Kremlin, the costly decade-long Russian occupation ended and, with the consent of the US, France and Britain, the country was granted full sovereignty under a Second Republic and was declared neutral by the Austrian State Treaty.[3]

The economy was a shambles. Harry Lime, the unscrupulous dealer in penicillin in Graham Greene's *The Third Man* (1949), was typical of the black-marketeers who thrived in this context. In early May 1945 the bread ration was set at half a kilo per head per week. In Wiener Neustadt, a reporter documented the diet of an eight-year-old boy two weeks before Christmas: a cup of black coffee for breakfast, half a liter of soup from the school for lunch, and in the evening another cup of black coffee. It took until November 1946 for the daily calorie intake per head to rise to 1500 everywhere in Austria. In 1945 it had been officially 800.[4] At the time, 1600 calories was the amount considered necessary for survival.[5]

In spite of the destruction and suffering and the subsequent military occupation, after the Second World War Austria was soon on the path to prosperity. In fact this period has gone down in history as the 'Austrian Miracle'. Inflation swiftly came under control. The country's GDP doubled between 1946 and 1950. By 1951 it had risen above the pre-war level. The growth rate between 1953 and 1957 was 7.7 per cent, and from 1968 to 1975 it was 5.6 per cent.[6]

Austria occupied a privileged position in the globalized postwar 'Golden Age' of sustained economic growth.[7] Next to Japan, it had the fastest rate of economic growth in the developed world between the end of the Second World War and 1980, and the fastest increase in real income per head – in sharp contrast to the period after the First World War, when the country's economy was mostly stagnant, with heavy unemployment.[8]

The general perception was that the Austrian Miracle was due to the industrious character of Austrian workers. This was partly correct, but other factors were involved. In the first place, like Japan, because Austria had lost the war, it was excluded from NATO at its inception in 1949. This gave the country the distinct advantage, unlike the nations that had won the war, of not being permitted to re-arm. What it saved on military expenditure it was free to invest in more economically productive sectors.[9]

A second factor was the inheritance of the reorganization and modernization of Austria's industrial base carried out by Nazi Germany after the Anschluss in 1938. The chief case in point was the Reichswerke Hermann Göring in Linz, which had not recovered its pre-First World War level of production until the Nazi takeover. The mills were bombed by the Allies, and the Marshall Plan then supplied funds for reconstructing the steel production of the mills, now under Austrian state ownership.[10]

The third reason was that Austria was disproportionally favored by the Marshall Plan during the Cold War because of geopolitics. The policy of the victors was the opposite of the one that Keynes had so vociferously condemned after the First World War. Instead of asphyxiating the losers, the Marshall Plan was intended to kickstart all the economies of Europe, including Germany and Austria.[11]

Austria received more money from the Marshall Plan per head of population than any other country except Denmark. On a per capita basis, each American taxpayer invested $80 in the Plan and, amazingly, each Austrian received $133 from it.[12] The financial aid was used to buy raw materials, foodstuffs and new technologies but also went toward balancing the state budget.[13] The funds began arriving in late 1948 and promoted rapid development.[14] It provided for the completion of the construction of the Kamprun hydroelectric dam in the Tyrol, which had been begun by the Nazi regime, besides turning the steel industry in Linz into one of the most modern in Europe. In addition to giving the country a long-term economic boost, it also provided social cushioning for economic reconstruction. This weakened the Communist Party in Austria, which like everywhere else had made inroads with the electorate following the renewed economic crisis of 1947, when famine threatened the country.

The fourth factor responsible for Austria's exceptional economic revival was, as was the case with all European states at the time, postwar Keynesianism. Austria adhered to government-managed welfare-state economic policies, often resorting to anti-cyclical measures such as deficit spending. These policies were pursued by the postwar coalition government of the Socialist Party and the conservative Christian Socials. The economic historian Nicholas Kaldor credited the remarkable economic dynamism of Austria to the role played by the state, noting that 'the public sector of Austria, accounting for 16% of all employees, 20% of total output, and 25% of exports, is the largest (in relative terms) among the developed countries of the West.'[15] This was true throughout the period when the country was occupied, and continued after the Vienna State Treaty of 1955. The national debt was 9 per cent of GDP in 1957.[16] Public sector building programs for social housing and public transportation were the great beneficiaries of these policies.

The material damage inflicted by the war was far easier to overcome than the psychological trauma. The death toll of the Second World War dwarfed the figures of the First. About 37 million Europeans had been killed, more than half of them civilians. This is excluding the war dead in Japan and North America. Sixteen million Russians alone were killed.[17] But such was the brain drain in Austria due to the decimation of the pre-war cultural elite at this time that the first and most outstanding artistic expression of postwar 'noir' was produced by foreigners, the 1949 film of Graham Greene's *The Third Man*, made by the Hungarian Alexander Korda with the American David O. Selznick and a British director, Carol Reed. Local expressions of Austrian angst by Ingeborg Bachmann, Thomas Bernhard, Elfriede Jelinek and Helmut Qualtinger came later – all rebellious literary figures.

The first casualty of the Cold War in Austria was the truth about its Nazi past. What occurred was what Freud termed a 'memory problem' or a 'false memory'. Its major symptom was the fantasy that Austria had been the first victim of the Third Reich's aggression.[18] The resulting commonplace assumption was reinforced by Cold War geopolitics. Austria's successful case for claiming victim status was largely the result of Allied wartime planning in 1943, in particular by an official in the British Foreign Office, Geoffrey Harrison, who proposed this narrative as a means of postwar nation-building for Austria. This scenario was favored by the prime minister, Winston Churchill, in opposition to US president Franklin D. Roosevelt, who argued for postwar rapprochement between the West and Russia. The resulting sanitized Austria, supposedly made up of loyal and virtuous heroes, had the potential to become the administrative center of a grand Middle European confederation, impeding any renewed Anschluss with Germany by enhancing Austria's self-perception as an independent country. An irreproachable Austria offered not only a physical buffer between the former allies Germany and Italy but also a showcase for the economic benefits of political 'goodness' or capitalism, strategically located on the fringe of the Soviet Bloc in the build-up of the Cold War, not to mention a convenient base for intelligence gathering and recruiting in countries to its east.[19]

Austria had never been anything but a willing ally of Adolf Hitler.[20] It was complicit from the beginning to the end in the Third Reich. Its role in the Holocaust was disproportionately high. Although Austrians comprised only 8 per cent of the population of Hitler's Reich, they made up 14 per cent of SS members and 40 per cent of those involved in the Nazis' killing operations.[21] At the Nuremberg trials, it was declared that 25 per cent of Nazi war criminals were Austrian, although the country's population was a fraction of Germany's. In spite of this, Austria's confrontation with the Nazi past and the Holocaust was delegated to what has been called a 'private do-it-yourself history workshop, where the administration of liberal doses of self-justification was the rule.'[22]

The selective amnesia was institutionalized. No effort was made to return property that had been 'Aryanized' by the Nazis and was now in the hands of the state.[23] In her 1440-page *Was einmal war* ('What Once Was', subtitled 'Handbook of Vienna's Plundered Art Collections') Sophie Lillie uncovered 148 significant collections, based on Gestapo seizure inventories, including pieces by Rembrandt, Tintoretto, Schiele, Klimt and Oskar Kokoschka. Few have found their way back to their owners or their descendants. In the catalogues of the Dorotheum auction house, the names of the original owners were omitted and sales of objects from 'Aryanized' apartments were listed as 'voluntary'. The personalities of Viennese Jews come to life as one reads these itemizations of collections of both valuable art and miscellaneous household objects.[24]

Under the Nazi regime the Jewish community of Vienna was almost completely wiped out. Approximately 200,000 Jews had been living in Austria before 1938, 180,000 of them in Vienna, where they made up 9.4 per cent of the city's population. About 65,000 were exterminated by the Nazis, almost 130,000 were forced to emigrate, and only a few survived in hiding. In December 1945, months after the country was liberated, the Jewish community consisted of a mere 4000 members. Less than half of them were survivors of concentration camps, and only some hundreds had returned from emigration. In the following years, about another 5000 émigrés returned. Today's Jewish community in Vienna is no larger than 10,000.

The politics of the Cold War created a culture in denial of its Nazi past, reinforcing nostalgia for the good old days as a means of restoring pride and reshaping national identity.[25] *Heimatkultur*, an assertion of the patriotism and fundamental good-heartedness of Austrians, dominated.[26] This constructed, highly parochial national identity hinged on 'past greatness', portraying Austria as a country of jovial, light-hearted music lovers. This is how it was presented in 1955 in a state-sponsored brochure called *Kulturland Österreich* that identified Haydn, Mozart, Beethoven and Schubert as the great cultural forebears of contemporary Austria.[27] The biggest popular success of this period was the *Heimatfilm* movie trilogy *Sissi* (1955–7), about the Empress Elizabeth, consort of Emperor Franz Josef.

The real beneficiaries of the Cold War memory problem were the pre-war Austro-fascists. Novelist Robert Menasse describes the result:

> The very fact that Austro-fascists had been also persecuted by the National Socialists made it possible for them to return immediately to the posts they had held until 1938, claiming to have been victims of the Nazi regime. The continuity between Austro-fascism and the Second Republic, in terms of the individuals involved, guaranteed that everything Nazi fascism had put into practice, much more consistently than Austro-fascism, ended up being reformulated in a more patriotic mold, but was not retracted. Instead, it remained as what might be called a historical achievement of bourgeois society, although here a pragmatic alliance was established in the corridors of intellectual life between Austro-fascists and immigrants returning from the USA as CIA agents.[28]

Postwar Austria had more than a psychological problem. The brain drain that had begun in the 1920s was now close to complete thanks to the Aryanization policies imposed under Hitler. The scientific and cultural quality of Austrian universities, once so internationally celebrated, was obliterated. Most of the high-achieving academic meritocracy, the enlightenment figures, overwhelmingly Jewish, either emigrated or perished in the death camps. Aryanization turned Austria's great universities into dumbed-down, parochial backwaters. Still among the lowest-ranking in the world,[29] they continue to pay the price of the replacement of Jewish academics and students with Nazi supporters who conformed to 'Aryan science'.[30] Postwar Austria did little to rectify this. After the fall of the Reich, the Austrian Academy of Science expelled those of its members who had been part of the Nazi regime, but in 1950 they were all reinstated.[31]

Typical of what replaced the flourishing pre-war cultural modernity in Austria was the bestselling *Verlust der Mitte* ('Loss of the Center'), published by an art historian and prominent former Nazi, Hans Sedlmayr, in 1948. In the tradition of the Nazi writer Schultze Naumburg, it was an attack on modern culture – including the Vienna Secession – as degenerate and Jewish.[32] The ultra-conservative book ends with the hope that time will 'heal' Austrian culture and bring it back to Catholic values.

As late as 1965 even the legal scholar Hans Kelsen, by then a professor at Berkeley and previously at Harvard, who had written the Austrian constitution in the 1920s, was not invited to participate in the official celebration of the sixth centenary of the University of Vienna. He had to give a lecture at a side event.[33]

The effect of the brain drain on architecture was devastating. Most of the outstanding pre-Anschluss architects had emigrated or perished, leaving what the architectural critic Friedrich Achleitner called 'the unloved generation'.[34] With the absence of the great avant-garde figures, disorientation ensued and mediocre architecture sprouted up everywhere. There was no architectural criticism in Austrian newspapers before 1962 when Achleitner started writing for *Die Presse* and Günther Feuerstein for *Kurier*.

Among the most touted projects of the period were the Strandbad Gänsehaüfel (1948–9) by Max Fellerer and Eugen Wörle, described by Achleitner as 'not very inspired'.[35] Oswald Haerdtl (1899–1959) designed the Messepavillion for Felten & Guillaume in 1953 but really left his mark on the period as the copycat importer into the Austrian café world of postwar Italian modernist espresso bar aesthetics – the master of which was Gio Ponti – with such iconic projects as the Arabia Espresso on the Kohlmarkt (1950, since destroyed), the Milchpavillon in the Volksgarten (1951), the Arabia Café (1954) and Café Prückel (1954).[36] The most interesting project was Clemens Holzmeister's design for the concert hall (1956–60) of the Grosse Festspielhaus, the prestigious concert house of the Salzburg Music Festival, for which 55,000 cubic meters of the Mönchsberg mountain were excavated, thus leaving the historical fabric of the town intact while accommodating a gigantic public.

In 1988 Günther Feuerstein looked back and decried 'the vacuum' of the time 'characterized by clumsy helplessness'.[37] Sokratis Dimitriou, another architecture critic, wrote that 'the first years of the liberation belong to the darkest period of Austrian architectural history'.[38] It was as if the modernists of the pre-Anschluss period had never existed. The architect Ottokar Uhl wrote in his *Moderne Architektur in Wien* (1966) that it was 'totally tragic that in the need of the postwar period the two most important buildings were a beach house and an exhibition pavilion'.[39] He also asserted that of the 23,066 buildings put up during the first 20 years after the war, no more than seven were architecturally outstanding.[40]

Another factor, besides the general amnesia and disorientation, that held back innovation at the time was the ultra-conservative Catholic Church, which, according to Achleitner, became one of the major clients of postwar architects. The most active builders of unremarkable churches of the time were Holzmeister and his student at the Academy of Fine Art, the Tyrolean architect Josef Lackner.

As for the architecture schools, according to Friedrich Achleitner, they 'limited themselves to transmitting a subjective knowledge, often irrelevant and obsolete,' causing the 'young generation to suffer from a lack of information.'[41] Hans Hollein attests to the impact of post-Austro-fascist, post-Anschluss 'purification': during his studies at the Academy of Fine Art between 1952 and 1956, no one had told him about Adolf Loos. He learned about Loos from a bookstore owner in Vienna whose shop he happened to enter. Moreover, the first lecture he attended on Loos was at Berkeley, where he was a student, in 1959. Hollein also recalls attending, along with notable architects of the city, an event in Vienna in honor of Alvar Aalto in 1953. Before Aalto's arrival, an elderly man entered the room. Hollein (then a student) asked who he was and no one knew. Upon his own arrival, Aalto looked around and, instantly recognizing the man, addressed him as 'Master'. It was Josef Hoffmann.[42]

Amnesia in postwar architectural academia was selective. Catholics like Holzmeister and Ernst Plischke, who had chosen to go into exile after the Anschluss, were each welcomed upon their return, respectively, from self-imposed exile in Turkey and New Zealand and rewarded with university professorships. Margarete Schütte-Lihotzky, a Jew, on the other hand, was met with a cold shoulder, although she had been more prominent both locally and internationally than either. The fact that she was a woman was also a marked disadvantage. The University of Vienna had once been a 'Mecca' for women,[43] but in post-Anschluss, Aryanized Viennese universities, the situation was reversed. In fact, women are still in the minority today when it comes to full professorships (17 per cent of full professors were women in 2011).[44] Thirdly, she had been a member of the anti-Nazi underground, which was led by Communists. In the climate of the Cold War, the result was that in spite of the feverish pace of reconstruction, she received no commissions from the government. The two she did receive were for the Globus building (1954–6), for a Communist publishing house, and a primary school in the low-income Eleventh

District. She was forced to go far afield in search of work, to Mexico and Turkey, for example, and was involved in the planning of new cities in the east of the Soviet Union.[45]

It was not until Schütte-Lihotzky had reached the age of 99, in 1996, that she was honored. Peter Noever, Director of the MAK (Museum of Applied Arts), went against the mainstream and dedicated a one-woman show to her, accompanied by a richly documented catalogue of her achievements.[46]

As for Richard Neutra, who returned to Vienna after a fire destroyed his house in Los Angeles, he had no work at all in Austria between 1966 and 1969. He did receive commissions from Switzerland, including his masterpiece the Rentsch House in Wengen, overlooking the Jungfrau, and the Bucerious House in Brione on Lake Maggiore, both nestled in the breathtaking natural surroundings.

One refuge from the intellectual vacuum of the architecture schools was the Salzburg Summer Academy, founded in 1953 by Oskar Kokoschka and the art dealer Friedrich Welz, whose gallery had been Aryanized by the Nazis. The head of the architecture section was Hans Adolf Vetter, who had been a student at the Kunstgewerbeschule of Oskar Strnad and Josef Hoffmann, then participated in the Vienna Werkbund housing project and subsequently took up a teaching position at the Carnegie Institute of Technology in Pittsburgh, from 1948 to 1963. Salzburg was chosen because of the relative ease of opening a new school there; in 1953, unlike Vienna, it was under American occupation. The first professors were Holzmeister and the Swiss architect Hans Hofmann. The tutor who made the biggest impact on the architecture students, however, was the engineer Konrad Wachsmann, who had, like Vetter, emigrated to the USA in 1941. Wachsmann was teaching at Illinois Institute of Technology and was to become visiting lecturer at the overwhelmingly American-funded Ulm School of Design, also founded in 1953. He taught in Salzburg for five summers, between 1956 and 1960. It was here, according to Friedrich Kurrent, that 'a whole generation of young Austrian architects [got] in touch with international architects'.[47] Wachsmann was not only a leading influence, along with Richard Buckminster Fuller, in postwar prefabrication of houses, but also one of the great structural engineers of the twentieth century, renowned for his three-dimensional tetrahedral truss structures and lightweight long-span cantilevers.[48]

Another light at the end of the tunnel was shone by Sigfried Giedion. Born in Austro-Hungarian Prague and a graduate of the Technical University of Vienna, he gave a series of lectures to a select group of students (among them Hans Hollein) in the winter of 1956, which provided them with an exposure to the history of the twentieth century that they could not possibly have had in Vienna.[49]

A final respite was the less Teutonic environment of the postwar CIAM. Schütte-Lihotzky and her husband Wilhelm Schütte were the only Austrians present at the first postwar CIAM meeting in 1947, in Bridgwater in Somerset, England. Postwar CIAM meetings were largely made up of architects who had been on the winning side in the war – Dutch, French, Greek, Italian and British. They included Alison and Peter Smithson, Shadrach Woods, Giancarlo de Carlo, Aldo van Eyck and Jerzy Soltan.[50] Austrians had only a minor role. By 1951, the leadership of the Austrian branch of CIAM was taken over from Schütte and Schütte-Lihotzky by the head of the Hochschule für Angewandte Kunst, Otto Neurath's former disciple Franz Schuster (1892–1972), who was, along with Oswald Haerdtl, Max Fellerer, Roland Rainer and Karl Schwanzer, among the organization's most active members. Eduard Sekler, who took the unusually cosmopolitan step of leaving Vienna to do a doctorate on Christopher Wren at the Warburg Institute in London, became the group's most prominent presence internationally. He read a paper at the historic breakaway conference at Otterlo in 1959 which gave birth to Team Ten, eventually becoming Professor of Architectural History at the Harvard Graduate School of Design for the next half-century.

But it was the Salzburg School, and Wachsmann in particular, who had the greatest influence on the young postwar generation of architects. The creation of Arbeitsgruppe 4 ('Workgroup 4', because there were four members) in the late 1950s brought together four of his professed disciples: Friedrich Kurrent (b. 1931), Johannes Spalt (1920–2010), Wilhelm Holzbauer (b. 1930) and Otto Leitner (b. 1930). Although none of their designs, carried out in reinforced concrete, made use of Wachsmann's metallic structures, their buildings were well conceived from an engineering point of view. Their most adventurous and noteworthy building was in the Catholic Center of Steyr-Ennsleiten in Salzburg, designed by a non-member of the team, Johann Georg Gsteu. It used tilted cross-like elements made out of reinforced concrete as the structural support for the building (fig. 93).[51]

94 Karl Schwanzer, 20er Haus, 1958, restored in 2010

Two architects of the late 1950s who did break out of the mediocrity of the time were Karl Schwanzer (1918–75) and Roland Rainer (1910–2004). Schwanzer's first big commission was for the Austrian Pavilion at the Brussels International Fair of 1958. Designed in the idiom of Mies van Rohe's Crown Hall of 1956 at Illinois Institute of Technology, the steel-frame building created an almost uninterrupted space. The difference between the two buildings was that Mies's structure was elegantly exoskeletal while Schwanzer's more rhetorically high-tech approach exhibited its muscle, in the form of monumental internal pylons. This allowed him to produce two open-plan, airy storeys whose sliding panels could be moved in order to accommodate different exhibition programs. Although it was meant to be a temporary structure, the building was so successful that it was subsequently taken to Vienna where it was renamed the 20er Haus ('Museum of the Twentieth Century') and is still an exhibition space, restored in 2010 by Adolf Krishanitz and now run by the Belvedere Museum (fig. 94). Schwanzer's most important works were exercises in the inventive exploitation of pre-fabrication. His masterpiece is his metal-clad megastructural BMW headquarters in Munich, built between 1968 and 1972 in an over-the-top techno-optimistic spirit close to Archigram and the Japanese Metabolists. The lower, large rotund structure, 20 meters in diameter, housing the BMW Museum, is supposed to mimic the shape of a car tire, while the four vertical cylinders housing the administration offices rising above it resemble four colossal spark plugs, the implication being that this was the starting point for the combustion of the creative engine of the company. Again the structural system was remarkable. Schwanzer conceived of each of the separate cylinders as independent units assembled on the ground from pre-fabricated elements and then suspended from a central tower.

Roland Rainer's range was remarkable. At one extreme was his reinforced-concrete Wiener Stadthalle or Vienna Stadium (1953–8), which he competed for against Alvar Aalto, and which was one of the first so-called 'flexible', multipurpose neo-brutalist megastructures (fig. 95). Rainer exploited the potential offered by technology to create a sophisticated facility capable of meeting different requirements. The vast octagonal hall can accommodate up to 20,000 people for all kinds of activities, from boxing, tennis, ice hockey and equestrian events to pop concerts. Its lattice steel structure is in the form of an enormous suspended hyperbolic paraboloid with a saddle-shaped roof, the stage is made of wood and steel and the cladding is aluminum. The building features smaller aditional mobile roofs, along with stands and playing areas, so that it is capable of being quickly converted to offer optimum configuration and maximum comfort for spectators, whatever the event. In the wake of the stadium's success, sport halls became Rainer's specialty and he went on to build even more structurally daring examples in Germany, such as Bremen stadium (1961–4) with its flying buttresses, the one in Kassel in 1962 and the Friedrich Ebert Halle in Ludwigshafen (1962–5), culminating with the gigantic ORF Zentrum Wien (1968–76). At the other extreme, his own house in Steinbruch in Lower Austria (1957) fits most sensitively into the gentle rolling landscape with its low-profile stone walls and sympathetic use of concrete and wood.[52]

Social housing was another area which suffered a surprising dumbing down in Vienna after the Second World War. As we have seen, 20 per cent of the city's apartments had been destroyed and 35,000 people left homeless. In 1950, a *Schnellbauprogram* ('fast construction organization') was created to meet the urgent needs of over 55,000 people. Between 1945 and 1960 Franz Schuster was responsible for redressing the housing shortage, along with Leopold Thaller, a city councilor who devised an eight-point program for reconstruction. Mayor Felix Slavik played a key political role in implementing Schuster's guiding principles.

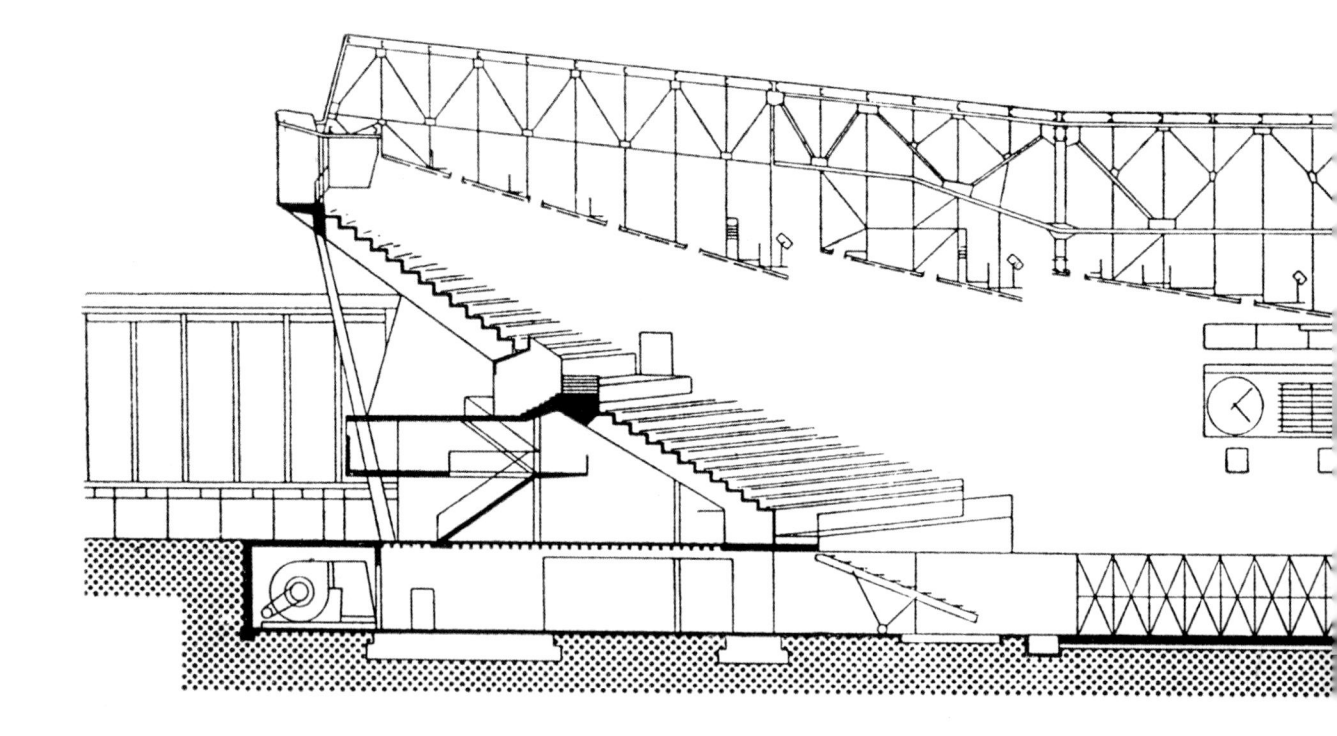

The sheer number of housing units created by the postwar municipal government is remarkable. The city of Vienna reconstructed over 50,000 housing units in the first two years after the war – almost as many as the 60,000 that Red Vienna had built in 12 years, from 1922 to 1934. Of all new housing built between 1954 and 1962, 66 per cent was by the city, 26 per cent by other public agencies and private cooperatives, and only 8 per cent by individuals.[53]

The first massive postwar housing project was the Per Albin Hansson estate (1947–54), subsidized by the Swedish government and designed by Stephan Simony, Friedrich Pangratz, Eugen Wörle and Schuster himself. Not surprisingly, given that Schuster shared his mentor Otto Neurath's inclinations, the new housing had characteristics of the old Siedlungen, though the only project that conformed to Red Vienna's standards (because it followed pre-war plans) was the massive Hugo Breitner Hof by architects Erwin Fabrici, Georg Lippert, Fritz Purr and Paul Widmann, comprising 12 blocks on a parcel of land of which 85

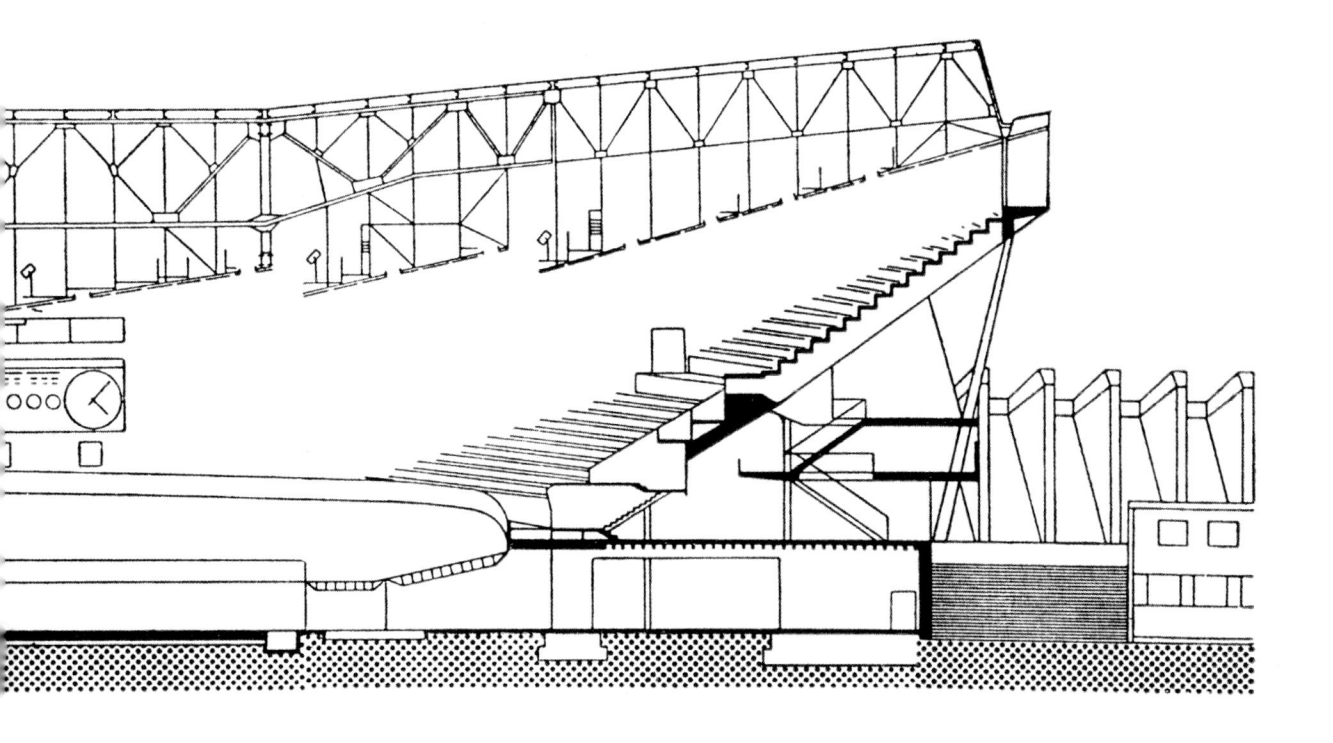

95 Roland Rainer, Stadthalle interior, 1953–8. Drawing

per cent was given over to a shared open space with playing fields, playgrounds and gardens.

A second phase of housing policy began in 1960. Again under Felix Slavik, at that time the councilor in charge of housing, Viennese housing told were told to look into the 'Camus' heavy prefabrication technique that was being applied all over Western and Eastern Europe. The system had been developed and patented by the French engineer Raymond Camus, who founded a construction and development firm based on the technique. It was first applied in Le Havre in 1949. Although the Camus system did not increase the number of housing units built, it did mean a 90 per cent reduction in manpower costs.[54]

The result was a new company, Montagebau Wien, of which 51 per cent was owned by the city of Vienna, 26 per cent by French construction firm Camus–Dietsch and 23 per cent by an Austrian construction firm, Maba. It built 1000 housing units a year. The use of the crane was integral to the plan. The parallel slabs stood in line along the street, with the green areas in between – in contrast to the intimacy created by the traditional closed courts – creating unfriendly empty spaces that were given over to circulation. The construction of large new housing areas at the city's northern and southern

96 (above) The promise held out by prefabricated social housing of the 1960s. Poster Collection, Vienna Municipal Library

97 (opposite) The monotonous reality of prefabricated housing. Vera Mayer (ed.), *Plattenbausiedlungen* (Vienna, 2006), p. 27

peripheries started with the opening of the first prefabrication plant in 1961. In the early 1960s GESIBA in Vienna abandoned its historic Siedlung and Gemeindebau models in favor of an approach more suited to prefabrication, and 105,000 apartments were built in this manner, mainly in the Twenty-first and Twenty-second Districts. The prefabricated model resulted in a vastly shorter construction period. It remained dominant up until the 1970s (figs 96 and 97).

This was Austria's answer to the international shift towards prefabrication, the most high-profile examples of which were Gordon Bunshaft's Lever House in Manhattan (finished 1952) and Mies's Lake Shore Drive apartment buildings in Chicago (1952). Some of the Viennese versions of prefabrication proved more successful, thanks chiefly to the work of Oskar and Peter Payer. The Payer brothers were chief proponents of so-called *Bau- und Wohnkultur* ('Building and Domestic Culture'). In 1963 they won a competition to establish standardized plans for apartments for single people, couples and families. All had cross-ventilation and bathrooms with windows, and the bathrooms were big enough for washing and drying clothes. In their Siemensgründe, they supplied some split-level apartments of 102 square meters, each with a loggia. Most of the apartments were intended for two to six people, however, each measuring between 58.4 and 97.3 square meters, with a loggia or terrace of between 5 and 17 square meters.[55]

Because these apartments were large and well equipped, they were well received by the residents (fig. 98). In fact, the rate of social mobility in these estates was no higher than the Vienna average – very low, in other words. These housing estates never became slums or ghettos like

98 Payer Brothers, a master bedroom in a prefabricated social housing project of the period with floor-to-ceiling windows on two sides. Vera Mayer (ed.), *Plattenbausiedlungen* (Vienna, 2006), p. 134

the neighborhoods on the outskirts of Paris, for example, as had often been predicted. Later attempts to increase their density were opposed by the residents.[56]

The Payer brothers have become synonymous with Viennese prefabricated design of the 1960s. They were responsible for the eastern component of the Per Albin Hansson-Siedlung estate in 1967 and designed the biggest of all the prefabricated housing complexes, Grossfeldsiedlung, with 5788 units, built between 1966 and 1972.[57] In 2004 a survey found that 72.7 per cent of Grossfeld's occupants were happy with the size of their apartments, and 40 per cent of the residents of the prefabricated units said that the size of the apartments was the most important factor for them. The survey also found that 73 per cent were happy with the transport infrastructure. It has since been readapted, with swimming pools, playgrounds and further amenities.[58]

By the early 1970s, whatever their relative advantages, prefabricated housing units were being widely condemned in Austria for their deadening uniformity. Indeed, during the first phase of prefabrication, the use of cranes allowed for the construction only of uniform parallel blocks, which the Viennese unflatteringly referred to as 'Emmental' or *Emmentaler* buildings as they were lined up like so many thick slices of that Swiss cheese. Perhaps this nickname also referred to the foreign character of the paradigm, rooted in the German modernist tradition of the *Zeilenbau* ('slab housing') and epitomized by Siemensstadt Siedlung, constructed by Hans Scharoun, Walter Gropius and Hugo Häring, among others, near Berlin between 1929 and 1934. This building type was at odds with the more traditional perimeter block, with its community-enhancing shared central space typical of the Red Viennese style of social housing. Hans Hollein ridiculed structures of this type with a collage showing a big slice of cheese towering over the skyline of Vienna. Nevertheless, the 1960s did see an increase in the quantity, if not the quality, of housing, and the enormous volume of construction produced over 10,000 public apartments per year, which relieved housing pressure in the densely populated inner city and created the pre-conditions for the vast urban renewal program of the next decades.

There was one exception to the general disorientation in Viennese architecture of that time: urban planning. This was an area where postwar architects excelled, in particular in their adoption of restoration and preservation policies. When Franz Schuster became Vienna's first director of planning in 1945, the influence of Otto Neurath and Red Vienna was added to the tradition initiated by Otto Wagner.[59] Like Neurath, his mentor, Schuster had been critical of the Gemeindebau phase of Red Vienna's housing policy, and faithful to the Garden City Siedlung phase. He had worked on the Winarsky housing development along with Loos, Frank, Schütte-Lihotzky and Behrens, and had also contributed a design for a house in 1931 for the Wiener Werkbund. Moreover, Schuster and Neurath had co-authored two major policy articles in 1923 and 1924, which, among other things, had advocated the creation of the position of chief planner for the city of Vienna, a role which Schuster became the first to fill. Schuster founded the journal *Der Aufbau* in 1926 to promote modern city planning in Austria but, like Schütte-Lihotzky, he left the city to work for Ernst May in 1937. He returned to Vienna during the war with no qualms, regarding either himself or the cultural establishment as a whole, to succeed Josef Hoffmann as director of the Hochschule für Angewandte Kunst (previously the Gewerbeschule, today the University of Applied

Arts) under the Nazis. After the war, again with no qualms, he revived Otto Neurath's people-friendly anti-CIAM approach – although without attributing it to its author.

Indeed, when it came to the inner city, Schuster forcefully resisted the dominant trend in postwar planning in heavily bombed Germany, which was to follow the old pre-war CIAM model, based on radical reconstruction. In fact, he dismissed it as 'a utopian romantic attachment to skyscrapers' which 'ignored the needs of ordinary people' as early as July 1945, much earlier than Team Ten's humanistic pronouncements of the late 1950s. He added in his journal *Der Aufbau* (Construction), that 'the human being, the single individual, should be the standard against which all reconstruction concepts and planning must be measured.'[60] In an unpublished manuscript, he went on to declare that '[o]ne cannot simply follow in the footsteps of Le Corbusier, Frank Lloyd Wright or Neutra. They are mavericks who were on the offensive. One must not follow weakly in their subjective pursuit of a general line of work which in general is at odds with the built environment.'[61]

Of course, Schuster's task was facilitated by the fact that the bombing damage of Vienna by the US Air Force had been far lighter than that of Dresden, Cologne, Hamburg or Berlin. As a result, Vienna was not left with gaping empty spaces. Instead of turning its back on historical antecedents, the city set to work restoring and preserving its architectural heritage. The major projects in this line were the Stephansdom, the Burgtheater, the Kunsthistorisches and Naturhistorisches museums, the Albertina, the Staatsoper and the Parliament building.

But in rejecting the pre-war CIAM model and adhering instead to a more enlightened, multi-faceted, people-oriented one, combining the legacy of Wagner, Neurath and Red Vienna in general, Schuster set the tone for the planning policies still in place today. Consistent with the position papers he had written with Neurath in the early 1920s, and with the City Council Act of 1921, Schuster believed that planning should not be limited to the city, but should be included in a broader regional scheme.[62] As in the Act of 1921, however, there was no provision for public transportation.

Schuster's successor followed in his footsteps. Karl Heinrich Brunner took over from him in 1948 and stayed on until 1958 as head of the city's planning department, retaining Schuster as a consultant. Brunner had trained as an urban planner at the Technical University, had gone into voluntary exile after the Anschluss and pursued town planning in Latin America. He echoed Schuster's views when he criticized some of the proposals for the reconstruction of Berlin. In Berlin, as in Vienna, he wrote, the degree of destruction was not great enough to warrant so-called 'utopian' planning. 'It is not our task', Brunner argued, 'to give the city a new structure through the abstract application of all of the theories of modern city planning.'[63]

What Brunner was criticizing was the kind of radical planning proposed by former CIAM members, such as the 'ribbon plan' for Berlin put forth by a collective of planners headed by Hans Scharoun. The 'ribbons' were high-capacity roads carving up the site of the pre-war city.[64] His own plan of 1950 called for minimal intervention, simply proposing the widening and straightening of streets, the revitalization of unhealthy slums, and the separation of housing and industry, while sticking to existing building densities. On the other hand, his traffic planning embodied a revived vestige of Neurath's Garden City policy, advocating new satellite towns set in greenery and indirectly supporting increased private vehicular traffic rather than the public transportation system advocated by Otto Wagner.[65]

In 1958, Brunner was succeeded by Roland Rainer, who had recently published *Die gegliederte und aufgelockerte Stadt* ('The Diffused and Fragmented City', 1957), arguing for decentralization within the city and the reduction of urban densities. Rainer, who had spent the war in Germany as a Nazi, had no ties with Wagner's visions for public transportation, to which the pre-war planners of Red Vienna had been so receptive when designing the Gemeindebau program. Instead, he favored one of the planning ideas of Hitlerian Germany, namely car-intensive highways. Although Rainer is generally recognized as a very early proponent of an ecologically responsible approach to urban planning, he was misguided when it came to implementing this vision. He opposed underground transportation and was in favor of suburban sprawl under the erroneous belief that this was consistent with ecological principles. He published the plan he submitted to the planning commission in 1962 under the title *Planungskonzept Wien*,[66] unwittingly calling for the opposite of what were in fact ecologically sound ideas, namely urban decentralization, lower housing densities and automobile traffic planning. By 1964, frustrated by the inactivity of the municipal Social Democratic council to act on his plans, Rainer resigned his post as city planner.[67]

Rather than favoring sprawl as Rainer did, the members of Arbeitsgruppe 4 reconnected with the ideas Otto Wagner had put forward in *Die Grossstadt* in 1911. They took sides in articles and public statements in heated debates throughout the 1960s, defending the construction of an underground public transportation U-Bahn network and the densification of the urban fabric along the new lines.

Another architect had a positive impact on Vienna's planning policy at this time. Surprisingly, given his historic role in the rise of shopping centers in the postwar period, Victor Gruen supported the particular approach of Vienna to preservation. Gruen had cemented his reputation as the champion of suburban development after making his fortune with the Northland Center mall in the US. But by the late 1960s, in the wake of urban crises and the impact of various books arguing for an alternative to postwar planning policies – such as Jane Jacobs's bestselling celebration of urban street life in her *Death and Life of Great American Cities* of 1963 – he underwent a conversion. The expression of this conversion was his book *The Heart of Our Cities: The Urban Crisis, Diagnosis and Cure* of 1965,[68] an indictment of the automobile, of suburban sprawl and mid-city urban blight and a call for the transformation of city centers into walkable, people-friendly areas. The manifesto-like text was clearly a riposte to Jose Luis Sert's *The Heart of Our Cities* (1952), which took the automobile for granted as the only form of transportation in cities.

Gruen moved back to Vienna in 1968, where he was commissioned by his friend Felix Slavik, the Social Democratic Mayor of Vienna, to draw up a plan for the city's historic center, the First District. Slavik had been Gruen's stage assistant in the Politische Kabarett (Political Cabaret), founded by a group of Socialist Youth a block away from Gruen's family apartment on the Riemergasse (now the renowned jazz venue Porgy and Bess).

As a new apostle of pedestrianized urban centers, Gruen had returned to his original vision of the shopping mall, which he had intended to be far more multi-functional, with housing, schools, medical services, a park and a lake making up the urban pedestrian zone. This notion was first developed immediately after the war as the 'Lijnbaan' by the Dutch architect Johannes van den Broek for the tabula rasa of Rotterdam, which had been totally flattened by German bombing. In Vienna, Gruen was instrumental in creating an urban design which was to become imitated worldwide, namely the pedestrian zone of Vienna's First District. As opposed to the usual mono-functional approach, exclusively based on shopping, it includes residential and work areas, all made accessible by public transportation. Gruen's great innovation was to adapt the multi-functionality of the Wollzeile, interweaving shopping, residential, cultural and work activities in a richly textured, historic urban fabric, and to impose strict zoning whereby shops were integrated in a fine-grained, cellular pattern with housing and workplaces, and access via the metro. These ideas shaped the final plan for the urban center of Vienna and explain why it has remained lively, with a broad social mix.[69] Irony of ironies, this pioneer of the shopping mall also opposed the invasion by the car into the city center (fig. 99).[70]

Based on his Viennese experience, Gruen wrote more works advocating his new approach to urban planning. One was his *Charter of Vienna* (1972),[71] conceived as a challenge to Le Corbusier's *Athens Charter* of 1931 and to 'the developers and promoters, specialized consultants, each wearing blinders with regards to other specialized fields'.[72] His *Lebenswerte Stadt* of 1975 advocated mixed uses in a cellular model not only for urban districts but also for regional settlements. Unfortunately, he never got to publish one of his most intriguing works, an urban planning game based on Monopoly, in which all the players, from the mayor to the developers to the users, negotiate over the shape of a city, its monuments, transportation network, pedestrian traffic, housing and shops. It remains in his archive in Vienna. He died in 1980, before he could actively promote these ideas to other municipal administrations, ideas based on a prototype of his native city to which he had always clung throughout his professional life as an architect of large-scale projects.

99 Victor Gruen, proposal for turning the center of Vienna into a multi-functional pedestrian area and banning automobile traffic. From his *Centers of the Urban Environment* (1973), p. 345

8

The Kreisky Era
From the Late 1960s to the Present Day: Economic Prosperity and Culture Wars

With the election of Bruno Kreisky to the post of Chancellor of Austria in 1970, the country entered what is generally referred to as a second phase of Austro-Keynesianism, even more dynamic and innovative than the first.[1] No one left a greater mark on the history of postwar Austria than the charismatic Kreisky, trained as a lawyer, who governed until 1983. He had joined the youth wing of the Social Democratic Party in 1925 at the age of 15 and after the party was banned by the fascist government of Dollfuss in 1934, he became a member of the underground. He fled to the neutral and social-democratic Sweden after the Anschluss but returned to Austria after the end of the war and quickly rose inside the party. No doubt drawing from his first-hand experience of Hugo Breitner's policies, he also imported welfarist economic ideas from Sweden, but infused them with an Austrian character to create a stabilizing macro-economic policy mix which balanced anti-austerity spending with business friendly policies, carried out under finance minister Hannes Androsch, which encouraged entrepreneurship.[2] Whatever the fluctuations in the economy or in the make-up of political coalitions since then, the fundamental structure – based on a commitment to full employment,

100   Zünd-Up, *Auto Expander*

universal social services and a minimum standard of living[3] – has remained the same. The result was an unabated outpacing of the earlier postwar 'Austrian Miracle', continuing up until the very recent past, marked by the collapse of bad banks in 2015 and the refugee crisis of 2016.[4] Because this cohesive approach to the economy has been maintained throughout almost the past 50 years, I have treated it as a single period.

    Indeed, against the international current, the Kreisky government doggedly clung to classical Austro-Keynesianism with its heavy state expenditure as a shield against economic crisis and as a stimulus for industrial development and economic growth. Faced with the first oil price shock that sent inflation soaring and caused stagflation in the mid-1970s, it did not adopt the kind of austerity policies implented, most notably, in Britain and the United States during the Thatcher and Reagan period.[5] It eschewed the tendency to shift priorities away from jobs and social welfare toward a policy of higher unemployment, spending cuts, tax reduction and the slashing of budget deficits.[6] In fact, Austria not only pursued a business-as-usual agenda, it redoubled its commitment to Keynesianism in the belief that, just as it had helped create an economic miracle in the immediate postwar period, it would continue to maintain prosperity if permitted to run its course. Throughout that period and up until the present, Austria has adhered unwaveringly to a welfare-state social contract in spite of opposition both on the far right and the far left.

Unlike most other Western countries, Austria's history of the past 50 years has been one of continuity rather than one of rupture. In 2015 it ranked tenth among the most prosperous of all the OECD countries,[7] its level of unemployment was the lowest in the EU, and the budget deficit, which had risen sharply after 2008, had fallen back to below the 3 per cent threshold by 2014.[8] Social cohesion remains high.[9]

The case of Austria appears to confirm the view that, although welfare-state expenditure has generally been blamed in the West for the economic crisis of the mid-1970s, the real cause was external. Globalization meant competition from China and India, with their low cost of labor, and the resulting growth of the 'Asian tigers' drew an increasingly mobile capital and labor market away from the Western economies. By not retrenching from Keynesian policies, Austria fared better than countries that followed neo-liberalism.[10] Taking advantage of the great economic gains of the immediate postwar period, the Kreisky administration continued to invest in infrastructure – transportation, schools, hospitals and, most importantly here, social housing schemes – on which the economy still rests today.[11]

An equally dramatic feature of this long period was the coming to grips with the 'memory problem' that had accompanied the dominant postwar culture of denial. There was a reawakening of the tradition of *Kulturkampf* of the kind that Karl Kraus, Adolf Loos and Otto Wagner had led between the 1890s and Kraus's death in 1936. It first emerged among a small but vocal minority of artists but it was to become increasingly strident, acrimonious and widespread with time. Theodor Adorno's declaration in 1949 that 'to write poetry after Auschwitz is barbaric'[12] played a major role in sparking the so-called *Sprachkritik* ('language critique') movement. Every historical period has its own voice, its own language, and Adorno's statement captured the zeitgeist that marked the output of German-speaking artists at the time.

Sprachkritik provided postwar artists with a tool for breaking down the wall of silence that hid the harrowing realities of Austria's involvement in the Second World War. The fact that this had to be carried out in an oblique, coded, elliptical way is an indication of the existentialist, angst-filled, suffocating culture of the times. *Sprachkritik* was to become the mainstay of all major Viennese intellectuals and artists from the 1950s to the 1980s. In the literary sphere, the poets Paul Celan and Ingeborg Bachmann, who became lovers, were among the earliest in the German-speaking world to attempt to write poetry, in spite of Adorno's pronouncement, after the war. Celan, a Jew from the former Austro-Hungarian city of Czernowitz, whose pen name derives from a partial anagram of his real name, Paul Antschel, had moved to Vienna in 1952, where he met Bachmann. His haunting poems were necessarily halting and litotic in the extreme because they were conceived as an attempt to invent a new language. Meanwhile the composer Peter Kubelka was an early explorer of the breakdown of the familiar musical language of pre-war Vienna.

But the subsequent artistic output of what the Viennese embraced as *Sprachkritik* translated less into this kind of understatement and lyricism and far more often into an uncompromising and extreme expressionism characterized by a cacophonous, incoherent, often obscene, even self-mutilating fury. Among the first stirrings of the artistic manifestations to emerge was the provocative, but still relatively tame Art Club. Among its most prominent members were the poet Gerhard Rühm, the artists Herbert Boeckl, Maria Lassnig and Arnulf Rainer, and the writers Friedrich Achleitner and Friederike Mayröcker.

Active between 1946 and 1953, the Art Club, according to Rühm, reached only a small group of people. In contrast to the German equivalent, Gruppe 47, its members were not only literary; thanks to what had become the second nature of Viennese high culture, it was multi-disciplinary, bringing together painters, sculptors and musicians as well as writers. Their meeting place was a jazz club under Loos's American Bar, just off the Kärntnerstrasse, which also served as an exhibition center, visited by Jean Cocteau, Orson Welles and Benjamin Britten. As Rühm wrote:

There was an urgent need to recover lost ground and for us, the young ones, to discover modern art, which had been largely ostracized up to then, even before 1938, when it had reached merely a small minority, especially in Austria; the big libraries had failed to collect its most important documents, or they had been 'purged'; we had to rely on sparse material scattered in private archives; the fragmented information on expressionism, Dadaism, surrealism, constructivism, was lapped up eagerly, passed on, pieced together with difficulty to provide a picture, first the important names and titles [needing] to be identified in order to know what to look for; this made every clue, even the shortest statement, an exciting discovery.[13]

The Art Club's performance art had an impact. In 1951, a parliamentary debate was held in which one member launched an attack against it as a 'miasma of perversities'.[14] Art theoretician Ernst Fischer fulminated that:

> . . . this world is so replete with ugliness, with infamy, so tinged with eerie disgust, that any artist worth his salt must revolt against it and would be a liar if he attempted to whitewash it . . . What passes for cultural policy in Austria is clearly unable to provide even the slightest impetus for a new, emerging culture. In this Austria of the coalition, there is the danger that capable young people will slip deep into despair, hopelessness, nihilism. Ladies and Gentlemen, if you see ghosts grinning down at you from the walls of some art exhibition, you should ask yourself if you have deserved any better . . .'[15]

One of the subsequent waves of convulsive *Kulturkampf* came in the form of the Vienna Group (Wiener Gruppe), composed of Gerhard Rühm (again), H. C. Artmann, Konrad Bayer and Oswald Wiener. It began to constitute itself in 1952 at the Café Hawelka, a couple of blocks away from the American Bar. Friedrich Achleitner joined in 1955: to put things in perspective, this was the year Allen Ginsberg performed *Howl* at the Six Gallery in San Francisco. Drawing perhaps on Viennese prewar precedents such as Kraus's *avant-la-lettre* 'performance art' based on nonsense rants against the political and cultural status quo of the

1930s (which sounded like the contemporary rants of Adolf Hitler), the Wiener Gruppe combined literary cabaret, concrete poetry and collage in their own incensed, raucous performance art (fig. 101). One of the group's most painfully compelling pieces, Konrad Bayer and Gerhard Rühm's performance *'Bissen Brot'* ('A Bite of Bread'), a phrase associated in the collective memory with the starving victims of the Second World War, expressed a complete breakdown of even the ordinary German language, indissociable from Austria's complicity in the war.[16] The group dissolved in 1964 after existentialist angst pushed Bayer to suicide.[17]

The visual arts were shaken up by the Seckau Abbey Symposium held in early July 1958, entitled 'Situation-Konfrontation'. The meeting was organized by a Catholic priest, Monsignor Otto Mauer, director of the only modern art gallery in Vienna at the time, the Galerie Nächst St Stephan, which exhibited the work of artists such as Peter Kubelka, Maria Lassnig, Joseph Beuys and Friedensreich Hundertwasser. Arrested repeatedly by the SS during the German occupation, Mauer emerged as part of the postwar Catholic Enlightenment, the Austrian equivalent of Père Couturier, Le Corbusier's patron for the monastery at La Tourette (1959) in France.[18] Mauer's main concern was to denazify the Austrian Catholic Church, whose reputation was tainted in particular by the Archbishop of Vienna, Theodor Innitzer, who had welcomed the Anschluss in 1938.

Besides bringing together local cultural figures, such as Maria Lassnig and Gerhard Rühm, along with foreign participants such

101 Wiener Gruppe, second Literarisches Cabaret (literary cabaret) performance, involving the smashing of a piano, 15 April 1959, by Friedrich Achleitner and Gerhard Rühm

as Pierre Restany, the Seckau symposium was also the setting for the first major critiques of architecture in Austrian postwar history, not by architects but by three Austrian artists. One was made jointly by Markus Prachensky and Arnulf Rainer and another, far more provocatively, by the combative, warrior-like Hundertwasser. The year before, in 1957, Hundertwasser had already written in an article entitled '*Mes Yeux sont fatigués*' that 'It would be better to kill people or murder them in their mother's belly than to put them in mass-produced housing units.'[19] In his Seckau statement, entitled 'Mould Manifesto against Rationalism in Architecture', he now declared that 'art and sculpture have been liberated and everyone can produce all kinds of things . . . But in architecture, this basic freedom, the condition of all artistic creation, still does not exist.'[20]

Hundertwasser's personal rebellion against what he saw as the oppressive mediocrity and technocratic regimentation of postwar architecture in Austria was to be a departure point for him, as an artist who eventually became an architect. The 24-year-old Hans Hollein was one of the only two architects in attendance. Both were to serve as conduits through which this critique of postwar architectural mediocrity eventually entered the Austrian mainstream later in the 1960s.

By the mid-1960s these sporadic expressions of counter-cultural ferment evolved into an explosive cultural crisis. The group of artists known as the Vienna Actionists were active between 1960 and 1976, although different figures associated with it continued in a similar vein afterwards. These artists called themselves after the 'Actions' or 'happenings' they performed and often filmed. The group was founded in 1960 by Otto Mühl, Hermann Nitsch, Rudolf Schwarzkogler and Günter Brus.[21] Drawing, as the Austrian art historian Werner Hofmann pointed out, on such Viennese precedents like the contorted, grotesque representation of bodies by Alfred Kubin, Oskar Kokoschka and Egon Schiele,[22] and on Karl Kraus's extraordinarily violent *The Last Days of Mankind*, they saw themselves as cultural guerrilla warriors, using shock tactics to pit their radical, subversive, taboo-breaking works against Austria's guilt-laden complicity in the Nazi regime. The ultimate aim was to tear away the willful amnesia veiling the country's past by expressing what they saw as the deep, hidden reality of wartime Austria.

What all the Actionists shared, along with painter Arnulf Rainer, was the concept of guilt-laden body-centric performances, involving extreme exhibitionism. Among the Actions was Brus's *Wiener*

Spaziergang ('Vienna Walk') of 1965, in which he walked through the streets of Vienna dressed up to look like a corpse. During another Action he got himself arrested for singing the Austrian National Anthem while masturbating and then vomiting. Eventually Brus was awarded the Grand Austrian State Prize in 1997, as was Nitsch in 2005.[23]

Beginning in 1957, Hermann Nitsch had begun to conceive of the 'Theater of Orgies and Mysteries', a travesty of Catholic liturgical themes, from which his artistic practice flowed. In his Action I of 1962, he suspended himself with his arms spread out as if he were Christ and had his body splashed with blood. In Action II of 1963 he replaced his own 'crucified' body with the slaughtered, skinned and disemboweled carcass of a lamb.[24]

With Otto Mühl, who had served in the German army during the Second World War, the grotesque was at its most unrestrained. What he portrayed in his works was the world as an orgiastic Sadean insane asylum. He smeared his own excrement on canvas instead of paint. The bodies of participants in various 'happenings' became the surface and site of his art-making. Besides excrement, he brought in menstrual blood, vomit and afterbirths. Nitsch wrote of him that 'bearing in mind the "inter urinas et faeces nascimur", we are born between piss and shit – he deliberately replaced paint with blood and intestines. From shit to blood: it takes only one step. After all, when blood dries up, it equally becomes brown.'[25]

The early 1960s performances of Peter Weibel and Valie Export added to the taboo-breaking Actionist performances a new, carnivalesque edge, such as in *Aus de Mappe der Hundigkeit* ('From the Dogness File') of 1968, during which Export walked Weibel along the central shopping streets of Vienna like a dog on a leash.[26] During another happening, *Zochfest*, organized by Weibel on 21 April 1967, Nitsch suspended a dead lamb from the ceiling and swung it around the room, Oswald Wiener shouted out literary utterances while throwing dumplings at the audience and Otto Mühl smashed up kitchen furniture and put a cockerel down his trousers, leaving its head dangling from his waistband.[27]

The Viennese theater and cabaret world also saw its own version of *Sprachkritik*. One must single out the outstanding performance work of the actor/author Helmut Qualtinger. His masterpiece is *Herr Karl*, a play in the form of a monologue written by himself and Carl Metz for Austrian television that premiered in 1961.[28] The entire performance takes place in the storage cellar of a food shop. Herr Karl, the fat and slovenly assistant of the shopkeeper, drunkenly narrates the ultimately despicable story of his life to an invisible listener. His narrative extends from the First World War to the present, during which he portrays himself switching political alliances from fascism to Nazism and from Nazism to postwar apoliticism, without the slightest afterthought. Among Qualtinger's other cabaret performances were an imitation of Hitler reading *Mein Kampf* and a rendition of Karl Kraus's *Last Days of Mankind*.[29]

In the heat of this *Kulturkampf,* the fog of forgetfulness began to lift in the public mind. One of the biggest blows to the fantasy of victimhood came from without. It was a reference by Edgar Bronfman, the president of the World Jewish Congress, to the wartime record of Chancellor Kurt Waldheim, whom he called 'part and parcel of the Nazi killing machine' in 1985.[30] But the myth was not officially put to rest by the government until 8 July 1991, when Federal Chancellor Franz Vranitzky used a parliamentary debate on the war in Yugoslavia to disown the Austrian doctrine of victimhood and accept the country's role in the Holocaust for the first time.[31] The message of the exhibition at the 1993 Venice Biennale, *Vertreibung der Vernunft – The Cultural Exodus from Austria,* organized by the Austrian Ministry for Education and Art, was clear: 'We must warn against only thinking of Germany when speaking of emigration and exile,' it declared. 'Austria itself created a holocaust of . . . culture on an enormous scale. Scores of geniuses were driven away from Austria and killed for reasons that have to do with Austrian history . . . The losses that resulted from such a holocaust of the intellect have been enormous.'[32]

Still, a residual anti-Semitism remained deep-seated, even among the cultural elite. When the grandson of Sigmund Freud, the artist Lucian Freud, refused to allow his paintings to be exhibited in Austria in 1999, the director of the KunstHausWien speculated that he 'doesn't want to be compared with his grandfather, and . . . fears that his grandfather's name will overshadow his. It could be a kind of envy, a complex.'[33] He omitted to mention that Lucian Freud's five great-aunts, Sigmund's sisters, had died in Auschwitz and Treblinka.[34]

The architectural world witnessed a *Kulturkampf* of its own, carried out by a group of architects whom the English architect Peter Cook referred to collectively in 1970 as the 'Austrian Phenomenon'.[35] This was an explosive, turbulent time of modernization internationally as much in architecture as in the economy, in society and in culture as a whole. While the late 1960s and early 1970s were a period when the young generation was desperate for new ideas and strove to break away internationally from all conventions, this was even truer in Austria. The economy had heated up, there was upward mobility, there were industrial and scientific breakthroughs, yet movements involving ecological concerns, peace and sexual liberation predominated. Added to this set of issues, Austria's young generation demanded the truth about its past.

Not surprisingly, given the generalized cultural crisis affecting postwar Austria by the early 1970s, the number of architectural counter-cultural groups in Austria by far exceeded those in other countries. Most countries produced one or, at most, two similar movements. England had Archigram, the US had Animal Farm, Japan had the Metabolists, Italy had Archizoom and Superstudio. But Austria had Haus-Rucker-Co, Coop Himmelb(l)au, Heidulf Gerngross, Zünd-Up/ Salz der Erde, Missing Link, the School of Graz (Grazer Schule) – and these were just the second generation.[36] The first generation of so-called 'veterans' included Raimund Abraham, Friedrich St Florian, Günther Domenig, Walter Pichler and, last but not least, Hans Hollein.[37]

What the Austrian Phenomenon had in common with the other architectural counter-cultural movements of the time was its exuberant subversive satire of a postwar architecture that had become, in its view, mired in sloppy thinking. Chantal Beret writes:

> There was a sense that architecture had not kept up with the times, that it was stuck in a time warp, that it was incapable of finding an alternative to technocratic standardization and of taking advantage of technological innovation. In a climate of generalized agit-prop, these architectural groups pursued an anti-architecture stance against the tedium of an administrated world and its authority. It engaged in the screwball econstruction of the allegory of the technocratic, stifling regimentation. They took aim at the architecture of the conveyor belt, and overturned the vapid, simplistic dogmas that underlay it.[38]

But the Austrian Phenomenon featured two characteristics that set it apart from most other national movements and that can be seen, if not as influenced by the art scene, at least as parallel to it and grounded in the same sensibility. The first of these is what Beret called 'pathos', that is a distinctively dystopian feeling, at odds with the 'playful optimism and apolitical positivism' of the other architectural movements.[39] Its members were not seduced by the things that preoccupied other movements: the new space travel, the ubiquitous car culture, consumerism, mass production, the urban condition, the loss of traditional architecture and urban tissue, the destruction of durability, drive-ins, comics, gadgets, television, Yuri Gagarin's Sputnik trip into outer space – all of which had forced their way into the simple world of architecture. Although their antics were madcap and funny, they also betrayed what was becoming a typically Viennese sense of distressing angst. Technology was sensed as ominous, oppressive, threatening, rather than as a source for madcap fantasizing. In the exhibition organized by Feuerstein in 1966 called *Urban Fictions*, Haus-Rucker-Co's Günter Zamp Kelp used a device he called an *Architekturschleuder* ('architecture hurler') to throw rotating images of architecture onto the surface of the surrounding walls, like grenades.

The other distinguishing feature of the Austrian Phenomenon was that, in addition to the usual 'paper' projects, collages and manifestos, its members made widespread use of intentionally provocative performance art, staged outside the confines of gallery and museum walls, on the streets of Vienna. Architects themselves referred to these as 'interventions' or 'actions', often involving their own bodies, and often filmed – as had been the case with the Vienna Actionists. Feuerstein has stated that the architecture scene and the art scene were worlds apart, socially at least, even if the architects drew inspiration from the artists, but this is not entirely correct.[40] The one exception was Friedensreich Hundertwasser, who did bridge the two worlds.

Hundertwasser never deviated from the straight and narrow path he had set for himself toward a non-rational architecture. The year 1967 saw him in Munich in the first of two performances in which he appeared naked, declaring:

> I don't care if I seem ridiculous or not. I am perfectly aware of all this . . . Personally I feel sick when I pass windows that are all alike in streets that are all alike . . . We live in buildings that are criminal, built by architects who are criminals. I cannot understand why people accept to live in these prisons, I come back to this again and again, and that they don't revolt.

101 Haus-Rucker-Co, *Mind Expander*, 1967

The second time he appeared naked was at a performance at the International Student Center in Vienna in January 1968. 'I disrobed for the following reasons: I am convinced man is surrounded by three layers: his skin, his clothes and a building. In the past centuries clothes and buildings have undergone an evolution that has nothing to do with nature and with basic human needs ... Naked man returned to his natural state is a harbinger of protest to come.'[41]

In a more ludic and carnival spirit, among the earliest, wildest, most striking images and performances of the Austrian Phenomenon were those of Haus-Rucker-Co. The group was founded in 1967 by architects Laurids Ortner, Günther Zamp Kelp and Klaus Pinter, who were later joined by Manfred Ortner. The aim of their installations and happenings, which used soft, pneumatic bubbles or prosthetic devices that altered perceptions of space, seems to have been to serve as a critique of the regimented spaces of bourgeois life by creating comforting, womb-like architecture. They were exploring the potential of architecture, creating experimental environments and utopian cities as a critique of the uniform, prefabricated buildings that had come to dominate social housing. In 1967 they came up with the *Pneumacosm*, 'a living unit that functions like a light bulb . . . conceived to be delivered ready to install and plug into the special holding unit of a vertical urban structure.' It was a 'spherical balloon, 12 meters in diameter, made of reinforced-polyethylene skin segments

welded together, kept in shape by an elevated inner pressure.'[42] Among their most striking projects were the *Mind Expander* (1967), a 'communication plastic' installation in which two people would sit in a certain position inside a helmet-like balloon that was tipped over their heads, and *Fly Head*, which distorted the wearer's perceptions. Their *Gelbes Herz* ('Yellow Heart') of 1968 was a pneumatic, 'vibrant communication space capsule' for two people (figs 102–4).[43] With *OASIS No. 7* at Documenta 5 in Kassel, Haus-Rucker-Co created a transparent sphere with a diameter of eight meters that emerged from the main façade of the Fridericianum. Their *Green Lung* of 1973 was 'an artificial respiratory organ for town dwellers. Used air produced here is filtered and cleaned, enriched with chemical aromas, imbued with illusions of fresh green. What you inhale is synthetic nature.'[44] Works like these had a popular, almost cult following because of their playfulness, in contrast to the performances of the Actionists.

103 (opposite)   Haus-Rucker-Co, *Gelbes Herz* ('Yellow Heart'), 1968

104 (above)   Haus-Rucker-Co, *Ballon für Zwei* ('Bubble for Two'), 1967

105 (above)   Coop Himmelb(l)au, *Villa Rosa*

106 (opposite)   Coop Himmelb(l)au, *House with Flying Roof*, London, 1973

Coop Himmelb(l)au, founded by architects Wolf Prix and Helmut Swiczinsky, paralleled the impertinently mischievous pranks of Haus-Rucker-Co. They created large balloon-like pneumatic structures from 1968 to 1972, such as their *Villa Rosa* (1968; fig. 105), a design for a 'Living Unit', and their *Wolke* ('Clouds'; fig. 106). In 1971 they installed *City Football*, in which giant single-storey balls rolled back and forth in the street, mimicking an enormous billiard table (*Riesenbilliard*) that Haus-Rucker-Co had put up in 1970. In *Hard Space*, they set off a series of explosions triggered by heartbeats, and in their *Soft Space* vast quantities of foam spilled out into a street. After an initial period marked by an anti-intellectual, clownish spirit, Coop Himmelb(l)au became increasingly aggressive over time. As they explained: 'The initially amicable interventions in Basel and Vienna triggered, much to our surprise, violent, aggressive reactions in the audience, so that our interventions became increasingly aggressive too.'[45] In 1980, they staged a pyrotechnic event entitled *Architecture Must Burn* at a rave in Graz, using a steel construction that burned apocalyptically atop an abandoned building for a couple of minutes.

Zünd-Up – based on the German word *zünden*, meaning 'to ignite' – was founded in 1969 by former students of Günther Feuerstein: Timo Huber, Hermann Simböck and Michael Pühringer. The word set the agenda, according to Feuerstein: the focus was on igniting ideas.⁴⁶ Subsequently Salz der Erde was formed in 1970 when members of Zünd-Up were joined by Wolfgang Brunbauer, Günter Matschiner and Johann Jascha. Their first action was a protest scene in the U-Bahn, filmed to produce their first video. Zünd-Up/Salz der Erde were among the artists who made coherent and articulate calls for the control of cars in the city, and criticized the power politics of architecture through their performances and collages, which equated urbanism with devastation (fig 100 and color plate 22).

Missing Link, the group formed by Adolf Krischanitz, Angela Hareiter and Otto Kapfinger, produced artistic objects, graphics, actions, performances and experimental films. One gets the sense that their interventions were directed toward finding realistic solutions to the sorry state of the urban environment rather than indulging in phantasmagoric architectural visions. They were the most intellectual of all the groups, prolific producers of serious essays, and their references were to the enlightened generation of American writers on postwar urban culture. Grounded in the works of contemporary American authors, such as Jane Jacobs's *Death and Life of Great American Cities* and Erving Goffmann's *The Lonely Crowd*, and novels like James Joyce's *Dubliners*, they moved away from Pop Art themes and adopted a position that engaged with the sociological dimensions of urban life.

This generation of the Austrian Phenomenon was shaped by its forerunners. All the members of the above groups had been students of Günther Feuerstein at the Technical University of Vienna. He was not only the main theoretician of these groups, which he called collectively 'Visionary Architects' in his many publications about them, but he was their main impresario, presenting them at the Galerie nächst St Stephan in 1968 in an exhibition called *Urban Fiction*.

Besides Günther Feuerstein, the younger generation drew inspiration from the manifestos and art works of Raimund Abraham and Friedrich St Florian. The uncompromising artist Walter Pichler (1936–2012), in particular, played an important role in this respect. An architect trained at the Technical University, he had already become a sculptor and illustrator by 1962 when he introduced himself to Hans Hollein, who had given a lecture on his work at the Galerie nächst St Stephan. The two remained close friends. Of all the architects of the time, Pichler was the most rooted in a dystopian, anti-technocratic angst, set off by a paranoid phobia of technological surveillance preoccupied by the militarization of everyday life on the border between the Eastern and Western Blocs under the threat of thermonuclear warfare. His works included a white, torpedo-shaped helmet with a television inside it (*Portable Living Room*), a rusty bed frame supporting a humanoid form, divided by sheets of jagged glass, and numerous drawings and models of fantastical structures, including floating cities and underground buildings. His architectural drawings were not just plans; they were also works of art in and of themselves. Other images – 'dream drawings,' as he called them – were dark and loaded. His figures were often skeletal or robotic.

Of all the rebellious figures of the Austrian Phenomenon, it was Hans Hollein who played the most important role. Born in 1934, he spent his childhood in such deprivation that he was one of a group of starving Austrian children sent to England after the war in order to be fed. His father died when he was six. Although his mother could barely afford it, she enrolled him in a mechanics' training school and then the avant-garde school of Franz Čižek,[47] a pioneer of art teaching for children as well as a professor at the Kunstgewerbeschule, the center of multi-disciplinary crossovers, alongside Josef Hoffmann, Oskar Kokoschka, Gustav Klimt and Koloman Moser. Hollein credited Čižek as one of his most formative influences.

In the late 1950s, the international art world saw the almost simultaneous eruption of Pop Art, Film Art, Video Art, Photography Art, Minimal Art and Land Art. It was the era of the crossover and of 'everythingizing'. Harald Szeeman's show *Live in Your Head: When Attitudes Become Form* of 1969 at the Kunsthalle Bern is remembered as one of the first exhibitions to dissolve the boundaries between art forms. Here the medium became the message and the message was cross-disciplinary, a polymorphic blurring between different movements and media, bringing together Walter de Maria, Bruce Nauman, Sol LeWitt, Richard Serra and Joseph Beuys. And of course, happenings, performance art, conceptual art and installation art had surfaced by the mid-1950s. These movements dissolved the boundary between the curator and the artist. Artists took charge and they did so outside the confines of the gallery and the museum, adding to the breaking down of barriers the one separating art from the world at large. Curating became an art form in its own right.

Between 1959 and 1976, Hans Hollein served as the main conduit for these ideas to flow into architecture, not only in Vienna but internationally, and he became one of the earliest and most consummate crosser-overs or 'everythingizers' of his generation. It is difficult to draw the line between Hollein's work as an architect and his work as an artist; and also, for that matter, from his work as a curator, a collage artist, a sculptor, a designer, a writer and a magazine editor. The line is difficult to draw, first, because Hollein is so exceptionally multi-faceted, constantly crossing over from one field to another. One measure of his agility is that, during this period, besides becoming the architect we all know, he was also an artist whose work was exhibited by Sidney Janis in 1963, by Richard Feigen in 1964, by Johannes Cladders in 1972 at the Mönchengladbach Museum, by Leo Castelli in 1989, and selected by curators Harald Szeemann and Rudi Fuchs to be part of an exhibition representing Austrian art with five other

Austrian artists in the early 1970s (though this did not materialize).[48] His paintings, collages and graphic works are held by MoMA and the Pompidou Center, among others.

Hollein's ultimate statement in this respect was his '*Alles ist Architektur*' ('Everything Is Architecture') issue of *Bau* magazine of April 1968. In this publication, structured like an exhibition, he opened up the closed world of architecture to the realities of the time. He recategorized architecture. Things not usually associated with 'architecture' or the concept of the 'architect' were suddenly and startlingly equated. Never before had architecture been identified with the most pressing issues of contemporary culture: the Vietnam War, war criminals, sexual liberation, sexual exploitation, the third world, oil cartels, political revolution, pop culture, transience, violence, consumer society, space technology, computer technology, thermonuclear technology, the loss of tradition, labor unrest, Dada, public space, disastrous urban renewal and ecological disaster.[49]

Being from Vienna was an advantage for someone who was going to embark on a creative rethinking of what architecture should be. There was one inventive Viennese artist/architect/curator in particular whom Hollein could look back to as a precedent. This was the correalist crossover artist/architect/set designer/furniture designer Friedrich Kiesler, whom he met in New York in 1959 or 1960.[50]

In addition, Hollein was at least as widely exposed to the American art scene as he had been to the Austrian one. Thanks to a Harkness Commonwealth travel grant, he spent two years in the US, between late 1958 and late 1960. After one year he enrolled at Berkeley at the invitation of Joseph Esherick and William Wurster. There he completed a Master's degree in architecture in 1960 with Esherick and the sculptor James Prestini, both of whom he much admired.

During his stay in the US, Hollein gravitated toward American poets and artists, largely staying clear of the world of architects except for the Bay Area school of Esherick and Wurster, which he believed to be the most modern of all. In fact, he expressed disappointment with American architecture's 'East Coast establishment'. The 26-year-old's final report to the Harkness Foundation was categorical:

> People like Eero Saarinen, Philip Johnson, Marcel Breuer, Yamasaki, Rudolph, are altogether overestimated in their importance and competence. Recent efforts of some of

them to get off the beaten track and break away are more an intellectual realization that something else has to be done than a genuine new way and attitude, which comes from the heart. Of course . . . one man whose work has great potential is Louis Kahn. Certainly no potential has Edward [Durell] Stone . . .

Never one to shy away from controversy, the young provocateur then went on to dismiss the entire output of Stone, by then perhaps the great doyen of 1950s American neo-monumental architecture, comparing it to Hitler's Reichskanzlei (Reich Chancellery) and to the Foro Mussolini (Mussolini's Forum), no less.[51] He was taking up the stance already adopted by the non-conformist Kahn, and, of course, by his teachers at Berkeley. It was at this time, in 1958, in Chicago, that he produced his two designs for 'Skyscrapers' as comments on neo-monumentalism (color plates 23 and 24).

If Hollein avoided the mainstream architectural scene, he was drawn to the most innovative artists of the time, such as Allan Kaprow. Hollein recollected having attended some of Kaprow's earliest 'happenings'.[52] After he returned to Austria in 1960, he must have attended *Eighteen Happenings in Six Parts*, presented in 1959 at the opening of the Reuben Gallery.

One has to read contemporary accounts to get an inkling of the shock Kaprow's happenings provoked. Susan Sontag, one of the most alert minds of the time, wrote: 'There has appeared in New York recently a new and still esoteric genre of spectacle. At first sight apparently a cross between art exhibit and theatrical performance, these events have been given the modest, somewhat teasing name of "happenings".' She goes on to describe the work:

> . . . assemblages, a hybrid of painting, collage, and sculpture, using a sardonic variety of materials, mainly in the state of debris, including license plates, pieces of glass, machine parts, newspaper clippings, and the artist's socks. From the assemblage to the whole room of 'environment' is only one step further. The final step, the Happening, simply puts people into the environment and sets it into motion.

The purpose, Sontag surmised, was to 'destroy conventional meanings, and create through radical juxtapositions (the "collage principle")'.[53]

The idea of crossing over and of everythingizing was indeed central to Kaprow's happenings. In 1965 Kaprow explained the importance of collages in inspiring him. As an undergraduate at New York University, he had been much influenced by John Dewey's book *Art as Experience* (1934). He did graduate work in art history at Columbia University with Meyer Schapiro, for whom he wrote a doctorate on Piet Mondrian. But most importantly of all he started off as the student of John Cage, who formulated the famous dictum that 'Everything we do is music.'

This, along with Berkeley's radically multi-disciplinary and regionalist School of Environment Design founded by William Wurster, is the context in which Hans Hollein's own 'everythingizing' *forma mentis* was shaped. These ideas translated into his remarkably diverse oeuvre. Hollein's first exhibition, in 1960, was his graduation Master's thesis at Berkeley, called *Plastic Space: Space in Space in Space* (color plates 11 and 12). It is the matrix from which all his other works of art, architecture and curation sprang forth between 1960 and 1976. It was the first time he transferred concepts from the field of art 'curating' to the field of architecture 'curating'. The thesis was written in the form of concrete poetry and was around 1000 words long. The desired effect was to bend the definition of architecture, to challenge current *idées reçues* and to break down the boundaries that separated it from art, sculpture, urban design and concrete poetry and, as one might expect from the regionalist mold of Berkeley, vernacular architecture, in this case Hopi Indians and the Incas, and landscape design and regional planning. It included an example of installation art, or rather installation architecture, which he called *City*, made up of large pieces into which Hollein crawled. Moreover, like many of the happenings in the art world at the time, it was presented outside the confines of the gallery space. To this was added a series of clay sculptures, collages, paintings in Indian ink and more concrete poetry.[54] It is to the credit of Joseph Esherick that he accepted such a sui generis work. But then, as Esherick makes clear in the introduction to Hollein's catalogue at the Galerie nächste St Stephan in 1962, he thought of Berkeley as an everythingizing program.

Selection 66 was next, curated by Hollein at the request of MAK director Peter Noever in 1966. Although it was relatively small, it was groundbreaking. What is interesting about it is that Hollein transferred the concept of installation from art curation and applied it to the exhibition of chairs in the MAK collection, with design objects set like art works in specially made architectural environments.

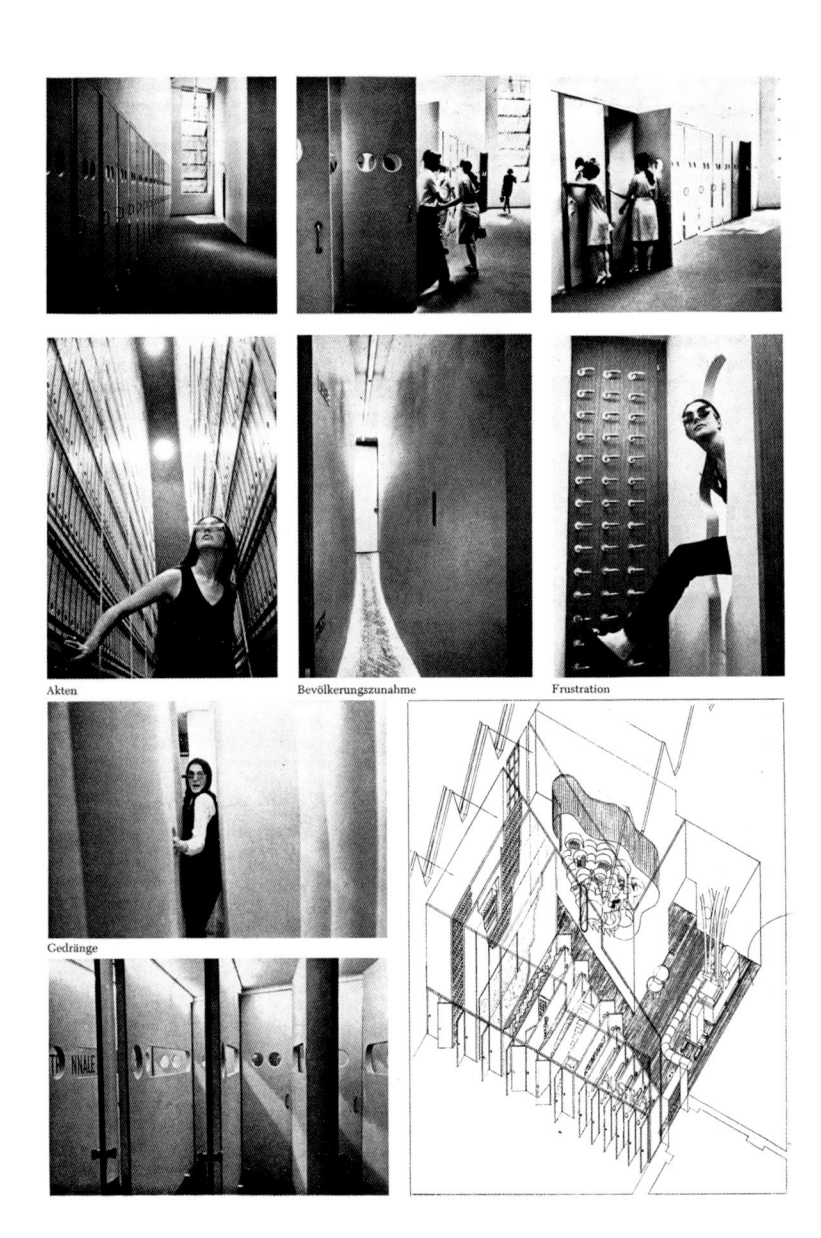

Nineteen sixty-eight was an *annus mirabilis* for Hans Hollein. This was the year when he put together the '*Alles ist Architektur*' issue of *Bau* magazine and also organized the Austriennale, the Austrian contribution to the Milan Triennale of 1968, directed by Giancarlo de Carlo, called 'The Greater Number.'[55] Apart from the theme of the Austriennale, an absurdist satire of Austrian conformity and bureaucracy, what singled it out from all the other architectural exhibitions at the Triennale was that it introduced concepts of curating from the art world, more precisely multimedia and interactive techniques (fig. 107 and color plate 14).

Hollein's next two architectural curating projects were polar opposites as far as content is concerned, although formally both were exercises in crossing over. The first was his Dada *Mobile Office* of 1969,

107 Hans Hollein, part of the Austriennale installation, featuring the celebrated Viennese model Katarina Noever imprisoned in the claustrophobic state bureaucracy and officialdom of Austria. With kind permission of Hans Hollein

108 Hans Hollein, *Mobiles Büro* ('Portable Office'), 1969, showing Hollein himself working in a bubble. MoMA

which was part pneumatic architecture, part performance and part video art. It saw him land on a small runway in a Cessna airplane and deploy an inflatable, transparent plastic office in which he was seen as talking on the phone and typing (fig. 108). The second, in 1970, was a disconcerting expansion of 'everythingizing'. It was about death. Although, viewed from outside Austria, the theme of death was unusual, it was had been commonplace in Viennese art since the early postwar period. The most shocking of Hollein's exhibitions, it was commissioned in 1969 by Johannes Cladders, the director of the avant-garde Mönchengladbach Museum. Lest anyone should doubt that this was an architecture exhibition, he entitled it *Alles ist Architektur:* TOT ('Everything is Architecture: DEATH'). It was, in Hollein's words, about 'archeological excavation sites, archeological burial grounds, mortuary shrouds, deathbeds, tombs and graves.'[56] With this exhibition, Hollein became, with Joseph Beuys, among the first artists in the German-speaking world to break the taboo and confront the realities of Germany's role in the Second World War. But whereas Joseph Beuys's art referred to his own experiences in the German Wehrmacht, Hollein dared to address the Holocaust, as he had also done two years earlier with his *Monument to the Victims of the Holocaust* of 1967. Anselm Kiefer, the artist most associated with the theme today, would begin his own reflections on the Holocaust about this time, with his symbolic *Occupations*, dressed in his father's Nazi army uniform, of different European countries between 1969 and 1975.

Naturally the 'catalogue' was conceived as a catalogue. It contained information about the exhibition, and about previous works of Hans Hollein. But it was also a work of art. It consisted of a funereal black box – a limited edition of 50 was produced – containing two pamphlets and two sprigs of grassy plants.[57] Hollein's curating consisted in scripting a performance, as in a happening. It was the first of the Mönchengladbach's exhibitions to break down the boundary between the museum and the real world. It took place, as Johannes Cladders explained in his introduction, not inside the museum, but outside.[58] It involved performance. Guests were invited to dig into the earth around the museum and search for archeological remains. Then Hollein relocated the guests to artificial archeological sites inside the museum. 'What will the objects buried in the earth in our time disclose to archeologists in the future? It contains a hard hat, a golf club, the shards of a Coca-Cola bottle, a crayon and a pair of crampons.' Some rooms exhibited shrouds hung from the ceiling, another a sarcophagus-like box covered with flowers that were to be left to wilt. Some objects had deliberately erroneous captions. A fool's cap, for example, was attributed to a king, a spiked helmet to a medicine man. A metal hose with a sprinkler attached was labeled as 'a cleansing instrument for the preservation of racial purity,'[59] a reference to the gas jets at Auschwitz.

With *Werk und Verhalten, Leben und Tot* ('Work and Behavior, Life and Death') at the Austrian Pavilion for the 1972 Venice Biennale, Hollein once again returned to the theme of death. The exhibition was divided into two. Part installation and part performance art, in the first section Hollein transformed the interior of Josef Hoffmann's building into a morgue. This was based on a childhood memory of the death of his own father when Hollein was a child of six. The other half of the exhibition was an installation based on extreme elation. It was a raft on the canal at the back of the pavilion, fitted with a chair, a reconstructed memory of the artist as a small child with his father on an Austrian lake. Here Hollein, with his own six-year-old son, re-enacted the scene.[60]

Man Transforms was the opening exhibition of the Cooper Hewitt design museum in 1976.[61] It consisted of 24 interlocking displays, all concerned with real-life situations, by ten leading international architects and designers from different fields. Besides Hollein there was Arata Isozaki, Richard Buckminster Fuller, Richard Meier, Murray Grigor, Ettore Sottsass, Oswald Mathias Ungers, Peter M. Bode, Karl Schlamminger and the German Nader Ardalan. Some used sculptures, some used film. Among the different media were door handles and bread, a sculpture by Isozaki, another sculpture by

Meier and films by Grigor. There were no designers' names on items, no famous manufacturers, no labels of good or bad. 'The role of the Cooper Hewitt Museum is to help people see design, to show how things are designed, and how they affect our lives,' wrote Lisa Taylor, the museum's director. 'The exhibition is different from a traditional object-show simply because it is "experiential" in nature . . . each visitor's reactions will be affected by his or her unique background of experience. It is participatory in the sense that it is demanding: there is nothing to tell the viewer whether this or that is to be looked at in a certain approved way.' In other words, it was like a happening. As Hans Hollein put it: 'Design is here understood as an approach to a problem, as an attitude toward action, shaping life and environment. Design as process, and design as product, encompasses practically any aspect of life. Design can be urban design or architectural design or product design or dressmaking but it can also be cooking or singing or making war or making love.'[62]

We find the same liberating, everythingizing approach in Hollein's published texts.[63] Between 1965 and 1971 Hollein took over *Der Aufbau* – the architecture journal founded in 1926 by Franz Schuster – along with Günther Feuerstein, Oswald Oberhuber and Sokratis Dimitriou, among others, and transmogrified it into one of the major international periodicals of the day. Renamed *Bau*, each issue was deeply imbued with the globalized counter-cultural revolt of the 1960s against the narrow conformism of the 1940s and 1950s and was a manifesto for a new, experimental kind of architecture, sometimes Pop, sometimes High Tech, sometimes neo-brutalist. From the purely formal point of view, its extraordinary graphic design and collagist collection of images made it unique. The cover of the first issue is a collage of images of monuments – the Verrazano Bridge, Hollein's own design for a monument in the form of a colossal train coach of the kind that was used for deporting Jews to concentration camps, a drawing by the Austrian artist Walter Pichler for a dystopian underground city, the pyramids of Giza, and the colossal neo-brutalist auditorium of the late 1960s at the Technical University of Delft by Bakema and van den Broek – along with Roy Lichtenstein's *Whaam!* (fig. 110). Hollein was bent on breaking down boundaries. Inside the magazine one finds Ron Herron's *Walking City* next to Hollein's own collage, *Aircraft Carrier in the Landscape* (fig. 109), and an illustration of a fictional space station out of *Life* magazine. To this combination he added an article, 'The Future of Architecture', in which he called for 'space-plastic' buildings adapted to the realities of 'the contemporary city and the contemporary environment', an architecture that would be 'the expression of all kinds of human relationships, their achievements, their emotions and passions'.

The second issue placed the launching silos at Cape Canaveral on the cover, with the title *Cathedrals of Another Weltanschauung*, and argued for the machine aesthetic to be incorporated in contemporary architecture because it had, as he put it, 'plastic, dynamic, expressive, formal, and emotional potentials'. In this issue Hollein also assembled a visual essay bringing together photographs of the kind of machine-age buildings he had in mind: the Rocket Assembly Plant at Cape Kennedy, the Lowry air force base, a superhighway interchange at Crockett, California, the Radio Telescope in Puerto Rico, an amphitheater of the Incas near Machu Picchu, and the USS *Enterprise* aircraft carrier. The 1965 issue was *Background USA*. This contains a photographic essay juxtaposing a room full of hefty early computers, the Grand Canyon, a Hopi Indian on horseback, the Unity Temple by Frank Lloyd Wright, Le Corbusier's Carpenter Center, a portrait of Louis Kahn and Frank Lloyd Wright, Kahn's Richards Medical Research Building, Burnham and Root's Monadnock Building, Marilyn Monroe in front of Niagara Falls, highway advertisements from Las Vegas, and a portrait of Mies van der Rohe. Four issues later, the magazine placed a transverse section of the curved chamber of the

109 (above)   Hans Hollein, *Flugzeugträger in die Landschaft* ('Aircraft Carrier in the Landscape'), showing the USS *Enterprise*, the first nuclear-powered warship, used during the Vietnam War

110 (below)   Hans Hollein, an issue of *Bau* magazine, 1965, whose theme was technology and the military-industrial complex during the early years of the Vietnam War

ALLES IST ARCHITEKTUR

Bau

1/2 1968

human inner ear on the cover and juxtaposed it with early twentieth-century Viennese Thonet chairs in the name of both industrial, machine-age mass production and organic form. Then came a Romantic Hollein, as enamored with the Southwest as J. B. Jackson, and a Pop Hollein, as excited about popular culture as Reyner Banham and Tom Wolfe.

Bau not only brought the international architectural world to Austria; it lifted the veil of forgetfulness that enshrouded the roots of the architectural culture. *Bau* was the first Austrian magazine to publish the work of Rudolf Schindler and Frederick Kiesler, then unknown in their native Vienna, and to publish documents from the municipal archive of Vienna proving that the Wittgenstein House had really been built by Ludwig Wittgenstein – equally unknown up to that point in postwar Vienna. This made the magazine directly responsible for establishing Wittgenstein's authorship of the house and for saving, by one day, the house from the demolition crew already on the site.

Everything is Architecture is the title of the extraordinary 1968 issue, written entirely by Hollein (fig. 111). It served as the culmination of his thinking about architecture and was a clear and polemic manifesto. Hollein had been one of the earliest importers into architectural thinking of Marshall McLuhan's epoch-making 1962 *Gutenberg Galaxy: The Making of Typographic Man*, the first book to herald the information age and attempt to predict the profound impact it would have on traditional verbal culture. Hollein's manifesto is primarily an attempt to imagine what this age meant for architecture. He was fascinated with the artistic potential of the new electronic media. One of his schemes at the time, in fact, was to replace the University of Vienna with a television set. Hollein was eager to embrace the age of digital reproduction. In the optimistic 1960s, his manifesto was the first to oppose a novel e-topian alternative to the conventional, tired mainstream architectural practices of the day.

What he was calling for was the end of Austrian provincialism and the removal of all boundaries between architecture and other fields. His opening sentence translates as: 'The limited categorical foundations and tradition-bound definitions of architecture and its means have on the whole lost their validity.' His last paragraph translates as: '[A] true architecture of our time, then, is emerging, and is both redefining itself as a medium and expanding its field. Many fields beyond traditional building are taking over "architecture",

111 Hans Hollein, cover of the *Alles ist Architektur* ('Everything is Architecture') issue of *Bau* magazine, 1968

just as architecture and "architects" are moving into fields that were once remote. Everyone is an architect. Everything is architecture.' Hollein's aim was to increase architecture's 'scope and understanding by supplying a basis for the associations it already divined' – with subjects including 'artificial climate', 'transportation', 'clothing', 'environment in the widest sense', 'the senses', 'self-centered clients', 'community', 'cultic architecture', 'control of bodily heat', 'development of science', 'simulated architecture', 'sewn architecture', 'inflatable architecture', 'the haptic', 'the optic', 'the acoustic', 'the expression of emotional needs' and even 'military strategy'.

Hollein assembled his basically visual (as opposed to verbal) manifesto in a collage-like manner and then placed the message 'This is architecture' under each one. One image was of a pill. Another image was of a spray can. Then a fresh stick of lipstick. Then photographs of Sergei Eisenstein; of former architect, Holocaust survivor and Nazi hunter Simon Wiesenthal; of fashion designer Paco Rabanne. Then came the famous photograph, *Guerrillero Heroico*, of Che Guevara by Alberto Korda. There was a caricature of Lyndon Johnson's face as an oil refinery. French-American painter Niki de Saint Phalle is photographed walking with Swiss artist Jean Tinguely out of the vulva of her giant Pop sculpture of a supine woman. Then the observatory of Jaipur. One of Tom Wesselman's *Great American Nude* series was shown next to a nude photograph of the artist/architect Hundertwasser, followed by photographs of a brassiere and a pair of sunglasses, and a computer printout of a digitized message transmitted from Mars by the *Mariner IV* spacecraft in 1965. Then a cartoon drawing of astronauts in a capsule in outer space, a Magritte painting of a giant comb lying in bed, a clenched fist, a soap bubble and a pair of scissors. Never had the definition of architecture been stretched to include these objects.

Hollein was pushing architecture toward the most burning issues of 1960s cultural-sexual liberation, rebellion, violence, the drug culture, futurism, revolution, the loss of tradition, consumerism, anti-Semitism, geopolitics, war, space technology, computer technology, hipness, political protest and bad urban planning. Out of this collagist mentality would come his greatest art pieces: *Superstructure over Vienna* (1960), *Monument for the Victims of the Holocaust* (1967), *Aircraft Carrier in the Landscape* (1964), *Architecture Pill* (1967) and *Urban Renewal in Manhattan* (1964) (fig. 112 and color plates 28 and 29).

112 Hans Hollein, criticism of the urban renovation in Lower Manhattan of the early 1960s

9
After the Shock Therapy
Renewal

Ultimately, the brutal *Kulturkampf* of the late 1960s and 1970s was therapeutic. Like the pent-up energy that was unleashed by Otto Wagner's manifesto in the late nineteenth century, the activists of the Austrian Phenomenon opened the floodgates and shook up the conservative, provincial backwaters of the establishment. They opened up paths away from the mediocrity that had marked the immediate postwar period and reconnected Vienna with its past history as well as with the rest of the world. This, and the fact that the national economy was robust, resulted in a return to the ambitions of *fin de siècle* Vienna to reinvent architecture in keeping with the new realities. This spirit of innovation has been constant over the next three generations of architects. As we shall see in this chapter, the 1970s also marked a time when the city and its architects reconnected to the housing tradition of Red Vienna and attempted to reinvigorate its Gemeindebau tradition.

The first building to surface from the 1960s counter-cultural ferment, not surprisingly, was by Hans Hollein. This was the Retti candle shop (1965–6). Hollein transferred his Pop Art collage technique to architecture in a wholly original way, bringing together many diverse references into his design. Reversing the amnesiac mindset of his 1940s and 1950s predecessors, he created a building that

113 Richard Feigen Gallery. Photo Franz Hubman

was deeply Viennese, replete with references to Otto Wagner and Adolf Loos. Rather than employing citations to mimic the masters, its all-aluminum façade, for example, was a direct quote from Wagner's aluminum- and glass-clad façade for the *Die Zeit* dispatch office of 1902 (color plate 30). Wagner, like Loos, had not balked at using materials and techniques from industry. All superfluous ornamentation disappeared. Only an assembly of dark wooden laths and aluminum strips animated the surface or highlighted the structure. And although it was tiny in comparison to Adolf Loos's Goldman & Salatsch and Knize shops nearby, with a floor plan of barely 25 square meters and a façade 4 meters wide, its extreme nakedness and lack of ornamentation, so at odds with the opulently decorated, *fin de siècle* historicism of its surroundings, was likewise planned from the very start as a provocation whose purpose was to create a media sensation. Located just doors down from Loos's shop, it was also within view of the imperial residence of the Hofburg, on the traditionally patrician shopping street of the Kornmarkt, while its use of mirrors to create an illusionistic infinity effect in a tiny interior was a direct citation of Adolf Loos's infinity mirrors in his equally diminutive American Bar nearby. It also tapped into the fine art of provocation that had been refined by Wagner and Loos. Before its opening, its façade was hidden behind a paper wrapping, with images of a London-based icon of the 1960s, the model Jean Shrimpton, in a space suit, implying that what lay behind was something far out. The controversial shop created a sensation internationally, earning Hollein the US-based Reynolds Prize for 1967. He was the first of his contemporaries to reconnect with Vienna's architectural past.

The collage technique that Hollein had come up with in his art work was to become, through his crossover tendency, the signature feature of all of his architecture. The Retti candle shop was followed by the Christa Metek boutique (1966–7), also in the shopping area of the First District. It collaged Super Graphics into the architectural structure. His design for the Schullin jewelry shop (1972–4) was a cross between a shop and a gigantic piece of jewelry, which in turn represented a gold vein in a mine. As time went on and the scale of his projects grew, Hollein brought together more elements into his schemes. His commission from the Richard Feigen Gallery in 1967–9 was for the renovation of a town house on East 79th Street in New York, the bottom two floors of which were a gallery. Here he sheathed the bearing element of the entrance in highly polished stainless steel and then warped it to look like a double column which acted as a playfully distorting mirror on all that passed (fig. 113). Also featured was a Buckminster Fuller-like design for an all-stainless-steel plug-in bathroom, made to emulate an interplanetary space capsule. Even the ceiling was made of small, parabolic, polished stainless-steel mirrors which filtered the fluorescent lighting above. The lighting was an important part of the design in another way. At a time when neon light had been taken from the world of street advertising and inserted into Pop Art by the sculptor Chryssa, Hollein used bare fluorescent tubes in circular and wiggling patterns on the ceiling of the ground floor. He also playfully introduced pop science-fiction elements in the building. Prefiguring the trend for conspicuous ducts and pipework in buildings today, he had a pipe running along the ceiling of the top floor of the gallery that he called the Plug-in Media Spine, which carried telecommunications and lighting cables. When it came to the nitty-gritty reality of ventilation, Hollein exposed all the shafts he could and either made them out of polished stainless steel or painted them *Yellow Submarine* yellow.[1]

Hollein's Mönchengladbach Museum (1972–82), his largest-scale commission at the time, was another assembly of elements from different sources. Internally, in contrast to the idea of a museum as a universal generic container, a 'white box' where objects float in a seemingly unlimited space, arrested at will by mobile panels, his approach was the opposite. In the Loosian *Raumplan* tradition, his aim was to provide a variety of spaces to serve the specific attributes of the objects exhibited there. The partition into individual and distinct spaces inside the building was reflected on the building's exterior, also broken down into a cluster of units, some in brick, some in chrome or aluminum, some in glass, some orthogonal, some curved. Moreover, nestled as it was into the topography and urban fabric of the surrounding townscape, with its multiple pathways and entrances, interconnected with pre-existing circulation, it was a work of both urban design and of Land Art that succeeded in visually anchoring the entire town with its inviting pathways, leading from the foot of the hill to the top of the building. It was an example of what Hollein called 'walk-on' architecture inspired by the Pueblo architecture he had encountered as a Harkness fellow in 1959.[2] Yet another collage was his Neues Haas Haus (1985–90) that stands opposite the Stephansdom. Clad in glass, it reflects like a mirror the different elements of its widely divergent surroundings, which include a medieval cathedral, an early twentieth-century emporium and a mediocre post-Second World War apartment house (color plate 31). And it also incorporates its historical precedents, namely an early medieval wall founded on the Roman fortification of the heart of Vienna and its turret.

These projects earned Hollein the Pritzker Prize in 1985. Following such success, almost immediately afterwards he entered the fold of the international postmodern architectural establishment. He curtailed his previously prolific artistic output and shed the *Kulturkampf* spirit which had been such a wellspring of formal innovation for him. Although he continued to produce some experimental works during the next decades – such as the Soravia Wing Structure at the Albertina in Vienna (2004), a design for the underground Guggenheim Museum for Salzburg (which was never built), a design for the SBF Fund Tower

(2014) and his Volcanic Museum in the Auvergne (2002) – increasingly he chose instead the path of mainstream commercial building.

Actually, the first major building to emerge out of the postwar Viennese *Kulturkampf* should not have been Hollein's Retti candle shop. It should have been the sculptor Fritz Wotruba's far more weighty Church of the Holy Trinity on the edge of the Vienna Woods in the Twenty-third District. It was conceived in 1964, but because of local resistance to the building it was not completed until after Wotruba's death in 1976, by the architect Fritz G. Mayr. Wotruba, who had escaped to Switzerland during the Second World War, was well known for his uncompromising stance toward the role of Austria in the Third Reich. This had resulted in the cancellation of several of his sculptures, for example the naked figure of a fallen soldier designed in 1934 for the Heroes' Memorial in the Burg Gate, Vienna. His design for the monument *To the Victims for a Free Austria* (1934–45) at the Vienna Central Cemetery was considered too aggressive and accusatory. But a number of his monuments are still on view, among them the controversial 1932 memorial *Man Condemns War in Leoben, Styria*, removed for political reasons in 1938 and re-erected in 1988.[3] With its 152 asymmetrically arranged colossal concrete blocks, each weighing between 1.8 and 141 tons with the largest block being just over 13 meters long, the church was obviously not intended to give the impression of unshakable faith. On the contrary, the arrangement of the concrete slabs evokes destruction and chaos.

A version of the international deconstructivist movement also grew out of the aesthetics of this church after an article on it was published in the *Alles ist Architektur* issue of *Bau* in 1967, although this movement had none of Wotruba's *profunditas*. The first example was a building by another major figure of the Austrian Phenomenon, the Graz School architect Günther Domenig, who, like Hollein, succeeded in making the transition from artist to architect. In 1974–6 he had designed the organic Zentralsparkasse on the Favoritenstrasse in Vienna to much acclaim. But more important was his Steinhaus (early 1980s–1990s), located in the spectacular Alpine landscape of Lake Ossiach near Graz, which was begun barely five years after Wotruba's church. It started off as a series of drawings in the 1980s depicting a structure made of rocks that seem to stand where some geo-tectonic force has thrust them helter-skelter, like the concrete slabs of the Wotruba church. Its overall form echoes the craggy crystalline rocks of the surrounding mountains, with its asymmetrical, disorienting polyhedrons of glass, steel and concrete (color plate 32).

The same concept, of a building made from a stack of chaotic, jagged polyhedrons, is to be found in many of Domenig's subsequent projects, notably his colossal 60-meter-high and 225-meter-long T-Centre in Vienna (2002–4), the headquarters for the Deutsche Telekom subsidiary of T-Mobile. This fractured architectural language seems, however, particularly appropriate to his Nuremberg Nazi Party Rally Grounds Museum (2000–2001), which contains a documentation center and congress hall focusing on the history of Hitler's mass rallies. Given that its permanent exhibition is entitled 'Fascination and Terror' and deals with the causes, context and consequences of Nazism, the jagged, unfinished, brutalist, almost freakish appearance of the building is an apt reminder of the megalomania of the Nazi regime.

Two more architects joined the deconstructivist fold. As soon as they received their first building commissions, Coop Himmelb(l)au's Wolf Prix and Helmut Swiczinsky turned away from the madcap antics inspired by Hans Hollein's pneumatic sculptures, such as their House with a Flying Roof of 1973, and joined another movement of architects, influenced by Frank Gehry's house in Santa Barbara of 1978 and Zaha Hadid's paintings and drawings as a student at the Architectural Association in London, which Wolf Prix came across in his networking visits to Los Angeles and London. The result is a series of diminutive, low-cost, cult buildings. One was their Roter Engel ('Red Angel', 1981), a small bar and music venue 130 square meters in plan in a rundown part of Vienna's First District, which was then dominated by tawdry establishments. Like Gehry's house, it had corrugated metal doors and interior wall panels; the lights were shaded by industrial guard rails, the bar wall was concrete and the floor asphalt. Their next project in the same vein was the unbuilt Merz School in Stuttgart (1981).

Their new aesthetic really came to fruition with their masterful Falkestrasse rooftop addition to the law offices of Schuppich, Sporn and Winischhofer (1983–9). It earned the firm an invitation to participate in the Deconstructivist Architecture exhibition organized in 1988 at MoMA, which launched a movement of the same name that became dominant in architecture schools for the next 15 years. The rooftop project was for the expansion of the existing office to include three new offices and a new conference room. Rather than resorting to the traditional Viennese practice of seamlessly adding on an extra attic to the existing building, Coop Himmelb(l)au's solution was to burst through and beyond the roof of the orderly nineteenth-century historicist building with a glazed roof fragmented as if in an explosion by a mass of light steel beams that seem to be shards or shreds (color plate 33). The architects themselves referred to the result as looking like a 'reverse lightning bolt' or a 'taut electric arc'.

Wolf Prix ended his partnership with Helmut Swiczinsky in the mid-2000s and the firm became Austria's most commercially successful on a global scale, from France to the US and China, with such high-end buildings as the BMW Welt (2001–7) and the European Central Bank in Frankfurt (2003–14), the Martin Luther Church in Hainburg, Austria (2011), with its elegant geometry (color plate 34), the Dalian International Conference Center (2008–12; fig. 114) and the Musée des Confluences in Lyon (2014).[4] Recently he has gained star architect status but seems to have increasingly indulged in an overwrought, almost cartoonish parody of the firm's first projects, typified by the recent Expo 2017 project for Astana, the capital of Kazakhstan (fig. 115).

Carl Pruscha, on the other hand, who studied under Roland Rainer at the Academy of Fine Art and then Eduard Sekler at Harvard, eventually becoming the Dean of Architecture at the former, began his career as United Nations Advisor to the government of Nepal between 1964 and 1974. There Pruscha devised a Katmandu Valley Development Plan and built a UNHCR housing project but he never abandoned his commitment to vernacular architecture in the tradition of Bernard Rudofsky, writing a book on the subject of Himalayan vernacular, as well as conservation, habitat and the environment.[5] This was also true of Günther Feuerstein. His architectural practice remained committed to his 1960s program, aiming to correct what he had seen as the ills of postwar Viennese architecture and planning. Between 1979 and 1985, he was put in charge of revitalizing the mega-prefab housing project of Grossfeldsiedlung by the City of Vienna. The new project focused on playgrounds as a means of creating a sense of community. Since the city did not implement the plan, Feuerstein resorted to doing so with the help of citizen participation. But it was Friedensreich Hundertwasser who was the most steadfast in his pursuit of the revolutionary stance he had assumed at the Seckau meeting of 1958, and later in his performances in the nude of 1967 and 1968. We will come to him and his milestone achievement, the Hundertwasserhaus social housing project, in the next chapter.

The one major architect of this generation who went against the current and decided to devote himself to building a socially conscious practice was Anton Schweighofer. Like his mentor, the Dutch architect Aldo van Eyck, with whom he formed a lifelong friendship, he sought to eschew grand gestures and what he perceived as empty rhetoric, and instead to try and transform the everyday into an understated architectural form, an architecture of community and encounter.[6] His entire career was spent in the service of 'the greater good' and in creating a humane form of architecture, concerned with the care of underprivileged children, university students and the elderly.[7] His most remarkable buildings were devoted to children: SOS Children's Villages in India (1965–9) and in South Korea (1966–7) and his Stadt des Kindes ('City of the Child', 1974) in Vienna, which was home to 260 children in care at any one time, from two to 19 years of age. Funded by the City of Vienna, it was inspired by the Austrian social worker

114 (opposite) Coop Himmelb(l)au, Dalian International Convention Center, China, 2008–12

115 (above) Coop Himmelb(l)au, Expo 2017, Astana, Kazakhstan, City of the Future. Competition entry, 2013

Hermann Gmeiner's work with orphans of the Second World War, and built in the bucolic patrician suburb of Hietzing near the Vienna Woods. Likewise influenced by Aldo van Eyck's famous Amsterdam Orphanage (1960), Schweighofer's design was based on the concept of the child as 'the lord of architectural space' and applied in particular to underprivileged children from broken families, but his complex was much bigger and more multi-functional than its Dutch precedent. Among the facilities were an Olympic-sized swimming pool, a sauna, a disco, a theater, sports grounds, playgrounds, a ceramics workshop and a doctor's surgery. The project itself was made up of five identical 'family units', each with its own mother figure who was head of the household. The buildings were white stucco with cheerful bright red handrails along the many terraces and balconies adjoining the bedrooms. In addition, bridges, some glazed and some roofed, linked the five buildings to each other and to the sports and cultural facilities, like streets in the sky. Over its 30-year history, around 5000 children went through the Stadt des Kindes. Today, there are 233 such complexes throughout the world. The building itself was demolished in 2008. In its place is a housing project into which is integrated a small part of Schweighofer's original complex, designed by Walter Stelzhammer and overseen by Schweighofer himself.

Most of the architects who had been part of the Austrian Phenomenon, like Hollein, Prix and Swiczinsky, did an about-face by the end of the 1970s, abandoning their confrontational fervor and embracing mainstream professional life. This was understandable – the culture wars had been fought and won. Given the sustained boom that characterized the Austrian economy in the late 1960s, they had much to gain in opting for a *retour à l'ordre*. They pursued commissions for high-end buildings, free of any cultural ambition, and were successful in obtaining them. The result was an extraordinary series of quality mainstream architecture. For example, Ortner and Ortner, former members of Haus-Rucker-Co, went on to design the monolithic Museum of Modern Art (2001; fig. 116), the Kunsthalle Wien and the Leopold Museum, all three in the Museumsquartier, the former site of the Baroque Imperial Stables, designed by Fischer von Erlach, and now the center of contemporary art in Vienna. Their Landesarchiv in Duisburg, Germany, and City Tower Vienna in Wien Mitte are more mundane, but well planned. They provide a functional backdrop for what has become a highly successful public space, the open, airy Wien Mitte shopping center. Missing Link's Adolf Krischanitz turned into a thoughtful, subdued radical in his monastic rejection of ornament, notably in his New World School in Vienna (1994) and his Rietberg Museum in Zurich (2006).[8]

Heinz Tesar, more of a fellow traveler of the *Kulturkampf* than an activist participant, also availed himself of a minimalist language to create unusually pure, airy and serene environments particularly well suited to church and museum design, such as his Essl Museum in Klosterneuburg (1998–9) and his Donau City Church of Christ (1999). Another member of the Graz School, Helmut Richter, designed the formally daring Secondary Science School at Kinkplatz (1994), characterized by blue glass walls and featuring a pair of wing-like masses that frame a lofty gymnasium, plus a series of classrooms with exposed-concrete ceilings and industrial detailing.

And finally, there was Hermann Czech. He too was discontented with the conservative and anti-intellectual bent of postwar Austrian architecture. Through a series of writings, beginning with a book dedicated to Adolf Loos's Goldman & Salatsch shop, mistitled *Das Looshaus*, co-authored with Wolfgang Mistelbauer in 1976, he pointed

116 Ortner and Ortner, Museum Moderner Kunst (Museum of Modern Art), Vienna, 2001

out the deeply ornamental aspect of the building. Czech's entire oeuvre as an architect is a hushed, elliptical, hermetic evocation of the lost world of the *fin de siècle*. The fact that this was by definition the world of Jewish Vienna could not be uttered by his generation. And so Czech's references are not spelled out but understated in the extreme. Whereas the architecture of the Austrian Phenomenon screamed, his architecture whispered. His architectural statements are, in fact, coded messages, which are always associated with a moral stance and are at odds with the empty posturing of the bombastic sophist. His designs are means of dredging up from its murky past Vienna's 'memory problem'. For someone like Czech, who grew up in post-Anschluss, Nazi Vienna, this questioning is also existential and autobiographical.

Czech's diminutive Kleines Café of 1970 serves as a strangely familiar, ghostly memory of past Viennese coffee-house life (fig. 117). Its way of dealing with architectural language is, in spite of its apparent ordinariness, highly charged and difficult to read. One needs to have prior knowledge of Viennese history in order to tease out the intricately integrated chinks-of-the-past meaning that the interior contains. One needs to know that some of the cafés evoked – the Griensteidl, the Café Central, the Museum Café, the American Bar – were where intellectual life happened in *fin de siècle* Vienna. One needs to know, as Carl Schorske pointed out, that these cafés are synonymous with the irredeemably lost world of Karl Kraus, Felix

Salten, Jung Wien, Klimt, Loos, Peter Altenberg, Arthur Schnitzler and Hugo von Hofmannsthal.⁹ One needs to know that Czech's use of mirrors is a direct reference to Loos's American Bar, and the tables to those of the Café Hawelka. The chairs too are the typical black Thonet chairs associated with the bygone cafés. The ground is made of tombstones, a comment perhaps on the fate of the intellectual life that once infused Vienna's celebrated cafés.¹⁰ A series of cafés and restaurants, Wunder Bar (1975–6), Lokal Salzamt (1981–3), Czech's bar at the Schwarzenberg Palais, the MAK Café (1993; fig. 118), the Theater Café (1998 and 2010), and Gasthaus Immervoll (2000), are all likewise replete with concealed references to the bygone era that take time to decipher, and that inevitably yield a profound sense of loss, but also an attempt to overcome the amnesia.¹¹

Czech has also designed a series of houses. They overcome the amnesia of his generation in a different way, by reviving the tradition of Loos, specifically his *Raumplan*, and of Josef Frank's accidentism, that is the celebration of ordinariness and everyday attachment to things. They too are characteristically understated and have not been widely publicized until now.¹²

117 (opposite)   Hermann Czech, Kleines Café, interior

118 (above)   Hermann Czech, MAK Café

The most dominant trend of the next generation of architects, who had been onlookers during the turbulent years of the *Kulturkampf,* steered clear of the boisterous uproar of their elders. By the time this new generation entered upon the professional scene in about 1990, the economy was going full tilt. These architects chose to pursue cool, frictionless, discreetly luxurious minimalism, placing the emphasis on expensive materials, rigorous detailing and gleaming finishes, all suited to high-end clients. The one notable exception was Next Enterprise, whose most celebrated building, the concert hall at Grafenegg close to Vienna, employed the deconstructive aesthetics of Coop Himmelb(l)au.

The firm most representative of this perfectionist current is the extraordinarily multi-faceted and versatile Delugan Meissl, founded by Roman Delugan and Elke Meissl, former students of the University of Applied Arts in Vienna. They excel in a large number of areas, including interior design, urban design, healthcare, retail, domestic and cultural buildings, and, as we shall see in the next chapter, social housing.[13] Their stunning EYE Film Institute in Amsterdam (2012) and their Festival Hall for the Tirol Festival of Erl (2014) display what has become their trademark emphasis on long, clean, white, sleek horizontal surfaces, angular cantilevers and smooth, flawlessly crystalline geometry (fig. 119). Their interiors have their own distinctive design feature. As opposed to their smoothly immaculate exteriors, here the material of choice is generally natural wood, with its warm texture and color (fig. 120).

Their most prestigious project is the Porsche Museum in Stuttgart (2009), next to the headquarters of the company. The museum's spectacular reflective membrane wraps around the façade into the entrance and onto the ceiling of the colossal foyer, revealing yet another update of Adolf Loos's (color plate 35). As in Knize and

Goldman & Salatsch buildings, this museum, which is ultimately a showroom, uses its seductively shimmering surfaces to incorporate the viewer into a gold-tinted paradise.

If the Porsche Museum is meant to stand out, Delugan Meissl's Casa Invisibile (2013), located in the countryside near Vienna, fits right in. In a register more akin to magic realism, the mirror-like skin of this 'invisible' house creates the illusion that it has become seamlessly fused with its natural surroundings (color plates 36 and 37).

The Viennese firm of Jabornegg and Pállfy is the most culturally sensitive expression of this understated trend. Their emphasis is on restraint, balanced by perfect construction detailing. Their materials are quietly luxurious: raw-edged concrete polished until it becomes mirror-like, reflecting the beholders as they move along long passages punctuated by buffed, gleaming stretches of stainless steel, past naked glass detailing under cool white fluorescent lighting. This aspect of their architecture was why the British artist Rachel Whiteread chose

119 (opposite)   Delugan Meissl, EYE Film Institute, exterior, Amsterdam

120 (below)   Delugan Meissl, EYE Film Institute, interior

121 Jabornegg and Pálffy, renovated National Council Chamber, Vienna, 2016–17

them to collaborate on her sculptural monument commemorating the Holocaust on the Judenplatz in Vienna (2000). Their Museum Judenplatz, located underground, directly below Whiteread's sculpture, is above the excavation of a synagogue destroyed in 1421. The excavation is accessible through the Mizrahi House, which is now the site of the Jewish Museum on the square. Gleaming galvanized steel and brass cladding precisely delineates the outer extent of the excavations. The simple industrial roof filters direct southern light through louvres. The white truss-supported artificial skin hides all technical installations between the roof and ceiling and ensures an even distribution of light. A bridge floats just four centimeters above the archeological remains.

The firm's innate sensitivity toward the archeological and architectural history of whatever site they work on, in sharp distinction to that of international star architects like Hollein and Wolf Prix, is the reason why in 2014 they won the competition for the extension of Hansen's Parliament building on the Ringstrasse (fig. 121).

A second memorial was the work of a team made up of artists Iris Andraschek and Hubert Lobnig and landscape architects Maria Auböck and Janos Kárász, who are responsible for some of the city's most prestigious landscaping projects, such as the restoration of the eighteenth-century Belvedere garden (1995–2009) and of the Augarten

(2003). The project arose from a plan to build a memorial on the site of the Turner Temple, designed by the Jewish architect Karl König in 1923 in the mostly Jewish Fifteenth District. It was burnt down during Kristallnacht, like most of the city's other synagogues, and the site was eventually turned into a gas station. A foundation called Herklotzgasse 21 joined forces with the Vienna Wiesenthal Institute for Holocaust Studies to restore it to the Jewish community and to organize a competition for the proposed memorial.[14] The winning project was inaugurated in November 2012. Like the rest of Auböck and Kárász's work, it is understated, subtly demarcating the original structural elements of the building, and creating a public place. A third memorial is Gabu Heindl and Hito Steyerl's *Unter Uns* ('In Our Midst'), an installation for Linz European City of Culture for 2009 in which the architects took the façade of what was once the SS headquarters and left marks on the plaster that appear to be laceration scars.

A new current has appeared among the third generation of architects, who entered practice in the late 2000s: a sense of responsibility to the urban environment and the need to move beyond individual building to considering the town or city as a whole. What makes these projects specifically Austrian is that they are all responses to municipally initiated projects and to responsible, top-down urban planning policies. The most pressing concern for these architects has been to improve the quality of the urban social community in which buildings are embedded. One such firm is Roland Gruber's non:conform. Their playful Mobile Grandstand (2008) was created for the small, picturesque, pastel-colored Baroque town of Haag in Lower Austria, where, in 1999, an open-air summer theater festival was founded which required a structure for the audience. These young architects came up with the idea of a temporary bandstand on stilts with a canopy to shelter 650 people. Made out of wood and steel, it can be disassembled and stored over the winter by the citizens themselves in a specially made shelter. The result is a bright red, exuberant structure that offers an unobstructed view of the stage as well as of the curving curlicues atop the surrounding buildings (fig. 122).

Viennese architects can have a particular feel for rusticity. Martin Feiersinger's reconversion of a farmhouse into a residential building (2010–13) in Ramsau, one of the small towns in the Zillertal Valley in the Tyrol, is a case in point (fig. 123). The immediately striking quality of the building is the profile and massing, almost identical to those of

122 (above)   Non:conform architects specialize in participatory projects. This was for the Summer Theater for the town of Haag in Lower Austria

123 (opposite)   Martin Feiersinger, converted barn in Ramsau, Styria, 2010–13

the old farm building next to it. Rather than mimicking its predecessor literally, Feiersinger, using the technique of the critical regionalist, 'makes it strange'. In order to emphasize its rusticity, the architect has cladded the building with reused untreated wood from a dismantled stable nearby. The former stable's sliding doors are echoed by the shutters that now slide across parts of the façade. Here we find an uncompromising insistence on retaining the rusticity of the building, close to the spirit of Walter Pichler, an intentional roughness that eschews the slickness or polish of the tourist structures beginning to invade the valley. Another young firm, AllesWirdGut, was given the commission of creating a pedestrian thoroughfare in San Candido ('Innichen' in German), a small Italian town in the area of Bolzano, in a valley of the Italian Dolomites. The result (1999–2003) not only accommodated the rhythm of the city, with provisions for adapting to varying volumes of pedestrians and cyclists, but used reflecting pools, surrealistically set in the middle of streets once dedicated to vehicular traffic, to mirror the surrounding Alps. The town's historic core is aerated, and its center not only freed from cars but turned into a kind of urban living room.

A new tone was first set by Silja Tillner, who has built her career around the idea that architects should have a solid grounding in the field of urban planning. In addition to her degree in architecture from Vienna's Academy of Fine Art, she earned a Master's in Urban Design from UCLA and then worked on projects with the office of Victor Gruen in Los Angeles. Upon returning to Vienna she worked on Vienna Urbion (1994), one of the first examples in the city of public space rehabilitation to counteract social blight, which was specifically concerned with transportation infrastructure, and then the Urban Loritz Platz (1998). Both are located on Otto Wagner's public transport line along the Gürtel, the main traffic artery of Vienna, which carries 85,000 vehicles a day across ten districts. For years its traffic, lack of street life and menace of social degradation had been the subject of numerous and inconclusive planning projects. Finally the municipality initiated a design competition for the area. Tillner's winning Urbion project recalls Wagner's agenda in more ways than one. It is based on the Stadtbahn Viaduct, an elevated railway whose arches Otto Wagner had intended to be used by small businesses. By 1900 the arches were filled with shops and restaurants, but after the First World War they were walled up, creating a barrier between the inner city and outlying neighborhoods, and found themselves in the middle of two major traffic thoroughfares going in opposite directions.

Tillner's aim was to preserve Otto Wagner's architectural heritage and also to create public spaces in the midst of traffic. She made the arched viaduct transparent once again, turning it into a meeting place instead of a barrier and updating Wagner's concept of the transportation hub that can absorb future developments. Today, the revitalized arches under the viaduct house a series of bars, art galleries, cafés and shops overlooking two rows of newly planted trees which frame pedestrian and cycle lanes, while Wagner's Stadtbahn stations provide public transport access. The inner and outer Gürtel are far more integrated than before.

Tillner's refurbishment of the Urban Loritz Platz is a larger-scale attempt to overcome functional defects in the public transport network and to create a public space in what had become a desolate transportation hub on the Gürtel. The square has been planted with rows of trees. Waiting zones and pedestrian routes have been covered by a white membrane roof floating above the square, dramatically illuminated at night by spotlights. Similar membranes are stretched between the double arches of the Main Central Library to provide shelter for the entrance to the underground station.

Gabu Heindl, another upholder of the Wagnerian vision, has dedicated her young practice to the aim of enhancing community, both on the small and large scale. Among the most remarkable of her design projects is the Fünf Höfe für die Zehnergasse ('Five Courtyards for the Zehnergasse', 2014) in Wiener Neustadt just outside Vienna, which was carried out on a minimal budget. Here she took the initiative of providing five luxurious, sun-drenched sports and recreation spaces on all levels of the building, including a roof that had not been requested in the initial brief. But it is her plan, with Susan Kraupp, for the Danube Canal which is the most noteworthy. The winning entry in another competition of ideas initiated by the City of Vienna, it is a set of guidelines for the development of the canal, and is to a large extent true to the regulatory plan drawn up by Otto Wagner. The competition sought answers to the question of whether to allow commercial development of the area, which extends over 16 hectares along 17 kilometers, or to maintain it as a kind of public park along the water's edge. Heindl and Kraupp convincingly proposed the latter. The subsequent Partitur plan preserved the original magnificent Otto Wagner design while opening it up to a range of leisure uses, guaranteeing access to the river bank for pedestrians and cyclists in a zone free of commercial exploitation.[15]

Possibly because of the disproportionate role architecture has played in the city, an exceptional number of contemporary Viennese artists have been involved with architectural representations or interventions. This tendency has roots in the work of Hollein, Hundertwasser, Friedrich Kiesler and the Austrian Phenomenon. Among the best-known contemporary architectural art works are Eva Schlegel's 2005 installation at the Secession building; Hans Schabus's installation at the Venice Biennale, *The Last Land*, curated by Max Hollein in 2005; Erwin Wurm's *House Attack* at the Museum of Modern Art of 2006; and Peter Weibel, Peter Kogler and Günter Brus's Art Lounge in the Café Korb (fig. 124). These also include Steinbrener/Dempf's *Jesuitenkosmos* of 2008–9 and *Limbo* of 2015, a gigantic rock that seems to be a homage to Magritte's floating stones (fig. 125).[16] It was commissioned by Gustav Schörghofer SJ, the head of the Jesuitenkirche, who has used the funding of the Otto-Mauer-Fonds to support avant-garde religious art. Among the other projects he has subsidized are an altar by Michael Kienzer and a cross made of Lego by Manfred Erjautz that had to be moved close to the pulpit in order to save it from vandalism.

124 (opposite)   Peter Weibel, Günter Brus and Peter Kogel, Art Lounge in the basement of the Café Korb, 2005

125 (above)   Steinbrener-Dempf, *Limbo*, a site-specific sculpture in the Jesuitenkirche, 2015

10

Good Social Housing is Good for the Economy

During the Kreisky Era, from 1970 to the early 1980s, Vienna remained committed to the two priorities it had adopted during the immediate postwar period: social housing, and the preservation and restoration of Vienna's historic buildings and monuments, such as the Stephansdom, the Burgtheater, the Kunsthistorisches and Naturhistorisches museums, the Albertina, the State Opera and the Parliament building. The latter imperative was reinforced in 1971 by an official law protecting the city's historic center. To these older priorities was added a new one. This was the construction of the underground transportation network that began in 1970 with federal funding. In the tradition of Otto Wagner's design for the late nineteenth-century Stadtbahn, the underground transportation system is outstanding, and its hubs tend to be used to create public places. Most of these are above ground, but one in particular is underground, namely the Karlsplatz, where three lines intersect, along with the Opernpassage, providing links to the Opera, the Secession building, the Karlskirche, the Technical University and the Albertina: a masterpiece of planning and engineering (fig. 126).

During this period of massive public spending, real estate speculation was low. Of the five big architectural projects in the city, only two were private sector. The first was in 1955, when the 73-meter-

126 Pedestrian roundabout in the underground: the Karlsplatz metro station, a transportation hub at the intersection of three underground metro lines, which in addition links the Secession building, the Opera, the Albertina, the University of Fine Art and the Technical University, while forming a shopping destination and public area

high Ringturm opened on the Danube Canal – and was reviled in the press. It was designed in Allied-occupied Vienna by Erich Boltenstern for the Vienna Insurance Group. It was not until almost ten years later, in 1964, that a second high-rise was built: the Intercontinental Hotel, one of the biggest hotels in the world at the time. Such was the public concern that the hotel would threaten the visual integrity of the cherished historic view of Vienna, especially as seen from the Hildebrandt's eighteenth-century Belvedere Palace, that its height had to be lowered from 50 meters to 39.

The year 1964 also saw the commission for the General Academic Hospital of Vienna in the Ninth District. The main building was begun in 1974, but not opened until 1994. It consisted of two large, 22-storey towers which accommodated 2200 beds. The fourth major project of the time was the United Nations building designed by the Austrian architect Johann Staber, opened in 1979, and the fifth, the Business School of the University of Vienna, was built in 1983. As in the La Défense area of Paris, the UN building was intended to serve as the anchor of a concentrated skyscraper zone outside the city center, in this case on the northern side of the Danube, with public transport links to the center.

In the late 1980s the situation changed dramatically with an unprecedented global building boom fueled by what has been called 'impatient capital'. Money pursued landed property as never before. Thanks to the wave of privatization of public property, the price of urban real estate acquired through 'land grabs' skyrocketed.[1] In the words of Rahul Mehrotra, cities became a landscape where the 'global whims of international investors favoring the rich monopolized urban design issues' and where the role of architects was limited to representing 'the power of capital and its universalizing symbolism'. Architecture in the form of 'shopping malls, IT parks, gated employment enclaves, gated communities, and luxury hotels by local and foreign architects' disrupted the existing fabric and were 'out of scale, out of proportion', epitomizing 'the crassness of capital expressing itself on the landscape'.[2]

Vienna became a magnet for impatient capital. Architects, along with developers and construction firms, lobbied for relaxation of the building codes in order to accommodate new construction. In 1991, the administration of Mayor Helmut Zilk commissioned Coop Himmelb(l)au to prepare a high-rise concept for the Urban Development Plan of 1994. Smarting from the loss of a megaproject that the firm had submitted jointly with Hans Hollein for the buildings of the Expo '95 that had just been canceled thanks to a referendum, Coop Himmelb(l)au recommended changing the legal and economic conditions for high-rise projects.[3] In 1994 Werner Faymann became councilor for urban renewal and began to put these recommendations into practice, and in 2002 he was instrumental in the sale of communal land to private interests. He left the municipal government to join the federal government, eventually becoming prime minister of the country in 2008. His task was taken over almost single-handedly by Rudolf Schicker, who became deputy mayor in charge of urban development in 2001. It was under his direction that the building boom reached its most fevered pitch. Major building projects were initiated, including the new main train station, the new town of Aspern, business parks such as Donau City, shopping areas such as Wien Mitte, Wienerberg City and Monte Laa, the Gasometer housing projects and the new Business School of the University of Vienna. Coop Himmelb(l)au's Wolf Prix served as a kind of impresario for potential clients, both private and public, as did Hans Hollein, introducing to the municipality star architects like Zaha Hadid, Jean Nouvel, Peter Cook, Odile Decq, Carme Pinos, Hitoshi Abe, Thom Mayne and Dominique Perrault – all of whom were given prestigious commissions in Austria. Coop Himmelb(l)au and Hollein also received commissions.

In just two decades of fevered construction, the number of highrises in Vienna has climbed to 173.[4] This number does not include the city's countless shopping malls. The first entrepreneur with the acumen to realize the potential of real-estate speculation on a large scale was local building contractor Richard Lugner, who had previously specialized in the construction of gas stations. In 1990, he built Vienna's first colossal shopping mall and named it Lugner City – a reference to Donald Trump's upscale Trump Tower, but located in the multicultural, working-class Fifteenth District. In the wake of Lugner's success, there appeared a far more ambitious generation of real estate developers. The one who stands out for the quality of his ventures is structural engineer Thomas Jakoubek. Perhaps his most daring commission was Günther Domenig, Hermann Eisenköck and Herfried Peyker's design for the T-Center St Marx, with its novel use of steel that required him to hire bridge-building engineers. Jakoubek was also behind Ortner and Ortner's Wien Mitte and most of the new buildings in Donau City, including the DC Towers by Dominique Perrault and Hans Hollein's Saturn Tower.

In 2007, Viennese urbanist Reinhard Seiss published a damning invective of the building projects commissioned under Schicker. His *Wer Baut Wien?* ('Who Builds Vienna?'), introduced by two of the city's most respected architecture critics, Friedrich Achleitner and Christian Kühn, became a bestseller and went through four editions in quick succession,[5] reflecting the mood of the Viennese electorate. During the municipal elections of 2010, the public's disapproval was clear and Schicker was replaced by the Green Party candidate, Maria Vassilakou.

Whatever the benefits and disadvantages of the building boom – these projects are well serviced by public transportation; many are clustered in high-quality mixed-use environments, including housing projects; one, due to be completed in 2017 by Rüdiger Lainer, is the highest wooden 'green' building in the world (fig. 127) – the fact is that Vienna redoubled the influx of private capital with a massive increase of investment in the public sector. The list of infrastructure and investment projects undertaken is long, particularly in the wake of the 2008 financial crisis. The city undertook to maintain public buildings, improve transport and services, finance new research, provide universal free kindergartens and, generally, 'put money in people's pockets and indirectly in the tax base', according to Ewald Nowotny, the head of the Austrian National Bank.[6] These projects include a new airport, additions to the Museumsquartier, an expansion of the public transport network and, as we shall see in more detail, massive social housing. According to Nowotny, the balancing of private and

127 RLP Rüdiger Lainer + Partner, HoHo Wien, the highest wooden high-rise in the world. Rendering A3ZO

public investment was positive, and the resulting growth in public-sector amenities, especially in social housing, has been a 'stabilizing factor with regard to the current unprecedented growth of real estate speculation at the macro-economic level'.[7]

The result of these projects is that Vienna is an exceptional example of a socially just city. The positive effect has also been recognized internationally. Since 2011 the city has been officially ranked the most livable in the world in three surveys. The first is the *Global Livability Survey* published yearly by the *Economist*'s Intelligence Unit, which measures stability, healthcare, culture and environment, education and infrastructure. The second is *State of the World Cities 2012/2013*, the report of the United Nations Settlements Program, based on a city's productivity, infrastructure development, quality of life, social equality and environmental sustainability. Third, and the most robust of all, is the *Mercer Survey*, based on 39 factors, including political and social environment, economic environment, socio-cultural environment, medical and health considerations, schools and education, public services and transport, recreation, consumer goods, natural environment and housing.

Of all the public sector areas that have benefited from these spending policies it is Vienna's social housing that is the most unique internationally. At a time when other European countries cut spending on housing, Austria not only maintained fundamental postwar spending levels but reinforced them. Just as the Kreisky Era's transport system was based on an updating of Otto Wagner's achievements, its social housing policy renewed that of Hugo Breitner, the first to use the sector not as a charity but for counter-cyclical investment aimed at stimulating the economy as a whole.

As a result of this now 40-year-old policy, wedded to a Keynesian model, 60 per cent of Vienna's population today lives in social housing, compared to 10 per cent at the height of Red Vienna. This makes Vienna Europe's largest property manager, with more than 220,000 apartments.[8] The country's housing situation is officially better than the EU average, with the majority of the population having access to affordable housing, and the level of public spending on housing is lower than the European average, that is, 1 per cent of GDP. Austrians enjoy 41 square meters of living space per capita, and 90 per cent of the housing stock is 'A-standard' (minimum size or above, with central heating and a bathroom). Moreover, there is almost no segregation, no ghettos, and homelessness is rare. Finally, the average rent is no more than 18 per cent of household income, again below the European average.[9]

The reason Vienna's housing budget is so high is that the country can afford it.[10] Austria as a whole has been a robust economic performer since 1970, as we have seen. Until 2014 it managed to remain relatively stable following the global economic recession of 2008, and it is still one of the world's most prosperous nations, with the highest GDP in the Eurozone after Luxembourg.[11] Of all the OECD countries, it is also the one with the highest expenditure per capita on welfare. Recently the federal government has been providing between 450 and 600 million euros a year in federal funds to the city for housing. In addition, the city contributes its own funding to the effort, increasing its total public housing spending to 640 million euros for 2013 and 689 million for 2014.[12]

But the reverse is also true. The reason the country is so economically robust is because of its public spending. The tax money collected as a result of this stimulus policy has allowed Vienna to invest in infrastructure up to now – although externalities such as the misguided overexpansion into risky East European markets by Austrian banks such as Raffeisen, Erste Bank and Hypo Alpe Adria damaged the overall Austrian economy as of 2014.[13] The municipal government has adhered to an anti-cyclical public spending model rather than an austerity-based policy. Renate Brauner, the deputy mayor under Michael Haüpl from 2007 to 2015, has claimed that Vienna is 'investing its way out of a crisis, instead of saving [its] way into the next one'. The rationale for such a policy has to do with cultivating a tax base.[14] The point is reiterated by Michael Ludwig, the deputy mayor in charge of housing, who constantly stresses that investment in housing is a major driver of the general economy. Spending on housing and other infrastructure creates jobs; jobs create income, and the higher the income level, the bigger the tax base.[15] The result is that 'while the crisis has resulted in unemployment rates in the rest of the European Union above 10 per cent in the Eurozone, it is 4.3 per cent in Austria.'[16] Vienna reduced its debt by hundreds of millions in the economically good years preceding the crisis. This put the city in a solid position to inject a powerful counter-cyclical stimulus package directly into the crisis-hit economy. Moreover, according to Brauner, Vienna's debt as a percentage of regional GDP is only 6 per cent, a level she describes as 'absolutely manageable', and only a tenth of the debt ceiling of 60 per cent set as the objective for EU members.[17]

Ten years ago, an EU law and associated procurement rules made it illegal for the municipality to pay for social housing directly. The last social housing project fully funded by the city was opened on 1 May 2004, a facility with 74 apartments in the Rösslergasse in the Twenty-third District. One alternative would have been to privatize social housing. But the municipality has clung to the idea that housing is a civil right so important that it should not be left to the free market. Instead, the city rejected privatization in favor of 'social housing in a social Europe',[18] and became a non-profit developer. A scheme was worked out whereby the model of publicly funded housing was transformed into one of subsidized housing. Since then the city of Vienna has not undertaken to build itself, but it continues to indirectly promote social housing finance.

The high quality of social housing relies on a complex set of strict regulations. Austria combines long-term public loans at favorable conditions and grants defined at the level of federal provinces, with commercial loans raised via bonds and developer/tenant equity. Promotion of social housing is also supported by municipal land policy. Rents are calculated on the basis of costs combined with limitations defined by the subsidy schemes. A typical project comprises the following elements of finance: 20–60 per cent conditional subsidies (grants, low-cost loans) with limits to keep construction and financing costs down; 5–15 per cent equity from developer(s); 0–15 per cent equity from future tenants (with the right to buy in some circumstances); 50–70 per cent commercial loans, today financed by commercial bonds and via Housing Banks, which refinance via housing construction convertible bonds (HCCBs) with very favorable conditions.[19]

A particularity of the process of building a social housing project in Vienna today is the proviso that the competition should always involve an architect, a developer and a non-profit housing association. This ensures that economic, social and ecological costs are realistically taken into account, and that the costs declared at the outset are respected.[20]

According to Ryan Holeywell, 'there is no mortgage interest deduction in Vienna, as there is in the US. Vienna chooses to subsidize buildings rather than residents, which also explains the high percentage of social housing.' Because public housing is so widespread in the city, private developers of unsubsidized units must provide good prices and high quality in order to be competitive. The result is that although Viennese apartments are of exceptionally high quality, rents are low for a European capital. Monthly rent is generally capped at 25 per cent of a family's income, half the rate of in European cities such as Barcelona, Berlin and Zurich. A recent study by the financial firm UBS backs up Holeywell's assertion that Vienna's rents are among the lowest in Western Europe.[21] Judging from rental rates readily available on the web, monthly rent for apartments today ranges between 7.25 and 7.90 euros per square meter. This means that the rent on a 70-square-meter apartment is about 500 euros a month.

Finally, through an energy standard enforced in all recent projects of a maximum of 50kWh per square meter a year,[22] and the provision of subsidies bound to rigid quality standards, the social housing sector in Austria has been able to adhere to fairly ambitious Kyoto goals. In addition, a growing number of projects are heated from non-fossil-fuel sources.[23]

Besides its economic rationale, Vienna's social housing since the early 1970s has been committed to the tradition of community. This has translated into providing not just mono-functional dormitory residences but a uniquely wide array of shared amenities intended to bring people together. The set of standard amenities is extraordinary, as we shall see.

In addition, in an effort to avoid ghettoization, social housing has been incorporated into the urban fabric all across the city. What is remarkable about a number of these projects, in particular since the mid-1980s, is their level of quality in design and detailing. Neues Leben, for example, one of the 200 non-profit housing associations active in Austria, has a record of architectural excellence. It manages the establishment of new housing projects, recruits the tenants, architects and builders, and obtains funding from the city and from developers. It has been responsible for commissioning the following: Helmut Richter's Brunnerstrasse design (1986–91) and Rataplan's Autofabrikstrasse (1996–8), both in the Twenty-third District; Heidulf Gerngross's Wiener Loft Siedlung in the Twenty-first (1996–7); Geiswinkler & Geiswinkler's Am Hofgartel (1998–2003) in the Eleventh and their two housing projects for the Alxingergasse (2002–4 and 2005–6) in the Tenth; ARTEC's Bremer Stadtmusikante (2008–10; color plate 38) and Walter Stelzhammer's Odenburgerstrasse (2008–12) in the Twenty-first. Rüdiger Lainer's House with Porches (2006–8) in the Eleventh District, with its balconies jutting out at irregular intervals in a multitude of different colors, not only allows for outdoor access but also includes a day-care center, playgrounds, a sauna on the roof, and a communal space for planting vegetables (color plate 39).

Other housing projects are conceived to create centers of community inside peripheral areas. This was the case, for example, with Karrée St Marx (2008–10), on the border between the middle-class Third District and the old industrial Eleventh District, otherwise known as Simmering, and once the site of a slaughterhouse which subsequently became an urban wasteland. It has become the heart of a future urban development zone, Eurogate, the largest energy-efficient 'passive house' settlement in Europe. In addition to new residential buildings, the development also includes a children's day-care center, offices and a food market. The residential projects are located in a natural park, adjacent to the green area of 'urban wilderness'. The master plan was developed by Geiswinkler & Geiswinkler, who proposed the creation of an L-shaped bulwark against traffic noise in the form of offices and commercial buildings. Thus protected within a quiet park area are housing units by three different architects, one by Querkraft, one by Elsa Prochazka and the third by Geiswinkler & Geiswinkler. In Querkraft's concept, all apartments have a double aspect and overlook a glazed atrium.

The present success of social housing units goes back to the early 1970s, as we have seen. One of the earliest projects to replace mediocre postwar housing and to embody the new concern for community through shared amenities was Wilhelm Holzbauer's Wohnen Morgen ('Tomorrow's Living'), built between 1976 and 1980 in the low-income, multicultural Fifteenth District of Vienna. It consisted of four parallel rows of six- or seven-storey houses. Instead of dreary prefab concrete buildings, these were painted the yellow ochre typical of Biedermeier Vienna, and separated by generous strips of leafy garden equipped with playground facilities. A central pedestrian street was intended to house shops and community facilities. The apartments, which ranged in size from 45 to 120 square meters, all have a terrace facing the front gardens.

The most successful project of this type was a colossal complex made of 18 prefabricated towers. Named Alt-Erlaa, it was built between 1973 and 1985 in the Twenty-third District. Its designer, ironically, was one of the staunchest critics of prefabrication systems, Harry Glück. Conceived explicitly as an updated version of Red Vienna's perimeter Gemeindebauen, the project, built and managed by the city, covers 24 hectares and comprises 3200 apartments (65 per cent of which have at least three bedrooms, with an average size of 74.5 square meters) housing about 9000 people (fig. 128 and color plate 40).

The Alt-Erlaa complex was the first to display what has since become a mainstay of Viennese social housing, namely the rejection

128 Alt-Erlaa, detail

of the dominant commuter dormitory model of social housing and the promotion of an astonishing multi-functionality expressed in an extraordinary range of amenities. The colossal project has its own underground station, a shopping center, medical centers, schools, kindergartens, playgrounds, tennis courts and other recreational facilities, large green spaces, approximately 3400 parking spaces, administrative offices, a library, restaurants, 32 halls for community activities and a ballroom. Glück's most imitated innovation was the inclusion of rooftop swimming pools, accompanied by a tepidarium, a solarium and infrared saunas. The sense of community inside this megalith is reinforced by a tenants' council whose members are elected every three years, giving every tenant has a stake in the running of the complex.[24] As for the internal arrangement of the apartments, it follows Glück's concept of the 'stacked single-family home' in the form of terraced apartments. All the apartments are supplied with densely stocked planters up to the twelfth floor. All the other apartments have a loggia as private open space. The façade is slightly concave, allowing 180-degree views to the north and south. The apartments have open kitchens and a large amount of storage space; the larger ones have a second bathroom. The widely varying apartments have no fewer than 35 different floor plans to accommodate individual preferences.

Not all attempts to apply the Gemeindebau idea were so felicitous or well designed. The system's worst failure, contemporary with Alt-Erlaa, was Am Schöpfwerk ('At the Pumping Station'), designed by Viktor Hufnagl and a team of architects and built between 1976 and 1978 in the Twelfth District. Its construction was shoddy, public space was in the lower percentiles, the apartments lacked soundproofing. The result is a rare Viennese example of the overcrowding, filth and danger associated with slums.[25]

The early 1970s in Vienna also witnessed the emergence of another, very different, innovative and successful facet of Vienna's social housing policy, *Sanfte Planung* or 'soft planning'. It adopted citizen participation, advocacy planning and a small-scale, interstitial approach to the traditional nineteenth-century urban fabric. Its aim, again, was to enhance the sense of community, or *Grätzel*,[26] not in new projects but in existing, rundown neighborhoods.

Sanfte Planung was initiated in 1974 through the institution of the *Gebietsbetreuung* ('area renewal office'), run on advocacy planning principles adopted by architects or social workers commissioned by the city. These *Gebietsbetreuungen* have a neutral position in relation to all actors involved, and they are not allowed to carry out their own private planning business in that area – a significant difference from rehabilitation commissioners in many other European cities. They were placed in each of the city's neighborhoods in order to coordinate and promote urban renewal programs, which have proven successful economically and socially. One notable example was Spittelberg in the Seventh District, once rundown but now the thriving home of galleries and studios. Spittelberg was used by the city as a model project for not only saving eighteenth-century historical fabric but reviving it by providing affordable social housing, preventing it from falling into the hands of speculators. Equally successful was the working-class district of Ottakring in the Fourteenth District in integrating people and finding solutions to conflicts typical of a multicultural neighborhood.[27] *Sanfte Planung* also brought non-profit associations of people together to develop urban revitalization projects in a participatory way. The result was indeed the revitalization of 80 per cent of the nineteenth-century architecture which had become rundown in Vienna.

Through *Sanfte Planung*, the city achieved the world's largest housing regeneration program, with more than 170,000 apartments refurbished, an average of 10,000 per year. The program was based on an extraordinary subsidy system in the 1970s with an annual budget equivalent to 218 million euros deriving from national tax revenues. Most of the projects involved the renewal of old private rental buildings, but housing estates from the 1920s – and increasingly from the 1950s to 1970s – were also completely refurbished. The overall modernization of Red Vienna's social housing schemes included such significant complexes as the Karl Marx Hof, Rabenhof, George Washington Hof and Sandleiten.[28]

Among the earliest individual planning participatory housing projects of the early 1980s was Walter Stelzhammer's renovation of a picturesque U-shaped Biedermeier house of 1780, erected around a garden in the Second District neighborhood of the Karmeliterviertel (fig. 129). The original building had fallen into disrepair and was slated for demolition. An association of six families bought it and succeeded in convincing the municipality not only to allow them to keep the building, but to provide three grants which covered up to 30 per cent of the costs. Subsequently the building was split up into apartments ranging in size from 90 to 150 square meters.

129   Walter Stelzhammer, Karmeliterhof, Second District, Vienna

Friedensreich Hundertwasser's so-called 'alternative' Hundertwasser Haus, built between 1983 and 1985 in the Third District, was another high point. Since 1976, the charismatic, outspoken and rebellious conceptual artist had put forth a series of highly publicized manifestos for a more humane and ecological alternative to social housing – of his own design. 'Without a people-friendly environment and without peace with nature a decent existence is impossible,' he wrote. 'These peace talks with nature must begin soon, otherwise it will be too late.'

Amazingly, Hundertwasser's call was heeded by the President of Austria, Bruno Kreisky himself, who suggested to the then mayor, Leopold Gratz, that the city fund the project. The result is the third most visited building in Vienna. Instead of hostile concrete, it has walls at ground level for children to draw on. Grass and trees grow on all its horizontal levels, including balconies and roofs, to which every apartment has access. It incorporated the previous building rather than destroying it, as a 'sign of respect' so that 'the spirits of the old house may move into the new one'. The terraces are aligned with the base of the windows, so that the resident has the lawns at eye level while sitting and can reach out and touch the grass and the flowers. In keeping with his sui generis hyper-decorative approach to style, based on precedents by Klimt and Gaudí, Hundertwasser chose to adorn the exterior and interior walls with ceramic and mosaic tiles 'so that the geometric rectangular windows, edges and other structural lines lose some of their famous aggressive terror' (color plate 41).[29] Hundertwasser subsequently received commissions to design what have become iconic landmarks in Vienna, including the KunstHaus

Wien and the District Heating Plant of Spitellau with an exhaust chimney ending in what looks like a colossal genie's lamp.

The 'alternative' spirit of the Hundertwasser Haus, embracing a green lifestyle, along with a sense of community, sensuality, child-friendliness and cultural expression, struck a deep chord in Vienna, harking back to the spirit that had shaped Red Vienna and set the agenda for much of what is best in the subsequent social housing in the city. Vienna's social housing policy has allowed for an extraordinarily community-enhancing component: so-called 'themed housing' projects, created by groups of people who want to share their life with others who have the same social, gender-based, cultural or ecological concerns. Although themed housing represents approximately 5 per cent of the total output, it represents one of the most unusual features of Viennese social housing. The tendency keeps developing, as we shall see.

The first example of themed housing, arising out of community-building *Sanfte Planung*, was the Sargfabrik ('Coffin Factory'), designed by the artists' collective BKK and led by the architect Johnny Winter. This project, located in the Fourteenth District and carried out in 1996, was commissioned by the Verein für Integrative Lebensgestaltung ('Association for Integrative Lifestyle'). It was a redevelopment of a former manufacturing site that kept only the original coffin factory's chimney as a memento (fig. 130). The complex is home to a wide range of people, all members of an association in which each is an owner, builder and landlord of the complex. This unique arrangement means that the tenants do not pay rent, but instead pay off the building's loan and maintenance fees. Tenants participated throughout the design process, including developing their individual floor plans. This was intended to encourage pride in the outcome and to contribute to the high standard of living in the Sargfabrik.[30] Such was its success that more than half of its 100 units were rented out before construction was complete, and a second Sargfabrik adjacent to the first, called Miss Sargfabrik, was completed in 2000 (color plates 42 and 43).[31]

The complex has many popular 'green' features, such as a parking area for car-sharing, plenty of storage for bicycles and a roof garden. There was an effort made to ensure that the materials used in the construction were ecologically certified and non-hazardous. To make the building economically and environmentally efficient, the

130 (above)   BKK-3 and Johnny Winter, the Sargfabrik

131 (opposite)   Miss Sargfabrik, part of the spa

insulation used was a homogenous non-vapor-retarding system with no thermal leaks.³² In the first Sargfabrik, access to each apartment is via the weather-protected staircases, which lead to communal balconies which fulfill a dual function for the residents: they are both circulation routes for the apartments and an outdoor seating area, since none of the apartments are equipped with private balconies. To further encourage community involvement, the complex is fitted with communal facilities, which include a kitchen, library, media room, laundry room and a club room for young adults.³³

In Miss Sargfabrik, the more formally adventurous of the two buildings, the new units were conceived in such a way as to accommodate many different types of family: traditional, multi-generational, same-sex, single-parent or 'patchwork', as well as senior citizens, adolescents, refugees, pensioners and disabled people. Three of the 39 apartments are wheelchair-accessible, the rest being maisonettes, some of which have their own entrance from the street. The ceiling height can range from 2.26 to 3.12 metres in the same apartment. There is even one apartment designed to accommodate adolescents who prefer to live together rather than with the rest of their families in the complex. A brochure for the project reveals the spirit that animates it:

> We interact with the room as much as we act in space – space moves with you . . . The folding walls interconnect sloping floors – a sensation of landscape. No room is like any other, because the tenants are the co-architects of their own apartments and of the complex they live in. The common rooms are a logical addition to the apartments and reflect the needs and desires for a new lifestyle. Our basic principle for this new living is to support a social mix as a platform for communication – a merger of living, working and culture – ways of unconventional living. But we also have a place for multi-generational living for the integration of minority groups, obstacle-free design for disabled people and for places for sharing emotions.

Finally they boast 'noise reduction thanks to the type of windows, and low energy consumption.'[34] From the start the complex was renowned for its amenities, which reinforce the sense of *Grätzel* or community. These include a restaurant that serves a two-course dinner for 7.30 euros, a café bar that provides barista training, a concert hall that hosts 30 concerts a year, a global dance class and a spa (fig. 131). The entrance fee to the women only night at the spa includes one glass of champagne, as well as use of the tepidarium, ice bath, pool for swimming laps, sauna and three baths with a choice of bath oil. In addition, you can book a half-hour massage for about 28 euros. There is a special night for gay men and daytime hours for baby swimming lessons. The rest of the time is for mixed public bathing.

The first feminist-themed housing project in Vienna was launched in 1997. Frauen-Werk-Stadt ('Women-Work-City') was conceived and designed by women architects and planners, who happened to be some of the most prominent professionals in the city. The master plan was by Franziska Ullmann, Gisela Podreka and Elsa Peretti, the architecture by Elsa Prochazka, and the landscaping by Maria Auböck. To ensure child safety, it reverted to the perimeter-block layout typical of the Gemeindebau program of Red Vienna. All leases were given to women, although they were free to have male partners. Such was its success that it was followed by a series of three similar, self-organized so-called Ro*sa projects, initiated by Sabine Pollak, an architect, planner and professor at Vienna's Technical University. The first, called Kalypso, comprised 43 apartments inside one of the most extensive social housing projects in Vienna, Am Kabelwerk (see below), built in 2003; the second was in Donaustadt in 2009, and a third in Semmering in 2015. They are explicitly based on Virginia Woolf's feminist principle of 'A room of one's own', based upon her essay of that title, where women are freed from patriarchal family ties and their particular economic and social needs are taken into account. As in the first project, the main target group is single women with or without children, although women with a partner, male or female, are also welcomed. In addition, the project has adopted a 'Ro*sa Seniora' policy, which means that retired women are given a high priority, as are women with disabilities. The complexes are equipped with a communal kitchen as well as private ones, in addition to a laundry room, shared gardens and safe playgrounds for children. Shared workplaces with office equipment are also provided for women who work at home.[35]

However, it is the inter-ethnic-themed housing project called In der Wiesen ('In the Fields') that has garnered most attention. Built between 1998 and 2000 by the architectural firm of Peter Scheierfinger, it is, according to the architect, 'neither a ghetto nor a melting pot'.[36] Its aims are to encourage multicultural integration based on mutual respect and understanding, and to make a new urban district attractive to immigrants and to those moving from other districts. The complex contains 140 apartments for 300 people (including 126 children). Half of the tenants are Austrian and the other half are immigrants from Afghanistan, Bangladesh, Bosnia, Bulgaria, China, the Czech Republic, Egypt, France, Germany, Hungary, India, Iran, Iraq, Macedonia, Montenegro, Pakistan, Poland, Romania, Serbia, Slovakia, Syria and Turkey, as well as various African countries. The communal areas of the building include a Turkish bath, a swimming pool, games rooms, banquet hall, loggias, terraces, gardens, including the 'Garden of Paradise', and an orchard of apricot trees with a fountain powered by photovoltaic panels. The roof is split up into a series of tea-houses. Angelika Fitz has pointed out that one of the major factors responsible for the social harmony in the community is the presence of a full-time, live-in 'culture manager' in charge of conflict resolution.[37] According to a recent survey, 80 per cent of residents feel a 'personal gain in quality of life' and would recommend this kind of home to friends.[38]

'Intergenerational Living' is another housing theme that has been developed to respond to the demographic changes that are affecting the city. The complex called Generation: Wohnen am Mühlgrund ('Generations: Living on the Grounds of the Mill', 2007–14) was designed by three of Austria's leading architects, Hermann Czech,

132 Hermann Czech, Am Mühlgrund, interior inspired by Adolf Loos's *Raumplan*

Adolf Krischanitz and Werner Neuwirth (color plate 44). As a result of the extension of the U2 metro line, the location, once on the urban periphery, is now just a 20-minute train ride from the city-center Volkstheater station and has become far more attractive. Am Mühlgrund was one of the first projects to go up as subsidized rather than municipally funded social housing, as a result of the European regulation that came into effect in 2006, and is the setting for another theme that has emerged against the background of demographic change: how to include elderly people with special needs in intergenerational housing. All its apartments are obstacle-free and to some extent flexible (fig. 132). In one of the buildings, collapsible partition walls enable changes be made in response to different needs, for example to accommodate a growing teenager, an elderly family member or live-in helpers. The quality of detailing is very high. The load-bearing frame and floor slabs are of reinforced concrete, which offers excellent thermal insulation and protection from noise. The walls are insulated 'sandwich' constructions; externally all the buildings are clad with rough-sawn larch battens. The window frames and reveals are also of wood, and the parapets are galvanized steel. Between the storeys there is a clean separating joint along which water can drain off. Hermann Czech's units boast a ceiling height of 4.10 meters, in an arrangement dominated by a Loosian layout.

A relatively new trend since the late 1990s is to cluster a variety of themed projects together in one big complex. This also means amalgamating amenities targeted at different groups, as a means of integrating the increasingly diverse cultural, gender-related, economic, religious and medical needs of the population. Among these are Karrée St Marx (see above), the Nordbahnhof (2009) and the Sonnwendviertel (ongoing since 2008), but the first of this kind was Am Kabelwerk (1997–2005) in the Twelfth District. Built on the site of an old cable plant company, it contains 937 apartments in eight buildings represented by eight different tenants' associations – one of these being the Ro*sa Kalypso project mentioned above. The competition for the master plan was won by the team of Rainer Pirker and Florian Haydn and the architects of the different buildings are Mascha & Seethaler, Schwalm-Theiss Gressenbauer, Hermann & Valentiny, Pool Architektur, Martin Wurnig, Branimir Kljajic, and Spiegelfeld & Holnsteiner.[39] The old cable factory was preserved and renovated. Now it combines residential loft units, whose ceilings are almost 4.5 meters high, with workspaces for IT companies. The project has particularly large communal areas, and residents participated in the design of the floor plans. Among its amenities are a pizza restaurant, rooftop saunas and pools, a kindergarten, a weightwatchers' club, a medical center, 12 playgrounds, a children's garden, three new parks, several new shops, a hotel, nightclubs and, as of summer 2014, an avant-garde theater called Am Arsch der Welt ('At the Asshole of the World'). Am Kabelwerk also caters to youth culture. A center called Jam has featured 30 break-dance groups from all over Europe and 60 graffiti writers. The entire complex is fully accessible and has its own underground station.

Among the more original features of Am Kabelwerk is a 'dementia garden' designed by Anna Detzholler, enclosed in the courtyard between three of the housing units, for inhabitants with age-related mental problems. The first therapeutic dementia garden in Austria opened in January 2006 in a geriatric housing facility. They are now being introduced more frequently into housing projects in an attempt to integrate senior citizens within the broader social environment. Spending time in a garden is known to be both stimulating and relaxing. The gardens are tailored to users' needs, include handrails, different sensory zones, and opportunities for physical exercise as well as social encounters.[40]

As we have seen, one of the unique features of Red Vienna's housing policy was to build Gemeindebauen along Otto Wagner's train lines. The area of the former Nordbahnhof station in the Second District of Vienna is slated to become an entirely new urban center by the year 2025, offering approximately 10,000 apartments for 22,000 residents and as many jobs. The urban site is exceptional, close to the center as well as the Danube Island. The south-west façade of the house will run alongside a new park intended to become the recreation center of the district.

Of the two projects that have been built so far on the Nordbahnhof site, one is Bike City, conceived for cycling enthusiasts. Underground parking is, of course, an obligatory component of a housing project, but Bike City includes only half the usual car parking facilities. The large sum of money thus saved was invested in a 'wellness area' that covers the entire ground floor, complete with sauna and spa, solarium and relaxation room, along with a community room, a children's play area and youth facilities. The complex also includes large bicycle rooms, free outdoor workbenches with compressed air and water

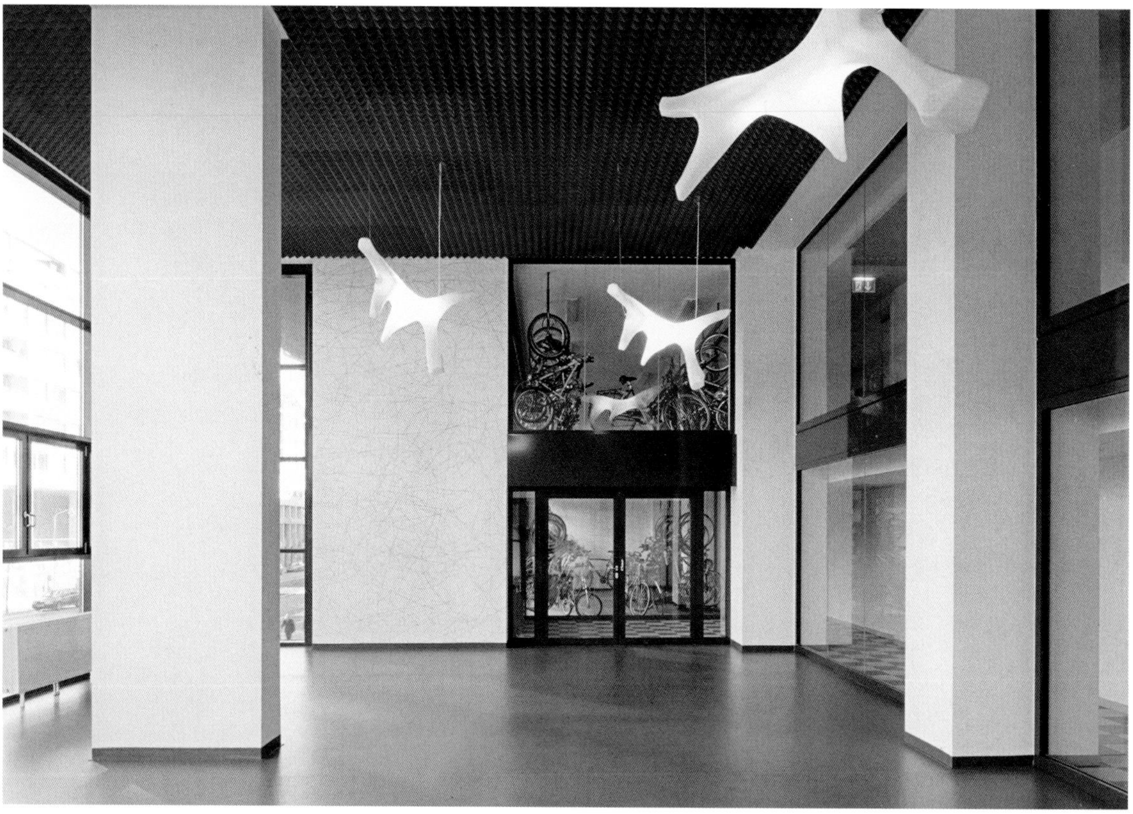

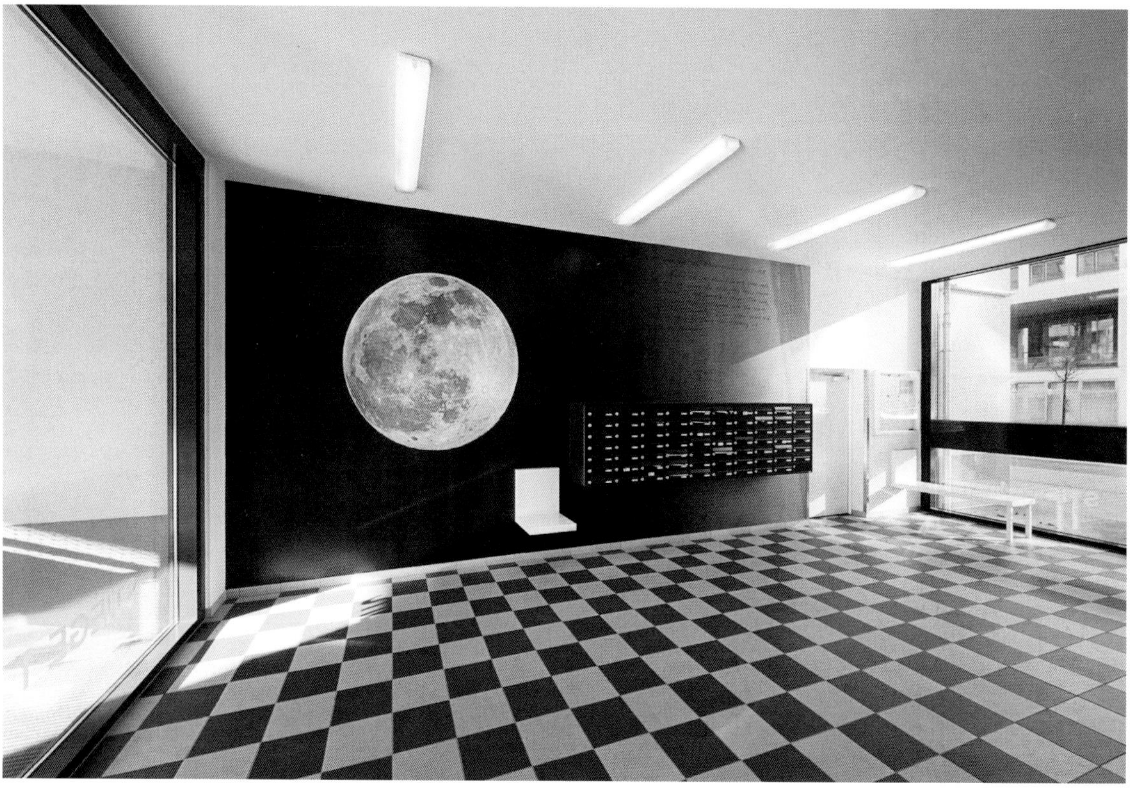

supplies, and a car-sharing contact point. There is bicycle parking at the front door and bikes can be taken up to apartments in the spacious elevators.[41]

Next door is Wohnen am Park ('Living by the Park') by PPAG, the inventive and prolific young architecture firm of Anna Popelka and Georg Poduschka, for approximately 1000 residents. The layout, with 274 flats on ten storeys, does not follow a single typology. Each flat is different, defined either by a special view, by its orientation or by its relationship to its immediate neighbors. All south-facing flats have a view of the park, while those apartments facing north are maisonettes, compensating for their less privileged position with additional height. The flats placed between the four staircases run from the back to the front of the building (figs. 133–5 and color plates 45–7). Instead of acting as a smooth enveloping skin, the façade reveals the internal structure. The project is located in the courtyards of the former imperial stables, home to many cultural organizations and cafés since its renovation. In addition, the main courtyard houses two new museums of modern art. Even more remarkably, the building is themed and its theme is *Kunst im Bau* ('Art in the Building'), a permanent art project curated by Li Tasser and involving 22 artists, including Clegg & Guttmann, Chloe Potter, Hans Schabus and Heimo Zobernig, which is accessible to all tenants and to visitors. The majority of the works were created in 2013 especially for this building.

This level of multi-functionality and high architectural quality is becoming more widespread in Vienna. The most ambitious multi-faceted housing project to date is the Sonnwendviertel ('Midsummer Solstice Neighborhood') near the newly overhauled Central Station in the Tenth District. It will eventually house 13,000 people in a total of 5000 apartments spread among a cluster of seven housing projects in an eight-acre park around the transport hub. Initiated by Deputy Mayor Michael Ludwig, its theme is social sustainability, alongside 'the usual criteria of ecology, economy and good architecture'. The design brief underpinning all the projects is to accommodate different uses, user groups and housing types through diverse or flexible floor plans and communal areas, with the intention of encouraging 'social mix, participation, multi-generational family life, and community-building'. All the contracts were awarded through competitions between different architect–developer teams. The rent per square meter ranges from approximately 7.50 to 9.90 euros, excluding heating and hot water.[42]

133 (opposite, top)   PPAG, Wohnen am Park, entrance

134 (opposite, bottom)   PPAG, Wohnen am Park, work of art integrated into the foyer

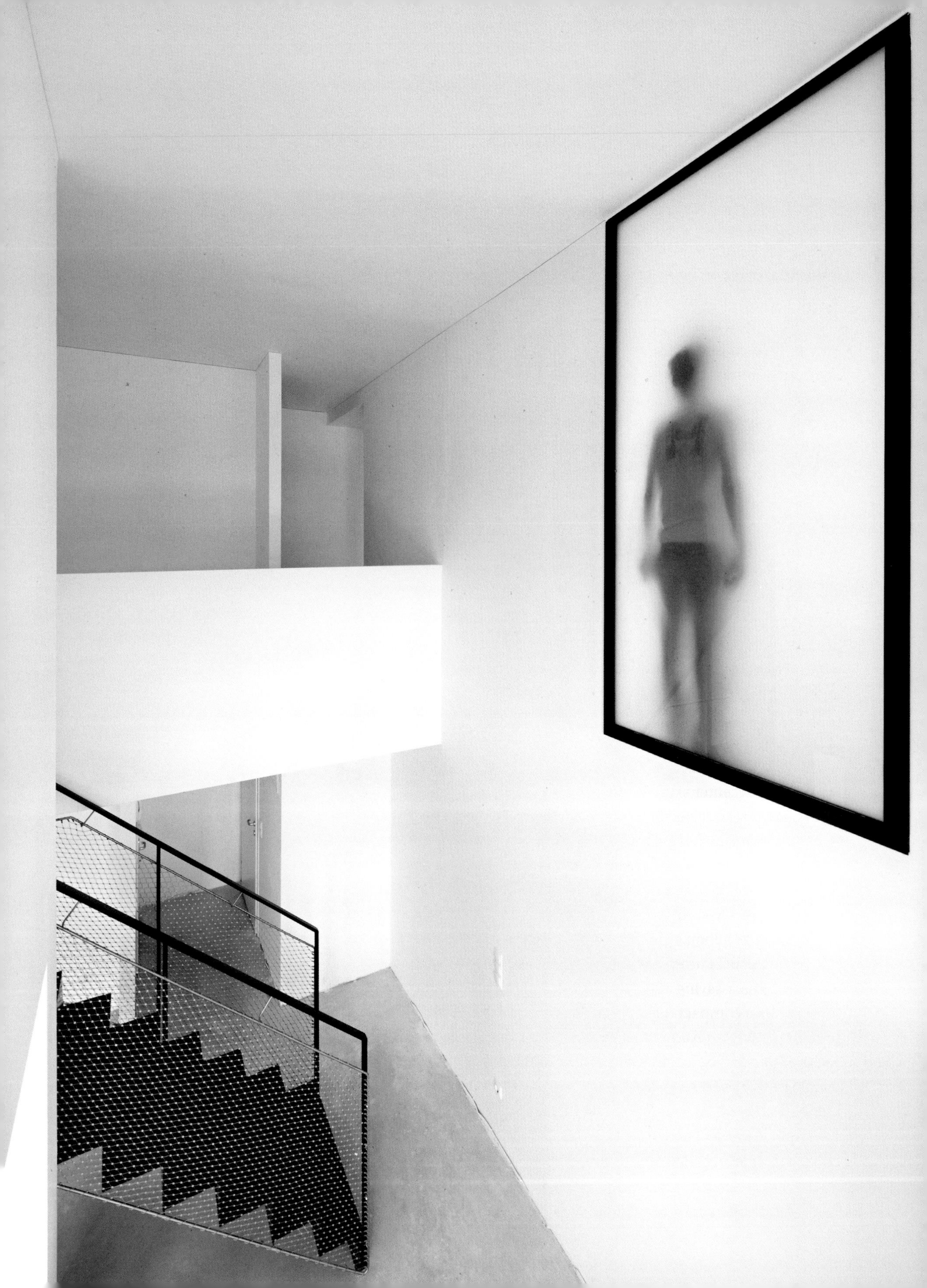

Among the architects of the Sonnwendviertel units are some of Austria's most renowned. Klaus Kada's winning entry in the residential complex (2012–14) is characterized by an exceptional concept of community and open space, with a library and a lounge that can be used as a meeting room, a gallery-like mezzanine floor which can become a stage for theater, music, films and lectures, and a spa and wellness center which will be open to non-residents. The free space is seen as an extended 'living room'. Additional services include a climbing wall, a greenhouse with a seating area, a youth club with a skateboard ramp, an observation gallery, a café terrace, a pool, a rehearsal space for musicians and a communal kitchen for celebrations and parties.

Another of the winning projects, by Kallco, is particularly aimed at young professionals and families with children. In addition to 74 apartments with two to four rooms, it will include 20 mini-lofts, mainly intended as starter homes for young people. A further target group is those who come to Vienna to work for a limited period. They can move in immediately, because the lofts are partly furnished and equipped with kitchen, bath and bed. Meanwhile Delugan Meissl's 192 single-unit apartments (2012–14) are conceived of as a multi-purpose jigsaw puzzle. These include combined home/office units, multi-generational homes, family houses, terraced houses, lofts and a two-storey leisure center on the roof that can be used for parties. The building also includes a daycenter and assisted-living facilities, with communal garden areas with raised beds that are fully wheelchair-accessible (color plates 48 and 49).

Federal funding for housing has suffered since 2010 because of the measures taken to salvage banks like Erste Bank, Raffeisen and especially Hypo Alpe-Adria, which alone has cost the federal government 18 billion euros. Instead of cutting back on new housing projects, Michael Ludwig instituted so-called 'Smart Building' in May 2012, a new cost-saving approach which allows the building of units that are more compact that the previous social housing standards (ranging in size from 40 to 70 square meters). In Ludwig's words, 'SMART apartments ... represent a tailored offer for all those people who have low reserves and want to take out a loan, such as young people just starting their careers, single parents or elderly people who seek a compact and inexpensive apartment.'[43] It aims to provide affordable housing while maintaining the principle of integration

135 PPAG, Wohnen am Park, apartment interior

and allowing tenants to experience high-quality social, ecological and cultural environments. At present the plan is to ensure that all subsidized housing projects must include 33 per cent 'Smart' units.

The inspiration and pilot project for the new policy was Trans_City's inventive and innovatively cost-cutting Lorenz-Reiter-Strasse in Simmering (2012). Trans_City's Christian Aulinger and Mark Gilbert were used to working under drastic economic constraints. The office's first projects were in New Orleans (2005–8), Hyderabad in India (2006) and emergency housing in Haiti (2010). One of Trans_City's Viennese projects, Modell Anger/Shared Space in the Twenty-second District, reduced the rent per square meter to 6 euros by raising its 60 units on pilotis – a novelty in Vienna – and using the space this created for parking rather than digging an underground facility, thus reducing the building costs by 15 per cent without sacrificing amenities such as balconies and front gardens.

What is 'smart' about the Lorenz-Reiter-Strasse project, where in fact half of the 182 apartments are 'Smart', is that it is more compact than standard housing and the living space is clustered around a central wet wall for the kitchen and bathroom. As a result, the living space, although smaller, is a versatile open plan that can be divided up according to the preferences of the user. All apartments, on the other hand, have generous balconies, many of which are wrap-around. The same is true of Geiswinkler & Geiswinkler's housing project at the Sonnwendviertel (fig. 136).

The conclusion to this chapter, following a century-long history of the varying success of the Viennese model to adapt to unprecedented crises, must come in the form of a question. Up until now the Viennese economy has been presented as relatively buoyant. However, in the past two years the global economic crisis has deepened in Vienna, as it has elsewhere in Europe and beyond. This has been exacerbated by the refugee crisis Austria shares with a large part of the first world, which almost brought a far-right president to power in the election of May 2016 for the first time since the Second World War.

The issue is hopefully not whether the policies forged over the past century will be able to adapt to worsening global economic conditions. If anything, the number of social housing units is increasing at present. The city is in the process of building a colossal new extension in Aspern, called Seestadt, on the other side of the Danube with underground transport links to the center of the city, a project whose benefits are too early to evaluate. Indicative of the ongoing dedication of Viennese architects to the tradition of social housing is the Austrian contribution to the Venice Architecture Biennale of 2016. Delugan Meissl, who were commissioned for the Austrian Pavilion, explained that the budget earmarked for an exhibition had partly been invested in social housing:

> Due to the refugee crisis, this contribution to the 2016 Architecture Biennale is not limited to the pavilion in Venice, but also includes three ongoing projects in Vienna. More concretely, three teams have been commissioned to work together with NGOs not only to design the conversion of empty buildings into temporary accommodation for people whose asylum claims are being processed but also to accompany these buildings in the longer term. The objectives of these interventions are to subject the social responsibility of architecture to a reality check, to provide humane places to live for those affected and to present the results in Venice to a broader public.
>
> Extraordinary situations demand extraordinary measures. The current wave of refugees, which will probably continue for some time, represents an enormous challenge not only for Europe's public institutions but also for civil society. Offering protection, creating humane places to live and establishing the basis for good social coexistence have always been amongst the central roles of architecture.'[44]

This statement of Elke Delugan's, and the projects we have just surveyed in this final chapter, indicate the extent the tradition of exceptionally inventive, well-conceived and well-managed social housing, glimpsed over a century ago by Otto Wagner, Vienna's first modernist rebel, and carried out by the social-democratic municipal civil servants against the great odds of the 1920s and the early 1930s, has not only become deeply ingrained in the mentality of the architectural profession today but also has kept evolving and adapting to the new realities. One cannot help but see it as an example of how a well-run municipal Keynesian anti-austerity policies, wedded to an investment in high-quality architecture, can maintain the economy as a whole along with a relatively dynamic, harmonious and fair social order.

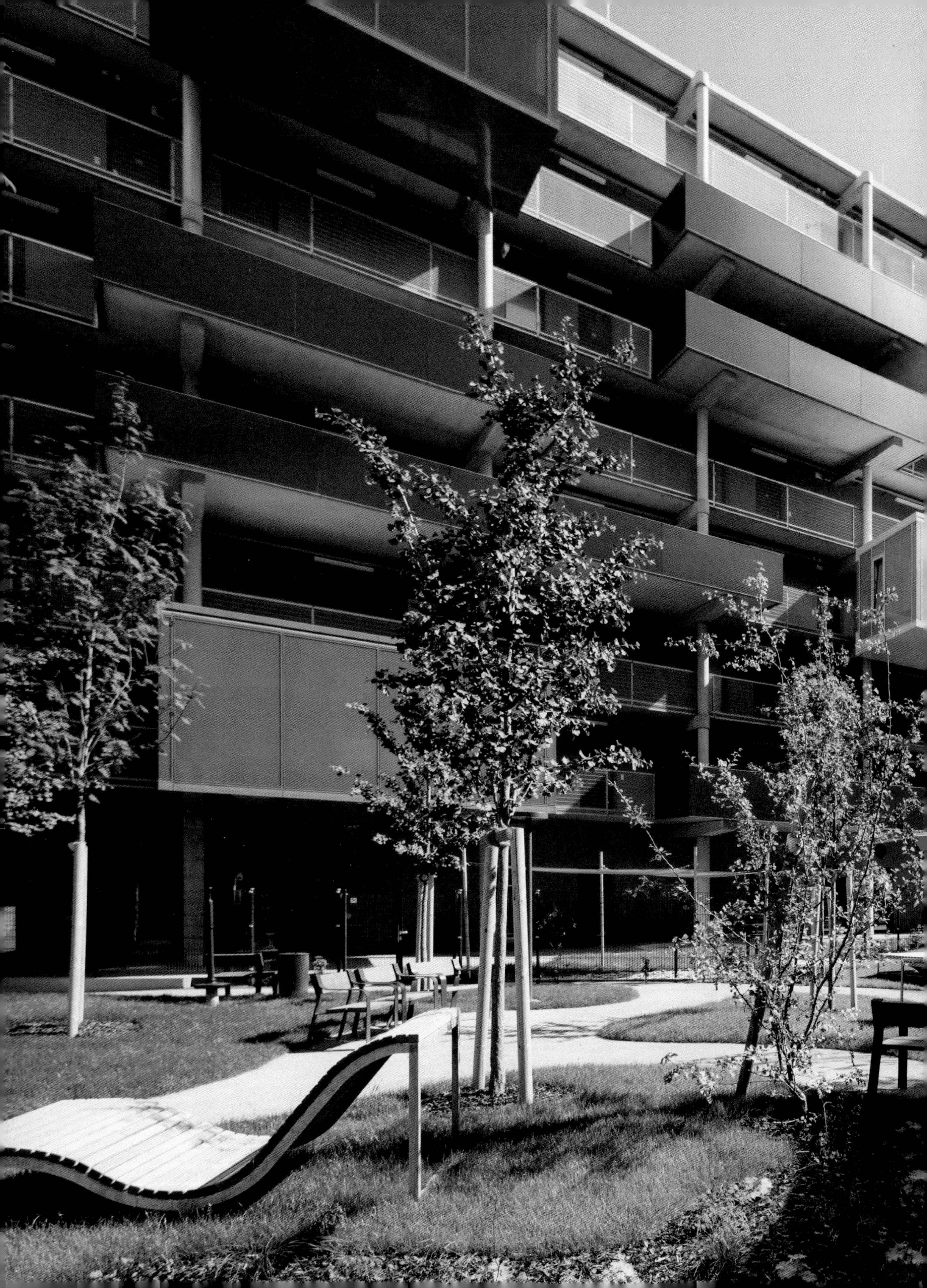

136 Geiswinkler & Geiswinkler, 'Smart' housing at Sonnwendviertel, 2016. Rendering Daniel Hwelka

Color plates

22 Timo Huber, *St Stephens Countdown II*, 1969, collage. Wien Museum

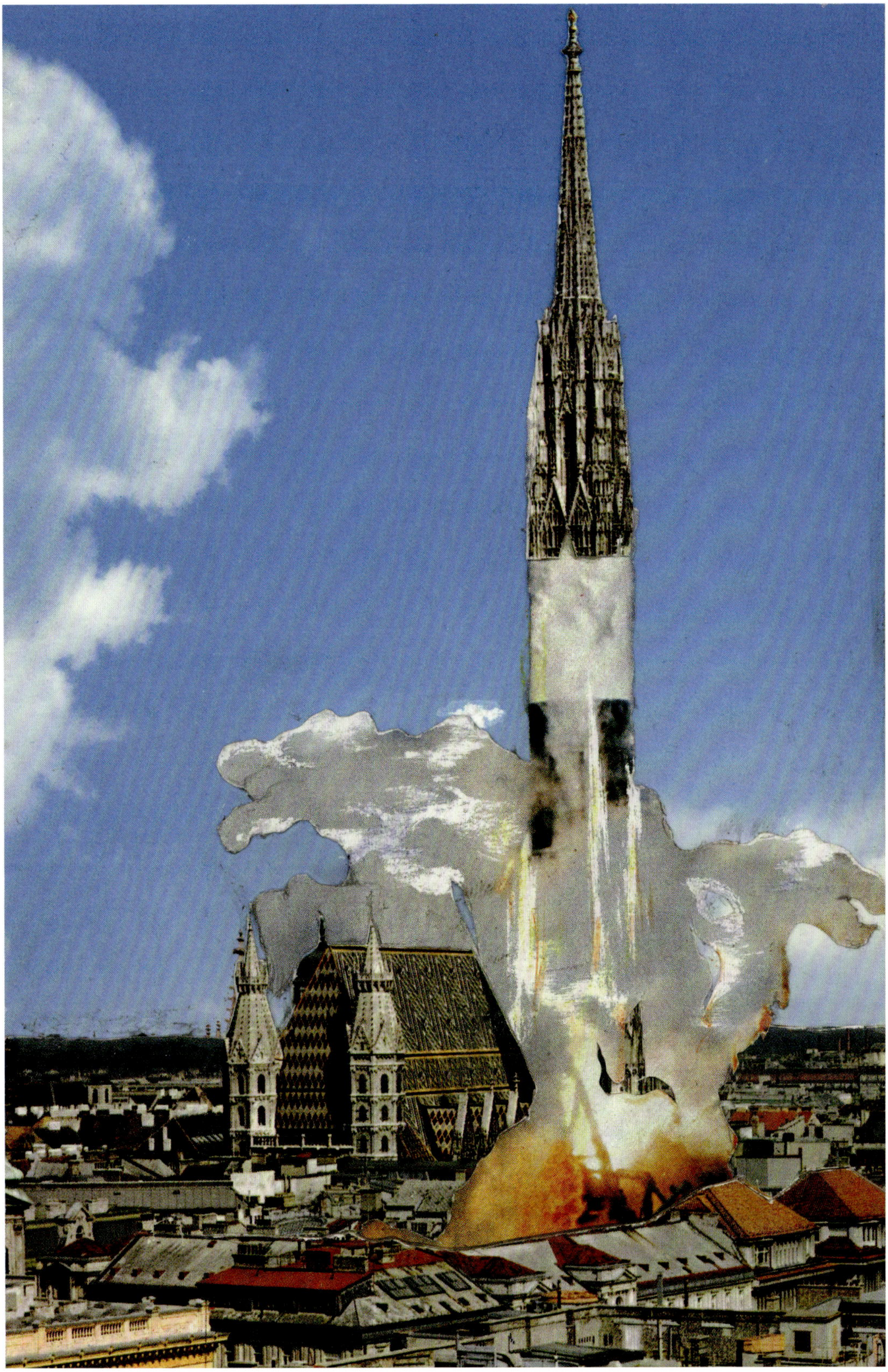

23 (left, top)   Hans Hollein, *Skyscraper*, 1958

24 (left, bottom)   Hans Hollein, *Skyscraper*, 1958

25 (right, top)   Hans Hollein, installation, part of his anti-neomonumental Master's project at Berkeley, 1960

26 (right, middle)   Hans Hollein, part of the installation at Berkeley, 1960

27 (right, bottom)   Hans Hollein, installation of doors leading nowhere at the Austriennale curated by Hollein at the 1968 Milan Triennale

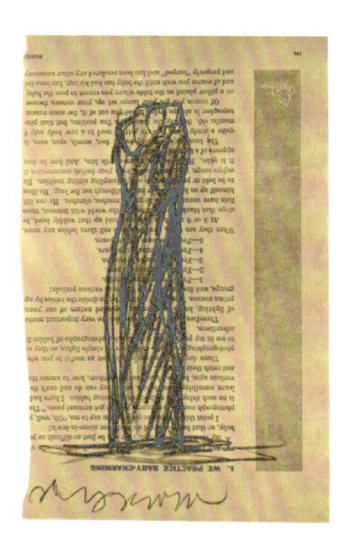

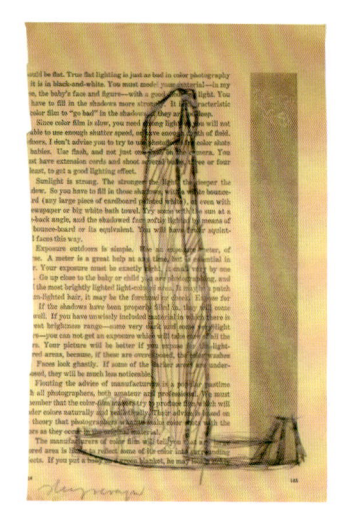

28 (top) Hans Hollein, *Superstructure over Vienna*, 1960, depicting the threat posed to the historic fabric of Vienna by the brutalist neo-monumentalism then in vogue, in the architecture of Karl Schwanzer and Roland Rainer, which he had criticized in his report to the Harkness Foundation. Georges Pompidou Center Collection

29 (bottom) Hans Hollein, *Untitled*. Architectural encroachment on nature

30 (top)   Hans Hollein, Retti candle shop

31 (bottom)   Hans Hollein, Neues Haas Haus

32 (opposite, top)   Fritz Wotruba's Church. Photo Thomas Ledl

33 (opposite, bottom)   Coop Himmelb(l)au, addition to the law offices of Schuppich, Sporn and Winischhofer on the Falkestrasse ('Falcon Street'), resembling a falcon taking flight

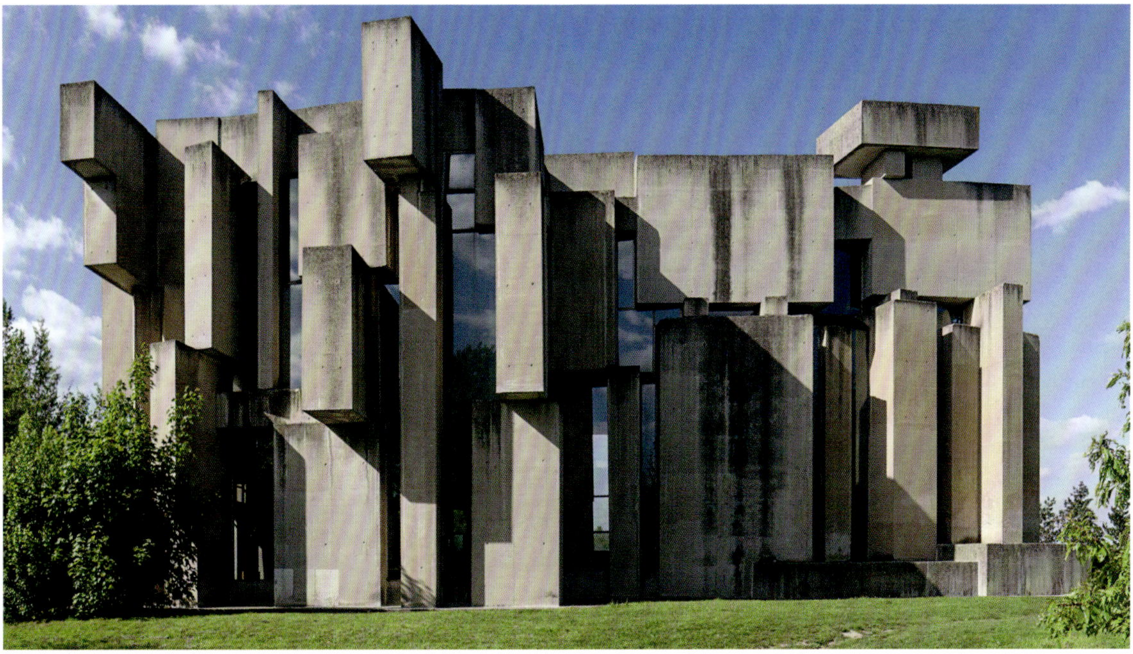

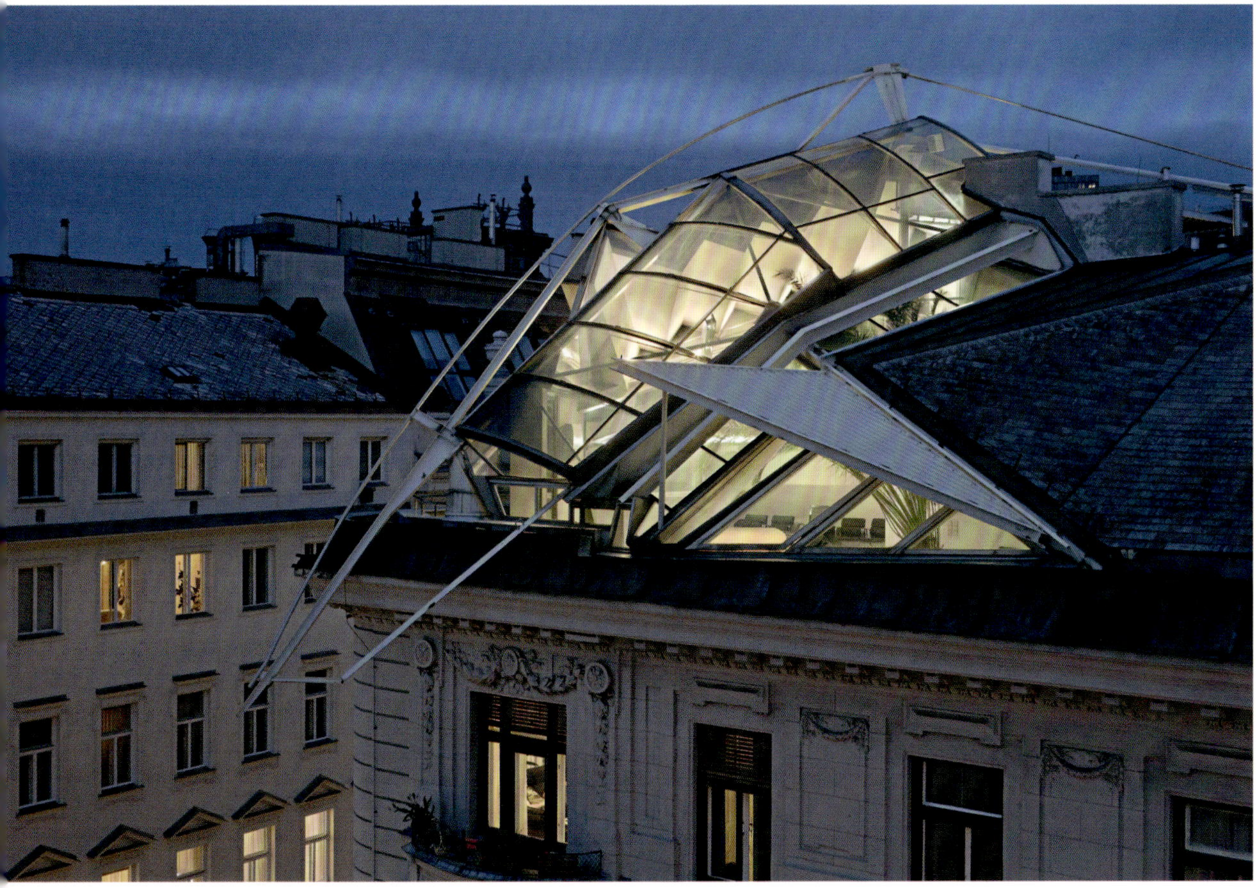

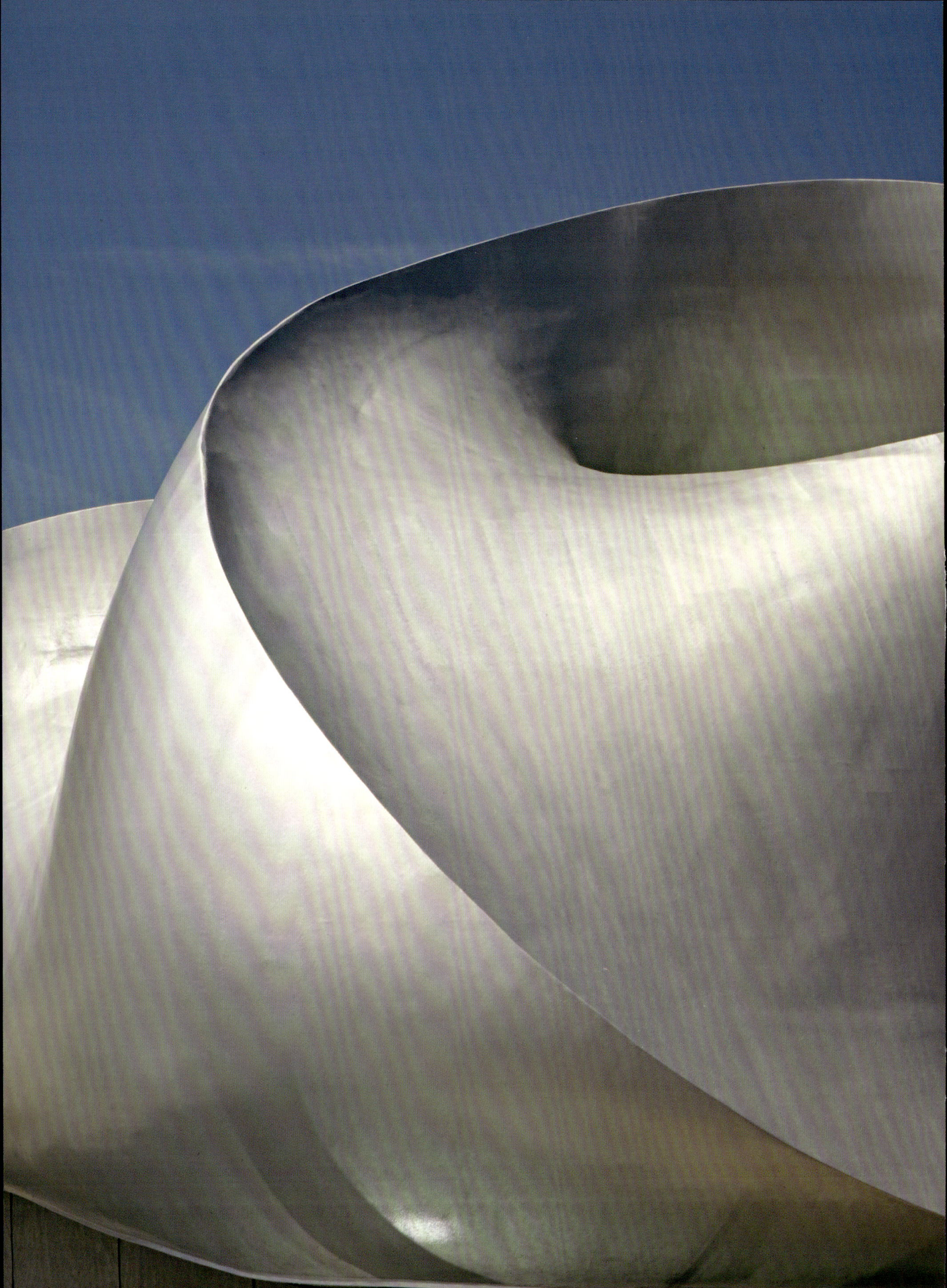

34 Coop Himmelb(l)au, Martin Luther Church, Hainburg. The complex, swirling geometry of the roof opens up around a skylight that illuminates the hall below

35 (top)   Delugan Meissl, Porsche Museum, Stuttgart

36 (bottom, left)   Delugan Meissl, Casa Invisibile, conceived as a prefabricated house, easy to transport and assemble

37 (bottom, right)   Delugan Meissl, Casa Invisibile

38 (opposite, top)   ARTEC, social housing Bremer Stadtsmusikanten, Tokiostrasse

39 (opposite, bottom)   RLP Rüdiger Lainer + Partner, House with Porches

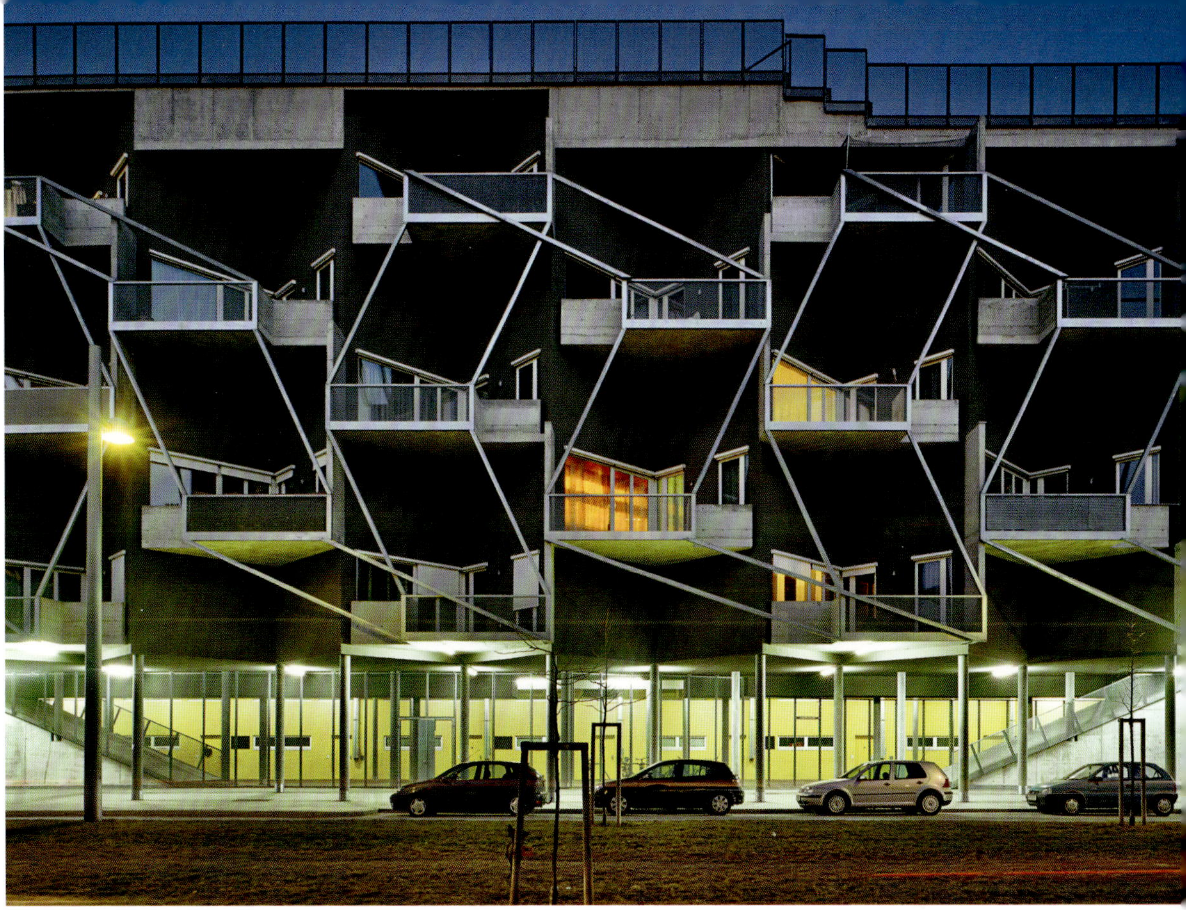

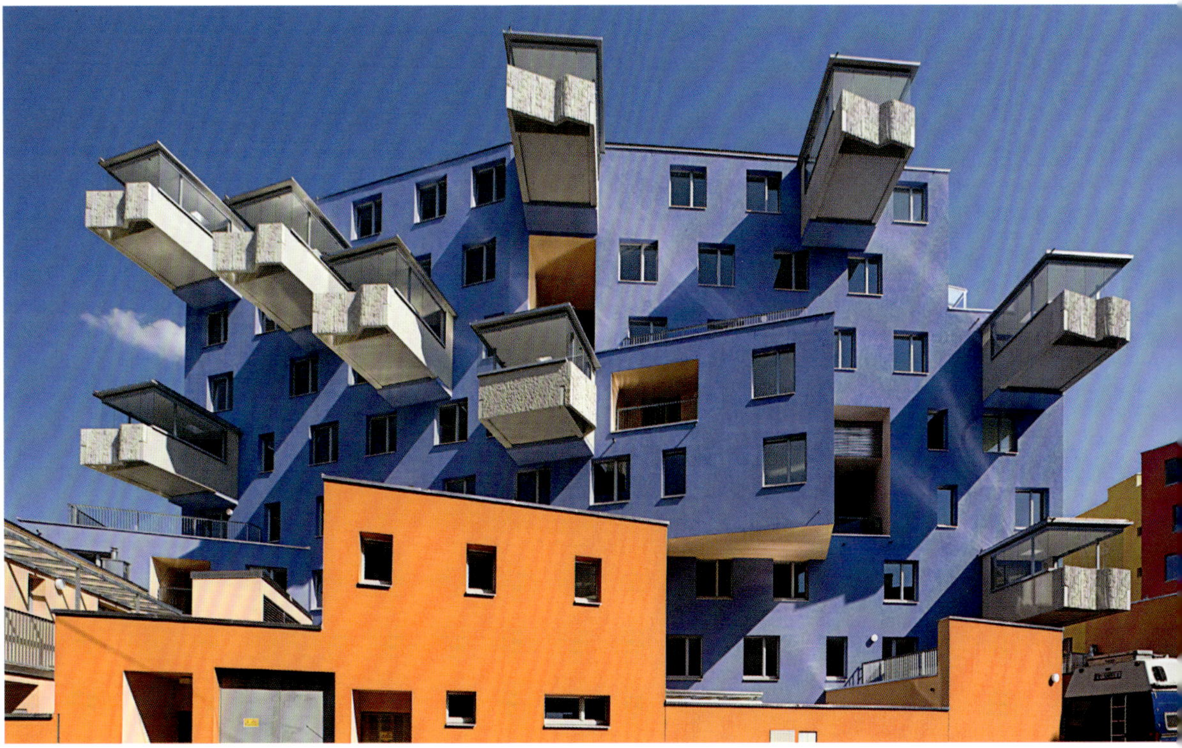

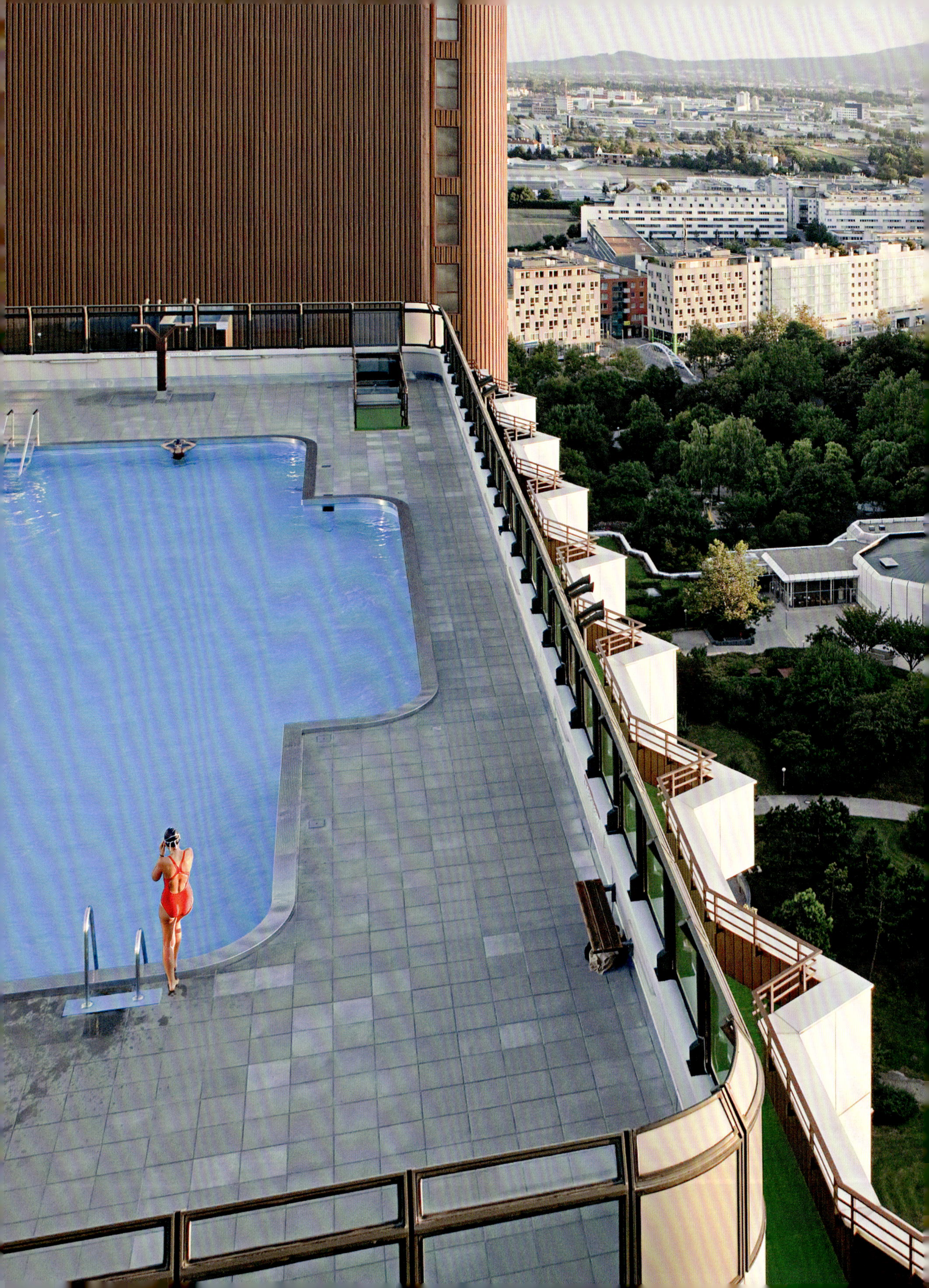

Harry Glück, Alt-Erlaa

41 (above)   Friedensreich Hundertwasser and Joseph Krawina, Hundertwasser House

42 (opposite, top left)   BKK-3 and Johnny Winter, Miss Sargfabrik

43 (opposite, top right)   BKK-3 and Johnny Winter, Miss Sargfabrik, typical non-standard apartment layout

44 (opposite, bottom)   Hermann Czech, Adolf Krischanitz and Werner Neuwirth, Am Mühlgrund, intergenerational social housing on the outskirts of Vienna, exterior

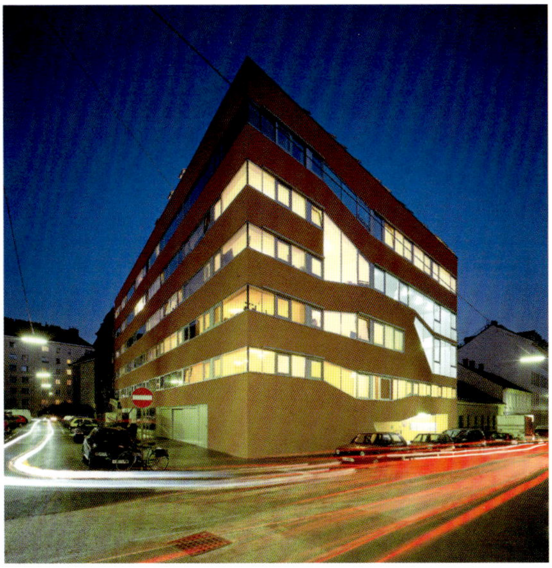

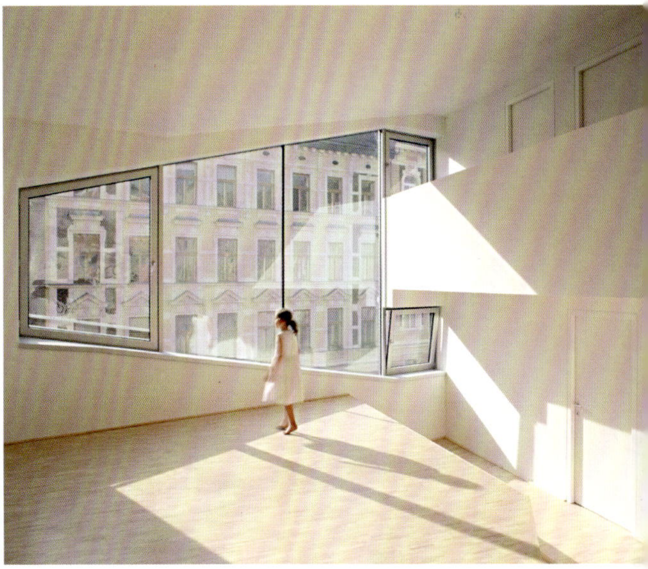

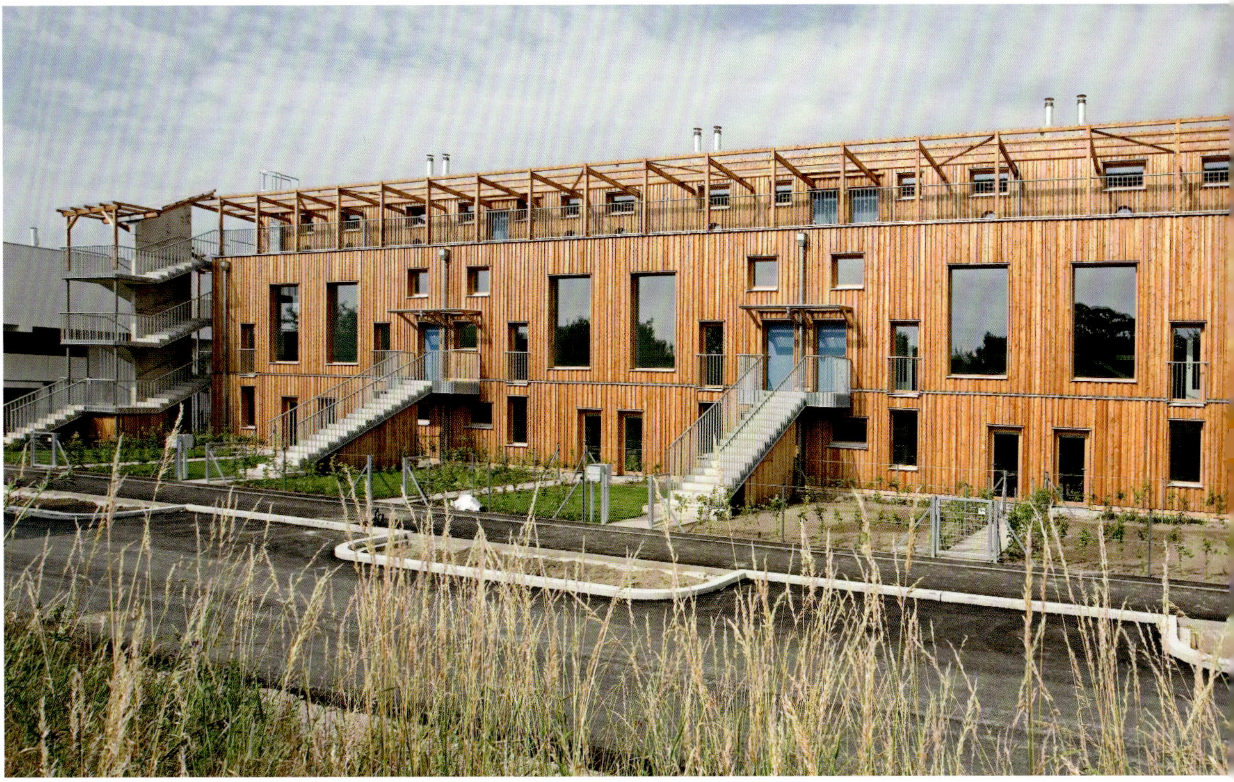

45 PPAG, Wohnen am Park seen from Bike City

46 (top) PPAG, Wohnen am Park, apartment interior

47 (bottom) PPAG, Wohnen am Park, work of art integrated into a lobby

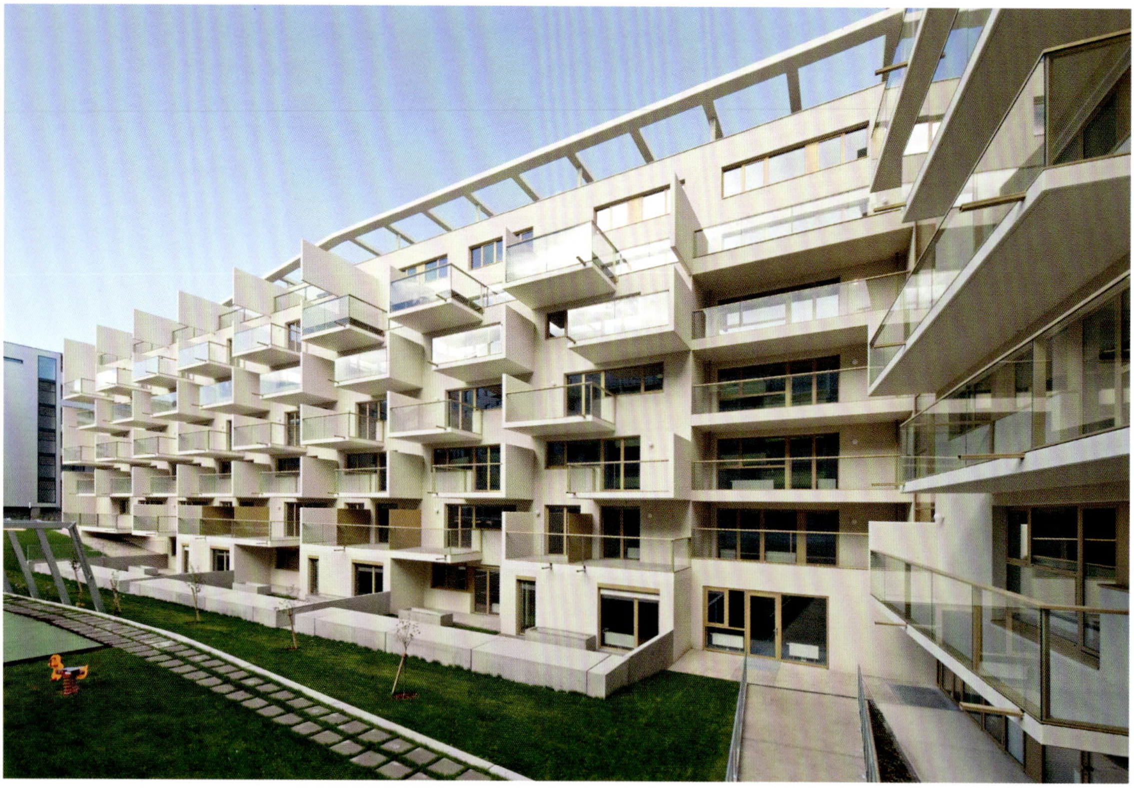

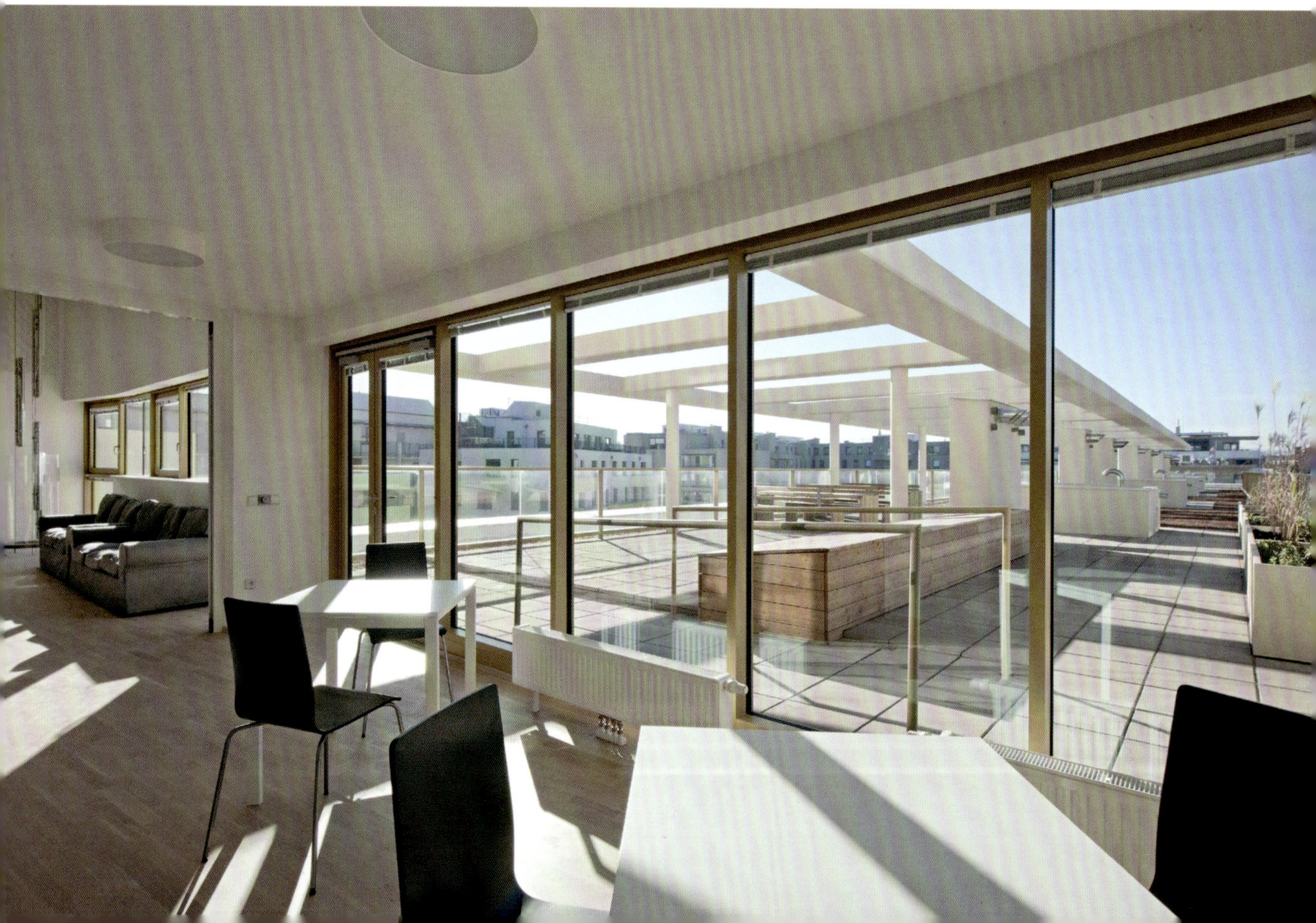

Conclusion

Chapter 10 of this book concluded with the developments in Vienna's social housing program since the 1970s. Much emphasis was placed on the community-enhancing amenities increasingly on offer to residents over the years. Among them are swimming pools, bars, saunas, spas that serve champagne, rooftop gardens, playgrounds, in-house social psychologists specializing in conflict resolution, works by Vienna's most acclaimed artists, computer-equipped business centers, inexpensive health-conscious restaurants, espresso bars, concert stages and cinemas, avant-garde theaters, immediate access to public transport, women- and child-friendly environments, LGBT events, safety from crime, intergenerational and inter-cultural living, and so-called dementia gardens for residents with memory problems.

Many of these buildings were designed by Vienna's most renowned architects – Friedensreich Hundertwasser, Johnny Winter, Geiswinkler & Geiswinkler, Anna Popelka and Georg Poduschka, ARTEC, Hermann Czech, Adolf Krischanitz, Elsa Prochazka, Rüdiger Lainer, and Elke Delugan and Roman Meissl. This means they share the same architect-designed feel and afford the same visual and spatial pleasure as the more upscale works we saw in earlier chapters, such as those by Hans Hollein, Coop Himmelb(l)au and Jabornegg and Pálffy.

That chapter also presented what is perhaps the most remarkable feature of Vienna's social housing. This is the fact that 60 per cent of Vienna's population lives in it, that they pay around 7 euros per square meter in rent, and that, thanks to its efficient Austro-Keynesian municipal government, it is a highly productive sector that stimulates the economy of Austria as a whole.

48 (opposite, top)   Delugan Meissl, social housing at Sonnwendviertel, exterior, 2016

49 (opposite, bottom)   Delugan Meissl, interior of a rooftop apartment at Sonnwendviertel

The aim of the last two chapters has been to present Vienna's current architecture, and in particular its social housing since the 1970s, as a culmination of the 'modern rebellion' initiated 120 years ago by Otto Wagner's manifesto, *Modern Architecture*, where this book began. This is the last of three periods of astonishing Viennese architectural creativity, three golden ages of modern architecture since the time of Otto Wagner.

To go back to the beginning, the first golden age began in the mid-1890s and lasted until the First World War. It is synonymous with some of the most epoch-making architecture of the twentieth century, beginning with Wagner's Stadtbahn, his Majolica House, his Postsparkasse, his façade for the *Die Zeit* dispatch office and his Steinhof church. Josef Olbrich's Secession building was another high point. It was followed by Josef Hoffmann's Palais Stoclet, his Purkersdorf Sanatorium, his house for Sonja Knips and his Fledermaus collection. Adolf Loos built his Goldman & Salatsch and Knize shops at this time, along with his American Bar and Scheu House.

The second golden age lasted from after the First World War until the Anschluss in 1938. This was when 'Red Vienna' produced its innovative social housing programs as well as universally renowned architecture such as the Wittgenstein House and Adolf Loos's houses for Tristan Tzara and Josephine Baker in Paris, as well as his Moller House in Vienna and and his Müller House in Prague. It was the time when Richard Neutra and Rudolf Schindler began to build, when Victor Gruen designed his first commercial buildings, when Margarete Schütte-Lihotzky designed her Frankfurt Kitchen, when Friedrich Kiesler designed his Space Stage, his City in Space, his Film Guild Cinema, his Space House and his Mobile Home Library. The list goes on.

A list of such masterpieces, disproportionate for such a small city, raises a few questions. One is whether there might be a family resemblance – to borrow Ludwig Wittgenstein's term, a certain 'Vienneseness' – running through the architecture of the last 120 years.

There is. It goes back to Otto Wagner. His direct influence is clear when it comes to the contemporaries who idolized him, for example in Josef Hoffmann's and Josef Frank's love of ornament. It is also clear in the work of his student Hubert Gessner, who transferred Wagner's perimeter block housing model to Red Vienna's Gemeindebau housing program in the early 1920s, after which it became the dominant building type.

Then there is Otto Wagner's unique socially conscious idea of what the modern city should be. It too went against the exclusively technocratic grain followed by other contemporary major architects, again most obviously Le Corbusier, van Eesteren and Hilberseimer. Wagner, true to form, was alone in favoring the new technology of public mass transit over that of the equally new technology of the automobile. He conceived of transportation hubs as meeting places for public life. In Garnier's, Le Corbusier's and van Eesteren's drawings of the city, the streets are devoid of humans. Otto Wagner's are full of people caught up in urban social life.

Among the other Viennese architects for whom this holds true are almost the entire Wagner School, Josef Hoffmann, Adolf Loos, Margarete Schütte-Lihotzky, Richard Neutra and Josef Frank, who all contributed to the social housing of Red Vienna, as much as it does for postwar architects like Hermann Czech, Jabornegg and Pálffy, Adolf Krischanitz, ARTEC, Geiswinkler & Geiswinkler, Popelka and Poduschka, Hundertwasser, Silja Tillner and Gabu Heindl.

And finally, again as opposed to his international modernist contemporaries, having witnessed the social inequality and poverty created by the Gilded Age in Vienna, Otto Wagner called for strong state interventionism as a means of regulating excessively exploitative real-estate speculation.

A hard-won combination of good architecture, social consciousness and sound economics, has worked for Vienna over the last 120 years.

Acknowledgements

I am grateful to a number of friends, colleagues and family members for their help in putting this book together. Hans Hollein, my colleague at the University of Applied Arts, generously shared his unequalled knowledge of the city's history. In the early phase of writing, in the spring of 2010, I had the good fortune to correspond with Tony Judt in spite of his illness. His views on social democracy and his encouragement are at the heart of this study. I had the opportunity to air the views developed in the book in the stimulating environment of Tsinghua University in Beijing and at the Li Kuan Yu Center for Innovative Cities in Singapore. I would like to thank Professors Wu Lianyong, Liu Jiang, Li Xiaodong, Yeo Kangshua and Chan Heng Chee for their invitations. I also was lucky enough to be able to deliver lectures on different chapters of the book at the conference of the Indian Institute of Architects in Mumbai and at Yale, thanks to Durganand Balsavar, Eeva Llisa Pelkonen and Karla Britton respectively. Borislav Petranov, and his kind colleagues at the Bulgarian Cultural Center, allowed me to stay at the Wittgenstein House over a period of four years from 2003 to 2007. David Baum helped with the research into recent social housing in Vienna. Eva Blšáková and Hu Yongheng were resourceful volunteer research assistants in the last phase of the book. The collaboration of my doctorate students, Eva Kuss and Valentina Sonzogni, has been very fruitful. For sharing their views and knowledge over the long period this book took to prepare, I also would like to thank Jeffry Diefendorf, Mark Gilbert, the late Madeleine Jenewein, Adrian Jolles, Erna Jolles, Winfried Kallinger, Otto Kapfinger, Christian Kühn, Antoine Lefaivre,

Micha Levin, Isben Önen, Mary Otis Stevens, Mara Reissberger, John Sailer, Vincent Scully, Reinhard Seiss and Monica Wittgenstein. Since one of the main topics of the book is the social housing tradition, I am especially grateful to Eve Blau, whose work on the topic is unsurpassed. I am also grateful to all the architects and artists who supplied material for this book and to the librarians of the MAK, the Austrian National Library in Vienna, the Vienna Museum, the Waschsalon of the Karl Marx Hof, and the library of my university, the University of Applied Arts in Vienna, as well as its archival collection under Patrick Werkner, the Architekturzentrum Wien and the Albertina. From Gerald Bast, rector of my university, I received a grant for the photographs, and from the Austrian Ministry of Culture's Austrian Science Fund (FWF) a research grant which partly funded my research. Special mention goes to the StadtWien and Wohnfonds-Wien and other websites supported by the municipality of Vienna for the plethora and transparency of information related to contemporary housing projects and policies. I hope I have honored the unexpected inheritance from my cousin, Denise Lefaivre, by using it all in the preparation of the book. Lucie Ewin and Sarah Thorowgood managed the production with meticulous expertise, and I am amazed at Eleanor Rees's painstaking copy-edit and Kate Parker's proofread of the text. Adrian Hunt's graphic design is a delight. As for Val Rose, I could not have wished for an editor with more kind patience, sound judgement and good advice. Alexander Tzonis, as ever, has been my greatest inspiration, critic and support.

Notes

Quotes in English from German works are the translation of the author.

Prologue

1. Charles Gulick, *Austria from Habsburg to Hitler*, 2 vols (Berkeley, 1948), p. 1.
2. Karl Kraus, *Die Fackel*, no. 400 (Summer 1914), p. 2
3. As I write this, it is still the first-ranking city in the world for livability according to the Mercer Scale 2016.
4. Helmut Weihsmann, *Das Röte Wien* (Vienna, 1985–2002); Eve Blau, *The Architecture of Red Vienna, 1919–1934* (Cambridge, Mass., 1999).

1. *Fin de Siècle* Vienna and the Culture Wars

1. The 'sleepwalkers' image comes from Hermann Broch, *The Sleepwalkers* (1931–2; trans. W. Muir and E. Muir, San Francisco, 1985) and the 'gay apocalypse' from his *Hugo von Hofmannsthal and His Times, 1860 to 1920* (1947–8; trans. and ed. Michael P. Steinberg, Chicago, 1984), p. 59.
2. Edward Timms, *Karl Kraus: Apocalyptic Satirist, Culture and Catastrophe in Hapsburg Vienna* (New Haven, 1989). See also Jonathan Franzen, Daniel Kehlmann and Paul Reitter, *The Kraus Project* (New York, 2014), an annotated translation of some of Kraus's best-known satirical articles criticizing the manipulative mass media of the time, in particular *Die Neue Freie Presse*, and defending his own often overwrought, febrile, unstrung, sometimes even intentionally incomprehensible prose, the equivalent of the expressionism of the paintings of Kokoschka. Later, in the 1930s, Krauss gave performances satirizing Adolf Hitler's style of public speaking. See www.youtube.com/watch?v=U20oHROPdLI.
3. Karl Kraus, *Die Fackel*, no. 400 (Summer 1914), p. 2. The best biography of Kraus is Edward Timms, *Karl Kraus: Apocalyptic Satirist* and *Karl Kraus: Apocalyptic Satirist, Volume Two: The Postwar Crisis and the Rise of the Swastika* (New Haven, 2005).
4. Karl Kraus, *The Last Days of Mankind* (trans. Michael Russell, Kindle, 2013).
5. ibid., Act IV, Scene 45.
6. ibid., Act V.
7. ibid., Act V.
8. Anthony Atkinson and Thomas Piketty, *Top Incomes over the Twentieth Century* (Oxford, 2007). Quoted in Roman Sandgruber, *Traumzeit für Millionäre: Die 929 reichsten Wienerinnen und Wiener im Jahr 1910* (Vienna, 2013). See also Elizabeth Lichtenberger, *Wirtschaftsfunction und Sozialstruktur der Wiener Ringstrasse* (Vienna, 1970).
9. Sandgruber, *Traumzeit für Millionäre*.
10. Christopher Clark, *The Sleepwalkers: How Europe Went to War in 1914* (London, 2012), pp. 69–70.
11. Carl E. Schorske in *Fin de Siècle Vienna* (New York, 1980) equates the rise of the modern Vienna with the failure of 'liberalism'. Schorske's analysis does not make clear the potential ambiguity of the term. He could have pointed out to an overwhelmingly American audience, used to equating liberalism with the reformist Kennedy era, embodied by the Rooseveltian economist John Kenneth Galbraith, that, in the case of Austria, it was a laissez-faire, libertarian conservative movement, close to the doctrine of the Vienna School of Economics, personified by Friedrich von Hayek, which was the origin of the conservative Chicago School of Economics led by Milton Friedman.
12. Wolfgang Maderthaner and Lutz Musner, *Unruly Masses: The Other Side of Fin de Siècle Vienna* (New York, 2008; first published in German, 1999). Chapter 1 describes the 'Hunger Revolt'.
13. Eugen von Philippovich, *Wiener Wohnungsverhältnisse* (Vienna, 1894). Cited in Gulick, *Austria from Habsburg to Hitler*, vol. 1, p. 354.
14. Patrick Decaix and Cornelia Redeker, 'Otto Neurath. Isotopia' in www.Architekturtheorie.eu.
15. Catherine Bauer, *Modern Housing* (New York, 1934), p. 294.
16. ibid.
17. Gulick, *Austria from Habsburg to Hitler*, vol. 1, p. 354.
18. ibid.
19. ibid., p. 412.
20. Alexander Gerschenkron specialized in the subject of economic backwardness during his long career as professor of economics at Harvard University. See his *An Economic Spurt that Failed: Four Lessons in Austrian History* (Princeton, 1977), p. 44 in particular: 'I deal with the central problem of Körber's policies which, to repeat, was the economic backwardness of Austria.' See also Chapter 2, 'The Economic Backwardness of Austria'. Gerschenkron is best known for his *Economic Backwardness in Historical Perspective* (Cambridge, Mass., 1962). He does not provide detailed examples of economic backwardness in Habsburg Austria in this work, however. For his intellectual roots, see Marcel van der Linden, 'Gerschenkron's Secret: A Research

Note', *Critique: A Journal of Socialist Theory* 40, 4 (2012), pp. 553-62.
21. Geoffrey Wawro, *A Mad Catastrophe: The Outbreak of World War I and the Collapse of the Habsburg Empire* (New York, 2014), Introduction, pp. 15-49.
22. See Felix Butschek, *Österreichische Wirtschaftsgeschichte. Von der Antike bis zur Gegenwart* (Vienna, 2011). Cited in Ewald Nowotny, 'The Austrian School of Economics and Austrian Economic Policy', Zilk Lecture, Hebrew University of Jerusalem, 31 May 2015.
23. William M. Johnston, *The Austrian Mind: An Intellectual and Social History* (Berkeley, 1972), p. 34.
24. Simon Winder's *Danubia* (New York, 2014) ascribes the ineptitudes of Franz Josef to the long tradition of the Habsburg monarchy.
25. Wawro, *A Mad Catastrophe*, p. 15.
26. Mark Twain, 'Stirring Times', *Harper's New Monthly Magazine*, March 1898.
27. Gerschenkron, *An Economic Spurt*, p. 15.
28. See Gerschenkron, *An Economic Spurt*, p. 8, where he quotes the playwright Johann Nestroy's *Judith and Holofernes*, in which the devil orders, 'Take the corpses away. I can't stand any *Schlamperei*.'
29. ibid., p. 9.
30. ibid., p. 26.
31. ibid., pp. 24 and 38. For the role of Bismarck in founding the welfare state in Germany, see Hermann Beck, *Origins of the Authoritarian Welfare State in Prussia* (Ann Arbor, 2007).
32. Gerschenkron, *An Economic Spurt*, p. 54.
33. ibid., p. 28.
34. Hermann Kuprian, 'On the Threshold of the Twentieth Century: State and Society in Austria before World War I', in Rolf Steininger et al. (eds), *Austria in the Twentieth Century* (New Brunswick, 2009), pp. 11-35, esp. p. 33.
35. This is the thesis that underpins Gerschenkron's *An Economic Spurt*.
36. Karl Polanyi, *The Great Transformation* (New York, 1944).
37. Richard Charmatz, *Österreichs innere Geschichte von 1848 bis 1907* (Leipzig, 1911-12, 2nd edn), vol. 2, pp. 153,
195. Cited in Schorske, *Fin de Siècle Vienna*, p. 275, nn. 27 and 28.
38. Gerschenkron, *An Economic Spurt*, pp. 57-60.
39. Wawro, *A Mad Catastrophe*, p. xx.
40. ibid., p. 24.
41. ibid., p. 25.
42. Clark, *Sleepwalkers*, p. 103.
43. This is the thesis of Geoffrey Wawro in *A Mad Catastrophe*. The counter view is that of Christopher Clark, who argues in *Sleepwalkers* that, on the contrary, the imperial army was well organized.
44. Wawro, *A Mad Catastrophe*, p. 25.
45. William O. McCagg Jr., *A History of Habsburg Jews, 1670-1918* (Bloomington, 1992) provides the best overview of the waves of upward mobility and Judeophilia and subsequent crisis. See also Allan Janik and Stephen Toulmin, *Wittgenstein's Vienna* (London, 1996), 'Karl Lueger and the Christian Social Party', pp. 53-7; George E. Berkley, *Vienna and Its Jews: The Tragedy of Success 1880-1980s* (Cambridge, Mass., 1988); Robert S. Wistrich, *The Jews of Vienna in the Age of Franz Joseph* (Oxford, 1989); Peter Pulzer, *The Rise of Political Anti-Semitism in Germany and Austria* (Cambridge, Mass., 1988); Paul Hofmann, *The Viennese: Splendor, Twilight and Exile* (New York, 1989); Steven Beller, *Vienna and the Jews, 1867-1938* (Cambridge, 1991).
46. See Schorske, *Fin de Siècle Vienna*.
47. See the passages by Schorske, ibid., on the relationship between Lueger and Schönerer. Also Andrew G. Whiteside, *The Socialism of Fools: Georg Ritter von Schönerer and Austrian Pan-Germanism* (Berkeley, 1975).
48. See Sophie Lillie, *Was einmal war: Handbuch der enteigneten Kunstsammlungen Wiens* (Vienna, 1982). Also Oliver Rathkolb (ed.), *Der lange Schatten des Antisemitismus. Kritische Auseinandersetzungem mit der Geschichte des Universität Wien im 19. und 20.s Jahrhundert* (Vienna, 2013), including Birgit Nemec and Klaus Tashwer, 'Terror gegen Tandler. Kontext und Chronik
der antisemitischen Attackem am I. Anatomischen Institut der Universität Wien', p. 147; and a study of the anti-Semitism aimed against Kammerer at the Vivarium, at the *Hundert Jahre Biologische Versuchsanstalt* symposium, held at the Vienna Academy of Sciences, organized by the German scholar Sabine Brauckmann, 6-7 February 2014.
49. Johnston, *The Austrian Mind*.
50. Friedrich Stadler, 'Spätaufklarung und Sozialdemocratie in Wien 1918-1938', in *Aufbruch und Untergang: Österreichische Kultur zwischen 1918 und 1939*, ed. Franz Kadrnoska (Vienna, 1981). See also Friedrich Stadler (ed.), *Vertriebene Vernunft*, 2 vols (Vienna, 2004, 2nd edn).
51. See the excellent Janek Wasserman, *Black Vienna: The Radical Right in the Red City 1918-1938* (Ithaca, 2014).
52. Timms, *Karl Kraus*, vol. 1, p. 6.
53. www.youtube.com/watch?v=rg-uGpBhs2g; www.youtube.com/watch?v=omoufyXm3ig.
54. Karl Kraus, 'Heine und die Folgen' ('Heine and the Consequences'), *Die Fackel*, 1911.
55. www.youtube.com/watch?v=rg-uGpBhs2g; www.youtube.com/watch?v=omoufyXm3ig.
56. https://archive.org/stream/dasandere01wienuoft/dasandere01wienuoft_djvu.txt.
57. Timms, *Karl Kraus*, vol. 2, p. 107.
58. Heinrich Kulka, *Adolf Loos: Das Werk des Architekten* (Vienna, 1931), p. 31.
59. Janik and Toulmin, *Wittgenstein's Vienna*, p. 105.
60. ibid., p. 104.
61. ibid.
62. This is the thesis of Christopher Long, *Der Fall Loos* (Vienna, 2015).
63. Klaus Taschwer, paper delivered at the *Hundert Jahre Biologische Versuchsanstalt* symposium at the Academy of Sciences, Vienna, in February 2014.
64. Wasserman, *Black Vienna*, pp. 188-9.
65. Eric Kandel, for one, has referred to this modernization as the result of 'the productive interaction of Christians and Jews': Eric Kandel,

'The Productive Interaction of Christian and Jews that Led to the Creation of Modernism in Vienna 1900', in Rathkolb (ed.), *Der lange Schatten des Antisemitismus*. See Beller, *Vienna and the Jews*, for an exception to the tendency to underrate the importance of Jewish contributions.
66. Johnston, *The Austrian Mind*, Introduction. See also Lichtenberger, *Wirtschaftsfunction und Sozialstruktur der Wiener Ringstrasse*. For an encyclopedic view of the biographical details of the Jewish population of Vienna before the Anschluss, see Georg Gaugusch, *Wer einmal war. 500 Jüdische Familien Wiens* (Vienna, 2011), vol. 1.
67. Sandgruber, *Traumzeit für Millionäre*.
68. Fredric Bedoire, *The Jewish Contribution to Modern Architecture, 1830–1930* (Stockholm, 2004), p. 301; Georg Gaugusch, 'Jewish Real Estate Ownership in the Vienna City Center and the Ringstrasse Area until 1885' in *Ringstrasse, A Jewish Boulevard* (Vienna, 2015), pp. 89–134.
69. Lillie, *Was einmal war*.
70. Rebecca Houze, 'Fashionable Reform Dress and the Invention of Style in Fin de Siecle Vienna', *Fashion Theory* 5, 1 (2001), pp. 29–55; Jill Lloyd, 'Feminists and Femmes Fatales: Representing Women in Turn-of-the-Century Vienna', in Jill Lloyd and Christian Witt-Dörring, *Birth of the Modern* (New York, 2011), pp. 121–41. An issue of *Deutsche Kunst und Dekoration*, vol. 19 (October 1906–March 1907), contains photographs of Flöge wearing loose-fitting gowns. The designs are attributed to 'Prof. Gustav Klimt' and the execution to the 'Atelier of the Flöge Sisters'. See also Wolfgang Georg Fischer, *Gustav Klimt and Emilie Flöge: The Artist and His Muse* (London, 1992).
71. Sophie Lillie, *Drei Frauen fördern die Wiener Moderne. Die Sammlungen Serena Lederer, Jenny Steiner und Aranka Munk*, PhD thesis, University of Vienna. In progress.
72. Elana Shapira, *Style and Seduction: Jewish Patrons, Architecture and Design in Fin de Siècle Vienna* (Boston, 2016).
73. Manu Miller, *Sonja Knips und die Wiener Moderne* (Vienna, 2004).
74. Meyer Schapiro, 'The New Viennese School', in *The Vienna School Reader: Politics and Art Historical Method in the 1930s*, ed. Christopher S. Wood (New York, 2000). Originally published in *Art Bulletin* 18 (1936), pp. 258–66.
75. Janik and Toulmin, *Wittgenstein's Vienna*, p. 92. They argue that the US owes its current pre-eminence in the medical sciences to the students who traveled to Austria at the time: William Osler, William Halsted and Harvey Cushing.
76. *Hundert Jahre Biologische Versuchsanstalt* symposium, February 2014; Wolfgang L. Reiter, 'Destroy and Forget: The Biological Research Institute and Its Scientists', *Austrian Journal of History* 10, 4 (1999), pp. 585–614; Veronika Hofer, 'Rudolf Godscheid, the Biologist Paul Kammerer and the Prater Vivarium in the Liberal Education of the Viennese Modernists', in Mitchell Ash (ed.), *Science, Politics and Public Life from Viennese Modernism to the Present* (Vienna, 2002), pp. 149–84.
77. This account is based on Maria Rentzi, *Trafficking Materials and Gendered Experimental Practices: Radium Research in Early Twentieth Century Vienna* (New York, e-publication, 2007).
78. ibid.
79. Wolfgang Reiter, 'Österreichische Wissenschaftsemigration am Beispiel des Instituts für Radiumforschung der Österreichischen Akademie der Wissenschaften', in Stadler (ed.), *Vertriebene Vernunft*, pp. 709–29.
80. Peter Galison, 'Marietta Blau: Between Nazis and Nuclei', *Physics Today* 50, 11 (1997), pp. 42–8.
81. Peter Galison, 'Aufbau/Bauhaus: Logical Positism and Architectural Modernism', *Critical Inquiry* 16 (Summer 1990), pp. 709–52. See also Robert Rosner and Brigitte Strohmaier, *Marietta Blau – Sterne der Zertrümmerung. Biographie einer Wegbereiterin der modernen Teilchenphysik* (Vienna, 2003) and http://jwa.org/encyclopedia/article/blau-marietta.
82. Deborah Holmes, *Langeweile ist Gift. Das Leben der Eugenie Schwarzwald* (Vienna, 2012).
83. Beller, *Vienna and the Jews*, pp. 33–70.
84. Richard Rhodes, *Hedy's Folly: The Life and Breakthrough Inventions of Hedy Lamarr, the Most Beautiful Woman in the World* (New York, 2011). For more on the multi-faceted Antheil, see: George Antheil, *Bad Boy of Music* (New York, 1945); Robert Morse Crunden, *Body and Soul: The Making of American Modernism* (New York, 2000); Noel Riley Fitch, *Sylvia Beach and the Lost Generation: A History of Literary Paris in the Twenties and Thirties* (New York, 1985).
85. Iris Meder, *Vienna's Shooting Girls*, exh. cat., Jewish Museum (Vienna, 2014); Anna Auer and Carl Aigner, *Trude Fleischmann. Fotografien 1918–1938* (Vienna, 1988); Anna Auer (ed.), *Übersee. Flucht und Emigration Österreichischer Fotografen 1920–1940* (Vienna, 1997); Heike Herrberg and Heidi Wagner, *Wiener Melange: Frauen zwischen Salon und Kaffeehaus* (Berlin: 2002); Hans Schreiber, *Trude Fleischmann. Fotografin in Wien 1918–1938* (Vienna: 1990); Duncan Forbes (ed.), *Edith Tudor-Hart: Im Schatten der Diktaturen*, exh. cat., National Gallery of Scotland and the Wien Museum (Berlin, 2014).
86. *Kinetismus – Wien entdeckt die Avantgarde*, exh. cat., Wien Museum (Berlin, 2006).
87. See Markus Oppenauer, *Der Salon Zuckerkandl im Kontext von Wissenschaft, Politik und Öffentlichkeit* (Vienna, 2012); Helga Peham, *Die Salonièren und die Salons in Wien. 200 Jahre Geschichte einer besonderen Institution* (Vienna, Graz and Klagenfurt, 2013); Michael Schulte, *Berta Zuckerkandl. Saloniere, Journalistin, Geheimdiplomatin* (Zurich, 2006); Lucian O. Meysels, *In Meinen Salon ist Österreich: Berta Zuckerkandl und ihre Zeit* (Munich, 1984).
88. Galison, 'Aufbau/Bauhaus', p. 710.

2. Otto Wagner

1. Otto Wagner, *Modern Architecture*, first delivered as a lecture given at the Academy of Art, then published as a book in four editions: 1896, 1898, 1902 and, under a different title, in 1914. See the annotated translation by Harry Francis Mallgrave (Santa Monica, 1988).
2. Karl Kraus, 'Die demolierte Literatur', *Wiener Rindschau* 1, 15 (1896). See the text in http://de.wikisource.org/wiki/Die_demolirte_Literatur. Mark Twain, 'Stirring Times', *Harpers New Monthly Magazine*, March 1898.
3. Wagner, *Modern Architecture*, p. 76.
4. ibid., p. 108.
5. ibid., p. 108.
6. ibid., p. 78.
7. ibid., p. 109.
8. ibid., p. 75.
9. ibid., pp. 78–9.
10. See Ian Boyd Whyte, 'Modernist Dioscuri?', in Harry Francis Mallgrave (ed.), *Otto Wagner: Reflections on the Raiment of Modernity* (Santa Monica, 1993), pp. 157–98.
11. Carol Herselle Krinsky, *Synagogues of Europe* (Cambridge, 1985).
12. Ines Müller, *Die Otto Wagner-Synagoge in Budapest* (Vienna, 1992), pp. 42–3.
13. The best book on Hansen is Renate Wagner-Rieger and Mara Reissberger, *Theophil von Hansen* (Vienna, 1998). It is volume 4 of Wagner-Rieger's monumental 12-volume study of the Ringstrasse architecture, *Die Wiener Ringstrasse* (Vienna, 1969–80).
14. Quoted in George Niemann and Ferdinand von Feldegg, *Theophilos Hansen und seine Werke* (Vienna, 1893), p. 71.
15. Mara Reissberger was the first to point this out in Wagner-Rieger and Reissburger, *Theophil von Hansen*, p. 235. It was then noted by the Ephrussi family member Edmund de Waal in *The Hare with Amber Eyes* (London, 2011), p. 125.
16. Architekturzentrum Wien, *Encyclopedie der Architekten*, 'van der Nüll', www.architektenlexikon.at/de/1197.htm. See also Wagner-Rieger and Reissberger, *Theophil von Hansen*, and Nicholas Parsons, *Vienna: A Cultural History* (Oxford, 2008), p. 209.
17. Wawro, *A Mad Catastrophe*, p. 2.
18. Louis Gonse, 'Le Nouveau Palais des musées à Vienne', *Gazette des beaux-arts*, 3rd per., 6 (1891), pp. 392–403, esp. pp. 395–6. This is quoted in J. Duncan Berry, 'From Historicism to Architectural Realism: On Some of Wagner's Sources' in Mallgrave (ed.), *Otto Wagner*, pp. 243–80 and fn. 50, p. 275.
19. Timms, *Karl Kraus*, vol. 2, p. 374.
20. See Parsons, *Vienna*, p. 209. See also Architekturzentrum Wien's most informative online dictionary of architects under 'Sicardsburg', www.architektenlexikon.at/de/1282.htm, and 'van der Null', www.architektenlexikon.at/de/1197.htm.
21. The information is gleaned from Jutta Pemsel, *Wiener Weltausstellung von 1873* (Vienna, 1989); Karlheinz Roschitz, *Wiener Weltausstellung 1873* (Vienna, 1989); and Wolfgang Kos and Ralph Gleis (eds), *Experimente Metropole: 1873. Wien und die Weltausstellung* (Vienna, 2014).
22. Norbert Rubey and Peter Schoenwald, *Venedig in Wien, Theater- und Vergnügungsstadt der Jahrhundertwende* (Vienna, 1996); Markus Kristan, *Oskar Marmorek: Architekt und Zionist, 1863–1909* (Vienna, 1996), pp. 186–91.
23. Thomas Grey, 'Wagner and the "Makart Style"', *Cambridge Opera Journal* 25, 3 (November 2013), pp. 225–60. See also Janik and Toulmin, *Wittgenstein's Vienna*, pp. 35, 94–5.
24. Grey, 'Wagner and the "Makart Style"', p. 225.
25. ibid.
26. Sigfried Giedion, *Space, Time and Architecture* (Cambridge, 1947), pp. 505–6.
27. Liane Lefaivre, *Leon Battista Alberti's Hypnerotomachia Poliphili* (Cambridge, 1996). All the information concerning Sitte is gleaned from the classic book on Sitte: George Collins and Christiane Collins, *Camillo Sitte: The Birth of Modern City Planning* (New York, 1986); see p. 67.
28. Collins and Collins, *Camillo Sitte*, p. 10.
29. ibid., p. 128.
30. ibid., 157.
31. Elisabeth Lichtenberger, *Die Wiener Altstadt* (Vienna, 1977), quoted in Kurt Mollik, Hermann Reining and Rudolf Wurzer, *Planung und Verwirklichung der Wiener Ringstrassenzone* (Wiesbaden, 1980), p. 29.
32. Paul Goodman and Percival Goodman's *Communitas* (New York, 1960) in particular expressed admiration for Sitte. See Collins and Collins, *Camillo Sitte*, p. 420.
33. Camillo Sitte, *City Planning According to Artistic Principles*, trans. George R. Collins and Christiane Graseman (London, 1965), p. 45.
34. ibid., p. 48.
35. The best description of Wagner's engineering excellence is in Heinz Geretsegger and Max Peinter, *Otto Wagner 1841-1914* (New York, 1979).
36. Ludwig Hevesi, *Eight Years of Secession* (Vienna, 1906).
37. Geretsegger and Peinter, *Otto Wagner*, pp. 79–104.
38. Richard Neutra, *Life and Shape* (New York, 1962). Cited in Thomas Hines, *Richard Neutra: The Search for Modern Architecture* (New York, 2006, 4th edn).
39. This is the expression of Anthony Alofsin in *When Buildings Speak* (Chicago, 2006), p. 79.
40. See Ludwig Hevesi, *Moderne Architektur, Prof. Otto Wagner und die Wahrheit über Beide* (Vienna, 1897), p. 8.
41. Charmatz, *Österreichs innere Geschichte*, cited in Schorske, *Fin de Siècle Vienna*, p. 275, nn. 27 and 28.
42. These quotations are cited by Alofsin, *When Buildings Speak*, p. 78. He refers, in turn, to Àkos Moravánszky, *Competing Visions: Aesthetic Invention and Social Imagination in Central European Architecture, 1867-1998* (Cambridge, Mass., 1998), p. 166.
43. Adolf Loos, 'Otto Wagner', *Reichpost*,

13 July 1911. Joseph August Lux also takes up this observation in his biography, *Otto Wagner* (Munich, 1914).
44. 'Otto Wagner', www.architekten lexikon.at/de/670.htm
45. Duncan Berry, 'From Historicism to Architectural Realism', p. 252.
46. www.architektenlexikon.at/de/670. htm. See Lewis Mumford, *Sticks and Stones* (New York, 1955, first published 1924), pp. 123-34. See also Robert Twombly, *Louis Sullivan: His Life and Work* (New York, 1986).
47. See Müller, *Otto Wagner-Synagoge*, p. 91. Cited in Alofsin, *When Buildings Speak*, p. 51.
48. Moravánszky, *Competing Visions*, p. 97.
49. Wagner, *Modern Architecture*, p. 69.
50. Gottfried Semper, *Der Stil in den technischen und tektonischen Künsten; oder, Praktische Ästhetik: Ein Handbuch für Techniker, Künstler und Kunstfreunde*, 2 vols (Munich, 1861-3); in English: *Style in the Technical and Tectonic Arts; or, Practical Aesthetics*, trans. Harry F. Mallgrave and Michael Robinson (Santa Monica, 2004).
51. Dieter Weidmann, 'Sempers Verhältnis zum Eisen', in Winfried Nerdinger and Werner Oechslin (eds), *Gottfried Semper 1803-1879. Architektur und Wissenschaft vol. 1* (Munich, 2003), pp. 321-9. See also his *Gottfried Semper und das Eisen* (Zurich, 2000).
52. This point of view stands at odds with that of architectural historians who look upon Wagner's relationship to Semperian historicism as one of evolution rather than radical rejection. Among these historians is Werner Oechslin.
53. Wagner, *Modern Architecture*, p. 91.
54. ibid., p. 93.
55. ibid., p. 96.
56. Semper, *Der Stil*, third section: 'Textile Kunst'.
57. Wagner, *Modern Architecture*, p. 121.
58. Adolf Loos, 'Interiors in the Rotunda', *Neue Freie Presse*, 12 June 1898; English translation by Jane Newman and John Smith in Adolf Loos, *Spoken into the Void: Collected Essays 1897-1900* (Cambridge, Mass., 1987).
59. Peter Haiko, Harald Leopold-Löwenthal and Mara Reissberger, '"Die Weisse Stadt". Der Steinhof in Wien', *Kritische Berichte* 9, 6 (1981), pp. 3-37.
60. Christian Schuhböck, *Otto-Wagner-Spital 'Am Steinhof'* (Vienna, 2013).
61. ibid.
62. See the passage on Hoffmann's Puckersdorf Sanatorium in the next chapter.
63. Otto Wagner, *Die Grossstadt: Eine Studie über diese* (Vienna, 1911), published in English as *The Development of the Great City*, Architectural Record, 31 (May 1912), pp. 495-500. The version quoted here is from http://urbanplanning.library.cornell.edu/docs/Wagner.htm
64. Blau, *Architecture of Red Vienna*, p. 171.
65. Wagner, *The Development of the Great City*, http://urbanplanning.library.cornell.
66. Blau, *Architecture of Red Vienna*, p. 171.
67. See Otto Wagner's comments in *Modern Architecture*, p.64.
68. From Otto Wagner, *Development of the Great City*. See http://urbanplanning.library.cornell.edu/docs/wagner.htm
69. ibid.
70. This point is made by Blau, p. 171.
71. ibid.
72. Wagner, *The Development of the Great City*, http://urbanplanning.library.cornell.
73. ibid.

3. The Next Generation

1. It has been intimated by Carl Schorske in *Fin-de-Siecle Vienna*, pp. 90-1, that Wagner's Postsparkasse was associated with anti-Semitism. This is because it was held up by Karl Lueger's Christian Social Party as an alternative to the kind of financial enterprises associated with the Liberals, whom he called the 'Rothschild party' because the owner of the Creditanstalt, the richest man in the world at the time, Albert Salomon von Rothschild, had made his fortune during the days of laissez-faire liberalism. The bust of the founder, Georg Coch, in the square in front of the bank, supposedly turned Coch into a 'martyr-hero for the Christian anti-Semites' and became the 'first monument to an anti-Semitic culture on the Ringstrasse'. The bust may have been used as a pawn in the mayor's anti-Semitic campaign, but this has nothing to do with Otto Wagner or with Georg Coch. The bank Wagner built in 1907 was founded in 1882 by the Imperial Assembly – 15 years before Lueger became mayor and, indeed, 30 years before the installation of Coch's bust.
2. Alofsin, *When Buildings Speak*, p. 82.
3. L. Hevesi, 'Das Haus der Secession', *Kunst und Kunsthandwerk* 1 (1898), pp. 405-7; J. A. Lux, *Josef M. Olbrich* (Berlin, 1919). See also www.architektenlexikon.at/de/441.htm.
4. Josef Maria Olbrich, 'Das Haus der Seccession', *Der Architekt*, vol. v, Jan 1899, p. 5. Quoted in Schorshe, *Fin de Siècle Vienna*, p. 217.
5. Wilhelm Schölermann, 'Neue Wiener Architektur', *Deutsche Kunst und Dekoration*, vol. III, 1898-9, pp 205-210. Quoted in Schorsche, *Fin de Siècle Vienna*, p. 219.
6. See Sandgruber, *Traumzeit für Millionäre*.
7. Liane Lefaivre and Alex Tzonis, *The Emergence of Modern Architecture: A Documentary History of Architecture 1000 to 1810* (London, 2004). The first defence of rigorism, between Bernard against Suger in the 12th century, is covered in pp. 32-37. The second, involving 18th-century defences of rigorism, by Algarotti, Cordemoy, Laugier and Lódoli are covered on pp. 265, 344, 362 and 428.
8. This is the structuring commonplace of the exhibition devoted to this quarrel at the Museum für Angewandte Kunst: *Josef Hoffmann–Adolf Loos. Ornament and Tradition* (Vienna, 2007).

9. Michael Huey, 'Art Itself: The Private Lives of Josef Hoffmann', in Christian Witt-Dörring (ed.), *Josef Hoffmann Interiors 1902–1913* (New York, 2005), pp. 74–97.
10. Agnes Husslein-Arco and Alfred Weidinger (eds), *Gustav Klimt/Josef Hoffmann – Pioneers of Modernism* (Munich, 2011).
11. Josef Hoffmann, *Selbstbiographie*, ed. Peter Noever and Marek Pokorny (Vienna, 2009).
12. The importance of the 1908 *Kunstschau* is emphasized by Kirk Varnedoe (ed.), *Vienna 1900: Art, Architecture & Design*, exh. cat., MoMA (New York, 1986). See the review in the *New York Review of Books* by Carl E. Schorske, 23 September 1986, pp. 19–24.
13. Eduard Sekler's classic monograph *Josef Hoffmann* (Princeton, 1985) is the source for all the treatment of Hoffmann's architecture here.
14. ibid.
15. See Markus Kristan, *Josef Hoffmann – Villenkolonie Hohe Warte* (Vienna, 2004).
16. Sekler, *Josef Hoffmann*, p. 54.
17. ibid., p. 65. See also Kristan, *Josef Hoffmann*.
18. Sekler, *Josef Hoffmann*, pp. 54, 67, 101, 110–11.
19. Eduard Sekler, 'The Stoclet House by Josef Hoffmann', in Douglas Fraser et al. (eds), *Essays in the History of Modern Architecture Presented to Rudolf Wittkower* (London, 1967), pp. 228–44; Peter Noever (ed.), *Yearning for Beauty: The Wiener Werkstätte and the Stoclet House* (Cologne, 2006); Jill Lloyd, 'Feminists and Femmes Fatales', p. 131.
20. Sekler, *Josef Hoffmann*, pp. 127–31.
21. ibid., pp. 318–19.
22. The best books on Loos are: Benedetto Gravagnuolo, *Adolf Loos: Theory and Works* (New York, 1982, first published in Italian, 1899); Heinrich Kulka, *Adolf Loos. Das Werk des Architekten* (Vienna, 1931); Burkhardt Rukschcio and Roland Schachel, *Adolf Loos. Leben und Werk* (Salzburg, 1982); Ralf Bock and Philippe Ruault, *Adolf Loos: Works and Projects* (Milan, 2007); and Werner Oechslin, *Otto Wagner, Adolf Loos and the Road to Modern Architecture* (Cambridge, Mass., 2002, first published in German in 1994).
23. Adolf Loos, 'Ornament and Crime' ('*Ornament und Verbrechen*'), in Adolf Loos, *Ornament and Crime: Selected Essays* (Riverside, 1997), p. 204.
24. Adolf Loos, 'Die Überflüssigen' (1908), *Sämtliche Schriften I* (Vienna, 1962), pp. 267–75.
25. Walter Gropius, 'Adolf Loos zum 60 Geburtstag', *Frankfurter Zeitung*, 10 December 1930.
26. Le Corbusier, 'Adolf Loos zum 60. Geburtstag', *Frankfurter Zeitung*, 10 December 1930.
27. Sigfried Giedion, 'Adolf Loos zum 60 Geburtstag', *Frankfurter Zeitung*, 10 December 1930.
28. Reyner Banham, *Theory and Design in the First Machine Age* (New York, 1960), p. 86. Fedor Roth, *Adolf Loos und die Idee des Ökonomischen* (Vienna, 1995), pp. 10–12, and Hildegund Amanshauser, *Untersuchungen zu den Schriften von Adolf Loos* (Vienna, 1985), p. 209, are other authors among many who have remarked on the contradictions in his writings.
29. Adolf Loos, *Trotzdem* (Innsbruck, 1931).
30. Adolf Loos, 'Architektur' (1910), in *Trotzdem* (Innsbruck, 1931), p. 104.
31. Loos, 'Ornament and Crime', p. 216.
32. *Raumplan* or 'space plan' was a term invented by Loos's student and subsequent biographer Heinrich Kulka. See Kulka, *Adolf Loos*, p. 18,
33. Koerner's interpretation in *Vienna, City of Dreams* (BBC, 2007) is at variance with Christopher Long's contention in *The Looshaus* (New Haven and London, 2011).
34. Elana Shapira, 'Assimilating with Style: Jewish Assimilation and Modern Architecture and Design in Vienna. The Case of the Outfitters Leopold Goldman and Adolf Loos and the Making of Goldman & Salatsch (1909–1911)', PhD thesis, Universität für Angewandte Kunst, Vienna, 2004. Last chapter.
35. An unpublished text by Loos reproduced in Elana Shapira, 'Tailored Authorship', in *Leben mit Loos*, ed. Inge Podbrecky and Rainer Franz (Vienna, 2008), pp. 53–76.

4. After the Apocalypse

1. According to George Kennan, the reason for the outbreak of the First World War was the abandonment of Bismarck's skillful balance of power which kept Russia isolated from France. Once that isolation was broken, Europe was divided between two rival systems, on one hand France and Russia, and on the other Germany, Austria-Hungary and Italy. See his *The Fateful Alliance; France, Russia, and the Coming of the First World War* (New York, 1984).
2. Barbara Tuchman, *The Guns of August* (New York, 1962) is the classic account of how Europe slipped into the First World War. For the best-researched analysis of the Austrian role in the war see Wawro, *A Mad Catastrophe*, and Clark, *Sleepwalkers*. See also Forbes (ed.), *Edith Tudor-Hart*.
3. John Maynard Keynes, *The Economic Consequences of the Peace* (London, 1919).
4. Charles Gulick, in *Austria from Habsburg to Hitler*, mentions his debt to Alexander Gerschenkron on p. xvii. Jeremy Adelman mentions Gerschenkron as the ghostwriter of the book in *Worldly Philosopher: The Odyssey of Albert O. Hirschman* (Princeton, 2014).
5. See http://socialdemocracy21stcentury.blogspot.co.at/2011/12/krugman-hayek-versus-keynes-and.html.
6. Felix Czeike, 'Wien', in Erika Weinzierl and Kurt Skalnik (eds), *Österreich 1918–1938, Geschichte der Ersten Republik*, vol. 2 (Graz, 1983), pp. 1043–78.
7. Wolfgang Maderthaner, '12 February 1934: Social Democracy and Civil War', in Steininger et al. (eds), *Austria in the Twentieth Century*, p. 67.

8. Gulick, *Austria from Habsburg to Hitler*, p. 357.
9. ibid., pp. 717-71. See also p. 7.
10. Anson Rabinbach, *The Crisis of Austrian Socialism: From Red Vienna to Civil War, 1927-1934* (Chicago, 1983), p. 27. He points out that, faced with a lack of power at the federal level, the Social Democrats directed their energies toward 'the construction of a model city in Vienna'.
11. Vienna, 1921.
12. Blau, *Architecture of Red Vienna*, p. 78.
13. Wolfgang Förster, 'Theophilos Hansen – A Nineteenth-century European Star Architect', in *Theophil Hansen. Ein Stararchitekt und seine Wohnbauten and der Wiener Ringstrasse* [*A Star Architect and his Tenement Palaces on the Viennese Ringstrasse*], exh. cat. (Vienna, 2013), pp. 68-9.
14. See Fritz C. Wulz, *Stadt in Veränderung: Eine architektur-politische Studie von Wien in den Jahren 1848 bis 1934*, 2 vols (Stockholm, 1977), vol. 1, p. 273.
15. Pointed out by Eve Blau in *Architecture of Red Vienna*, pp. 81-3.
16. ibid., p.82.
17. Decaix and Redeker, 'Otto Neurath. Isotopia'.
18. Frederic Morton, *Thunder at Twilight: Vienna 1913-1914* (New York, 1989), p. 2.
19. Klaus Novy and Wolfgang Förster, *Einfach Bauen. Genossenschaftliche Selbsthilfe nach den Jahrhundertwende: Zur Rekonstruktion der Wiener Siedlerbewegung* (Vienna, 1991); Blau, *Architecture of Red Vienna*, p. 85.
20. Blau, *Architecture of Red Vienna*, p. 84.
21. For the first detailed study of the phases of the settler movement see Klaus Novy and Günther Uhlig, 'Baugenossenschaften zwischen Tradition und Aufbruch', *Stadtbauwelt* 75 (1982); also Klaus Novy, 'Der Wiener Gemeindewohnungsbau: "Sozialisierung von unten"', *Arch+* 45 (1979); 'Selbsthilfe als Reformbewegung', *Arch+* 55 (1981).
22. Gulick, *Austria from Habsburg to Hitler*, vol. 1, p. 90.
23. Wasserman, *Black Vienna*, p. 158.
24. Blau, *Architecture of Red Vienna*, p. 92
25. ibid.
26. ibid., p. 110.
27. Cited in ibid., p. 112, n. 109.
28. ibid., p. 112.
29. ibid., p. 99.
30. ibid., p. 101.
31. ibid., p. 128; Novy, *Einfach Bauen*.
32. Leopold Bauer, *Gesund Wohnen und Freudig Arbeiten: Probleme unsere Zeit* (Vienna, 1919).
33. Blau, *Architecture of Red Vienna*, p. 102.
34. Peter Noever (ed.), *Margarete Schütte-Lihotzky, Soziale Architektur, Zeitzeugin eines Jahrhunderts* (Vienna, 1993).
35. Susan Henderson, 'A Revolution in the Woman's Sphere: Grete Lihotsky and the Frankfurt Kitchen', in Debra Coleman, Elizabeth Danze and Carol Henderson (eds), *Architecture and Feminism* (Princeton, 1996), pp. 221-53.
36. Noever (ed.), *Margarete Schütte-Lihotzky* .
37. Sabine Plakolm-Forsthuber, 'Ein Leben, Zwei Karrieren', in Matthias Boeckl (ed.), *Visionäre und Vertriebene* (Berlin, 1995), pp. 295-310.
38. Jeffrey S. Gaab, *Munich: Hofbräuhaus and History* (New York, 2006).
39. Nader Vossoughian, *Otto Neurath. The Language of the Global Polis* (Rotterdam, 2008).
40. ibid.
41. The best history of GESIBA is Barbara Feller and Monika Vlach, *75 Jahre GESIBA* (Vienna, 1996).
42. Otto Neurath and Franz Schuster, in *Osterreichs Kleingärtner* 3, no. 12 (1923), p. 1, and *Siedler und Kleingartner* 4, no. 1 (1924). Quoted in Blau, *Architecture of Red Vienna*, p. 99.
43. See Blau, *Architecture of Red Vienna*, p. 87; Peter Marcuse, 'A Useful Installment of Socialist Work: Housing in Red Vienna in the 1920s', in Rachel G. Bratt, Chester Hartman and Ann Meyerson (eds), *Critical Perspectives on Housing* (Philadelphia, 1986), p. 565. See also his 'The Housing Policy of Social Democracy: Determinants and Consequences', in A. Rabinbach (ed.), *The Austrian Socialist Experiment. Social Democracy and Austromarxism 1918-1934.* (Boulder, Co., and London, 1985), pp. 201-21.
44. Willem Korthals Altes and Andreas Faludi, 'Why the Greening of Red Vienna Did Not Come to Pass', *European Planning Studies*, 2, 3 (June 1994), pp. 205-25.
45. Blau, *Architecture of Red Vienna*, p. 131.
46. Friedrich Achleitner, 'Wiederaufbau in Wien, Innere Stadt', in Elizabeth Waechter-Boehm, *Wien 1945* (Vienna, 1985), pp. 106-25.
47. Michel Geertse, www.academia.edu/1984339/Garden_Cities_to_the_World_The_international_propagation_of_thegarden_city_idea_1913-1926. Undated
48. Christopher Long, *Josef Frank: Life and Work* (Chicago, 2001), p. 175.
49. ibid., p. 58.
50. Christopher Long, 'The Wayward Heir: Josef Frank's Vienna Years, 1885-1933', in Nina Stritzler-Levine (ed.), *Josef Frank, Architect and Designer* (New Haven, 1996), pp. 44-61, esp. pp. 56-7.
51. Blau, *Architecture of Red Vienna*.
52. This point was documented by Korthals Altes and Faludi in 'Greening of Red Vienna'.
53. Blau, *Architecture of Red Vienna*, pp. 222-3; Markus Kristan, *Hubert Gessner* (Vienna, 2012); Peter Haiko and Mara Reissberger, 'Die Wohnhausbauten der Gemeinde Wien 1919-1934', *Archithèse* 12 (1974), pp. 49-55.
54. Hans Bobek and Elisabeth Lichtenberger, *Wien* (Vienna, 1966).
55. Wulz, *Stadt in Veränderung*, p. 274.
56. ibid., p. 237.
57. ibid.
58. Vincent Scully, *Modern Architecture: The Architecture of Democracy* (New York, 1974), pp. 53-5.
59. Alastair Grieve, *Isokon: For Ease, For Ever* (London, 2004).
60. Helmut Gruber, *Red Vienna: An Experiment in Working-Class Culture* (Oxford, 1991).
61. Long, *Josef Frank*, pp. 80-82.
62. Blau, *Architecture of Red Vienna*, pp. 303-4.

63. Elizabeth Danto, *Freud's Free Clinics: Psychoanalysis and Social Justice, 1918–1938* (New York, 2005).
64. ibid.
65. Timms, *Karl Kraus*, p. 269.
66. Rukschcio and Schachel, *Adolf Loos*, pp. 258–66 and 290.
67. Malachi Haim Hacohen, *Karl Popper – The Formative Years, 1902–1945: Politics and Philosophy in Interwar Vienna* (Cambridge, 2001), p. 57.
68. Gulick, *Austria from Habsburg to Hitler*, vol. 2, p. 515.
69. Blau, *Architecture of Red Vienna*, p. 204.
70. See, for example, 'Einer Mahler Anekdote', *Kunst und Volk* 3, 3 (November 1928), p. 62.
71. Karen Painter, *Symphonic Aspirations: German Music and Politics, 1900–1945* (Cambridge, Mass., 2007), pp. 142–4.
72. ibid. See also *Die Musik* 26, 9 (June 1934), p. 712.
73. *Der Kuckuck*, January 1931 (Victor Gruen), August 1932 (on Greta Garbo), March 1931 (on Charlie Chaplin).
74. See Felix Czeike, 'Wirtschafts- und Sozialpolitik der Gemeinde Wien in der Ersten Republik, 1918–1934', *Wiener Schriften* 6, 11 (Vienna: Jugend und Volk, 1958, 1959). Also Gerhard Melinz and Gerhard Ungar, *Wohlfahrt und Krise: Wiener Kommunalpolitik 1929–1938* (Vienna, 1996); Robert Danneberg, *Vienna under Socialist Rule* (Vienna, 1929); and Rabinbach, *Crisis of Austrian Socialism*.
75. 'Millionstädte ohne Breitner – bankrott', *Der Kuckuck*, 1 December 1929.
76. Wolfgang Maderthaner, '12 February 1934: Social Democracy and Civil War', in Steininger et al. (eds), *Austria in the Twentieth Century*, pp. 45–71, p. 58.
77. ibid.
78. Bauer, *Modern Housing*, p. 81.
79. Gulick, quoted in Blau, *Architecture of Red Vienna*, p. 81.
80. ibid., p. 87.
81. ibid., p. 144.
82. ibid., p. 146.
83. The best description of Hugo Breitner's economic thinking and policies is Gulick, *Austria from Habsburg to Hitler*, vol. 1, pp. 357–406. See also Wolfgang Fritz, *Der Kopf des Asiaten Breitner: Politik und Ökonomie im Roten Wien* (Vienna, 2006).
84. This is the opinion of Gulick, ibid.
85. Sandgruber, *Traumzeit für Millionäre*, p. 43; Fritz, *Der Kopf des Asiaten Breitner*, pp. 51–86.
86. Fritz, *Der Kopf des Asiaten Breitner*, p. 78.
87. Blau, *Architecture of Red Vienna*, pp. 138 and 140. As Blau points out, in a US dollar equivalent, a pre-war rent of $600 would have been reduced to approximately $0.04.
88. Gruber, *Red Vienna*, p. 22; Gulick, *Austria from Habsburg to Hitler*, vol. 1, p. 369.
89. Gottfried Pirhofer, 'Wirtschaftspolitik', *Ausstellungskatalog Zwischenkriegszeit – Wiener Kommunalpolitik 1918–1938* (Vienna, 1980), pp. 13–23. See also Wolfgang Maderthaner, 'Politique communale à Vienne la Rouge', in *Vienne 1880–1938: L'apocalypse joyeuse*, ed. Jean Clair (Paris, 1986), exh. cat., pp. 596–607.
90. Gulick, *Austria from Habsburg to Hitler*, vol. 1, pp. 357, 164–171.
91. ibid., pp. 354–406.
92. ibid., pp. 369–70. See also Hugo Breitner, *Kapitalistische oder sozialistische Steuerpolitik* (Vienna, 1926).
93. Czeike, *Wirtschafts- und Sozialpolitik*, vol. 2, pp. 45–50. Cited in Blau, *Architecture of Red Vienna*, p. 140.
94. Bauer, *Modern Housing*, p. 79.
95. The evolution of social democratic housing policy as well as the new tax structure and the roles played by Danneberg and Breitner are elucidated by Charles Gulick in *Austria from Habsburg to Hitler*.
96. See Günther Sandner, *Otto Neurath. Eine politische Biographie* (Vienna, 2013), pp. 240–45.
97. Peter Oberlander and Eva Newbrun, *Houser: The Life and Work of Catherine Bauer* (Vancouver, 1999), pp. 70–71.
98. See Fritz, *Der Kopf des Asiaten Breitner*.
99. Tony Judt, 'What is Living and What is Dead in Social Democracy?', *New York Review of Books*, October 2009, pp. 86–8, 92.
100. Gulick, *Austria from Habsburg to Hitler*, vol. 1, p. 402.
101. John Maynard Keynes, *Collected Writings*, vol. 19: *Activities 1922–29* (Cambridge, 2012), p. 220.
102. See Mark Gimein, 'The Great Compression: How War and Taxes Made Us All Middle Class, and Why That's Changed', *Bloomberg Businessweek*, 14 December 2011. The argument is repeated in Thomas Piketty, *Capital in the Twenty-first Century* (Cambridge, Mass., 2014).
103. Robert Danneberg, *Der Finanzplan der Regierung Seipel. Wiederaufbau?* (Vienna, 1922). Here he qualifies the federal budget as 'an assault on industry' (p. 1). He calls on the federal government to 'improve the productivity of the export industry' and to make the country 'less dependent on foreign countries' (p. 7) by increasing taxation at the federal level (p. 12).

5. Between Two Wars

1. Ursula Prokop, *Margarethe Stonborough Wittgenstein* (Vienna, 2005).
2. Jorn K. Bramann and John Moran, 'Karl Wittgenstein, Business Tycoon and Art Patron', *Austrian History Yearbook* 15–16 (1979–80). See also Sandgruber, *Traumzeit für Millionäre*, pp. 84–7, which ranks Wittgenstein in thirty-seventh place in 1910.
3. Michael Nedo makes this point. See vimeo.com/28725163.
4. See the most informative book on the house: Paul Wijdeveld, *Ludwig Wittgenstein: Architect* (London, 1993); also Prokop, *Margarethe Stonborough Wittgenstein*.
5. Hermine Wittgenstein, *Family Recollections*, quoted in Wijdeveld, *Ludwig Wittgenstein*, p. 39.
6. Wijdeveld, *Ludwig Wittgenstein*, pp. 64–7.
7. The verbal source for the repainted lips is the Austrian historian Otto Kapfinger. Michael Nedo makes the point that the painting was not shown in the house. See vimeo.com/28725163.

8. Peham, *Die Salonièren und die Salons in Wien*.
9. Prokop, *Margaret Stonborough-Wittgenstein*; Wijdeveld, *Ludwig Wittgenstein*.
10. Ray Monk, *Ludwig Wittgenstein: The Duty of Genius* (London, 1991).
11. ibid., p. 54.
12. Alexander Waugh, *The House of Wittgenstein: A Family at War* (New York, 2008), p. 283.
13. Wijdeveld, *Ludwig Wittgenstein*, p. 38.
14. Wijdeveld makes the point about the absence of *Raumplan* in the Wittgenstein House and its presence in Engelmann's Müller House in Olomuc of 1927: ibid., p. 56. See Judith Bakacsy (ed.), *Paul Engelman and the Central European Heritage: The Path from Olomouc to Israel* (Vienna, undated), p. 79. The one building out of four still standing is the Yadlin House in Haifa. No drawings of the interior survive. I would like to thank the Israeli architecture historian Professor Michael Levin, an expert on the architecture of the 1930s in Palestine, for corroborating that the house adopts the *Raumplan*.
15. Ursula Schneider (ed.), *Paul Engelmann: Architektur, Judentum, Wiener Moderne* (Vienna, 1999), p. 208.
16. Wijdeveld, *Ludwig Wittgenstein*, p. 34.
17. ibid., p. 27.
18. I wish to thank Ian White for this information.
19. Hines, *Richard Neutra*, p. 29.
20. Wijdeveld, *Ludwig Wittgenstein*.
21. ibid., p. 186.
22. Galison, 'Aufbau/Bauhaus', pp. 709-52.
23. Ludwig Wittgenstein, *Tractatus Logico-Philosophicus* (New York, 1922. First published in German in 1921).
24. Wijdeveld, *Ludwig Wittgenstein*, p. 39.
25. Thanks to Michael Nedo for this information.
26. Michael Nedo first brought these photographs to light in 'Familienähnlichkeiten: Philosophie und Praxis', in Joseph Kosuth and the Vienna Secession, *Wittgenstein: Das Spiel des Unsagbaren*, exh. cat. (Vienna, 1989), pp. 147-57.
27. Kulka, *Adolf Loos*, p. 18. The best study of the *Raumplan*, besides Kulka's book, is Max Risselada, *Raumplan Versus Plan Libre* (Rotterdam, 1988).
28. Johan van de Beek, 'Adolf Loos - Patterns of Town Houses', in Risselada, *Raumplan Versus Plan Libre*, pp. 27-46, esp. p. 30.
29. Shorthand record of a conversation in Pilsen, 1930, from Villa Müller Museum and Study and Document Center website: www.mullerovavila.cz/english/raum-e.html.
30. The best graphic representation of the *Raumplan* of the Tzara House and its staircases is at https://vimeo.com/15376483.
31. Corinne Contini-Flicker, '*Mouchoir de Nuages* (1924) de Tzara, collage de *Hamlet*: Une re-écriture Dada', in Isabelle Chol (ed.), *Poétiques de la discontinuité de 1870 à nos jours* (Clermont-Ferrand, 2004), explains the formal poetics of discontinuity in Tzara's play.
32. *Zentralblatt für Psychoanalyse* 1 (1921).
33. Adolf Loos, 'Die Interieurs in der Rotunde', *Neue Freie Presse*, 5 June 1898, I. Quoted in Rukschcio and Schachel, *Adolf Loos*. Also reproduced in Loos, *Spoken into the Void*. 'The bathing unit is actually made out of plate glass mounted with nickel. Even the cut-crystal faceted glasses on the washstand have been made according to Wagner's designs, as have the attractive fixtures, of course.' His admiration for Otto Wagner was boundless.
34. Christopher Long, lecture at the University of Applied Arts, May 2012.
35. Iris Meder, 'Formlos Formen. Oskar Strnad und seine Schule', in *Moderat Modern. Erich Boltenstein und die Baukultur nach 1945* (Salzburg, 2005), pp. 29-43.
36. Long, *Josef Frank*, p. 59.
37. 'Zu den Arbeiten Josef Frank', *Das Interieur* 13 (1912), pp. 43-5. Quoted in Christopher Long, 'Frank and the Vienna Years', in Nina Stritzler-Levine (ed.), *Josef Frank, Architect and Designer* (New Haven, 1996), p. 48.
38. Josef Frank, 'Accidentism', *Form* 54 (1958), pp. 160-65. Reproduced in Josef Frank, *Schriften/Writings* (Vienna, 2013), pp. 373-88.
39. Josef Frank, 'Das Haus als Weg und Platz', *Der Baumeister* 29 (1931), pp. 326-7, 319.
40. Kristina Wängberg-Eriksson, 'Life in Exile: Josef Frank in Sweden and the United States, 1933-67', in Leon Botstein et al. (eds), *Josef Frank, Architect and Designer* (New Haven, 1996), pp. 62-77.
41. See August Sarnitz, *Ernst Plischke* (Vienna, 2004).
42. Alofsin, *When Buildings Speak*.
43. See Georg Schwalm-Theiss, *Theiss & Jaksch, Architekten 1907-1961* (Vienna, 1986).
44. Iris Meder and Judith Eiblmayr, *Haus Hoch. Das Hochhaus Herrengasse und seine berühmten Bewohner* (Vienna, 2009).
45. Viktor Grünbaum, '1 Zimmer, 3 Zimmer', *Der Kuckuck* 25, 21 January 1931, p. 10: '. . . *und so den Grundstein zu einer neuen unverdorbene und nicht verlogenen Kultur legen.*'
46. Alex Wall, *Victor Gruen, From Urban Shop to New City* (Barcelona, 2005).
47. ibid.
48. ibid.
49. The best-documented, groundbreaking source on the topic is Boeckl (ed.), *Visionäre und Vertriebene*. Among the architects covered on pp. 155-70 are Liane Zimbler, Ernst Lichtblau and Paul Theodore Frankl.
50. Adolf Stiller, 'Rationele Systeme und Visionen. Anton Tedesko als konstruktiver Entwerfer', in Boeckl (ed.), *Visionäre und Vertriebene*, pp. 155-70.
51. All of Josef Urban's works are in the Josef Urban Collection in the Brander Matthews Dramatic Museum in the rare book and manuscript library at Columbia University. Also see John Loring, *Joseph Urban* (New York, 2010)
52. Barbara Lezák, *Die Kulisse explodiert: Friedrich Kieslers Theaterexperimente und Architekturprojekte 1923-1925* (Vienna, 1988); also Barbara Lezák and Thomas Trabitsch (eds), *Frederick Kiesler: Theatervisionär - Architekt - Künstler* (Vienna, 2012).

53. Frederick Kiesler, *Contemporary Art Applied to the Store and Its Display* (New York, 1930), p. 14.
54. Frederick Kiesler, 'On Correalism and Biotechnique. A Definition and Test of a New Approach to Building Design', *Architectural Record* 86 (1939), p. 59.
55. Francis O'Connor, Don Quaintance and Jasper Sharp (eds), *Peggy Guggenheim & Frederick Kiesler: The Story of Art of this Century* (New York, 2005), and especially Shirley Haines-Cooke, *Frederick Kiesler: Lost in History. Art of this Century and the Modern Art Gallery* (Cambridge, 2009).
56. Strasbourg, 1893.
57. Theodor Fischer, *Sechs Vorträge über Stadtebaukunst* (Munich, 1920), p. 78.
58. For a survey of Baumann's buildings see Horst Hambrisch, *Franz Baumann, Architekt der Modern in Tirol* (Vienna, 1998).
59. Arnold Reisman, *Turkey's Modernization. Refugees from Nazism and Atatürk's Vision* (Washington, 2006).
60. Hans-Joachim Dahms, 'Die Türkei als Zielland der wissenschaftlichen Emigration aus Österreich. Ein Überblick', in Stadler (ed.), *Vertriebene Vernunft*.
61. Sibel Bozdogan, *Modernism and Nation Building: Turkish Architectural Culture in the Early Republic* (Seattle, 2002).
62. ibid., p. 70.
63. Oya Atalay Franck, *Architektur und Politik: Ernst Egli und die türkische Moderne 1927-1940* (Zurich, 2012).
64. ibid., p. 43.
65. Michael D. Levin, *White City: International Style Architecture in Israel*, 2 vols (Tel Aviv, 1984).
66. I would like to thank Michael Levin, a specialist on Krakauer, for taking me to the Judean Hills and pointing this out to me. See the catalogue of an exhibition at the Israel Museum curated by him: *Leopold Krakauer, Painter and Architect* (Jerusalem, 1996).
67. Silvina Sosnovsky, *The Development of the Modern Architecture in Haifa, 1920-1940: The Design of the Commercial Centers* (Haifa, 1983).
68. I would like to thank Hu Yongheng, a student at the University of Applied Arts, for helping me with the Chinese texts related to the tea house of Feng, among others in translating the article by Professor Lu Yongyin on the tea house.
69. Arata Isozaki, *Japan-ness in Architecture* (Cambridge, Mass., 2008).
70. Arata Isozaki, *Katsura Imperial Villa* (London, 2007), p. 9.
71. I wish to thank Professor Peter Laurence, who showed me Greenville while I was visiting Clemson University in October 2013 and mentioned Max Heller to me. See also Katrina Daniel, 'A Tribute to Max Heller', *Greenville Business Magazine*, 1 August 2011 and http://library.furman.edu/specialcollections/southcarolina/heller_biography.htm.
72. Judith Sheine, *R. M. Schindler* (London, 2001).
73. ibid., p. 260.
74. From an interview with the author, July 2002.
75. Sheine, *R. M. Schindler*, p. 259.
76. The best book on Richard Neutra is Hines, *Richard Neutra*. It does not deal with Neutra as a regionalist, however. See also Liane Lefaivre, Alexander Tzonis and Bruno Stagno, *Tropical Architecture* (London, 1996), and Liane Lefaivre and Alexander Tzonis, *The Architecture of Regionalism in an Age of Globalization* (London, 2012).
77. Andrea Bocco Guarneri, *Bernard Rudofsky: A Humane Architect* (Vienna, 2003).
78. Antje Senarclens de Grancy and Heimo Halbrainer, *Totes Leben gibt es nicht: Herbert Eichholzer 1903-1943: Architektur - Kunst - Politik* (Vienna, 2004).
79. See Margarete Schütte-Lihotzky, *Erinnerungen aus dem Widerstand* ['Memories of the Resistance'] (Vienna, 2014).

6. Nazi Ostmark

7. Mark Mazower, *Hitler's Empire: How the Nazis Ruled Europe* (New York, 2008), pp. 46-7.
8. Evan Burr Bukey, *Hitler's Austria: Popular Sentiment in the Nazi Era, 1938-1945* (Chapel Hill and London, 2000), p. 38.
9. See Thomas Weyr, *The Setting of the Pearl: Vienna under Hitler* (Oxford, 2005), p. 35. See also Hans Safrian and Hans Witek, *Und keiner war dabei. Dokumente des alltäglichen Antisemitismus in Wien, 1938* (Vienna, 2008).
10. Bukey, *Hitler's Austria*, p. 146.
11. Adolf Eichmann was born in Germany but when he was seven years old his family moved to Linz, where he attended the same school where Adolf Hitler and Ludwig Wittgenstein had studied.
12. The most authoritative books on Eichmann are Bettina Stangneth, *Eichmann before Jerusalem: The Unexamined Life of a Mass Murderer*, trans. Ruth Martin (New York, 2014), and David Cesarani, *Becoming Eichmann: Rethinking the Life, Crimes and Trial of a 'Desk Murderer'* (Cambridge, Mass., 2007).
13. Mazower, *Hitler's Empire*, p. 47.
14. ibid.
15. ibid.
16. www.annefrank.dk/Schirach.
17. Ursula Prokop, *Rudolf Perco 1884-1942: Von der Architektur des Roten Wien zu NS Megalomanie* (Vienna, 2001).
18. All the information concerning the flak towers is from Edward B. Westermann, *Flak: German Anti-aircraft Defenses 1914-1945* (Lawrence, 2005).
19. Ingrid Holzschuh, *Wiener Stadtplanung im Nationalsozialismus von 1938 bis 1942* (Vienna, 2011), pp. 47-end. See also Winfried Nerdinger and Raphael Rosenberg (eds), *Hitlers Architekten. Historisch-kritische Monografien zur Regimearchitektur im Nationalsozialismus* (Vienna, 2012).

20. *Österreichisches Staatsarchiv, Aktenbestand Gruppe 04b. Karton 299*, quoted in Holzschuh, *Wiener Stadtplanung im Nationalsozialismus*, p. 23.
21. Dagmar Thorau and Gernot Schaulinski (eds), *Mythos und Verbrechen* (Berlin, 2014).
22. Eigruber's minutes, written down from memory, of speeches by Hitler 1941-3, Linz Oberösterreichisches Landesarchiv (OOLA), 'Politische Akten', box 49. Quoted in Brigitte Hamann, *Hitler's Vienna: A Dictator's Apprenticeship* (Oxford, 1999), p. 27.
23. Evan Burr Bukey, *Hitler's Hometown: Linz, Austria, 1908-1945* (Bloomington, 1986). See review by John Ries, *Journal of Historical Review* 9, 3 (Fall 1989), pp. 380-82 and www.ihr.org/jhr/v09/v09p380_Ries.html.
24. Hanns Christian Löhr, *Hitlers Linz. Der 'Heimatgau des Führers'* (Berlin, 2013), pp. 24-32; Michael Früchtel, *Der Architekt Hermann Giesler. Leben und Werk (1898–1987)* (Munich, 2008). See also Nerdinger and Rosenberg (eds), *Hitlers Architekten*; Brigitte Kirchmayr (ed.), *Kulturhauptstadt des Führers' Kunst und Nationalsozialismus in Linz und Oberösterreich* (Linz, 2008), the catalogue of an exhibition on Hitler's Linz on the occasion of Linz becoming European Capital of Culture; and Bukey, *Hitler's Hometown*.
25. Hamann, *Hitler's Vienna*.
26. Hermann Giesler, *Ein anderer Hitler* ['A Different Hitler'] (Leoni, 2004), p. 48.
27. Adolf Hitler, *Monologe im Führerhauptquartier* ['Monologues at the Führer's Headquarters'] *1941–1944*, ed. Werner Jochmann (Hamburg, 1980), p. 405, 25 June 1943. Quoted in Hamann, *Hitler's Vienna*. See also Löhr, *Hitlers Linz*; Bukey, *Hitler's Hometown*; Geoffrey P. Megargee (series ed.), *Encyclopedia of Camps and Ghettos, 1933–1945* (in association with United States Holocaust Memorial Museum, Bloomington, 2012); http://en.wikipedia.org/wiki/Mauthausen-Gusen_concentration_camp.
28. Giesler, *Ein anderer Hitler*, p. 99.
29. Josef Goebbels, diary, 13 March 1941, quoted in Hamann, *Hitler's Vienna*.
30. Giesler, *Ein anderer Hitler*, p. 216.
31. ibid.
32. For a list of the works of art, see Charles de Jaeger, *The Linz File: Hitler's Plunder of Europe's Art* (Ann Arbor, 1981). See also Kathrin Iselt, *'Sonderbeauftragter des Führers': Der Kunsthistoriker und Museumsmann Hermann Voss* (Vienna, 2010); Birgit Schwarz, *Hitlers Museum: Die Fotoalben Gemäldgalerie Linz* (Vienna, 2004); Hanns Christian Lohr, *Das Braune Haus der Kunst* (Berlin, 2005).
33. *Adolf Hitler's Drei Testamente* ['Adolf Hitler's Three Wills'], ed. Gert Sudholt (Leoni, undated), quoted in Hamann, *Hitler's Vienna*, p. 10.
34. Lohr, *Hitlers Linz*, pp. 94-8.
35. See Michael Ellenbogen, *Gigantische Visionen: Architektur und Hochtechnologie im Nationalsozialismus* (Graz, 2006); Kurt Tweraser, 'The Marshall Plan and the Reconstruction of the Austrian Steel Industry 1945-1953', in Günter Bischof et al., *The Marshall Plan in Austria* (New Brunswick, 2000), pp. 290-322; J. Bradford Delong, 'Nazis and Soviets', in *Slouching towards Utopia? The Economic History of the Twentieth Century* (Berkeley, 1997); Richard J. Overy, *The Nazi Economic Recovery* (Cambridge, 1996, 2nd edn), p. 50. See also L. Larry Liu, 'Economic Policy in Nazi Germany: 1933–45', *Penn History Review*, October 2013, www.academia.edu/4736105/Economic_Policy_in_Nazi_Germany_1933-1945.
36. Bukey, *Hitler's Hometown*.
37. ibid.
38. Lohr, *Hitlers Linz*, p. 120.
39. Taylor, *The Word in Stone*.
40. Hamann, *Hitler's Vienna*, p. 35. See also Paul B. Jaskot, *The Architecture of Oppression: The SS, Forced Labor and the Nazi Monumental Building Economy* (New York, 2000); Rudolf A. Haunschmied, Jan-Ruth Mills and Siegi Witzany-Durda, *St Georgen-Gusen-Mauthausen: Concentration Camp Mauthausen Reconsidered* (Traun, 2008).
41. Haunschmied, Mills and Witzany-Durda, *St Georgen-Gusen-Mauthausen*.
42. ibid., p. 37.
43. Ben Tufft, 'Secret Nazi Nuclear Bunker Discovered', *Independent*, 29 December 2014.
44. Bojan Pancevski, 'Vast Secret Nazi "Terror Weapons" Site Uncovered', *The Times*, 28 December 2014.

7. Reconstructing with a Memory Problem

1. Jeffry M. Diefendorf, 'Planning Postwar Vienna', *Planning Perspectives* 8 (1993), pp. 1–19.
2. Karl Ziak, *Wiedergeburt einer Weltstadt. Wien 1945-65* (Vienna, 1965).
3. James Clay Carafano, *Waltzing into the Cold War: The Struggle for Occupied Austria* (College Station, Texas, 2002); Günter Bischof, *Austria in the First Cold War 1945-55* (New York, 1999).
4. Tony Judt, *Postwar: A History of Europe since 1945* (London, 2005), p. 35.
5. Oliver Rathkolb, *The Paradoxical Republic: Austria, 1945–2005* (New York and Oxford, 2010), p. 219.
6. ibid., p. 58.
7. Eric Hobsbawm, *The Age of Extremes: The Short Twentieth Century 1914-1991* (London, 1994). The same point is made in Barry Eichengreen, *The European Economy since 1945: Coordinated Capitalism and Beyond* (London, 2008), and Herman Van der Wee, *Prosperity and Upheaval: The World Economy, 1945–1980* (London, 1987), p. 44.
8. N. Kaldor, 'Public or Private Enterprise – the Issues to be Considered', in W. Baumol (ed.), *Public and Private Enterprises in a Mixed Economy* (London and Basingstoke, 1980). Quoted in Ha-

Joon Chang and Ajit Singh, 'Public Enterprise in Developing Countries and Economic Efficiency', in Ha-Joon Chang, *Globalisation, Economic Development and the Role of the State* (London, 2004).
9. ibid.
10. Rathkolb, *Paradoxical Republic*, p. 54.
11. ibid., p. 35.
12. Günter Bischof, Anton Pelinka and Dieter Stiefel (eds), *The Marshall Plan in Austria* (New Brunswick, 2000), Introduction.
13. In the words of Ewald Nowotny: 'First of all – but not exclusively – the funds granted under the Marshall Plan Fund helped Austria to finance its initially persistent current account deficit. This made it possible to start the reindustrialization of the devastated industry. Nationalized industries took the key role in this process and the social partnership was crucial, with social partners being represented on the boards of the nationalized industry. At the beginning, the output of these industries grew much faster than that of the private industries. What is more, they were at the cutting edge of innovation and leading in the export sector.' 'The Austrian School of Economics and Austrian Economic Policy', lecture, Hebrew University of Jerusalem, 31 May 2015, www.bis.org/review/r150701e.htm.
14. Oliver Rathkolb, 'The Kreisky Era, 1970-1983', in Bischof, Pelinka and Stiefel (eds), *The Marshall Plan in Austria*, p. 266.
15. Kaldor, 'Public or Private Enterprise'.
16. Rathkolb, *Paradoxical Republic*, p. 76.
17. Judt, *Postwar*, p. 35.
18. There are many books on this topic. See Gerald Stourzh, *Um Einheit und Freiheit: Staatsvertrag, Neutralität und das Ende der Ost-West-Besetzung Österreichs 1945-55* (Vienna, 1998) and *1945 und 1955: Schlüsseljahre der Zweiten Republik* (Innsbruck and Vienna, 2005), and Rolf Steininger, *Austria, Germany and the Cold War: From the Anschluss to the State Treaty, 1938-1955* (New York and Oxford, 2008).
19. Günter Bischof, 'Allied Plans and Policies for the Occupation of Austria, 1938-1955', in Rolf Steininger, Günter Bischof and Michael Gehler (eds), *Austria in the Twentieth Century* (New Brunswick, 2002), pp. 162-89, esp. pp. 166-8. Fuller treatment is to be found in Steininger, *Austria, Germany and the Cold War*, Chapter 3.
20. See Heidemarie Uhl, *Das 'erste Opfer': Der österreichische Opfermythos und seine Transformationen in der Zweiten Republik* (Vienna, 2001).
21. Bukey, *Hitler's Austria*.
22. Rathkolb, *Paradoxical Republic*, p. 281.
23. Lillie, *Was einmal war*.
24. ibid.
25. Erika Thurner, *Nationale Identität und Geschlecht in Osterreich seit 1945* (Innsbruck, 2000), and Max Haller (ed.), *Identität und Nationalstolz der Österreicher* (Vienna, 1996).
26. Rathkolb, *Paradoxical Republic*.
27. ibid., p. 238.
28. Robert Menasse, *The Grand Synthesis. Comment on the Production of the New Austria* (1985). Quoted in Architekturzentrum Wien (ed.), *The Austrian Phenomenon. Architecture and Avantgarde Austria 1956-1973* (Zurich, undated), vol. 2, pp. 104-8.
29. www.timeshighereducation.co.uk/world-university-rankings/2012-13/world-ranking. Only one Austrian university ranks in the top 200 internationally: the University of Vienna, at 167. Two Austrian universities rank between 200 and 300. See also results for 2014.
30. Friedrich Stadler, 'The Emigration and Exile of Austrian Intellectuals', in Steininger, Bischof and Gehler (eds), *Austria in the Twentieth Century*, p. 131.
31. Uhl, *Das 'erste Opfer'*, p. 1. Uhl's project analyzes the transformation of the Austrian memory of war, Nazism and the Holocaust from 1945 to the present in the transnational European context. It focuses on the one hand on the negotiations and controversies surrounding the interpretation of the past, and on the other on cultural representations, both in material form, such as monuments, memorials and museums, and in popular media such as TV documentaries and movies. Two sub-projects deal with the Mauthausen concentration camp memorial and the Austrian memorial in the State Museum of Auschwitz-Birkenau.
32. For a description of Sedlmayr's increasingly public support of National Socialism before the war, see Wood (ed.), *Vienna School Reader*, Introduction, pp. 12-13.
33. Stadler, 'Emigration and Exile of Austrian Intellectuals', p. 129, and his magisterial collection of essays, *Vertriebene Vernunft II. Emigration und Exil österreichischer Wissenschaft 1930-1940*; Friedrich Stadler and Peter Weibel (eds), *The Cultural Exodus from Vienna* (Austria, 1995).
34. Friedrich Achleitner, 'Städtebau und Zigarettenpackung', in Adolph Stiller, *Oswald Haerdtl* (Salzburg, 2000), exh. cat., Wien Museum, pp. 53-61. See also his 'Wiederaufbau in Wien, Innere Stadt. Ein Stuck locale Architekturgeschichte wird besichtigt', in Liesbeth Waechter-Böhm (ed.), *Wien 1945-1985* (Vienna, 1985), pp. 108-15.
35. Friedrich Achleitner, *Österreichische Architektur im 20. Jahrhundert*, 3 vols, (Vienna, 1990-2010), vol. 3, p. 1.
36. See Stiller et al., *Oswald Haerdtl*.
37. Günther Feuerstein, *Visionäre Architektur in Wien 1958-1988* (Vienna, 1988), p. 26.
38. Sokratis Dimitriou, 'Die ersten Jahre nach 1945', *Bau* 1 (1965), p. 15: '*Die erste Jahre nach der Befreiung gehören zu den dunkelsten Epochen der österreichschen Architekturgeschichte.*'
39. Ottokar Uhl, *Moderne Architektur in Wien* (Vienna, 1966), p. 89.
40. Ottokar Uhl, 'Vienna: The Story of an Urban Landscape', *Landscape* 5 (1956), p. 13.
41. Friedrich Achleitner quoted in Otokar Uhl, *Moderne Architektur in Wien* (Vienna, 1986), p. 65.
42. Hans Hollein, interview with the author, October 2000.
43. Peter Galison, 'Aufbau/Bauhaus'; Rentetzi, *Trafficking Materials*.

44. http://genderinacademia.sabanci univ.edu/sites/genderinacademia.sabanciuniv.edu/files/birgit_sauer.pdf.
45. Noever (ed.), *Margarete Schütte-Lihotzky*.
46. ibid.
47. Friedrich Kurrent, 'Salzburger Sommerakademie', in Barbara Wally (ed.), *Die Ära Kokoschka* (Salzburg, 1993), p. 110. See also his *Einige Häuser, Kirchen und Dergleichen* (Salzburg, 2001), pp. 30-35.
48. Konrad Wachsmann, *The Turning Point of Building: Structure and Design* (New York, 1961); Dietmar Strauch and Bärbel Högner, *Konrad Wachsmann: Stationen eines Architekten* (Berlin, 2013).
49. Thanks to Hans Hollein for this information. Interview by the author, August 2000.
50. Liane Lefaivre and Alexander Tzonis, *Aldo van Eyck, Humanist Rebel: In-betweening in a Postwar World* (Rotterdam, 1999).
51. Architekturzentrum Wien (ed.), *Arbeitsgruppe 4. Wilhelm Holzbauer, Friedrich Kurrent, Johannes Spalt. 1950-1970* (Salzburg, 2010).
52. Roland Rainer, *Das Werk des Architekten 1927-2003* (Vienna, 2003).
53. See Harald Sterk, *Wohnbau zwischen Ideologie, Politik, und Wirtschaft* (Vienna, 1985), and Peter Marchart, *Wohnbau in Wien 1923-1983* (Vienna, 1984).
54. Vera Mayer (ed.), *Plattenbausiedlungen in Wien und Bratislava zwischen Vision, Alltag, und Innovation* (Vienna, 2006).
55. ibid.
56. Wolfgang Förster, *80 Years of Social Housing in Vienna*, www.wien.gv.at/english/housing/promotion/pdf/socialhous.pdf.
57. Marchart, *Wohnbau in Wien*.
58. Mayer (ed.), *Plattenbausiedlungen*.
59. Otto Neurath and Franz Schuster, *Siedler und Kleingärtner* 3, 12 (1923), p. 1, and *Siedler und Kleingärtner* 4, 1 (1924), cited in Blau, *Architecture of Red Vienna*, p. 99.
60. Franz Schuster, *Der Aufbau* (1945), vol. I, p. 4.
61. Franz Schuster, unpublished manuscript of 1949, Schuster Archive, University of Applied Arts, Vienna, p. 4.
62. Neurath and Schuster, in *Siedler und Kleingärtner* 3, 12 (1923), p. 1, and *Siedler und Kleingärtner* 4, 1 (1924), cited in Blau, *Architecture of Red Vienna*, p. 99.
63. Karl Heinrich Brunner, 'Die Aufgaben der neuen Stadtplanung für Wien', *Der Aufbau* 4 (1949), p. 203, referred to in the excellent article by Diefendorf, 'Planning Postwar Vienna', p. 14. Kindly suggested to me by Oliver Rathkolb.
64. Brunner, 'Die Aufgaben der neuen Stadtplanung für Wien', quoted in Diefendorf, 'Planning Postwar Vienna', p. 14. For the history of planning of postwar Berlin, see Jeffry M. Diefendorf, *In the Wake of War* (Oxford, 1993), pp. 83-100.
65. Brunner, 'Die Aufgaben der neuen Stadtplanung für Wien', quoted in Diefendorf, 'Planning Postwar Vienna', p. 12.
66. Vienna, 1962.
67. See Diefendorf, *In the Wake of War*, p. 16.
68. Published by Thames and Hudson in London, 1965. This conversion of Victor Gruen has also been documented by Alex Wall, *Victor Gruen: From Urban Shop to New City* (Barcelona, 2005).
69. The plea for a multi-functional pedestrian zone is clearly spelled out in Gruen's *Centers for the Urban Environment* (New York, 1973), pp. 223-329.
70. Liane Lefaivre and Alexander Tzonis, *Critical Regionalism* (Munich, 2003), pp. 41-2.
71. Victor Gruen, *The Charter of Vienna*, VGFEP (Los Angeles, 1972).
72. Gruen's *The Essence of Architecture* is quoted in Wall, *Victor Gruen*, p. 231.

8. The Kreisky Era

1. Wolfgang Maderthaner, *Wie Phönix aus der Asche* (Vienna, 2010); *Die Kreisky Ära* (Vienna, 2005); Wolfgang Maderthaner and Lutz Musner, *Der lange Weg in den Wohlstand* (Vienna, 2004); Wolfgang Maderthaner and Wolfgang C. Müller (eds), *Die Organisation der Österreichischen Sozialdemocratie 1889-1995* (Vienna, 1996); Brigitte Ungerer, 'Österreichs Wirtschaftspolitik: vom Austro-Keynesianismus zum AustroNeoliberalismus?', in Ferdinand Karlhofer and Emmerich Tálos (eds), *Zukunft der Sozialpartnerschaft – Veränderungsdynamik und Reformbedarf* (Vienna, 1999).
2. Rathkolb, *Paradoxical Republic*, pp. 78-80; 'Nowotny: Bankenabgabe darf nicht zu hoch werden', *Der Standard*, 5 September 2015. He is quoted as saying that '*Österreich habe einen starken gemeinnutzigen Sektor, der stabilisierend wirke*' ('Austria has a strong non-profit sector that has a stabilizing effect') on the overall macroeconomy.
3. Ramesh Mishra, *The Welfare State in Capitalist Society: Policies of Retrenchment and Maintenance in Europe, North America and Australia* (Toronto, 1990).
4. Ewald Nowotny (ed.), *Sozialdemokratische Wirtschaftspolitik. Die solidarische Leistungsgesellschaft* (Vienna, 1992).
5. Rathkolb, *Paradoxical Republic*, p. 79.
6. Mishra, *Welfare State*, p. 65.
7. OECD, *In It Together: Why Less Inequality Benefits All* (Paris, 2015), http://dx.doi.org/10.1787/9789264235120-en.
8. http://derstandard.at/2000018077431/Handelsbilanzdefizit-2014-mehr-als-halbier.
9. James Shotter and Eric Frey, 'Progress Belies Lack of Political Vision', *Financial Times*, 18 November 2012.
10. Mishra, *Welfare State*, p. 65.
11. ibid., pp. 79-80.
12. Theodor Adorno, 'Cultural Criticism and Society', *Prisms* (Cambridge, Mass., 1982), p. 17. First published in German in 1949.
13. Quoted in Weibel, *Die Wiener Gruppe*, p. 14.
14. 'The Austrian Cultural Crisis', in Architekturzentrum Wien (ed.), *The Austrian Phenomenon*, pp. 102-3.
15. ibid.

16. www.youtube.com/watch?v=oI7GboKpTQU. I thank Eva Kuss for this reference.
17. Weibel, *Die Wiener Gruppe*, provides the best documentation concerning the Wiener Gruppe. See also www.youtube.com/watch?v=oI7GboKpTQU.
18. Bernhard A. Böhler, *Monsignore Otto Mauer. Ein Leben für Kirche und Kunst* (Vienna, 2003).
19. Robert Fleck, *Avantgarde in Wien. Die Geschichte der Galerie nächst St Stephan 1954-1982* (Vienna, 1982). See also Architekturzentrum Wien (ed.), *The Austrian Phenomenon*, pp. 12-13. For the full text of Friedensreich Hundertwasser's two statements, see Angelika Taschen, *Hundertwasser Architecture. Pour une architecture plus proche de la nature et de l'homme* (Cologne, 2011), p. 34.
20. Fleck, *Avantgarde in Wien*; Architekturzentrum Wien (ed.), *The Austrian Phenomenon*, pp. 12-13; Taschen, *Hundertwasser Architecture*, p. 34.
21. Anna Schober, *Ironie, Montage, Verfremdung: Ästhetische Taktiken und die politische Gestalt der Demokratie* (Munich, 2008); Eva Badura-Triska (ed.), *Vienna Actionism, Art and Upheaval in 1960s Vienna*, exh. cat., Museum der Moderne Kunst (Cologne, 2012); Malcolm Green (ed. and trans. in collaboration with the artists), *Brus, Muehl, Nitsch and Schwarzkogler: Writings of the Vienna Actionists* (London, 1999); *Out of Actions: Actionism, Body Art & Performance 1949-1979*, exh. cat., MAK (Vienna, 1998); Danièle Roussel, *Der Wiener Aktionismus und die Österreicher* (Klagenfurt, 1995); Dieter Schwarz and Veit Loers, *Von der Aktionsmalerei zum Aktionismus. Wien 1960-1965* (Klagenfurt, 1988); Oliver Jahraus, *Die Aktion des Wiener Aktionismus. Subversion der Kultur und Dispositionierung des Bewusstseins* (Munich, 2001); Amos Vogel, *Film as a Subversive Art* (New York, 1974).
22. Werner Hofmann, 'Die Wiener Aktionisten', *Kunstforum* 89 (May–June 1987), pp. 202-11.
23. For a complete list of prize-winners, see John Sailer, *Kunst Kunst Kunst. Der grosse Österreichische Staatspreis* (Vienna, 2001).
24. http://d-sites.net/english/nitsch.htm#.VOy6QfnF8qk.
25. http://d-sites.net/english/nitsch.htm#.VOy6QfnF8qk. See also www.ubu.com/film/muehl.html; Günter Brus, *Viennese Actionism 1960-1971* (Vienna, 1989); Peter Noever (ed.), *Otto Mühl: Leben/Kunst/Werk*, exh. cat. (Vienna/Cologne, 2004).
26. Valie Export, 'Aspects of Feminist Actionism', *New German Critique* 47 (Spring-Summer 1989); Peter Weibel (ed.), *Wien: Bildkompendium, Wiener Aktionismus und Film* (Frankfurt, 1970); *Vienna Action Group: Performance Narratives from the 1960s*, exh. cat., Museum Moderner Kunst Stiftung Ludwig (Vienna, 2008); Jahraus, *Die Aktion des Wiener Aktionismus*; Vogel, *Film as a Subversive Art*.
27. Heinz Cibulka, Wolfgang Denk and Wieland Schmied, *Hermann Nitsch* (Berlin, 2007); Christian Höller, 'Zock, Aspects of a Total Revolution', in Badura-Triska (ed.), *Vienna Actionism*, pp. 174-83.
28. Helmut Qualtinger, *Herr Karl*, www.youtube.com/watch?v=giF4-aEprQQ (Vienna, 1961) and www.youtube.com/watch?v=96AeH9BJQvU.
29. These performances are viewable on YouTube.
30. 'Bronfman says Waldheim dropped suit', *Jewish Telegraphic Agency*, www.jta.org, 5 July 1988.
31. Rathkolb, *Paradoxical Republic*, p. 125.
32. Richard Calvocoressi, *Financial Times*, 4 October 2013.
33. ibid.
34. ibid.
35. Peter Cook, *Experimental Architecture* (New York and London, 1970), pp. 71 ff.
36. Martina Kandeler-Fritsch, *Zünd-Up* (Vienna, 2001).
37. Architekturzentrum Wien (ed.), *The Austrian Phenomenon*.
38. Chantal Beret, 'Does Pop Architecture Exist?', in Mark Francis (ed.), *Les Années Pop* (Paris, 2001).
39. ibid.
40. Feuerstein made this point during a discussion at an event organized on the subject of the relation between the Actionists and the so-called architectural Austrian Phenomenon at the FEA by Jan Tabor, 6 June 2013.
41. Both quotations are from Taschen, *Hundertwasser Architecture*, pp. 31-43. See also 'My eyes are tired' (1957), *Manifesto of Mold against Rationalism in Architecture* (1958), *The Line of Hamburg* (1959) and *Speech in the Nude* ('*Nacktrede*') for the right to a third skin (1967), *Summary* (Vienna, 26 January 1968).
42. Haus-Bucher-Co, 'Pneumacosm', in Dieter Bogner (ed.) *Denkräume-Stadträume*, 1967–1992 (Klagenfurt, 1992), p. 11.
43. See www.youtube.com/watch?v=lunN_Hl6EKE, 1972.
44. 'Haus Rucker Co, "Green Lung"', in Architekturzentrum Wien (ed.), *The Austrian Phenomenon*, p. 26; Elke Beilfuss, *Kunststoff als Design-Material: Wohnkultur im Stil der 1968er* (Berlin, 2014), pp. 49-51.
45. 'Interventions', reproduced in *The Austrian Phenomenon*, 1970–71, p. 17.
46. Günther Feuerstein, 'Notes on Zünd-Up', in Architekturzentrum Wien (ed.), *The Austrian Phenomenon*, p. 923.
47. Rolf Laven, *Franz Čižek und die Wiener Jugendkunst* (Vienna, 2006).
48. For more about the exhibition to be curated by Rudi Fuchs and Harald Szeeman, see John Sailer, interview with *Der Standard*, 21 January 2010.
49. Liane Lefaivre, 'Everything is Architecture: Hans Hollein, or the Fine Art of Crossing Over', *Harvard Design Magazine*, Spring 2003, available at www.dyd.com.ar/biblioteca/new/selecciona203.html.
50. Interview with Hollein by the author, 7 August 2000.
51. Hans Hollein, *Report to the Harkness Commonwealth Foundation*, 1960, p. 4. With kind permission of Hans Hollein.

52. Hans Hollein, interview with the author, 7 August 2000.
53. Susan Sontag, 'Happenings: The Art of Radical Juxtapositions' (1962), reprinted in *Against Interpretation and Other Essays* (London and New York, 2009), pp. 263–73.
54. Hans Hollein, *Plastic Space*, thesis submitted in partial satisfaction of the requirements for the degree of Master of Architecture, College of Environmental Design in the Graduate Division of the University of California, approved by James Prestini and Joseph Esherick, 19 July 1969.
55. Hans Hollein (ed.), *Austriennale*, exh. cat. (Vienna, 1968). The material on Hans Hollein as a curator is based on 'Hans Hollein curator', Eeva-Liisa Pelhoven (ed.), *Exhibiting Architecture: a Paradox*, Yale School of Architecture, 2015.
56. Hans Hollein, *Alles ist Architektur: TOT*, exh. cat. (Mönchengladbach, 1970).
57. ibid.
58. Johannes Cladders, 'Opening Lecture', in *Alles ist Architektur: TOT*. Reproduced in Architekturzentrum Wien (ed.), *The Austrian Phenomenon*, p. 872.
59. Hollein, *Alles ist Architektur: TOT*, exh. cat. (Mönchengladbach, 1970).
60. Hans Hollein, *Austria, XXXVI Biennale di Venezia*, exh. cat. (Vienna, 1972).
61. Hans Hollein, *Man TransForms. Konzepteeiner Austellung/Concepts of an Exhibition* (Vienna, 1989).
62. Lisa Taylor, 'Press Release', 1976. Cited with permission of the Cooper Hewitt Museum. Special thanks to archivist Elizabeth Broman.
63. The rest of this text is based on Lefaivre, 'Everything is Architecture'.

9. After the Shock Therapy

1. See www.rlfeigen.com. For a more detailed description of the Richard Feigen Gallery, see Liane Lefaivre, 'Hans Hollein's Richard Feigen Gallery, A Rare Instance of Pop Architecture', *Docomomo* 31 (September 2004), pp. 85–96.
2. Interview with the author, July 2002.
3. *Fritz Wotruba – Monuments, Sculpture and Politics*, exhibition, 21er Haus, Vienna, July 2015–January 2016.
4. For the list of design collaborators, see www.coop-himmelblau.at.
5. Carl Pruscha, *Himalayan Vernacular* (Vienna, 2004).
6. Alexander Tzonis, Foreword in Christian Kühn, *Anton Schweighofer* (Vienna, 2000). See also Lefaivre and Tzonis, *Aldo van Eyck*.
7. Kühn, *Anton Schweighofer*.
8. Otto Kapfinger (ed.), *Adolf Krischanitz* (Berlin, 2014).
9. Schorske, *Fin de Siècle Vienna*, p. 212, and, especially, Charlotte Ashby, Tag Gronberg and Simon Shaw-Miller (eds), *The Viennese Café and Fin de Siècle Culture* (New York and Oxford, 2013).
10. See Eva Kuss, *Hermann Czech and Sprachkritik*, doctoral dissertation supervised by Prof. Liane Lefaivre, University of Applied Arts (Vienna, 2014), and *Hermann Czech: Architekt in Wien* (Zurich, 2016).
11. Kuss, *Hermann Czech and Sprachkritik*.
12. ibid. See the last section of the book of 2016 on the houses of Hermann Czech.
13. www.dmaa.at/home.html.
14. www.herklotzgasse21.at/.
15. 'Eine Partitur für eine grüneren Donaukanal', *Der Standard*, 19 December 2014, http://derstandard.at/2000009626816.
16. www.steinbrener-dempf.com/public-projects/to-be-in-limbo/.

10. Good Social Housing Is Good for the Economy

1. Joseph Stiglitz, 'Property', www.alternet.org (undated).
2. Rahul Mehrotra, *Architecture in India since 1990* (Ostfildern, 2011), pp. 60–61.
3. Rudolf Schicker, *High-Rise Building in Vienna*, www.wien.gv.at/stadtentwicklung/studien/pdf/b007383c.pdf.
4. http://skyscraperpage.com/cities/maps/?cityID=983.
5. Reinhard Seiss, *Wer Baut Wien?* (Salzburg, 2007).
6. 'Nowotny: Bankenabgabe darf nicht zu hoch werden', *Der Standard*, 5 September 2015.
7. ibid.
8. www.iut.nu/FindOutMore/Europe/Austria/Socialhousing_finance_Amman_Mundt.pdf.
9. ibid., p. 22.
10. ibid.
11. John Authers, 'Austria's 97 Years of Loss Offer Lessons', *Financial Times*, 8 February 2013.
12. City of Vienna, *Gemeinde Baut. Wiener Wohnbau 1920–2020* (Vienna, 2014), p. 117.
13. Eric Frey, 'Österreichs Banken: Krugman hatte Recht', *Der Standard*, 6 July 2014.
14. Dardis McNamee, 'Renate Brauner: Keynesian in the Rathaus', *Vienna Review*, 4 March 2013, p. 4.
15. Michael Ludwig, 'Keine Privatisierung von Gemeindewohnungen durch die Hintertür' ['No Privatization of Social Housing through the Back Door'], www.spoe.wien/keine-privatisierung-von-gemeindewohnungen-durch-die-hintertür, (undated).
16. McNamee, 'Renate Brauner'.
17. ibid.
18. Michael Ludwig, quoted in Martin Putschögl, 'No Commercial Developers', *Der Standard*, 25 April 2014.
19. *Vienna Review*, 2012.
20. Vienna housing expert Wolfgang Förster sums up the complicated financial leveraging model thus: 'At present, about 200 non-profit housing associations are active in the whole country, managing some 650,000 apartments and building another 15,000 each year. In Vienna, they not only manage but own about 136,000 apartments, in addition to the city's own 220,000, and even the major part of the owner-occupied apartments

has been built within the subsidized housing program. These owner-occupied apartments are therefore also subject to certain limitations concerning the income per household and the later sale of the apartments. Non-profit housing associations enjoy tax-reliefs and have to re-invest profits back into housing. Rents are strictly regulated, the cost-rent covering financing, the running costs and the 10% value-added tax (consumer tax). The maximum monthly net rent for a subsidized apartment in Vienna is currently 3.54 euro/m2 (3.26 US dollars), or 5–6 euro/m2 (4.60 to 5.52 US dollars) in total. Low-income households are entitled to individual subsidies ensuring that they do not lose their apartments in case of a sudden illness or unemployment. To reduce financing costs most developers ask for a down payment, which in rental housing may not exceed 12.5% of the total construction costs, as well as a share in land costs. These contributions by the tenants are refunded with interest when the tenants move out. Low-income households are entitled to low-interest public loans or even to apartments without a down payment. All subsidized apartments are subject to certain income-limits at the time of completion, high-income households are mostly excluded from such housing, for example. On the other hand, a later increase of income does not lead to a loss of the apartment.' Quoted in Ryan Holeywell, 'Vienna Offers Affordable and Luxurious Housing', *Governing*, February 2013, www.governing.com/topics/economic-dev/gov-affordable-luxurious-housing-in-vienna.html

21. ibid.
22. *Housing in Vienna*, exh. cat., edited by Wolfgang Förster, Gabriele Kaiser, Dietmar Steiner and Alexandre Viehauser (Vienna, 2008), pp. 120–25.
23. www.iut.nu/FindOutMore/Europe/Austria/Socialhousing_finance_Amman_Mundt.pdf.
24. Reinhard Seiss, *Häuser für Menschen. Humaner Wohnbau in Österreich* (film, Vienna, 2013).
25. *Planen, Bauen, Wohnen, Zeitschrift fur Architektur und Bauwesen Gesellschaft* 6 (1980), p. 89.
26. Colloquial term for a residential area, one or more blocks, a street or a square. The word is related to the Middle High German *Gereiz*, which means something like 'radius'. But it is not just a geographical term; it is connected to identity or way of life. Each *Grätzel* has its own character, which has to do with the original village structure of Vienna. The city is trying to revive this idea – as with tours or promotions for neighborly '*Grätzel* havens' (*Der Standard*, 14 September 2015).
27. Concerning *Sanfte Planung*'s history see *Stadtverneuern. Das Magazin der Gebietsbetreuung Stadtverneuerung* 1 (June 2014); Heinz Dolanski, *35 Jahre Gebietsbetreuungen* (Vienna, 2009); Horst Berger, 'Gebietserneuerung 1974-1984: Das Wiener Modell', *Beiträge zur Stadtforschung, Stadtentwicklung und Stadtgestaltung* 15, 1984; Sandra Fleur Reimers, *30 Jahre 'Sanfte' Stadterneuerung in Wien* (Vienna, 2006); Walter Stangl, *Block- und Quartiersanierung als Teil der Stadterneuerung in Wien. Mit beispielhafter Untersuchung des Gebietes Wien – Fünfhausgasse* (Vienna, 2005).
28. Wolfgang Förster, *80 Years of Social Housing in Vienna*, www.wien.gv.at/english/housing/promotion/pdf/socialhous.pdf.
29. See Hundertwasser's text at www.hundertwasser-haus.info/en/.
30. Christian Schittich, *Im Detail. Integriertes Wohnen. Flexibel, Barrierefrei, Altengerecht* (Basel, 2007); Holeywell, 'Vienna Offers Luxurious and Affordable Housing'.
31. Eckhard Feddersen, Insa Lüdtke and Christel Kapitzki, 'Miss Sargfabrik', in *A Design Manual: Living for the Elderly* (Basel, 2009), pp. 92–5.
32. ibid.
33. Schittich, *Im Detail*.
34. BKK-3, undated brochure published with the support of Lafarge.
35. www.wien.gv.at/stadtentwicklung/alltagundfrauen/wohnbau.html; http://www.vcn.bc.ca/citizens-handbook/unesco/most/westeu19.html; www.frauenwohnprojekt.info.
36. See Peter Scheifinger's statement on his firm's home page concerning the project at www.ztg.at/projekte.html.
37. Angelika Fitz, *How to Live in Vienna*, http://vimeo.com/81858760.
38. Herbert Ludl (ed.), *Das Wohnmodell Inter-Ethnische Nachbarschaft* (New York and Vienna, 2003).
39. www.wien.info.
40. www.kabelwerk.at/info/objekte.
41. www.wien.gv.at/stadtentwicklung/projekte/nordbahnhof/.
42. For complete information, see www.sonnwendviertel.at/Overview.aspx.
43. Michael Ludwig, 'Keine Privatisierung von Gemeindewohnungen durch die Hintertür'.
44. www.dmaa.at/projekte/detail-page/places-for-people.html. This is a quote from Elke Delugan's official statement regarding her curating of the Austrian Pavilion at the Venice Architecture Biennale of 2016.

Select Bibliography

Achleitner, Friedrich, *Österreichische Architektur im 20. Jahrhundert*, 3 vols (Vienna, 1990–2010)

Achleitner, Friedrich, *Region ein Konstrukt? Regionalismus eine Pleite?* (Zurich, 1997)

Achleitner, Friedrich, *Wiener Architektur der Zwischenkriegszeit: Kontinuität, Irritation, und Resignation* (Vienna, 1998)

Alofsin, Anthony, *When Buildings Speak* (Chicago, 2006)

Anderson, Stanford, 'Sachlichkeit and Modernity, or Realist Architecture', in Harry Francis Mallgrave (ed.), *Otto Wagner: Reflections on the Raiment of Modernity* (Santa Monica, 1993), pp. 323–62

Architekturzentrum Wien (ed.), *The Austrian Phenomenon. Architecture and Avantgarde Austria 1956–1973* (Zurich, undated)

Ash, Mitchell, and Alfons Söllner (eds), *Forced Migration and Scientific Change: Emigré German-Speaking Scientists after 1933* (Cambridge and New York, 1996)

Atalay Franck, Oya, *Architektur und Politik: Ernst Egli und die türkische Moderne 1927–1940* (Zurich, 2012)

Atkinson, Anthony, and Thomas Piketty, *Top Incomes over the Twentieth Century* (Oxford, 2007)

Badura-Triska, Eva (ed.), *Vienna Actionism: Art and Upheaval in 1960s Vienna* (London, 2012)

Bakacsy, Judith (ed.), *Paul Engelmann and the Central European Heritage: The Path from Olomuc to Israel* (Vienna, undated)

Balamir, Aydan (ed.), *Clemens Holzmeister 1886–1983* (Istanbul, 2010)

Banik-Schweizer, Renate, *Zur Sozialräumlichen Gliederung Wiens 1869–1934* (Vienna, 1982)

Banham, Reyner, *Theory and Design in the First Machine Age* (London, 1960)

Bartetzko, Dieter, *Illusionen in Stein: Stimmungsarchitektur im Nazionalsozialismus* (Berlin, 2012)

Bauer, Catherine, *Modern Housing* (New York, 1934)

Bauer, Leopold, *Gesund Wohnen und Freudig Arbeiten: Probleme unsere Zeit* (Vienna, 1919)

Bedoire, Frederic, *The Jewish Contribution to Modern Architecture 1830–1930* (Stockholm, 2004)

Beller, Steven, *Vienna and the Jews, 1867–1938* (Cambridge, 1991)

Beller, Steven, *A Concise History of Austria* (Cambridge, 2007)

Beret, Chantal, 'Does Pop Architecture exist?', in Mark Francis (ed.), *Les Années Pop*, exh. cat., Pompidou Center (Paris, 2001)

Bettauer, Hugo, *The City without Jews* (first published in German, 1922; New York, 1997)

Bischof, Günter, *Austria in the First Cold War 1945–55* (New York, 1999)

Bischof, Günter, Anton Pelinka and Dieter Stiefel (eds), *The Marshall Plan in Austria* (New Brunswick, 2000)

Bischof, Günter et al. (eds), *New Perspectives on Austria and World War II* (New Brunswick, 2009)

Blau, Eve, *The Architecture of Red Vienna, 1919–1934* (Cambridge, Mass., 1999)

Bobek, Hans, and Elisabeth Lichtenberger, *Wien* (Vienna, 1966)

Bocco Guarneri, Andrea, *Bernard Rudofsky: A Humane Architect* (Vienna, 2003)

Bock, Ralf, and Philippe Ruault, *Adolf Loos: Works and Projects* (Milan, 2007)

Boeckl, Matthias (ed.), *Visionäre und Vertriebene* (Berlin, 1995)

Bogner, Dieter (ed.), *Friedrich Kiesler. Architekt - Maler - Bildhauer. 1890-1965* (Vienna, 1988)

Bogner, Dieter (ed.), *Inside the Endless House* (Vienna, 1997)

Bramann, Jorn K., and John Moran, 'Karl Wittgenstein, Business Tycoon and Art Patron', *Austrian History Yearbook* 15-16 (1979-80)

Breitner, Hugo, *Kapitalistische oder sozialistische Steuerpolitik* (Vienna, 1926)

Breitner, Hugo, *Seipel-Steuern order Breitner-Steuern?* (Vienna, 1927)

Broch, Hermann, *The Sleepwalkers*, (first published in German, 1931-2; trans. Willa Muir and Edwin Muir, San Francisco, 2001)

Butschek, Felix, *Österreichische Wirtschaftsgeschichte. Von der Antike bis zur Gegenwart* (Vienna, 2011)

Bukey, Evan Burr, *Hitler's Austria: Popular Sentiment in the Nazi Era, 1938-1945* (Chapel Hill and London, 2000)

Carafano, James Clay, *Waltzing into the Cold War: The Struggle for Occupied Austria.* (College Station, Texas, 2002).

Chang, Ha-Joon, and Ajit Singh, 'Public Enterprises in Developing Countries and Economic Efficiency', in Ha-Joon Chang, *Globalisation, Economic Development and the Role of the State* (London, 2004)

Clark, Christopher, *The Sleepwalkers: How Europe Went to War in 1914* (London, 2012)

Collins, George, and Christiane C. Collins, *Camillo Sitte: The Birth of Modern City Planning* (New York, 1986)

Croy, Otto R., and Josef Haslinger, *Leben in der Aschen. Trümmerjahre in Wien 1945-1948* (Vienna, 1948)

Czeike, Felix, 'Wien', in Erika Weinzerl and Kurt Skalnik (eds), *Österreich 1918-1938, Geschichte der Ersten Republik*, vol. 2 (Graz, 1983), pp. 1043-78

Dahms, Hans-Joachim, 'Die Türkei als Zielland der wissenschaftlichen Emigration aus Österreich. Ein Überblick', in Friedrich Stadler (ed.), *Vertriebene Vernunft II. Emigration und Exil österreichischer Wissenschaft 1930-1940* (Berlin, 2004)

Danneberg, Robert, *Der Finanzplan der Regierung Seipel. Wiederaufbau?* (Vienna, 1922)

Danneberg, Robert, *Kampf gegen die Wohnungsnot! Ein Voschlag zur Lösung der Ausfrechnunterhaltung der Mieterschutzes* (Vienna, 1924)

Danneberg, Robert, *Steuersadismus? Streiflicher auf die Rote Rathauswirtschaft* (Vienna 1925)

Danto, Elizabeth, *Freud's Free Clinics: Psychoanalysis and Social Justice, 1918-1938* (New York, 2005)

Darling, Michael, and Elizabeth A.T. Smith (eds), *The Architecture of R. M. Schindler* (New York, 2001)

de Waal, Edmund, *The Hare with Amber Eyes* (London, 2011)

Diefendorf, Jeffry M., 'Planning Postwar Vienna', *Planning Perspectives* 8 (1993), pp. 1-19

Dimitriou, Sokratis, 'Die ersten Jahre nach 1945', *Bau* 1 (Vienna, 1965)

Dreher, Thomas, *Aktionstheater als Provokation: Groteske Körperkonzeption im Wiener Aktionismus* (Vienna, 2006)

Eiblmayr, Judith (ed.), *Moderat Modern: Erich Bostenstern und sie Baukultur nach 1945* (Salzburg, 2005)

Ellenbogen, Michael, *Gigantische Visionen: Architektur und Hochtechnologie im Nazionalsozialismus* (Graz, 2006)

Engels, Friedrich, *The Housing Question* (first published in German, 1872)

Feldbauer, Peter, *Stadtswachstum und Wohnungsnot. Determinaten unzureichender Wohnungsversorgung in Wien 1848 bis 1914* (Vienna, 1977)

Feller, Barbara, and Monika Vlach, *75 Jahre GESIBA* (Vienna, 1996)

Feuerstein, Günther, *Visionäre Architektur Wien 1958-1988* (Vienna, 1988)

Feuerstein, Günther, *Visionary Architecture in Austria in the Sixties and Seventies* (Klagenfurt, 1996)

Fleck, Robert, *Avantgarde in Wien. Die Geschichte der Galerie nächst St Stephan 1954-1982* (Vienna, 1982)

Freisitzer, Kurt, and Harry Glück, *Sozialer Wohnbau* (Vienna, 1979)

Freud, Sigmund, *Civilization and its Discontents* (London, 2001; first published in German as *Das Unbehagen in der Kultur*, Vienna, 1930)

Fritz, Wolfgang, *Der Kopf des Asiaten Breitner: Politik und Ökonomie im Roten Wien* (Vienna, 2006)

Gaugusch, Georg, *Wer einmal War: Das jüdische Grossbürgertum Wiens 1800-1938* (Vienna, 2011), vol. 1

Geretsegger, Heinz, and Max Peinter, *Otto Wagner 1841-1914* (New York, 1979)

Gerschenkron, Alexander, *An Economic Spurt that Failed* (Princeton, 1977)

Gimein, Mark, 'The Great Compression: How War and Taxes Made Us All Middle Class, and Why That's Changed', *Bloomberg Businessweek*, 14 December 2011

Goldhagen, Daniel, *Hitler's Willing Executioners* (New York, 1998)

Gravagnuolo, Benedetto, *Adolf Loos: Theory and Works* (New York, 1982; first published in Italian, 1899)

Green, Malcolm (ed. and trans. in collaboration with the artists), *Brus, Muehl, Nitsch and Schwarzkogler: Writings of the Vienna Actionists* (London, 1999)

Gruber, Helmut, *Red Vienna: Experiment in Working-Class Culture* (Oxford, 1991)

Gulick, Charles, *Austria from Habsburg to Hitler*, 2 vols (Berkeley, 1948)

Hacohen, Malachi Haim, *Karl Popper - The Formative Years, 1902-1945* (Cambridge, 2000)

Hamann, Brigitte, *Hitler's Vienna: A Dictator's Apprenticeship* (Oxford, 1999)

Haunschmied, Rudolf Anton, Jan-Ruth Mills and Siegi Witzany-Durda, *St Georgen-Gusen-Mauthausen: Concentration Camp Mauthausen Reconsidered* (Traun, 2008)

Hayek, Friedrich A., *The Road to Serfdom. A Classic Warning against the Dangers to Freedom Inherent in Social Planning* (London, 1944)

Herrmann, Wolfgang, *Gottfried Semper. In Search of Architecture* (Cambridge, Mass., 1984)

Hevesi, Ludwig, *Moderne Architektur, Prof. Otto Wagner und die Wahrheit über Beide* (Vienna, 1897)

Hines, Thomas, *Richard Neutra: The Search for Modern Architecture* (New York, 2006, 4th edn)

Hobsbawm, Eric, *The Age of Extremes: The Short Twentieth Century 1914-1991* (London, 1994)

Hofmann, Werner, 'Die Wiener Aktionisten', *Kunstforum* 89 (May-June 1987), pp. 202-11

Hollein, Hans, *Plastic Space*, Master's dissertation, University of California, Berkeley, 1960

Hollein, Hans, 'Report to the Harkness Commonwealth Foundation', October 1960

Hollein, Hans, and Walter Pichler, *Hollein - Pichler - Architektur*, exh. cat., Galerie St Stephan (Vienna, 1963)

Hollein, Hans, 'Alles ist Architektur', *BAU* (Vienna, 1968)

Hollein, Hans, (ed.), *Austriennale*, exh. cat. (Vienna, 1968)

Hollein, Hans, *Alles ist Architektur: TOT*, exh. cat. (Mönchengladbach, 1970)

Hollein, Hans, *Austria, XXXVI Biennale di Venezia*, exh. cat. (Vienna, 1972)

Hollein, Hans (ed.), *Traum und Wirklichkeit 1870-1930. Sonderausstellung des Historischen Museums der Stadt Wien, Karlsplatz im Künstlerhaus 28. März bis 6 Oktober 1985* (Vienna, 1985)

Hollein, Hans: *Man TransForms. Konzepte einer Ausstellung* (Vienna, 1989)

Holzschuh, Ingrid, *Wiener Stadtplanung im Nationalsozialismus von 1938 bis 1942* (Vienna, 2011)

Janik, Allan, and Stephen Toulmin, *Wittgenstein's Vienna* (London, 1996)

Jaskot, Paul, *The Architecture of Oppression: The SS, Forced Labor and the Nazi Monumental Building Economy* (New York, 2000)

Johnston, William M., *The Austrian Mind: An Intellectual and Social History* (Berkeley, 1972)

Judt, Tony, 'What is Living and What is Dead in Social Democracy', *New York Review of Books*, 17 December 2009

Judt, Tony, *Ill Fares the Land* (New York, 2010)

Kaldor, Nicholas, 'Public or Private Enterprise - the Issues to be Considered', in W. Baumol (ed.), *Public and Private Enterprises in a Mixed Economy* (London and Basingstoke, 1980)

Kandel, Eric, *The Age of Insight. The Quest to Understand the Unconscious in Art, Mind and Brain in Vienna 1900 to the Present* (New York, 2013)

Kandeler-Fritsch, Martina, *Zünd-Up* (Vienna, 2001)

Kapfinger, Otto, (ed.), *Adolf Krischanitz* (Berlin, 2014)

Kapfinger, Otto and Adolf Krischanitz, *Die Wiener Werkbund Siedlung* (Vienna, 1985)

Kaufmann, Fritz, *Sozialdemokratie in Österreich. Idee und Geschichte einer Partei von 1889 bis zur Gegenwart* (Munich, 1978)

Keynes, John Maynard, *Economic Consequences of the Peace* (London, 1919)

Keynes, John Maynard, *Treatise on Money* (1930), in *Collected Writings*, vol. 13 (Cambridge, 2012)

Kiesler, Frederick, *On Correalism and Biotechnique. A Definition and Test of a New Approach to Building Design* (New York, 1939)

Kolb, G., *Otto Wagner und die Wiener Stadtbahn* (Munich, 1989)

Korinek, Karl, and Ewald Nowotny, *Handbuch der gemeinnützigen Wohnungswirtschaft* (Vienna, 1994)

Korthals Altes, Alexander, and Andreas Faludi, 'Why the Greening of Red Vienna Did Not Come to Pass', *European Planning Studies* 2, 3 (June 1995), pp. 205-25

Kos, Wolfgang, *Eigenheim Österreich. Zu Politik, Kultur und Alltag nach 1945* (Vienna, 1994)

Kraus, Karl, *Die Fackel* 400 (Summer 1914), p. 2

Kraus, Karl, www.youtube.com/watch?v=U200HROPdLI

Kraus, Karl, *The Last Days of Mankind* (1915-22), trans. Michael Russel (Kindle, 2014)

Krejci, Harald, Velentina Sonzogni et al., *Friedrich Kiesler: Endless House 1947-1961* (Cologne, 2003)

Kristan, Markus, *Oskar Marmorek: Architekt und Zionist, 1863-1909* (Vienna, 1998)

Kristan, Markus, *Joseph Urban: Die Wiener Jahre des Jugenstilarhitekten* (Vienna, 2000)

Kristan, Markus, *Josef Hoffmann - Villenkolonie Hohe Warte* (Vienna, 2004)

Kristan, Markus, *Die Sechziger. Architektur in Wien 1960-1970* (Vienna, 2006)

Kristan, Markus, *Hubert Gessner: Architekt zwischen Kaisersreich und Sozialdemocratie 1871-1943* (Vienna, 2012)

Kudrnofsky, Wolfgang, *Vom Dritten Reich zum Dritten Mann* (Vienna, 1973)

Kühn, Christian, *Anton Schweighofer* (Vienna, 2000)

Kühn, Christian, *Das Schone, das Wahre und das Richtige: Adolf Loos und das Haus Muller in Prag* (Basel, 2001)

Kulka, Heinrich, *Adolf Loos. Das Werk des Architekten* (Vienna, 1931)

Kuss, Eva, *Hermann Czech and the Shimmering of the Real*, doctoral dissertation with Prof. Liane Lefaivre, University of Applied Arts (Vienna, 2014)

Lazarsfeld, Paul, Marie Jahoda and Hans Zeisel, *Die Arbeitslosen von Marienthal. Ein Soziographischer Versuch* (Vienna, 1933)

Le Corbusier, 'Adolf Loos zum 60 Geburtstag', *Frankfurter Zeitung*, 19 December 1930

Lefaivre, Liane, 'Everything is Architecture: Hans Hollein, or the Fine Art of Crossing Over', *Harvard Design Magazine* Spring 2003

Lefaivre, Liane, 'Hans Hollein's Richard Feigen Gallery, A Rare Instance of Pop Architecture', *Docomomo* 31 (September 2004), pp. 85-96

Lefaivre, Liane, 'Hans Hollein Everythingizer, Hans Hollein Curator, 1960-1976', in Eeva-Liisa Pelkonen et al. (eds), *Curating Architecture* (New Haven, 2015)

Lefaivre, Liane, and Alexander Tzonis, *The Architecture of Regionalism in an Age of Globalization* (London, 2012)

Leontief, Wassily, 'The Distribution of Work and Income', *Scientific American*, September 1982, pp. 152-64

Les Années Pop, exh. cat., Pompidou Center (Paris, 2001)

Lezàk, Barbara and Trabitsch, Thomas, *Frederick Kiesler: Theatervisionär-Architekt-Künstler* (Vienna, 2010)

Lichtenberger, Elisabeth, *Die Wiener Altstadt* (Vienna, 1977)
Lichtenberger, Elisabeth, *Vienna* (London, 1993)
Lichtenberger, Elisabeth, *Wirtschaftsfunktion und Sozialstruktur der Wiener Ringstrasse* (Vienna, 1970)
Lillie, Sophie, *Was einmal war: Handbuch der enteigneten Kunstsammlungen Wiens* (Vienna, 1982)
Lillie, Sophie, 'Die Gustav Klimt Retrospective 1943. Ein Zurschaustellung enteigneter Kunst', talk delivered at *Das Künstlerhaus in Nationalsozialismus*, 20-1 October 2011
Long, Christopher, *Joseph Frank, Life and Work* (Chicago, 2001)
Long, Christopher, *The Looshaus* (New Haven and London, 2011)
Long, Christopher (ed.), *Joseph Frank: Schriften/Writings* (Vienna, 2013)
Loos, Adolf, *Spoken into the Void: Collected Essays*, ed. Jane Newman et al. (Cambridge, Mass., 1987)
Loos, Adolf, 'Ornament and Crime', in *Selected Essays* (Cambridge, Mass., 1997)
Loos, Adolf, *Why a Man Should Be Well Dressed* (Vienna, 2011)
Lützeler, Paul Michael, 'Theorie der Demokratie - Hermann Brochs wissenschaftliche Arbeiten im amerikanischen Exil (1938-1946)', in Friedrich Stadler (ed.), *Vertriebene Vernunft* (Vienna, 2004, 2nd edn)
Lux, Joseph August, 'The "Arbeitersheim" or Workman's Home, Vienna', *The Studio* 30 (November 1903), pp. 150-54
Lux, Joseph August, *Otto Wagner* (Munich, 1914)
Maimann, Helene, and Karl Stadler, *Mit uns zieht die neue Zeit. Arbeiterkultur in Österreich 1918-1934. Eine Austellung der Österreichischen Gesellschaft für Kulturpolitik* (Vienna, 1981)
Marcuse, Peter, 'The Housing Policy of Social Democracy: Determinants and Consequences', in A. Rabinbach (ed.), *The Austrian Socialist Experiment. Social Democracy and Austromarxism 1918-1934* (Boulder Co., and London, 1985)
Marcuse, Peter, 'A Useful Installment of Socialist Work: Housing in Red Vienna in the 1920s', in Rachel G. Bratt, Chester Hartman and Ann Meyerson (eds), *Critical Perspectives on Housing* (Philadelphia, 1986)
Maderthaner, Wolfgang, 'Politique communale à Vienne la Rouge', in *Vienne 1880-1938: L'apocalypse joyeuse*, ed. Jean Clair (Paris, 1986), exh. cat., pp. 596-607
Maderthaner, Wolfgang, *Die Organisation der Österreichichen Sozialdemocratie 1889-1995* (Vienna, 1996)
Maderthaner, Wolfgang, *Der lange Weg an den Wohlstand* (Vienna, 2004)
Maderthaner, Wolfgang, *Die Kreisky Ära* (Vienna, 2005)
Maderthaner, Wolfgang, *L' Autoliquidation de la raison* (Paris, 2010)
Maderthaner, Wolfgang, *Wie Phönix aus der Asche* (Vienna, 2010)
Maderthaner, Wolfgang, *Hubert Gessner und das Vorwärts-Haus* (Vienna, 2011)
Mallgrave, Harry Francis (ed.), *Otto Wagner: Reflections on the Raiment of Modernity* (Santa Monica, 1993)
Mallgrave, Harry Francis, *Gottfried Semper: Architect of the Nineteenth Century* (New Haven, 1997)
Marchart, Peter, *Wohnbau in Wien 1923-1983* (Vienna, 1984)
Mazower, Mark, *Dark Continent: Europe's Twentieth Century* (New York, 1998)
Mazower, Mark, *Hitler's Empire: How the Nazis Ruled Europe* (New York, 2008)
McNamee, Dardis, 'Renate Brauner: A Keynesian in the Rathaus', *Vienna Review*, 4 March 2013
Meder, Iris (ed.), *Vienna's Shooting Girls. Jüdische Photographie aus Wien*, exh. cat., Jewish Museum of Vienna (Vienna, 2014)
Meder, Iris, and Judith Eiblmayr: *Haus Hoch. Das Hochhaus Herrengasse und seine berühmten Bewohner* (Vienna, 2009)
Megargee, Geoffrey P. (ed.), *Encyclopedia of Camps and Ghettos, 1933-1945*, (in association with United States Holocaust Memorial Museum, Bloomington, 2012)
Menasse, Robert, *The Grand Synthesis. Comment on the Production of the New Austria* (1985). Quoted in Architekturzentrum Wien (ed.), *The Austrian Phenomenon. Architecture and Avantgarde Austria 1956-1973* (Zurich, undated)
Meysels, LucianO, *Berta Zuckerkandl. In Meinen Salon ist Österreich* (Munich, 1984)
Michel, Bernard, *Banques et banquiers en Autriche du début du 20e siècle* (Paris, 1976)
Miller, Manu, *Sonja Knips und die Wiener Moderne* (Vienna, 2004)
Mishra, Ramesh, *The Welfare State in Capitalist Society: Policies of Retrenchment and Maintenance in Europe, North America and Australia* (Toronto, 1990)
Mollik, Kurt, Herrmann Reining and Rudolf Wurzer, *Planung und Verwirklichung der Wiener Ringstrassenzone* (Wiesbaden, 1980)
Monk, Ray, *Ludwig Wittgenstein: The Duty of Genius* (London, 1991)
Moravánsky, Àkos, *The Architecture of the Danube Monarchy* (Cambridge, 1988)
Morton, Frederic, *Thunder at Twilight* (New York, 2001)
Müller, Ines, *Die Otto Wagner-Synagoge in Budapest* (Vienna, 1992)
Nedo, Michael, 'Familienähnlichkeiten: Philosophie und Praxis', in *Ludwig Wittgenstein*, exh. cat., Secession (Vienna, 1989), pp. 147-57
Nedo, Michael, *Interview with Michael Potter*, July 2011, https://vimeo.com/28725163
Nemec, Birgit and Klaus Tashwer, 'Terror gegen Tandler. Kontext und Chronik der antisemitischen Attackem am I. Anatomischen Institut der Universität Wien', in Oliver Rathkolb (ed.), *Der lange Schatten des Antisemitismus. Kritische Auseinanderdersetzungem mit der Geschichte des Universität Wien im 19. und 20.s Jahrhundert* (Vienna, 2013)
Nerdinger, Winfried, and Friedrich Achleitner, *Jabornegg & Pálffy* (Vienna, 2009)
Nerdinger, Winfried, and Werner Oechslin, *Gottfried Semper 1803-1879. Architektur und Wissenschaft* (Munich, Zurich, London and New York, 2003-4)
Neurath, Otto, and Franz Schuster, in *Österreichs Kleingärtner* 3, 12 (1923)
Neurath, Otto, and Franz Schuster, in *Siedler und Kleingärtner* 4, 1 (1924)

Neurath, Otto, 'Anti-Spengler' (1921), in Rudolf Haller and Heinrich Rutte (eds), *Otto Neurath: Philosophische Schriften*, vol. 1, pp. 209-12

Neutra, Richard, *Life and Shape* (New York, 1962)

Noever, Peter (ed.), *Margarete Schütte-Lihotzky, Soziale Architektur, Zeitzeugin eines Jahrhunderts* (Vienna, 1993)

Novy, Klaus, 'Der Wiener Gemeindewohnungsbau: "Sozialisierung von unten"', *Arch+* 45 (1979)

Novy, Klaus, 'Selbsthilfe als Reformbewegung', *Arch+* 55 (1981)

Novy, Klaus, and Wolfgang Förster, *Einfach Bauen. Genossenschaftliche Selbsthilfe nach der Jahrhundertwende: Zur Rekonstruktion der Wiener Siedlungbewegung* (Vienna, 1991)

Novy, Klaus, and Günther Uhlig, 'Baugenossenschaften zwischen Tradition und Aufbruch', *Stadtbauwelt* 75 (1982)

Nowotny, Ewald (ed.), *Sozialdemokratische Wirtschaftspolitik. Die solidarische Leistungsgesellschaft* (Vienna, 1992)

Nowotny, Ewald, 'The Austrian School of Economics and Austrian Economic Policy', Zilk Lecture, Hebrew University of Jerusalem. See www.oenb.at/en/Media/Speeches-and-Presentations/governor-ewald-nowotny.html (31 May 2015)

Oppenauer, Markus, *Der Salon Zuckerkandl im Kontext von Wissenschaft, Politik und Öffentlichkeit* (Vienna, 2012)

Out of Actions. Actionism, Body Art and Performance 1949-1979, exh. cat., MAK (Vienna, 1998)

Peham, Helga, *Die Salonièren und die Salons in Wien. 200 Jahre Geschichte einer besonderen Institution* (Vienna, Graz and Klagenfurt, 2013)

Philippovich, Eugen von, *Wiener Wohnungsverhältnisse* (Vienna, 1894)

Piketty, Thomas, *Capital in the Twenty-first Century* (Cambridge, Mass., 2014; first published in French, 2013)

Prokop, Ursula, *Margarethe Stonborough Wittgenstein* (Vienna, 2005)

Rabinbach, Anson, *The Crisis of Austrian Socialism: From Red Vienna to Civil War, 1927-1934* (Chicago, 1983)

Rainer, Roland, *Planungs Konzept Wien* (Vienna, 1964)

Rainer, Roland, *Das Werk des Architekten 1927-2003* (Vienna, 2003)

Rathkolb, Oliver, 'The Anschluss in the Rear-view Mirror, 1938-2008: Historical Memories between Debate and Transformation', in Bischof et al. (eds), *New Perspectives on Austria and World War II* (New Brunswick, 2009), pp. 5-19

Rathkolb, Oliver, *The Paradoxical Republic: Austria, 1945-2005* (New York and Oxford, 2010; first published in German, 2006)

Rathkolb, Oliver (ed.), *Der lange Schatten des Antisemitismus. Kritische Auseinandersetzungem mit der Geschichte des Universität Wien im 19. und 20.s Jahrhundert* (Vienna, 2013)

Reisinger, Gerhard, *Die Finanzpolitik Hugo Breitners: Entstehung und Ausformung des neuen Wiener Steursystems in Erstens Republik*, doctoral dissertation, Vienna University of Economics and Business (Vienna, 1990)

Reiter, Wolfgang, 'The Year 1938 and its Consequences for the Sciences in Austria', in Friedrich Stadler and Peter Weibel (eds), *Vertreibung der Vernunft: The Cultural Exodus from Vienna* (New York and Vienna, 1995)

Rentzi, Maria, *Trafficking Materials and Gendered Experimental Practices* (New York, e-publication, 2007)

Rubey, Norbert, and Peter Schoenwald, *Venedig in Wien, Theater- und Vergnügungsstadt der Jahrhundertwende* (Vienna, 1996)

Rudofsky, Bernard, *Architecture without Architects* (New York, 1964)

Rukschcio, Burkhardt, and Roland Schachel, *Adolf Loos. Leben und Werk* (Salzburg, 1982)

Sandner, Günther, *Otto Neurath. Eine politische Biographie* (Vienna, 2013)

Sandgruber, Roman, *Traumzeit für Millionäre* (Vienna, 2013)

Sarnitz, August, *Ernst Plischke* (Vienna, 2004)

Schapiro, Meyer, 'The New Viennese School', in *The Vienna School Reader: Politics and Art Historical Method in the 1930s*, ed. Christopher S. Wood (New York, 2000). Originally published in *Art Bulletin* 18 (1936), pp. 258-66

Schneider, Ursula A. (ed.), *Paul Engelmann: Architektur, Judentum, Wiener Moderne* (Vienna, 1999)

Schorske, Carl E., *Fin de Siècle Vienna: Politics and Culture* (London and New York, 1980)

Schumpeter, Joseph, *Capitalism, Socialism and Democracy* (London, 1942)

Schütte-Lihotzky, Margarete, *Erinnerungen aus dem Widerstand* (Vienna, 2014)

Schwarz, Dieter, and Veit Loers, *Von der Aktionsmalerei zum Aktionismus. Wien 1960-1965* (Klagenfurt, 1988)

Scully, Vincent, *Modern Architecture: The Architecture of Democracy* (New York, 1974)

Sekler, Eduard, *Josef Hoffmann* (Princeton, 1985)

Senarclens de Grancy, Antje, and Heimo Halbrainer, *Totes Leben gibt es nicht: Herbert Eichholzer 1903-1943* (Vienna, 2004)

Shapira, Elana, *Style and Seduction. Jewish Patrons, Architecture and Design in Fin de Siècle Vienna* (Boston, 2016)

Sheine, Judith, *R. M. Schindler* (London, 2001)

Sitte, Camillo, *City Planning According to Artistic Principles*, trans. George R. Collins and Christiane Graseman Collins (London, 1965)

Skidelsky, Robert, *John Maynard Keynes: The Economist as Saviour, 1920-1937* (London, 1997)

Skidelsky, Robert, *John Maynard Keynes: Fighting for Britain, 1937-1946* (London, 2000)

Sontag, Susan, 'Happenings: The Art of Radical Juxtapositions' (1962), reprinted in *Against Interpretation and Other Essays* (London and New York, 2009)

Stadler, Friedrich (ed.), *Vertriebene Vernunft II. Emigration und Exil österreichischer Wissenschaft 1930-1940* (Vienna, 2004, 2nd edn)

Stangneth, Bettina, *Eichman before Jerusalem: The Unexamined Life of a Mass Murderer*, trans. Ruth Martin (New York, 2014)

Steininger, Rolf, *Austria, Germany and the Cold War: From the Anschluss to the State Treaty, 1938-1955* (New York and Oxford, 2008)

Stiglitz, Joseph, *The Cost of Inequality* (New York, 2013)

Stiller, Adolph (ed.), *Oswald Haerdtl* (Salzburg, 2000)

Stourzh, Gerald, *Um Einheit und Freiheit: Staatsvertrag, Neutralität und das Ende der Ost-West-Besetzung Österreichs 1945-55* (Vienna, 1998)

Stourzh, Gerald, *1945 und 1955: Schlüsseljahre der Zweiten Republik* (Innsbruck and Vienna, 2005)

Stritzler-Levine, Nina (ed.), *Josef Frank, Architect and Designer* (New Haven, 1996)

Taylor, Robert R., *The Word in Stone: The Role of Architecture in the National Socialist Ideology* (Berkeley, 1974)

Taschen, Angelika, *Hundertwasser Architecture. Pour une architecture plus proche de la nature et de l'homme* (Cologne, 2011)

Tuchman, Barbara, *The Guns of August* (New York, 1962)

Twain, Mark, 'Stirring Times', *Harper's New Monthly Magazine*, March 1898

Tzonis, Alexander, and Liane Lefaivre, *Architecture in Europe since 1968* (London and Boston, 1992)

Uhl, Heidemarie, *Das 'erste Opfer': Der österreichische Opfermythos und seine Transformationen in der Zweiten Republik* (Vienna, 2001)

Uhl, Ottokar, *Moderne Architektur in Wien* (Vienna, 1966)

Ungerer, Brigitte, 'Österreichs Wirtschaftspolitik: Vom Austro-Keynesianismus zum AustroNeoliberalismus?', in Ferdinand Karlhofer and Emmerich Tálos (eds), *Zukunft der Sozialpartnerschaft - Veränderungsdynamik und Reformbedarf* (Vienna, 1999)

van der Linden, Marcel, 'Gerschenkron's Secret: A Research Note', *Critique: A Journal of Socialist Theory* 40, 4 (2012), pp. 553-62

Vienna Action Group: Performance Narratives from the 1960s, Museum Moderner Kunst Stiftung Ludwig (Vienna, 2008)

Vossoughian, Nader, *Otto Neurath. The Language of the Global Polis* (Rotterdam, 2008).

Wagner Otto, *Die Grossstadt: Eine Studie über Diese* (Vienna, 1911); engl. trans. 'Development of the Great City', *The Architectural Record* 31 (May 1912, pp. 485-500)

Wagner, Otto, *Einige Skizzen: Projekte und ausgeführte Bauwerke*, 4 vols (Vienna, 1889-22)

Wagner, Otto, *Modern Architecture*, trans. Harry Francis Mallgrave (Santa Monica, 1988; first published in German, 1896)

Wagner-Rieger, Renate, *Die Wiener Ringstrasse: Bild einer Epoche*, 12 vols (Vienna, 1969-80)

Wagner-Rieger, Renate, and Mara Reissberger, *Theophil von Hansen* (Vienna, 1998)

Waisserberger, Robert (ed.), *Traum und Wirklichkeit: Wien 1870-1930* (Vienna, 1985)

Wall, Alex, *Victor Gruen: From Urban Shop to New City* (Barcelona, 2005)

Wawro, Geoffrey, *A Mad Catastrophe: The Outbreak of World War I and the Collapse of the Habsburg Empire* (New York, 2014)

Weibel, Peter, *Wiener Gruppe/The Vienna Group* (Vienna, 1998)

Weibel, Peter (ed.), *Wien: Bildkompendium, Wiener Aktionismus und Film* (Vienna, 1970)

Weidmann, Dieter, 'Sempers Verhältnis zum Eisen', in Winfried Nerdinger and Werner Oechslin, *Gottfried Semper 1803-1879. Architektur und Wissenschaft* (Munich, Zurich, London and New York, 2003-4)

Weihsmann, Helmut, *Das Röte Wien. Sozialdemokratische Architektur und Kommunalpolitik 1919-1934*, (Vienna, 1985-2002)

Welzig, Maria, *Josef Frank 1885-1967. Das architektonische Werk* (Vienna, 1998)

Weyr, Thomas, *The Setting of the Pearl: Vienna under Hitler* (Oxford, 2005)

Whiteside, Andrew G., *The Socialism of Fools: Georg Ritter von Schönerer and Austrian Pan-Germanism* (Berkeley, 1975)

Wijdeveld, Paul, *Ludwig Wittgenstein: Architect* (London, 1993)

Wistrich, Robert S., *The Jews of Vienna in the Age of Franz Joseph* (Oxford, 1989)

Wittgenstein, Ludwig, *Philosophical Investigations*, trans. G. E. M. Anscombe (Cambridge, 1953)

Wittgenstein, Ludwig, *Philosophical Remarks* (ed. Rush Rhees, written 1927-9; Cambridge, 1975)

Witt-Dörring, Christian (ed.), *Josef Hoffmann: Interiors 1902-1913* (New York, 2005)

Wulz, Fritz C., *Stadt in Veränderung: Eine architektur-politische Studie von Wien in den Jahren 1848 bis 1934*, 2 vols (Stockholm, 1977)

Image Credits

Any errors or omissions to this list of image credits is entirely unintentional and the editor and publisher would be grateful if notified of any corrections that should be incorporated in future reprints or editions of this book.

Angelo Hornak/Alamy: color plate 9,
Architectural Forum, September 1941, p. 196: 83
Architecture d'Aujourd'hui, April 1938, p. 18: 82
@ ArchitekturZentrum Wien Collection: 80, 95, 96, 97, 98
Art Kowalsky/Alamy: color plate 14
Austrian National Library, Picture Archive: 2, 14, 47,
Bautechnische Zeitschrift, 18 January 1904: 45
© BAWAG PSK: 20
Boher/Alamy: 6
Camillo Sitte, *City Planning According to Artistic Principles*: 7
Catherine Bauer, *Modern Housing* (1934): 42
© Condé Nast: 90
With kind permission, Commons. Wikimedia.org: 5
With kind permission, © Coop Himmelb(l)au: 105, 106, 107, 114, 115; color plates 33, 34,
Das Interieur 39, (1914): color plate 10
© Delugan Meissl: 36, 37
Der Architekt XIV (1908): 31
Der Aufbau, nos 8–9 (1926), p. 129: 43
Der Kuckuck, November 10, 1929 : 53
Die Unzufriedene, 30 August 1930, no. 35, Year 8, Vienna: 48
© Dietmar Tollerian: 122
© Dorothea Stransky: 44
With kind permission, © Dothan Family: 91, 92
Duccio Malagamba: color plate 34
© Erich Lessing/ lessingimages.com: color plate 12
Harald Schönfellinger: 118
With kind permission of Hermann Czech: 117

Franz Hubman, © Municipal Library, Vienna: 101
Franz Hubman, with kind permission of Hans Hollein: 113
With kind permission © Geiswinkler and Geiswinkler, rendering Daniel Hawelka: 136
© Graphische Sammlung, Albertina, Vienna: 68, 69, 7, 72, 73, 74, 76; color plates 20, 21
With kind permission of Hans Hollein: 107, 108, 109, 110,111; color plates 23, 24, 25, 26, 27,28, 29, 30
© Hertha Hurnaus: 128, 130, 131, 133, 134, 135; color plates 35,40,42, 43, 45, 46, 47, 48, 49
© Hubert Dimko: 39
© Isben Önen: color plates 1, 2, 3, 5
© Iwan Baan: 119, 120
Janornegg and Pálffy: 121
© Josef Urban Collection, Rare Book and Manuscript Library, Columbia University: 84, 85, 86
© Katrin Bernsteiner: 277; color plate 44
© Lammerhuber: 124
© Liane Lefaivre: 17, 24, 54
Liane Lefaivre Archive: 8
With kind permission, © Lobmeyr Cristal, Vienna: 30
Man Ray Trust/ADAGP, 2017, Telimage/ Banque d'images de L'ADAGP: 70
Marburg Photoarchiv: 34
Margharita Spiluttini @ ArchitekturZentrum Wien Collection: 55, 57, 58, 59, 60, 61, 62, 93, 94; color plate 38
MoMA: 109, 112
© Monica Nicolic/ARTUR Images: 13
Moritz Nähr Photograph © Neue Galerie, New York: 12

Museum of Applied Art (MAK), Vienna: 18, 32, 33, 35, 36; color plate 11
Muzeum Josefa Hoffmanna, Brnice: 28
With kind permission of Ortner and Ortner: 102, 103, 104, 116
© PeterHoree/Alamy: 41
© Philippe Ruault: 37, 38, 39, 40, 41, 75; color plates 13, 16, 17, 18, 19,
© Photographic Masters Collection: 89
Roland Schlager/APA/picturedesk.com: color plate 15
© Rüdiger Lainer + Partner: cover, 127, color plate 39
© Rupert Steiner: 129
Stadt Wien, MA44: 52
© Steinbrener/Dempf: 125
Svenskt Tenn Archive, Stockholm: 77, 78
© The Austrian Frederick and Lillian Kiesler Private Foundation: 87, 88, 89, 90
© Thomas Ledl: 16, 25, 26, 27, 50, 51, 126; color plates 4, 6, 7, 8, 32
© University of Applied Arts, Vienna. Collection and Archive: 44
© University of Applied Arts, Vienna. Collection and Archive: 46
© Vienna Museum: 1, 4, 9, 10, 11, 15, 19, 21, 22; color plate 22
© Walter Zednicek: 125
© Werner Feiersinger: 123
With kind permission of Timo Huber: 100; color plate 22
Victor Gruen, Centers of the Urban Environment, 1973, p. 345: 99
Vienna Library, City Hall, Poster Collection: 3, 54
Vienna Municipal Library: 79, 81
Wiener-Werkstätte-Archiv-Fotoband 'Mode', MAK: 29
Wittgenstein Archive, Cambridge: 63, 64, 65, 66, 67

Index

Page numbers in *italics* refer to illustrations and captions.

20er Haus 198

Achleitner, Friedrich 194-5, 213, *215*, 263
Adler, Victor 13, 21, 123, 128
Aircraft Carrier in a Landscape 239
Alles ist Architektur, 1968 228, 231, *236*, 237, 244
AllesWirdGut 256
Alt-Erlaa 269, *269*, 298-9
Altenberg, Peter 181
Am Kabelwerk 276, 278-9
Amalienbad 76-7, 131-2
American Bar 9, *72*, 99, 213, 242, 250, *251*, 306
Androsch, Hannes 210
Animal Farm 219
Ankara 174
Anker building 9, 49-51, *51*
Anti-Semitism 12, 24, 27, 46, 161, 180-81, 192, 218, 239
Apotheke zum weise Engel 84
 Arbeitsgruppe 4 *188*, 197, 208
Arbeiter Zeitung 165
Archigram 219
Archizoom 219
Art Club 213-14
Art of this Century (Peggy Guggenheim's art gallery) 171, *172*
ARTEC 13, 268, *297*, 305, 307
Aryanization 28, 29, 137, 181, 192-5, *196*
Atatürk, Kemal 173, 174
Auböck and Kárász 255
Auböck, Maria 254-5, 276
Austrian Phenomenon 218

Austriennale 231, *231*, 290
Austro-Keynesianism 210-12, 305

Bachmann, Ingeborg 13, 191, 213
Bau magazine 228, 231, 234-7, *235*, *236*
Bauer, Catherine 18, 105, 130, 133, 136, 137
Bauer, Otto 13, 123, 128, 130, 165
Baumann, Franz 172, 175
Baumann, Ludwig 35, 38, 81-2, *82*
Bergkristall 186
Berkeley School of Environmental Design 228
Bernhard, Thomas 13, 191
Bike City 279-81
BKK-3 273-4, *274*, *301*
'Black Vienna' 25, *25*, 106-7, 137
Blau, Mariette 30
brain drain 168, 191, 193, 194
Brauner, Renate 265-6
Breitner, Hugo 130, 132-3, *133*, *135*, 135-9, 200-1, 210, 264
Bronfman, Edgar 218
Brunner, Karl Heinrich 0 206
Brus, Günter 9, 13, 216-17, 259, *259*
Buber, Martin 29

Cabaret Fledermaus *71*, 94
Café Central 250
Café Korb 8-9, 259, *259*
Café Griensteidl 250
Café Hawelka 214
Caliphate of Cordoba 35
Camus-Dietsch system 201
Cape Canaveral 168, 235
Casablanca (film) 165
Celan, Paul 13, 213
Churchill, Winston 191
Cladders, Johannes 232
Coch, Georg 81
Cold War geopolitics 189
Communist Party 190

Cook, Peter 218, 262
Coop Himmelb(l)au 13, 219, 224, *224*, *225*, 245-7, *246*, *247*, 252, 262, 293, *294-5*, 305
Correalism 171
culture of mediocrity 32, 127, 194, 198, 216, 240, 268
Czech, Hermann 10, 13, 249-51, *250*, *251*, 277, 277-8, *301*, 305, 307

Dadaist architecture 154-9, 228, 231-2
Danneberg, Robert 107, 130, 133-4, *135*, 137
Danube Canal 12, 42, 187, 259, 261
Das Andere, 1903 26, 95
Delugan Meissl 13, 252-3, *252*, *253*, 283, 285, 296, *304*, 305
dementia garden 279, 305
Der Kuckuck 131, *132*, *133*, 165
Die Fackel 16, 26
Die Zeit dispatch office 53-4, *54*, 241, 306
Dohány Street Synagogue 35
Dollffus, Engelbert 96, 107, 132, 137, 139, 164, 173, 180, 185, 210
Domenig, Günther 219, 244-5, 263
Dustmann, Hanns 182-3

Egli, Ernst 114, 175
Ehn, Karl 125, 181
Eichholzer, Herbert 179
Eichmann, Adolf 181
Endless House 171, *172*, *173*
Engelmann, Paul 29, 144, 175
Esherik, Joseph 228
Everythingising 227-239
Export, Valie 13, 217
EYE Film Institute, Amsterdam 252

Fabiani, Max 83
Feiersinger, Martin 255-6, *257*
Fellerer, Max 194, 197
Feng, Jizhong 176
Ferstel, Heinrich von 35, 37-8, 40

Feuerstein, Günther 194, 220, 224-5, 226, 234, 247
Film Guild Cinema 171, *171*, 306
Fischer, Ernst 214
Flakturm (pl. Flaktürme) 12, 182
Flöge, Emilie 28, *51*
Förster, Ludwig von 10, 11, 12, 28, 34-5, *35*, 37, 45, 46
Frank, Josef 13, 29, *80*, 90, 118, 121, *123*, 127-8, 144, 162-3, *163*, 251, 307
Frankfurt Kitchen 114-15, *115*, 306
Franz Ferdinand, archduke 22, 23, 24, 44, 104, 109
Franz Josef, emperor 12, 14, *17*, 20, 22-3, 24, 28, 34, 37, 39, 45, 58, 108, 133
Frege, Gottlob 148-50
Freud, Sigmund 8, 13, 29, 58, 128, 157-9, 181, 191, 218
Frauen-Werk-Stadt (Women-Work-City) housing for women 276
Fuchsenfeld Hof 105

Gänsehaüfel 194
Geiswinkler and Geiswinkler 13, 268, 284, 286-7, 305, 307
Gemeindebau 63, *105*, 110-12, *111*, 119, *120*, 122-37, *125*, 160, 164, 202, 205, 207, 240, 269, 269-70, 276, 279, 307
George Washington Hof 126, *126*, 271
Gerschenkron, Alexander 20, 21, 22, 23, 29, 106
Gerstel, Moshe 175
Gessner, Hubert 123-5, *125*, 127, 307
Ghega, Karl von 39
Giesler, Hermann 183-4
Gilded Age 14, 18, 21, 36, 48, 60, 141, 307
Glück, Harry 269-70, *269*, *298-9*
Goebbels, Josef 183
Goldman & Salatsch tailor shop 9, 27, 29, 60, *73*, 87, 99-101, *100*, 164, 241, 249, 253, 306
Göring, Hermann 184, 185, 189
Greene, Graham 188, 191
Grosstadt (Big City) 18-19
Gruen, Victor 10, 13, 29, 131, 165-8, *167*, 208-9, *209*, 257, 306
Gründerzeit 18, 21, 24, 87
Guggenheim, Peggy 171, *172*

Haerdtl, Oswald 10, 121, 194, 197
Hansen, Theophil von 10, 11, 28, 34-7, *35*, *36*, 44-5, 46, 108, 124, 187, 254

Hareiter, Angela 225
Hartel, Wilhelm von 22, 44, 58
Hasenauer, Karl Freiherr von 35, 38-9
Haüpl, Michael 265
Haus-Rucker-Co 13, 219, 220, *221*, 221, *223*, 223-4, 248
Hayek, Friedrich 29, 138-9
Heimatkultur 192
Heindl, Gabu 255, 258-9, 307
Heller, Max Moses 177
Herr Karl 218
Hilberseimer, Ludwig 18
Hildebrandt, Adolf von 172, 175, 176, 177, 178, 261
Hitler, Adolf 12, 14, 24, 27, 137, 139, 173, 177, 180-4, 191, 193, 207, 215, 218, 229, 245
Hochhaus 164-165
Holocaust Museum, Judenplatz 254
Hoffmann, Josef 86-96, *88*, *89*, *91*, 169-70
  Purkersdorf Clinic 12, 59-60, 92, *92*, 101, 130, 306
  Palais Stoclet *70*, 92-3, *93*, 102, 306
  Wiener Werkstätte 28, *71*, 88-96, *94*
  Skywa-Primavesi villa *71*, 87, 94
Hollein, Hans 178, 195, 205, 216, 226-39, *231*, *232*, 234-5, *235*, *236*, 239, 240-5, 259, 262-3, *290*, *291*, *292*
Holzbauer, Willhelm 197, 268-9
Holzmeister, Clemens 116, 121, 173-5, 179, 194-5, 196
Hötzendorf, Franz Conrad von 23
House with Porches 268, *297*
Huber, Timo 224
Hundertwasser, Friedensreich 215-16, 220-1, 238, 247, 259, 272-3, *300*, 305, 307

intergenerational housing 277-8, *301*, 305

Jabornegg and Pállfy 13, 253-4, *254*, 305, 307
Jacobs, Jane 226
Jahoda, Marie 29, 109
Jaksch, Hans 126, 163-4, *164*, 182
Jelinek, Elfriede 9, 13, 191
Josephine Baker House 53, 114, 153, 158-9, *159*, 306

Kada, Klaus 285
Kalypso, social housing for women 276
Kampffmeyer, Hans 112, 118
Kamprun Dam 190
Kapfinger, Otto 11, *54*, 225

Kaprow, Allan 229-30
Kárász, Janos 254-5
Karl Marx Hof *74-5*, 107, 125, 137, 181, 271
Kaufmann, Edgar Jr. 137, 179
Kaufmann, Edgar Sr. 137, *169*, 179
Kelsen, Hans 29, 194
Keynes, John Maynard 104-5, 138, 143, 189-90
Keynesian policy 107, 110, 135, 138-9, 185, 190, 210-12, 265, 285, 305
Kiesler, Friedrich 13, 29, 90, 169-72, *171*, *172*, 228, 237, 259, 306
Kleines Café 250, *251*
Klimt, Gustav 11, 12, 13, 22, 28, 31, 40, 45, 46, 51, *51*, 53, 86, 88, 89, 90, 94, 142, 166, 192, 227, 251, 272
Knips, Sonja 29, 91, 306
Kogler, Peter 9, 259
Kokoschka, Oskar 11, 27, 31, 90, 94, 140, 144, 155, 192, 196, 216, 227
König, Karl 255
Körber, Ernest von 21-2, 61
Köstlergasse House 51-3, *51*, *52*, 67, 159
Krakauer, Leopold 175, *177*
Kraus, Karl 13, 14, 16-18, 24, 26-7, 32, 95, 104, 129, 140, 212, 214, 216, 218, 250
Kreisky, Bruno 210-12, 260, 264, 272
Krischanitz, Adolf *55*, 198, 225, 249, 278, *301*, 305, 307
Kropotkin, Peter 112
Kubelka, Peter 215
Kurrent, Friedrich 197
Kulturkampf 13, 25, 100, 212, 214, 218, 240, 243, 244, 249, 252
Kunstschau, 1908 90, 95
Kupelwieser, Karl 30

Laboratory for the end of the world 14, 16-17, 24, 104
Lackner, Josef 195
Lainer, Rüdiger 13, 263, *264*, 268, 297, 305
Lamarr (born Kiesler), Hedy 30
Laske, Oskar 84
Last Days of Mankind 17, 104, 218
Late Enlightenment 25
Lazarsfeld, Paul 29, 109
Le Corbusier 18
Leitner, Otto 197
Lichtblau, Ernst 128
Linz 107, 139, 183-5, 189, 190, 255
Loos, Adolf 26-7, 86-7, 95-103, 113-14, 127-8, 129, 144, 152-66

Am Heuberg, Red Vienna social
  housing 114
riedenstadt, Red Vienna social
  housing 114
Hirschstetten, Red Vienna social
  housing 114
Goldman & Salatsch tailor shop 9, 27,
  29, 60, *73*, 87, 99–101, *100*, 164, 241, 249,
  253, 306
Knize tailor shop 9, 101, *101*, 166, 241,
  252, 306
American Bar 9, *72*, 99, 213, 242, 250,
  251, 306
Josephine Baker house 53, 114, 153,
  158–9, *159*, 306
Moller house *78*, 114, 153, 159, *160*, 306
Müller house *79*, 114, 153, 159–60, *161*,
  306
Ornament and Crime 95–9, 102, 144
Duschnitz house *102*, 102–3, 153
Scheu house 102–3, 113, 127, 153, 306
Rufer house 114, 152–4, *154*, *155*
Tristan Tzara house 114, 152, 154–9, *157*,
  158, 306
Loos, Lina 97, *97*
Ludwig, Michael 265–6, 281, 283
Lueger, Karl 12, 24, *44*, 48, 107, 135

Mahler, Gustav 13, 27, 29, 31, 92, 131
Majolica house 51–3, *51*, *52*, 66, 67, 306
MAK Café 10, 251, *251*
Makart, Hans 39–40, 45, 46
Marienthal, The Unemployed of 109
Marmorek, Oskar 39
Marshall Plan 189–90
Mauer, Otto 215, 259
Mauthausen-Gusen concentration camp
  185–6
May, Ernst 113
Mayer, Hugo 113
'memory problem' 191–3, 212, 250
Menasse, Robert 193
Metabolists 219
Migge, Leberecht 113–14
Mind Expander 221
Miss Sargfabrik 273, 274–6, *275*, *301*
Missing Link 11, 13, 219, 225, 249
Moller house *78*, 114, 153, 159, *160*, 306
Moorish architecture 35, 36, 46
Moravian regionalism 90, 94
Mühl, Otto 216, 217
Müller house *79*, 114, 153, 159–60, *161*, 306

Museum Café 250
Musikverein 35–36
Musil, Robert 26, 129, 140

Nähr, Moritz *51*, 152, *152*, *153*
Neue Freie Presse 26, 96
Neurath, Otto 13, 31, 109, 110, *111*, 112, 115,
  117–19, 121, 137, 162, 197, 200, 205, 206, 207
Neutra, Richard 13, 29, 44, 121, 144, 145–6,
  147, 153, 177, 178–9, 196, 206, 306, 307
New School for Social Research 169, *169*
Next Enterprise 252
Nitsch, Hermann 13, 216–7
Nobel Prize 29
Noever, Peter 10, 196, 230
Non:conform 255
Nordkettenbahn 173
Nowotny, Ewald 263–4
Nüll, Eduard van der 35, 37, 38, 45
Nuremberg Trials 191

Olbrich, Josef Maria 12, 13, 43, 58, 69, 84–6,
  88, 306
Orientalism 58, 85, 175
ornamentation 34, 36, 43, 51, 53, *57*, *84*,
  85, 87, 90, 94, 95–102, 132, 134, 162–3, 241,
  249–50
Ortner and Ortner 221–2, *223*, 248, *249*, 263
Ottakringer Bad 132

Pabst, Georg Wilhelm 26, 27, 110
Palais Stoclet 70, 92–3, *93*, 102, 306
Parliament in Vienna 37, 254
Payer Brothers 202–4, *204*
Peace Bricks (Pax Ziegel) 112
Peretti, Elsa 276
Pereira Mansion 35, *35*
Perco, Rudolf 128, *129*, 181–2
Philippovich, Eugen von 13, 18, 63, 108
Pichler, Walter 219, 226, 235, 256
Plečnik, Jože 63, 83, 84
Plischke, Ernst 163
Pollak, Sabine 276
Pop Art 226, 238
Porsche Museum 252
Postsparkasse 10, 22, 44, 49, 54–9, *55*, *56*, *57*,
  81, 84, 306
PPAG 13, *280*, 281, *282*, *302–3*, *303*
Prochazka, Elsa 13, 268, 276, *305*
Progressive Era 18
Pruscha, Carl 247
Przibram, Hans Leo 29–30

Pühringer, Michael 224
Purkersdorf Clinic 12, 59–60, 92, *92*, 101,
  130, 306

Qualtinger, Helmut 13, 191, 217–18

R.O.S.A. housing for women 276
Rainer, Roland 197, 198–9, *200–1*, 207–8,
  247, *291*
Raumplan 79, 99, 114, 144, 153, 155–6, 160,
  243, 251, 277
Regionalism 173–179, 257
Reinhardt, Max 29, 38, 161, 169
Reumann Hof 125
Reumann, Jakob 110
Richard Feigen Gallery *241*, 242
Ringstrasse of the Proletariat 123
Rix, Felice 90, 176
Roosevelt, Franklin D. 139, 191
Rothschild house 181
Rudofsky, Bernard 13, 29, 177, 179, 247
Rühm, Gerhard 213–15, *215*
Rumbach Street Synagogue 46, *47*, 49

Salz der Erde 13, 219, 225
Salzburg Summer Academy 196
Sandleiten Hof 125
Sanft planung 270–1, 273
Sargfabrik 273–4, *274*
Scheu house 102–3, 113, 127, 153, 306
Scheu, Gustav 28, 102–3, 112, 113, 118
Schimkowitz, Othmar 10, 51–3, 55, *55*, 59,
  65, 69, 86
Schindler, Rudolf 13, 84, 144, 177–8, 237,
  306
Schirach, Baldur Benedikt von 181, 182
Schlegel, Eva 259
Schlick, Moritz 27
Schnitzler, Arthur 25–6, 29, 31, 92, 181, 251
Schoenberg, Arnold 13, 27, 29, 31, 92, 129,
  131, 140, 152, 181
Schönerer, Georg 24
Schönthal, Otto 83, *83*, 126
Schörghofer, Gustav 259
Schuster, Franz 116, 119, 128, 197, 199–201,
  205–7, 234
Schütte Lihotzky, Margarete 11, 13, 29, 90,
  114–16, *115*, 118, 121, 127, 128, 161, 179, 195–7,
  205, 306, 307
Schwanzer, Karl 197, *198*, 198–9, *291*
Schwarzwald, Eugenie 13, 30
Schweighofer, Anton 247–8

Secession 22, 28, 40, 42–6, 51, 54, 58, 69, 84–90, *85*, 95, 142, 166, 193, 259, 260, *261*, 306
Seckau Abbey Symposium 215
Sedlmayr, Hans 193
Seitz, Karl Mayor of Vienna 111
Semper, Gottfried 38, 45–51, 54, 55, 58, 81, 185
shopping mall 166–7, 208–9, 262–3
Shrine of the Book 172
Shu, Wang 176
Sicardsburg, August Sicard von 35, 37, 38, 45
Siedlung 110–24, *111*, *121*, *122*, 128, 144, 152, 200, 202, 204, 205, 268
Simböck, Hermann 224
Sitte, Camillo 40–2, *42*, 62
Skywa-Primavesi villa *71*, 87, 94
Slum Clearance Project for New York by Josef Frank 80, 162–163
social housing projects for women 130–1, 276
Sonnwendviertel social housing 283–285
Sontag, Susan 229
Spalt, Johannes 197
Sputnik 220
Stadt des Kindes 247–148
Stadtbahn 12, 13, 42–4, *43*, 49, 54, 61, 62, *125*, 257, 258, 260, 306
Steinbrener/Dempf 259, *259*
Steinhof church 12, 22, 44, 55–8, *68*, 84, 306
Stelzhammer, Walter 248, 268, 271, 272
Strnad, Oskar 29, 114, 116, 121, 127, 128, 160–1, 196
Strzygowski, Josef 58, 85
Sullivan, Louis 34, 45, 46, 48, 87, 95
Superstudio 219
Synagogue, Dohány Street in Budapest 35
Synagogue, Rumbach Street in Budapest 49

Tamms, Friedrich 182
Tandler, Julius 130, 137
Taut, Bruno 113
Team Ten 197
Tedesko, Anton 168
Tesar, Heinz 249
Tessenow, Heinrich 11, 114, 116–17, *116*, 121
The Third Man 188
Theiss, Siegfried 126, 163–4, *164*, 182
Tillner, Silja 257–8, 307
Tony Garnier 18
Trans_city, 284
Tristan Tzara House 114, 152, 154–9, *157*, *158*, 306
Twain, Mark 11, 13, 18, 21, 24, 32
Tzara, Tristan 27, 152, 154–9, *156*

Ullmann, Franziska 276
United Nations Headquarters by Josef Frank 80, 162–163
Urban, Josef 84, 169, *169*, 172

Venice in Vienna 39
Vienna Actionists 216–17, 220, 223
Vienna Circle 27, 31, 142–3, 148
Vienna State Treaty, 1955 190
Vivarium 29–30
Vranitsky, Franz 218

Wachsmann, Konrad 196–7
Wagner, Martin 113
Wagner, Otto
  Anker building 9, 49–51, *51*
  Danube Canal 12, 42, 259
  Die Grossstadt, 1911 48, 60, 119, 124, 208
  Die Zeit dispatch office 53–4, *54*, 241, 306
  Köstlergasse House 51–3, *51*, *52*, 67, 159
  Majolica house 51–3, *51*, *52*, 66, 67, 306
  Modern Architecture, 1895 15, 32–4, 47–51, 83, 140, 306
  Neumann Department Store 49, 51
  Österreichische Länderbank interior 49, 135
  Postsparkasse 10, 22, 44, 49, 54–9, *55*, *56*, *57*, 81, 84, 306
Rumbach Street Synagogue 46, *47*, 49
Stadtbahn 12, 13, 42–4, *43*, 49, 54, 61, 62, *125*, 257, 258, 260, 306
Steinhof church 12, 22, 44, 55–8, *68*, 84, 306
Waldheim, Kurt 218
Wärndorfer, Fritz 28, 87, 89, 94
Weibel, Peter 9, 217, 259
Whiteread, Rachel 251
Wiener Gruppe 13, 214–15, *215*
Wiener Werkbund 80, *123*, 205
Wiener Werkstätte 28, *71*, 88–96, *94*
Wilder, Billy 29
Wimmer-Wisgrill, Eduard Josef 94, *94*
Winter, Johnny 273–4, *274*, *301*, 305
Wittgenstein House 11, 12, 128, 140–53, *141*, *145*, *146*, *147*, *150*, *151*, 160, 175, 237, 306
Wittgenstein, Helene 152, *153*
Wittgenstein, Hermine 142, *152*, *153*
Wittgenstein, Karl 26, 28, 84, 87, 91, 141–3, 185
Wittgenstein, Ludwig 11, 12, 13, 15, 26, 28, 29, 130, 140–53, *153*, 175, 237, 306
Wittgenstein, Margaret Stonborough 140–42, 144, *152*, *153*, *153*
Wittgenstein, Monica 12
Wittgenstein, Paul 91, 143
Wohnen am Park 281, *280*, *282*, 302–3
Woolf, Virginia, *A Room of One's Own* 276
Wörle, Eugen 194, 200
Wotruba, Fritz 12, 244–5, 293
Wurm, Erwin 259
Wurster, William 228, 230

Yellow Heart 221

Zeisel, Hans 29, 109
Ziegfeld Follies 84, 168–9
Zimbler, Liane 116
Zuckerkandl, Berta 13, 28, 31, 87, 92
Zuckerkandl, Emil 28, 29, 87, 92, 130
Zünd Up 13, *211*, 219, 224–5, *289*
Zweig, Stefan 13, 27